QUALITY AS
ALAN REMFRY
15th NOVEMBER 1995

REINVENTING
THE FACTORY II

REINVENTING THE FACTORY II

■■■

Managing the World Class Factory

ROY L. HARMON

Foreword by Leroy D. Peterson

THE FREE PRESS
A Division of Macmillan, Inc.
NEW YORK

Maxwell Macmillan Canada
TORONTO

Maxwell Macmillan International
NEW YORK OXFORD SINGAPORE SYDNEY

The Free Press
A Division of Macmillan, Inc.
866 Third Avenue, New York, N.Y. 10022

Maxwell Macmillan Canada, Inc.
1200 Eglinton Avenue East
Suite 200
Don Mills, Ontario M3C 3N1

Macmillan, Inc. is part of the Maxwell Communication Group of Companies.

Printed in the United States of America

printing number

2 3 4 5 6 7 8 9 10

Library of Congress Cataloging-in-Publication Data
(Revised for vol./open:2)

Harmon, Roy L.
  Reinventing the factory.

  Includes bibliographical references and indexes.
  Contents: v. 1. Productivity breakthroughs in manufacturing today—v. 2. Managing the world class factory.
  1. Industrial productivity. 2. Production planning I. Peterson, Leroy D. II. Title.
  HD56.H37 1990   658.5   89-16944
  ISBN 0-02-913861-2 (v. 1)
  ISBN 0-02-913862-0 (v. 2)

⬜⬜⬜

Contents

◨◨◨

Foreword

OPPORTUNITIES FOR MANUFACTURING productivity and quality have never been better. Manufacturing companies have at their fingertips a range of techniques that will give them competitive advantage over rivals anywhere in the world. In *Reinventing the Factory* we discussed techniques and highlighted the following opportunities for improvement:

Percent	Improvement
75–90	Manufacturing lead time
75–80	Setup/changeover time and cost
75–90	Work-in-process inventory
30–40	Indirect labor
20–30	Quality defects

These benefits and others were documented with examples from more than 130 factories in the appendix, entitled "The Achievers." In *Reinventing the Factory II*, "The New Achievers" appendix adds to the list of manufacturers applying the new technology in every imaginable environment—including not only repetitive manufacturers but also process companies, low volume job shops, government contractors, and small and large enterprises alike.

Clearly, Western manufacturing is rebounding, although many might question why the recovery pace is not faster. The U.S. manufacturing sector increased at a rate slightly faster than the rest of the economy in the 1977–88 period as reported by the U.S. Commerce Department. Manufacturing employment has unquestionably fallen. However, increased productivity of the reduced workforce led to overall growth of manufacturing output. During this period, annual increases of manufacturing's output averaged 2.5 percent while its portion of gross national product grew to 23 percent from 22.8 percent in 1977. However, manufacturing underwent notable shifts. Heavy equipment manufacturers, for example, lost ground in both business volume and employment, while business in nondurable goods such as food, paper, printing, rubber, and plastics swelled.

Disappointingly, the opportunities outlined in our earlier book and echoed by legions of other authors and practitioners have not spurred widespread efforts by U.S. factories to join the ranks of the superior achievers. Non-U.S. factories have made more and faster progress. We have used various statistics, surveys, and our own factory observations to develop an estimate, 15 percent, of U.S. factories that have implemented at least some of the new productivity techniques in portions of their plants. That leaves 85 percent that are sitting on the threshold of radical improvements in operating results and product quality and value. How they can complacently remain inactive with success virtually guaranteed is a mystery.

Granted, the recent business environment has made it difficult (yet all the more imperative) to spend personnel and monetary resources on the urgently needed improvement projects. Weak demand has put our clients under severe economic constraints. Tight capital and fierce competition have made it difficult to stay afloat, let alone to swim to the island paradise of productivity and quality. However, quantum improvements do not require a pipeline from the banks or investors. As many of our case examples have proved, a virtual sea of low cost improvements exists, from which projects can be structured to start increasing profitability in one year or less.

Incidentally, many of our plants have already improved the quality of their products and are doing better in international competition. However, to date progress in the quality arena is also distressingly slower than it can be, and too much has come from massive investments in inspection to cull defects from production and to rework or scrap them. Additional huge sums have been channeled into inspection-oriented quality training. Unwise emphasis on detection of quality problems has hindered efforts to get at the most important opportunities—specifically, improving product quality by producing better engineered products, and developing fail-safe manufacturing equipment and methods incapable of producing defects.

In Chapter 5, "Faster, Better Product Design: The Second Wave," and Chapter 6, "Quality Engineering: Replacement for Quality Control," Roy Harmon debunks the popular but outmoded quality fads that capture far too much attention. More importantly, he describes the new techniques that cut right through to the real problem sources with permanent solutions. This is the only way to avoid unwarranted cost and snail's-pace improvement in the quest for quality.

For many companies, snails-pace improvement is about all that can be managed as they struggle to find the best way to implement the new productivity technology. Perhaps a discussion of some of the reasons for limited success in improving plant productivity and applying time-tested, successful methods will help to give a better perspective.

KEYS TO SUCCESSFUL IMPLEMENTATION

The first key to success is to establish specific, lofty goals for improvement. The modest goals of just a few percent per year that in the past were deemed to be the limit must give way to new, considerably higher aspirations. Target increases in overall annual productivity in the range of 8 to 10 percent are necessary just to stay in the international competitive race. Aggressive, catch-up initiatives designed to achieve 20 to 30 percent improvement in one year are not unrealistic. Executive management must fuel the productivity engine by setting goals high enough to stretch the organization to its limits. They must ban the attitude that "it won't work in my plant" or "it won't work in my department." A giant infusion of the old-fashioned "can do" spirit can be injected into any organization by a top management that is committed and dynamically insists on identical commitment at all levels.

An often-asked question in every country where we work is, "What single benchmark best differentiates superior manufacturers from the also-rans?" In my experience, that benchmark is the time it takes to respond to changing market demands, without large anticipatory inventory investment. The plant that produces and ships customers' exact daily requirements each day is world class. Many factories take weeks and even months to produce their products and still fail to meet the customer's required dates. Although U.S. automobile manufacturers have been widely criticized for high cost and inferior quality, their problems go deeper. They are entrenched in the extremely high inventory and lead time in the entire pipeline of suppliers, factories, and dealer networks, which has not received the attention it warrants. Nevertheless, U.S. producers are in the top tier of all Western manufacturers. And, although they are better than commonly perceived and improving rapidly, opportunities for improvement abound. Improved control of finished automobile inventory alone has the potential for removing billions from idle investment and diverting it to productive uses. Ultimately, the best way to reduce finished inventory will be to reduce the time it takes to fill a vehicle order from several weeks to just a few days.

The second key to success is to focus on achieving the highest specific economic benefits possible. Too many factories are spending their people and economic resources unwisely—on products, components, and processes that have little potential for significant bottom line profit improvement. Early in the improvement process we systematically prioritize our clients' opportunities according to the magnitude of economic benefit. To do so means applying Pareto analysis to each aspect of every product and process.

The third key to success is to identify or create reengineering champions to lead the charge toward superior product quality and productivity status. The most important champion is the Chief Executive Officer, but champions must be nurtured at all levels if maximum results are to be achieved. The Vice President of Manufacturing, for example, must provide leadership, enthusiasm, and drive. It will follow that his organization will be infected with the fire to become champions in their own realms of responsibility. With the enthusiastic involvement of middle managers (the front-line officers) there will be a cadre of people getting the job done, supervising change and providing encouragement and motivation to their organizations. Nor can we afford to overlook the importance of the working men and women in the trenches. We have always relied too much on the backs and muscles of our workers to produce results, and too little on using their brains. It's time to put the entire person to work on improving quality and productivity!

Full-time teams are the fourth key to success. Too often improvement is viewed much like a hobby—something to be done in spare time or after the working day is finished. The normal job must always have priority, because if schedules are not met, if quality deteriorates, and if profits suffer from inattention, the company may have to cut back, further reducing the time available to work on superior manufacturing technology. As a result of treating the need to improve as a part-time activity, people work sporadically with bursts of activity shortly before target completion dates. By then, it is too late to produce world class results, if indeed they produce any results at all. Although *everyone* can have part-time involvement, only full-time teams can be assured of having enough time to achieve their companies' goals. The success of the team depends on its careful composition. Often, people who are expert in their own areas of the factory have an experience-based bias that might blind them to opportunities. For example, we frequently see people with career specialties in selecting equipment, designing tooling, participating in factory layout, and managing processes that close and lock their minds' doors when they are faced with changing the world in which they have so successfully operated in the past. But when such an individual is moved into a new, unfamiliar, unrelated area, his creative juices start to flow, and his vision and enthusiasm come alive. Finally, a project team needs the creative spark. Although each of us has some degree of this magic ingredient, very few have enough to produce results that push the limits of improvement potential. Thus, the brainpower of the team should be applied to improve upon every idea.

Design by committee, of a sort, is a reasonable alternative to brilliant, creative people. Even the most creative people need to recognize that they may overlook alternatives. The power of the group should routinely be used to enhance individual creative efforts. And, going beyond the formal team, marshaling the resources of every company employee has the potential for unleashing an unbeatable force for improvement. Thus, the faster a company can tap into the ideas and involvement of every employee, the sooner the company will advance to the forward ranks of superior manufacturers. A critical success factor is exuberant participation and buy-in of all of the people involved in the design, implementation, and subsequent operation of reorganized factory and office cells and lines. However, make no mistake, employees and their unions are rarely roadblocks to progress. It is middle managers in every functional discipline who are the most common culprits! Addressing this very serious problem and removing the roadblocks are key management challenges in building the successful team. It is fast becoming well-known that the vast majority of the world's people take pride in their daily work regardless of how boring or menial it may appear to observers who have never walked in the workman's shoes. Virtually every worker sees opportunities for improvement in his factory or office, but, sadly, many employees have given up on their immediate superiors and their company's willingness to listen to their ideas and put them into effect. The author and I, in discussions with thousands of factory workers in hundreds of factories, have heard this recurring complaint. It takes very little to turn this around. On our projects, workers' suggestions are always given priority over other business at hand. Regardless of how sketchy the definition of the suggestion is, every effort is made to implement the original idea as quickly as possible. The word then spreads like wildfire throughout the factory. Here is a project team that listens and acts on others' ideas—someone employees can talk to about ideas in their areas of the factory. The end result is often phenomenal, in terms of the outpouring of ideas and avid participation. When management works to perpetuate the new atmosphere of cooperative change, the flow of ideas never ends. Thus, it is not unreasonable to expect continuous improvement, year after year, in the range of 10 percent, compounded. Compounding of productivity can have the same mushrooming effect that interest compounding has on financial wealth. Even the most optimistic executives will look back ten years from now in utter amazement at the magnitude of the changes wrought.

The fifth key to successful projects is methodology brought to bear. A wealth of resources is available to help avoid reinventing the methodology wheel—countless existing books and video tapes, to which more are being added every day. However, in choosing *which* methodology to follow, it is important to select one that involves defining the best possible project scope. Some methodologies advocate projects much too small to be of reasonable value to the company. Others fall into the trap of defining projects of such breathtaking scope and complexity that the time required disillusions the executive decision makers. As a result, most of these projects are abandoned long before coming to fruition. Many engineers, consultants, and other experts actually believe that to convert an existing facility into a modern, superior factory is almost impossible. They advocate building new plants from the ground up in entirely different areas. By leaving old employees behind, they avoid conflicts with those who would resist change. In my mind this is nonsense! Big factories can be converted with the ease of small factories by simply breaking them into small pieces and attacking the pieces in a logical step-by-step approach. As to leaving old employees behind to avoid resistance, the key to winning people's cooperation is a strong leader who can drive all toward the common objective and save their jobs in the process!

The most practical projects have a reasonable combination of both narrow width and great depth. For example, selecting a significant product (and its components) from the broad universe of all products and their components can simplify the amount of effort required to work on improvements in all aspects of business operations related to the product chosen. Taking a complete view, starting at the customer, through engineering and order entry, back into the network of suppliers and company factories, and concluding at the end of the distribution pipeline, is normally only a practical reasonable-term option if the scope in each organization is limited. However, improvements that cover the entire network will ultimately be needed to achieve world class status.

The Menlo Park (California) Metals Division of Raychem (see "The Achievers" appendix of our prior book) is one example of a factory that has worked on most elements of the pipeline. David Taft, Corporate Vice President of Manufacturing, became quite enthused when I originally discussed a potential project with him. Dave chose a Raychem division and product of exceptionally good design and quality, a highly sophisticated metal coupling used in aerospace applications. The division management relished the notion of improving their timeliness of delivery (at the time, approximately one hundred days after receipt of a customer order). The project team, working on every link in the manufacturing and distribution chain, targeted delivery in ten days. The final result was two-to-three day delivery! Since the initial pilot project, improvements have been expanded to encompass all products. The new, speedier delivery is a prime factor behind a doubling of sales volume since the start of the first improvement project. The success story does not end there. After the results from the single small division were highlighted in the stockholders' quarterly financial report, other divisions were spurred to launch their own projects. For example, the Circuit Protection Division has achieved reductions of 90 percent of manufacturing lead time, and 40 to 50 percent of direct and indirect labor, respectively (see "The New Achievers" appendix). Obviously, Dave and his company are continuing to stress continuous improvement.

However, it would be misleading to imply that companywide improvement is easy. It requires the coordination and cooperation of a number of functional areas such as purchasing, marketing and sales, distribution, and product and process engineering. Winning meaningful participation and enthusiastic cooperation is most difficult in the largest organizations, simplest in those that are smallest. However, by beating the drum for the most vital organization, the customer, top management can start to change each organization's narrow self-interest into a force for uniting the company in common cause. Throughout the pipeline, from customer back to producers of raw materials, the unifying, common goal should be the cooperative, speedy planning and execution of all aspects of production improvement as a foundation for superb customer service. Andersen Consulting has coined a phrase descriptive of the new science of managing the minimization of time throughout the multiplicity of companies and their various functional organizations. The phrase is "time compression management." It serves as a rallying cry to all to achieve the new ideal: streamlined delivery of high value products to the end customers.

Timely, labor-saving, simple computer systems are the sixth success ingredient. In one company that already manufactured products to order in only two days, it took ten days to get a new order to the factory floor. Orders were channeled through branch and regional locations before being sent to engineering, order entry, credit department, and production control, then finally delivered to the factory. By creating order processing cells and matching systems, it was practical to reduce the time to process an order to several minutes and sharply reduce the staff level through simplification of both office and computer systems. Since overly complex systems and offices can drown our companies in oceans of paper, it is imperative that improvement projects include office simplification in their charter.

Last, but not least, the seventh key to success is the caliber of the project manager. It can make the difference between superb and disappointing accomplishment. Large, complex, and successful factories find it especially challenging to get all of the necessary people into one room in order to participate. Among other things, the number of functional areas involved and their wide geographic dispersion necessitates extraordinary generalship to coordinate schedules and master communications. The same type of individual is often the best candidate for manager of new focused subplants. These new factories-within-a-factory will have orgnizational resemblance to the outmoded large factory. Each will have not only its own storage, component machining, and assembly facilities but also its own support and staff personnel.

STRATEGIC ISSUES

The complex, multiple plant environment requires more effort to develop a fast-reacting network of interacting company and vendor factories. Many of our clients contend with as many as five tiers of factories through which products and their components flow. The process of receiving, inspecting, storing, issuing, storing again, and shipping at each level adds armies of nonproductive workers and legions of office staff, whereas a single, self-contained factory can operate with much less of these overhead expenses. Therefore, every multiple-plant company must reexamine its network with a view toward simplifying and streamlining it, as discussed in Chapter 2, "Strategic Planning: The Manufacturing

Network." However, eliminating the flow of production through multiple plants will not always be practical, thus procedures and systems to facilitate the flow of information and production are urgently needed. For example, passing requirements down the chain of plants and on to vendors often takes several weeks, by which time the lowest level tier gets requirement information that is several weeks old and out of date.

To have and follow long-range strategic plans is of vital importance. However, many companies go overboard on planning, to the detriment of actually getting to work on improvements. The grandiose plan must not be permitted to delay progress. A better approach is to start to work on projects of major, fast payback while concurrently working on the strategic plan. As mentioned earlier, pilot projects should encompass a complete cross-section of the manufacturing and distribution pipeline. However, such a broad initial project scope might be too large to permit rapid results (unless limited to a single product, a few of its manufactured and purchased components, and only the departments and vendors involved in their production). Many companies need to gain confidence that they too can achieve the radical improvements that characterize the project of superior achievers before they can rationalize setting longer-term companywide goals and plans of sweeping magnitude. They need to start with projects of limited scope to build confidence that they too can achieve 50, 75, and 90 percent improvements. Through substantial early payback, pilot projects can help to finance additional projects. They should do so by minimizing new and modified equipment expenditures. "Low cost automation" is a phrase of critical importance. For although simple automation is an important tool for improving quality and productivity while enhancing the quality of life and reducing exposure to hazards, complex, costly automation rarely achieves its objectives without increasing total cost. The longer-range strategic plan should be started only after pilot projects provide a company with the necessary base of experience and confidence. Incidentally, pilot project goals and achievements must be the highest possible if they are to set the stage for future plans. To achieve the utmost in results, management should assign some of the best available talent and experience to the pilot. Having done so will ensure developing the best possible team, which can then train others in the superior team techniques.

OVERCOMING RESISTANCE TO CHANGE

Successful companies are some of the most resistant to change, being supremely confident in their superiority based on their size, market share, and past successes. Even when they look over their shoulders and see their competitors inching up on them, they tend to find excuses and sometimes work even harder to make the old ways work. In looking over their shoulders, they all too often underestimate the pace of competitors' improvements, which is several orders of magnitude greater than their own. They fail to understand that yesterday's product or quality superiority, service network, or market dominance does not automatically ensure tomorrow's. One need only look at the turnover at the top of the Fortune 500 to see that the stockbrokers' darlings of last year too often become the duds of today.

Of all of the countries in which the author and I work, the United States leads those plagued by resistance to change. Factory and office staff workers are not the problem; middle and top management is where the problem lies. They are secure in their positions, and perhaps too comfortable in large homes, plush cars, and carefully manicured country clubs. Some middle managers have spent most of their careers specializing in a single discipline and working in a single department or section, where they are solid performers. They have come to be considered indispensable (not necessarily because they are, but more because they have not even tried to train subordinates in their experience-based knowledge). Relying on their experience at any rate, many have always been vital to delivering, designing, or producing a product. So management views them as key to future success. One of these types once told me, "If you can show me how to reduce inventory in my operation by 50 percent, I should be fired." My reply? "You should be fired if you don't jump at the opportunity to help make the 50 percent improvement happen!" I understand the reluctance of middle managers to accept these new concepts and the benefits that hundreds of successful companies have proved to be achievable. After all, the technology is new, having first come to the Western world about ten years ago. But this excuse is on its last legs. It's time for these managers to obtain education in the new technology and to adopt and improve it to become the superior manufacturer of the future.

The myth of the indispensable individual is one of the most assailable reasons for permitting a resistant individual to interfere with executive management's desire to become a superior producer. I do not intend to lay the main responsibility for the middle management roadblock at the feet of managers with the characteristics just described. Executive management must often shoulder most of the blame, because it has permitted the managers to operate in a mode that is detrimental not only to the enterprise's progress and the development of the manager's subordinates, but also to the manager's own career. Some might prefer to take a more comfortable approach to the problem by charging their improvement project teams with the responsibility of converting the manager into an advocate of change. This rarely works. Even when it does, it usually involves compromising the design of improved operations. Compromise of the basic productivity concepts always lowers or even negates the opportunities for improvement, delaying the company's goal of becoming the superior producer. Patience, understanding, and education should be used, but at some point a tough decision must be made to move the resister to another department or functional area—thus removing a roadblock to progress.

The most common way to dodge the problem of cautious or narrow-minded middle managers is to start initial projects in areas of the plant outside their responsibility, where the responsible managers are eager advocates of change and best suited to rapidly achieving results. If these areas have high payback potential, fine. However, if this detracts from either ongoing operations or business profitability, this only defers the necessary corrective changes to a later date.

The problem of reluctant managers would be minimized, if not eliminated, if a career-long process of cross-training managers were put into operation. After all, the role of the manager should not be that of the most skilled technician in a department, but rather the most skilled developer of the technical abilities of his employees and the ablest at bringing them to bear on the department's operations. The best managers are those who work hardest to train and educate others to assume ever greater resonsibility and authority. Every employee should strive to learn enough to become his boss' replacement. Only by developing replacements can the boss expect management to see that he has become promotable or ready for a broadening experience in a new area of the operation. The practice of cross-training is equally applicable to both managers and their employees. Cross-training can also be very important as a tool for reducing reluctance to change.

When factories and their machines start to become big and complex, specialization and centralization begin to run rampant, and overhead rates start to climb. In the small factory with a few simple machines, machinists are easily trained to operate several machines and even to maintain and repair them. When factories grow, it becomes more difficult to train every worker on every machine. Thus, machinists are almost permanently assigned, each to a single machine type. Since different machines have varying degrees of complexity, numerous pay grades and job classifications have evolved. As a result various machinists are paid on different pay scales based on the degree of machine complexity. When changes occur in scheduled volume and mix of products, and the load on some types of machines increases while other machine loads decrease, it becomes increasingly difficult to move people from one machine to another. Since people have machine-specific skills, it takes time to train them to man different machines. Productivity and quality suffer until workers achieve the required skill level and experience. When the work force has little flexibility in terms of its ability to move easily from one machine or assembly operation to another, dynamically reacting to current market demand is impossible. This inevitably leads to late deliveries of some products and shortages of others. By contrast, a cross-trained workforce has much greater value to the company since it helps the company achieve superior delivery performance while minimizing required inventory investment. Chief among the cross-training barriers is the typical job classification/pay grade scheme, which bases pay for different jobs on their relative levels of complexity and required skills. Some factories have dozens of different classifications and pay rates. These need to be reduced to a few, perhaps three or four. Typically, since every cross-trained worker's value and mobility have been raised as a result of mastering numerous operations, the new pay rate should reflect the highest pay from the group of job classifications to be combined.

Executive management and union leadership must start on the road to eliminating barriers, and that road may be longer than either would prefer. Even the best companies need to be energized, especially in the areas most critical to a manufacturing company—and tapping the people resources of their organizations is a tremendous force for progress.

SIMPLER, BETTER COMPUTER SYSTEMS

Modern plants need streamlined systems to help get material to the factory when it is needed. An assembler recently told me, "You know, it is really easy to assemble these products. The difficult part is finding parts or getting them from our supporting work centers or receiving inspection. Sometimes it is impossible to assemble because our vendors haven't even shipped the part, or the work center didn't make it because a machine was down." One role of modern computer systems is to help schedule and control component and material availability. Another is to help control labor imbalances and inefficiencies. Further, new systems need to be simplified to slash the ridiculous amount of paperwork heaped on the factory, including reporting factory transactions to the computer, and reports generated by the computer and sent to the factory. When factories took weeks and months to produce a product, it took tens of thousand of transactions to keep track of jobs in process. In modern factories that take only hours or days to complete any product and its components, even trying to track and monitor progress no longer makes sense. The job is already done before the paperwork can be processed! The best of the new factories can limit reporting to purchase receipts and production start and completion. On many lines and cells, the time between start and completion is so short that even production start reporting is unnecessary! Given the inventory and manufacturing lead time reductions of 70 to 90 percent, our objectives for computer input and output cuts should be in the same range. It would be disastrous to capture the massive volume of transactions used in outmoded factories in new, focused factories-within-a-factory. If we do so, we might find that reporting would take as much time as production.

In new cells that operate like assembly lines, it no longer makes sense to report time and pieces produced at each machine. Instead, one transaction will suffice for all machines and operators in a cell. In factories that are still too complex, where jobs are in process for weeks, some of the most intelligently designed systems simply cannot effectively control production. The problem is not the system but the factory. System developers will have a much easier task when their factories have completed the simplification process.

Incidentally, I would like to add a few words concerning the famous Japanese kanban system. Commonly misunderstood, the kanban card is not *the* system. The kanban system and computer material planning systems are not mutually exclusive. They must work together in synchronized harmony. The kanban card is used to control production and material movement based on the current (short-cycle) status of production. But the computer system is used to communicate longer-term requirements throughout the network. It transmits planned changes due to engineering releases and changes, as well as changes in customer and forecast demand. Without material requirement planning systems, the future could not be anticipated. Kanban and its electronic version are simple but powerful tools for communicating short-interval demands between a user and supplier, but they are not suited for planning future machine and manpower requirements. To exploit modern computer power, the best, simplest methods of input automation (bar code, on-line update, etc.) must be used in conjunction with 70–90 percent fewer transactions to reduce input labor even farther. Unfortunately, billions of dollars have been poured into complex systems—only because of unduly complex factories and factory automation. The Andersen Consulting method for minimizing automation cost and complexity requires sequential execution of three logical steps: (1) simplification of the present factory and office operations, (2) selective automation, mainly of the "low cost automation" type, and (3) integration to speed the flow of selected information throughout the network. Unnecessarily complex and costly systems can burden an otherwise prospering enterprise to the point of stagnation. The stakes are high, and the rewards of the low-cost approach are sufficient to help catapult companies into the ranks of the leaders. Unfortunately, many companies are now suffering under the burden of costly, complex operations. They need to heed the telltale signs of noncompetitive operations.

THE TELLTALE SIGNS

Fortunately, telltale signs that characterize a factory operating under outmoded methods are easy to learn and recognize. Below are ten self-examination questions designed to expose the telltale signs, followed by brief rationale for interpreting the answers.

1. *Is your manufacturing lead time weeks and months or hours and days? Whatever it is, is it shorter than competitors' lead time?* The most crucial factor for leading the competition in delivery performance, quality, and value is a rapid, delay-free continuous flow of production throughout the entire production and distribution pipeline. Squeezing every delaying factor out of the pipeline not only speeds the flow, it slashes unnecessary costs. Figuring the ratio of total payroll hours or cost to indirect hours and cost is an enlightening exercise. It helps us to understand how much of our organization's work adds zero value to the product while delaying its production. Today's "reinvented factories" are judged on their outstanding ability to deliver the right product, of the right quality and quantity, at the right time, and at the right cost. Long-range, complex forecasting systems are no longer needed because of drastically shorter manufacturing and distribution lead times.

2. *Do you organize your factories by grouping all similar machines?* That is the outmoded way! Today's factories no longer follow the time-honored (erroneous) concepts of workforce specialization. Focused factories, with cells containing all of the machines necessary for the production of a group of similar parts, make more sense. Parts flow from machine to machine in assembly line fashion, sharply reducing material handling

and inventories between operations that are unavoidable in the outmoded factory. An ideal focused factory consists of a cluster of machining cells and subassembly and final assembly lines, for a product or family of products and related components.

3. *Is responsibility for production and quality problems clear cut? Or is finger-pointing rampant?* Products that flow through many large, specialized departments make it tough to pinpoint sources of problems. In cells and clusters of subplants, teams have responsibility and authority for entire processes and products. Thus, they are empowered to make continuous improvements in quality and cost. The environment of finger-pointing and perpetually recurring problems is replaced by one of motivated teams dedicated to permanent problem elimination.

4. *Is a large fleet of lift trucks giving components and materials a plant tour?* Material movement adds cost to the manufacturing process and subjects the transported items to the possibility of damage in transit. Neither movement nor damage adds to the value of the product. Cells and subplant clusters almost always reduce transport in the 90 percent range, slash transport equipment and personnel, and virtually eliminate damage incurred by material handling. Also, finding things becomes easy since it is no longer necessary to track or search for an item throughout an entire factory. When quality problems occur, previous production is nearby and can be checked and corrected almost immediately.

5. *Are changeover costs so high that it is necessary to produce in large lot sizes—much larger than a customer needs?* When setup costs are high, lot sizes tend to average one month's requirement. Producing more causes a whole range of negative side effects: extra transport to and from formal or in-process storage areas, large amounts of storage space and equipment, people to move and to store it, and damage that occurs as a result of excessive handling. And, most noticeable of all, it causes a huge amount of inventory. When setup cost is reduced, all of these unnecessary cost-incurring results evaporate. Further, fast changeover capability can be used to increase responsiveness to new customer requirements, which is especially valuable to heavy equipment manufacturers that make to order. In factories with extremely long changeover times, slashing them will increase the hours available for production, which will be like getting an additional machine at almost no cost.

6. *Has it been necessary to build or lease additional storage space?* In superior factories, machined parts flow from one machine to another in hand-to-hand fashion and from cell to assembly just-in-time to meet production need. Vendors also deliver daily or even more frequently, and

final assembly produces to shipment, not to stock. Thus, the need for formal storage plummets.

7. *Do aisles and inventory occupy as much as half of the factory's area?* Eliminate 90 percent of the need for both storage and material movement, and the overall size of the factory required will drop accordingly. When starting from the ground up, companies must be miserly with space. When more space is provided than necessary, excess inventory and unnecessary material movement fills it. In addition, the occupancy costs of utilities and maintenance will be higher. Worse, the bigger the factory is, the harder it is to get people to work together as a team.

8. *How often do manufacturing people meet with customers and suppliers?* If the answer is seldom or never, the company cannot claim to be driven by customer interests, nor is it effectively working in partners-in-profit relationships with suppliers. Production people need to have frequent contact with customers to learn firsthand of changing demand patterns, quality and delivery problems, and productivity improvement opportunities. Product-oriented and customer-oriented cells, subplants, and focused factories help to simplify answering customers' needs and inquiries, by virtue of the simplicity of knowing the status of everything in the smaller, focused factory.

9. *Are design and process engineers located in widely separated areas?* That is a sign of poor integration! Lead times cannot be reduced if product designers work in virtual isolation, tossing completed designs "over the wall" to their process and tool design counterparts. Products must be designed with the process in mind if built-in quality and manufacturability are to be achieved. It's too late to start interaction after the design is finalized. A flood of engineering changes will swamp design engineers and delay production startup. The best way to get the job done fast and efficiently is not only to get product and process engineers into a common office (or better still, a common organization) but also periodically and systematically to involve customer and supplier engineers as well as other functions affected by new and changed product designs. True, effective integration requires expanding the traditional scope of design and manufacturing engineering roles. Designers will become more attuned to the realities of manufacturing processes, and manufacturing engineers will be much more involved in initiating ideas for improving the product's design through simplification, built-in quality and manufacturability. The net result will be an entire organization poised to slash product development cost and time, while fostering the reinvention of the factory.

10. *Do you haggle with multiple vendors and give the order to the lowest bidder?* If so, you are not getting the most from your vendors. Vendors should be part of the team—"partners in profit." "Just-in-time" is not a system for beating up on vendors. The new culture calls for mutual benefit, continuous productivity, and quality and value improvement at both ends of the customer–vendor pipeline. The focus should shift from a relentless fixation on price to interest and cooperation in reducing cost. After all, cost is a consequence of various operating factors, all of which are subject to continuous improvement. In the new environment the hallmarks of excellence are new long-term agreements with vendors for supplying entire commodities, not just selected items. Since both companies in the long-term relationship will have a stake in their mutual success, the emphasis of the relationship can switch from haggling to cost, service, and quality improvement.

SUMMARY

I hope this book will encourage readers to embark on an effort to improve their enterprises' productivity. It should provide helpful insights into what to do and how to do it. As in the previous book, *Reinventing the Factory,* an appendix of achievers lists companies that have made major improvements in customer delivery lead time, inventory reduction, employee productivity, space utilization, and many other areas. The purpose of the appendix is twofold: (1) to help convince the Western world that the new, superior techniques apply to every company and industry in every corner of the globe, (2) to identify sources of further information in those areas. We need to do a far better job implementing the techniques in all of our factories and offices. The tools and technology are here. Your factory brims with opportunities. Your chance to propel your factory into the ranks of world class manufacturers has never been better.

Leroy D. (Pete) Peterson
Managing Partner-Manufacturing Industry
Andersen Consulting
Chicago

Preface

THE REAL REASONS some companies are achieving superior manufacturing status are becoming increasingly clear as success stories all around the globe proliferate. Certainly there is overwhelming evidence that a nation's cultural and educational background is of minor importance. Proof of this can be seen in the giant strides being made by Andersen Consulting's clients in remote regions of Brazil, the South Pacific Basin, and other developing areas. Karatsu's[1] report of the superior performance of a color television factory in the countryside of Mexico should help to dispel any notion that the application of these techniques works in only one country or culture. The results in the Mexican factory were equivalent to those of the Japanese parent's factories in such key criteria as work pace and productivity, absenteeism, and loss through employee theft. However, the point of Karatsu's example was that the plant was purposely constructed in the countryside to take advantage of a workforce untainted by a long history of adversarial relations between management and labor. In addition to the quest for radical rationalization of its present factories, management's strategies in any country must sometimes also include consideration of new facilities in order to jettison the burdens of past mismanagement and to start anew. It is almost always faster to work with a new workforce and new factory management team than to change

---

[1]Hajime Karatsu, *Tough Words for America* (Cambridge, Mass.: Productivity Press, 1987), pp. 66–67.

the mind set of the original crew. The exceptions are those companies with progressive managements and workforces with long histories of harmonious relationships and the continuous quest for improvement.

Many of the themes central to the methodical pursuit of superiority, including simplicity of process and product design, organization of small factories within a factory, virtual elimination of machine and line changeover costs, and teamwork, are discussed in an earlier book[2] and in other publications. Although for every written word on the subject of productivity 10,000 more need to be put on paper, the author hopes that his books will be important cornerstones in the foundation of the new body of knowledge.

HOW TO USE THE BOOK

The organization of this book is structured to best serve the purposes of various individuals in a typical manufacturing company, including those responsible for its strategic direction and for improvement projects. The first three chapters address topics of primary importance to executive management:

Chapter	Title
1	Management Perspective: Strategy, Quality and Productivity
2	Strategic Planning: The Manufacturing Network
3	Managing and Supervising the Focused Factory

In addition, the executive should read the first subsection (zinger list) of each chapter. Each of these zinger lists highlights the most important messages detailed later in that chapter. They are intended to be management checklists, since these ideas are some of the vital weapons in the arsenals with which superior manufacturers can win competitive advantage in the twenty-first century.

Executives with the strongest motivation to become superior manufacturers will want to direct their attention to additional vitally important subjects that have not been widely published. These include:

Chapter	Title
4	Supplier Network: Pipeline to Profit

[2]Roy L. Harmon and Leroy D. Peterson, *Reinventing the Factory: Productivity Breakthroughs in Manufacturing Today* (New York: Free Press, 1990).

5   Faster, Better Product Design: The Second Wave
7   Cost Management for Focused Subplants

Individuals from various departments should also review these initial chapters, ultimately. However, they may find it more satisfying to start with the chapters that relate most directly to their daily responsibilities. The following list identifies the organizations that should find the corresponding chapters of primary interest. Executives, managers, and supervisors in the organizations indicated should become thoroughly familiar with these subjects. They should also encourage their employees and unions to assimilate the messages and help them get started on improvements. Achieving or continuing in superior manufacturer status depends on making quantum improvements. Thus everyone needs not only to "buy in" to the new methods but also to march in the new direction.

Chapter	Title	Organization
3	Managing and Supervising the Focused Factory	Factory
4	Supplier Network: Pipeline to Profit	Purchasing
5	Faster, Better Product Design: The Second Wave	Engineering (Design & Manufacturing)
6	Quality Engineering: Replacement for Quality Control	Quality, Engineering
7	Cost Management for Focused Subplants	Finance, Accounting
8	Capacity: Constraint or Opportunity? Plus Other Factory Issues	Factory
9	Instant, Free Machine Maintenance and Repair	Maintenance, Factory

Finally, many executives and managers want proof that the techniques described in this and in other books work in their countries. The author's previous book included an appendix, "The Achievers," that identified numerous companies, internationally, in which we played a major role helping to make their projects successful. Their achievements, expressed in percentages of improvement, are reported in the prior book and in "The New Achievers" appendix in this one.

The author's previous book is a frequently footnoted source of definitions and background for the subject matter covered in *this* book. Appendix 2 minimizes the clutter that numerous footnote references to one source might cause. Footnotes citing the first *Reinventing the Factory* will direct the reader to Appendix 2. Readers interested in selected chapters of *this* book may wish to first read selected portions of the prior book for important background material. Appendix 2 is organized to facilitate cross-referencing between the books, based on the organization of the chapters in this book.

ACKNOWLEDGMENTS

Knowledge is not a genetic data bank that passes from one generation to another but instead comes from a lifetime struggle to wrest the experiences of others from their minds and their books. The author, a lifelong avid reader, regrets that so much of great importance in life has not yet been written, and has the fervent wish that this book will make a small contribution to the written body of knowledge on the subject of manufacturing. Everyone with whom the author has ever worked has contributed a few more pieces of life's jigsaw puzzle, in the form of new knowledge. Without their contributions and those of the authors who have slaked his thirst for knowledge, the author's mind would be an empty, worthless vessel.

Were it practical, I would like to acknowledge every contribution, but because this would clearly be impractical, I would like to thank them collectively for making it possible to put their wisdom on paper. A handful of people made the most direct contributions to the book, and some are listed with their clients in the appendix, "The New Achievers." A special acknowledgement is in order for a few other individuals. M. Diane Harmon, my partner and my daughter, has not only contributed material but, as one of the earliest productivity consultants, has contributed in a more important way: she has been instrumental in helping to spread the practice to the far corners of the globe. My friend and colleague Leroy Peterson not only contributed the foreword to the book but also reviewed every page and gave me his insightful comments. His unswerving support and friendship for more than twenty years have always been a source of encouragement when it was most sorely needed. Leighton Smith, an Andersen Consulting partner (retired), was my mentor in my Tokyo years and was the first to recognize the importance of carrying the true reasons for the Japanese success story back to the West. Robert Halverson, another retired Andersen Consulting partner, encouraged me at every step of the way to build a new productivity practice in the dark days of consensus that said the "Japanese" fad would fade into obscurity. His encouragement included not only a liberal budget for producing the first Western methodology but also friendship and advice.

The author would have been unable to write the controversial Chapter 7, "Cost Management for Focused Subplants," had he not had the advice of his Arthur Andersen & Co. audit colleagues Robert Kutsenda and Charles Marx. He is indebted to them for taking time from their busy schedules to review the manuscript. In addition, I would like to give special recognition to Andersen Consulting partners Steve Kruger, Boston, and Tom Arenberg, Milwaukee. Both have been among the most dynamic disciples of the new productivity world order and have reviewed and commented on selected chapters. Finally, Molly Kinnucan worked tenaciously at editing the early and final book drafts. To all of those I have not acknowledged on these pages, I would like to say that, although your names are not printed on the paper, they are forever etched into my mind and my heart.

Roy L. Harmon

REINVENTING
THE FACTORY II

1

□□□

Management Perspective:
Strategy, Quality, and Productivity

THE IMMINENT DAWNING of the twenty-first century should serve to remind chief executive officers, their boards, and their fellow officers that they owe the stockholders, employees, and suppliers a road map for continuous improvement that will last well into the world of the future. The road map will be crucial to ensuring their future livelihood. In fact, the very viability of many businesses may be threatened should such plans be lacking. "Business as usual" is an operating philosophy that competitors are sure to reject. Bold, innovative changes were the precursors of past successes and will continue to be the hallmark of future giants of industry. Fortunately, the world of manufacturing is brimming with opportunities for improvement. The challenge is to find and develop executives who note a company's imperfections—in business operations, labor relations, supplier relationships, and product value and quality— and refuse to accept them as necessary evils. Recognizing the imperfections is the first step toward inventing strategies and tactics for eliminating them. The executive's responsibility does not stop with the limning of a future vision. It must extend into everyday planning and execution of the myriad tactics that, taken in concert, will propel the company into the ranks of the superior manufacturers of the world.

It would be easy to become complacent with the giant strides some of our factories and offices have already taken. The author, with experience in Japan and other countries, has participated in projects that have yielded even better results than those of Japanese companies. However, these improvements have not yet advanced the state of our operations to the exciting, achievable level of the global, systemwide economic benefits that lie ahead. For example, not one business executive would deny the enormous benefits that could be derived through radical reductions of the billions of dollars in the pipelines of production and distribution. However, these inventories (in the United States) have not dropped appreciably in any recent year, as shown in Exhibit 1-1. During these years, many businesses targeted, but failed to achieve, this very important business objective. Further, the strategies the *largest* companies pursued most aggressively had little to do with improving their operations. Too many paid insufficient attention to nuts-and-bolts issues like reducing inventories. Instead, many of the biggest businesses have pursued mergers, acquisitions, and divestitures as their route to success in the twentieth century—a road that turned out to be rocky for most. Those executives preoccupied with games designed to drain surplus resources from acquisitions or artificial gains from unrealistic increases in stock value have only diverted resources and executive attention away from vitally needed improvements in operations. The usual results have been to sap the vitality of the factories that have been traded from company to company like poker chips. By contrast, exceptional, successful companies have always focused most of their managerial talents and energies on their core business operations. The tide of success for the long term will continue to run with those executives dedicated to the operation, not

BUSINESS INVENTORIES

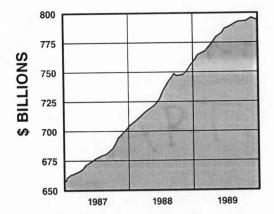

Source: U.S. Commerce Department

EXHIBIT 1-1

exploitation, of their businesses. Chief executive officers, therefore, must lead the charge to radically rationalized operations. To do so will require separating facts and myths.

EXECUTIVE OVERVIEW: KICKING THE SACRED COWS

A plethora of myths have arisen to explain why Japanese companies have been so competitive. In reality, they have no shortcuts to success, no single tricky gimmick to transform the rubble from a world war into a mighty industrial machine. Superior status was won and will continue to be won only by hard work and slogging, step-by-step progress spanning several decades of continuous improvement. The popular myths, each evolving from the compulsion to find an easy way to success, have caused many companies to detour from the path of hard, dedicated work. Sadly, their alternative paths have delayed achievement of the potential improvements. Several such myths—even today—are considered to be the sacred cows of "World Class Manufacturing." The author takes great glee in occasionally giving these sacred cows a not-so-subtle kick.

Manufacturers worldwide have listened to a confusing array of reasons for the emergence of Japan as an industrial superpower Initially, far too much emphasis was placed on "cultural" issues. Researchers such as Dore devoted entire books to analyzing the cultural differences between Western and Japanese factories.[1] And while these cultural issues are not completely unimportant, the first order of priority should be to focus on the easiest, fastest opportunities for improvement. Dore failed to note critically important hardware (tooling and equipment) differences such as fast setup (changeover) and poka-yoke (fail-safe) production methods. These low cost methods can be rapidly implemented, whereas changing cultural factors may require years. Eventually, however, initial studies led to a consensus that statistical quality control and quality control circles must have been the twin panaceas for solving deficiencies in productivity and quality. Unfortunately, these perceptions are passé. Statistical quality control advocates usually focus on the importance of maintaining various quality charts. Where applied with vigor, charts are found in profusion all over the factory. Shingo, the famous Japanese consultant, once told the president of an American company: "But these charts are like government statistics that tell you how many people died of cancer

---

[1] Ronald Dore, *British Factory–Japanese Factory: The Origins of National Diversity in Industrial Relations* (Berkeley: University of California, 1973).

. . . posting them is no more than displaying post mortem certificates."[2] He then proceeded, without charts and in a few minutes, to design a solution to one of the company's most persistent quality problems. As previously mentioned, state-of-the-art industry leaders have moved far beyond the perceived need for statistically sampling either products or processes to identify and solve problems. Today's best manufacturers *design and produce* perfect quality products and components, thus obviating the need for applying statistical techniques to the ongoing production process.

Another false and dangerous perception has been that management's highest priority should be increased spending on new state-of-the-art technology, commonly thought of as factory automation. For example, all but a few manufacturing executives in the world have seen a picture or film of a robot body-welding line like the one in Exhibit 1–2. Before people begin ooh-ing and ah-ing over such examples of advanced, state-of-the-art automation, they should note that process simplification could have reduced the line length, and thus the size of the factory, by as much

ROBOT BODY WELDING

EXHIBIT 1-2

[2]Shigeo Shingo, *The Sayings of Shigeo Shingo: Key Strategies for Plant Improvement* (Cambridge, Mass.: Productivity Press, 1987), p. 73.

as 50 percent. They see robots standing shoulder-to-shoulder, as densely as possible, working at top speed. What they fail to see as readily is that the factory designers fell into a common trap. Having been accustomed to human welders, they designed the line as though the robots had the same needs as humans. They do not! Robots do not need to stand on the floor. They are perfectly capable of "standing" on the ceiling and in holes, perhaps doubling the density of work on the line and cutting not only the length of the line, but also the part of the building occupied by the line, the time to weld a body, *and* the number of units in work-in-process inventory. In addition, the smaller physical area of each robot's work assignment should have reduced the size, complexity, and cost of the robots themselves. Programming each of the robots should also have been much simpler, since its part of the process should have been approximately one-half as complex.

While it is true that many factories have been penny wise and dollar foolish when it comes to upgrading processes through purchases of new equipment, far too little attention has been paid to the multiplicity of opportunities to achieve the "biggest bang for the buck"—that is, making low cost improvements to existing machines and equipment. Such low cost improvements have been proved capable of significantly increasing productivity and production capacity while conserving capital for the invention and acquisition of entirely new processes. The alternative to low cost modifications of present machines and tooling—massive investment in a few technologically advanced machines or processes—can yield results for only a small percentage of a factory's operations since few companies could afford to replace all existing equipment in less than twenty years at best.

Another persistent myth concerning Japanese success is that the Japanese have been willing to produce new products, at a loss, for a long time, in anticipation of long-term profitability. Critics of Western manufacturers have been beating them about the head and shoulders for placing short-term profitability ahead of investments that will first begin to produce profits in future years. Of course, although true in many instances, the whole notion that investments in improvements must always be huge and must always detract from short-term profitability is nonsense. Every improvement project can be planned in such a way as to begin paying for itself in the short term. To achieve this requires only that executive management make it a condition for designing and implementing improvements.

The most astute observers of Japanese methods have seen that factory equipment can be used indefinitely, if it is continuously improved by modification, is well maintained, and is periodically rebuilt when cumulative wear has caused general deterioration in its performance. Less experienced persons have seen the most modern of factories, with completely new equipment, and have failed to realize that they have obviously been put into operation to produce new product lines or to meet increases in sales volume that exceeded the company's older existing plants' capacities. Every major Japanese company has several factories, all of which vary in construction date and equipment age. In the past, the average age of equipment in the Japanese plant was much less than in the factories of Western counterparts. This was mistakenly attributed to higher levels of spending for new technology rather than the real reason, which is new and increased demand.

Yet another erroneous perception of some Western industrialists has to do with the myth of equipment flexibility. Product changes are the bane of every manufacturer. When the product is changed, or if there is a change in the mix of products sold, the process must also be changed, and/or its capacity must be revised. The myth of flexibility is that a machine or a number of machines can be designed and manufactured in a way that provides the flexibility to produce any product or product mix. In reality, flexible machine centers and flexible machine systems are rarely flexible since they are usually most economically and physically appropriate for a specific size range, set of shape characteristics, and necessary machining operations. Further, the presumed flexibility of the machine or system is almost always provided by a design based on using a single cutting tool at any one time. Contrasted to the conventional transfer line or multiple-spindle machines, the flexible machine or system is distressingly slow.

The equipment used by most factories, if adapted to a product and continuously modified to achieve perfect quality and superior productivity, will determine the cost of production, and hence the competitiveness of the company. Therefore, the development of a long-range plan for the purchase of new equipment and for upgrading existing equipment should be the core of every company's strategy for achieving superior manufacturing.

MANUFACTURING NETWORK: THE GLOBAL SUCCESS STRATEGY

The famous kanban[3] system is widely understood to be a vehicle for triggering shipments from vendor to customer. However, most research-

[3]Yasuhiro Monden, *Toyota Production System: Practical Approach to Production Management* (Atlanta: Institute of Industrial Engineers, 1983).

ers have failed to see and understand the requirement systems that work in harmony with kanban to broadcast the latest requirements to the network of suppliers at all levels of the manufacturing chain. Kanban (including electronically transmitted kanban) is an invaluable tool for triggering shipments between factories. However, each factory in the network needs a requirement schedule with which to schedule the capacity necessary to support the latest tempo of production.

The manuscript of the author's last book contained a statement that seemed too radical to the editor. The statement was that we should be able to reduce the cost of virtually any product by as much as 50 percent by implementing all of the improvements that are waiting to be designed. At the time, the author deleted the reference rather than delay the publication by taking the time to explain why this should be possible. The largest roadblock to achieving such an ambitious goal would naturally be that purchases are 50 to 60 percent of the cost of most companies' products. Thus, if in-house costs were slashed by 50 percent, over 75 percent of the original cost would be untouched. This being the case, no single company would be able to cut its product costs in half. Thus it is obvious that improvement efforts must encompass vendor operations as well as the operations of other company factories that are part of the manufacturing network. The "pipeline" of supply, from the lowest level in the supply chain to end customer, is the arena in which the most work remains to be done; it is also the area that holds the greatest potential for improving the cost of manufactured products. Initial pipeline projects have clearly demonstrated the impressive magnitude of improvements just waiting to happen in every corner of the world. For example, Nabisco's operations in Venezuela reduced the time and inventory in the pipeline by 30 percent in the first year of the project. The factory's contribution to this improvement sprang mainly from drastically slashing the time required to change production on cracker and cookie lines from one product to another. Samples of Nabisco's low cost line modifications are included in Chapter 8.

Superior performance of all factories in the pipeline makes vastly improved systems a paramount priority. The lightning response time of the pipeline cries out for corresponding lightning-fast transmission of the latest requirements through all levels in the network of vendor and company factories. Such systems, for many companies, will do even more to reduce pipeline inventories and slash lead times than will factory improvements. Nor do such systems need to be complex and costly. As discussed later, a short-term, manual transcription of requirements from computer output into vendor schedules permitted Harley-Davidson to get revised schedules to their first-tier suppliers in a few hours. Although better, faster schedule communication will provide immediate and substantial benefits, it will take considerably more time and numerous operating improvements to achieve anywhere close to the 50 percent cost reduction. In fact, the author believes that the effort will take most companies at least five to ten years. Therefore, because it will take so long to accomplish, will have such tremendous payback, and will require the cooperation and participation of so many company and vendor factories, developing and maintaining a strategic plan for its eventual achievement is of utmost importance. So much so that no company should be without such a plan today. Chief executive officers should all ask themselves if such a plan is in place and, if not, need to get the ball rolling.

SPEEDY VENDOR PIPELINE REQUIRES BOLD EXECUTIVES

It is relatively easy to cut manufacturing lead time, and therefore work-in-process inventory, by 90 percent or more. This should be a powerful incentive to implement rapidly the necessary changes to all manufacturing operations. However, in most factories, the inventory reduction is most often pushed back into raw material and forward into finished goods. To derive ultimate benefits from lowering work-in-process requires reductions in three areas: in materials stored at all levels of the pipeline, in manufacturing operations, and in finished goods. Few companies are able to marshal both the manpower resources and the courage to reduce all three in concert, and permanently. Many executives place a higher value on inventory availability and resulting customer service than on tight inventory control. Hence they are reluctant to gamble on approving pipeline inventory cuts until they see convincing proof that such reductions do not cause customer service to deteriorate.

Bold, informed executives, however, insist on moving to pipeline reductions as quickly as practical. They recognize the competitive advantage of being the producer with the shortest pipeline. These executives have heard enough success stories to understand that reducing inventory in the pipeline automatically increases customer service. A pipeline that is not clogged with inventory sharply reduces the amount of time required to respond to new and changed requirements. Thus, canny executives instruct their managers responsible for raw materials and for finished goods stock levels to play an important role in synchronizing material reductions with those of the factory inventory to get the inventory out of the *entire* pipeline. Even better, where practical, they can design improvements in their own areas for additional, permanent inventory reductions.

PRODUCT ENGINEERING: THE NEW FRONTIER

The world abounds with examples of poor product engineering. Design improvement therefore offers one of the most exciting opportunities for dramatically improving a company's competitive stance. As manufacturers, we see this most clearly in the large number of engineering changes that follow the first production of new products on production tooling. As consumers, we have almost come to expect that products will start to deteriorate or even fail shortly after we buy them. And, rather than complain, we buy replacements. Nor are we able to see products delivered to the marketplace right on the heels of innovative design breakthroughs. It takes years to get products like General Motors' Saturn automobile off the drawing board and onto the showroom floor. Further, every time our companies have taken the time to rationalize a product line and to standardize and improve the design of products and their components, the improvements have been startling. This is clear evidence that the first design was not as good as it might have been.

Too few companies have realized that improved productivity, cost, and quality start with improved designs. Nor have they realized that product designers—brilliant, imaginative people—have been working in isolation both from the factory engineers who must design equipment to produce their brainchildren and from others who could contribute valuable ideas—if only they had the opportunity. The results are often impressive and technologically advanced products that are more complex than they should be, more costly to produce than necessary, and laden with major opportunities for improvement in function and reliability. The solution lies in organizing a new design team similar in concept to that of a factory cell. The design team of the twenty-first century company will be crosstrained to work cooperatively. Its responsibilities will span both product and process design and will incorporate new techniques for controlling component standardization across all product families. Such standardization will help lower product costs by increasing the purchase leverage of the standard items used. In addition, emphasis on doing the design job right the first time will reduce the time spent in correcting previous oversights and errors. This will mean more time for new product development.

Further, all products have the potential for simplification. The most dramatic result of simplification is the reduction of components and materials. Fewer components means lower costs of material and of the labor and equipment required to manufacture and assemble the product. Perhaps equally important is the reduction of white collar personnel and system expense necessary to control the number of components. Even before simplifying product design, many companies need to redefine their product lines. The options include offering fewer products or increasing the modularity of design in such a way that a large number of product variations can be provided from a relatively small number of design modules.

PERFECT QUALITY: TODAY'S TECHNOLOGY MAKES QUALITY CONTROL OBSOLETE

All of us are inclined to look for the easy way out, the "magic bullet" medicine capable of curing all factory ills. Thus, when the first few Western observers heard about Japan's fabled quality control circle,[4] it was immediately adopted as fundamentally vital to factory improvement, perhaps because it had the advantage of not requiring factory management or responsible technicians to spend much time on developing and implementing new process designs. Working together in small groups was a traditional, cultural way of life in Japan centuries before quality circles. Therefore, forming small circles, training them, and using them to initiate operational changes was relatively easy. Nevertheless, it is a myth that the productivity and quality advances in Japan are solely or even mainly due to circle effects. In the first place, numerous Japanese companies have not found it necessary to operate circles but are nevertheless dazzlingly successful. Further, the accomplishments of most circles, while important, are seldom more than a small part of the story. When the author visits Japanese companies, for example, he always asks for an informal estimate of the circles' contribution to improved quality and productivity versus that of the full-time engineering staff responsible for process and product design. Estimates of the contribution of the engineering staff typically range from 80 to 95 percent! A Japanese-

[4]Masaaki Imai, *Kaizen: The Key to Japan's Competitive Success* (New York: Random House, 1986).

American joint venture case example will help explain the applicability of this lesson to the West. The New United Motor Manufacturing, Inc. (NUMMI), company, formed by General Motors and Toyota in a Fremont, California, plant, shows just how unimportant quality circles might be. Productivity in this factory was almost doubled and quality defects were virtually eliminated.[5] However, three years later, quality circles were demonstrated to have played no part in this phenomenal level of improvement. At Andersen Consulting's annual advanced manufacturing seminar in 1987, two NUMMI guest speaker executives, American and Japanese, somewhat ashamedly revealed that they had not a single circle and had no specific plans for establishing any at that time. (They had merely achieved the tremendous results previously mentioned).

What did and what did not contribute to this outstanding success is of extreme importance. NUMMI executives credit the engineering design, the kanban system,[6] and the human development philosophy. They are quick to point out that they used existing plant and equipment. Thus, massive investment in new factory automation played no role in the transformation of the plant from a troublesome loser to a superior manufacturer. This valuable NUMMI lesson is not unique. Hundreds of Andersen Consulting clients have had comparable experiences. The best results have occurred when fail-safe process and product designs, teamwork, and practical low cost automation have been among the focal points of management's strategy.

The Japanese, perhaps unintentionally, have hoodwinked the majority of industrial educators and even factory operations personnel. Those bamboozled have ardently pursued the holy grail of statistical quality/process control and even its companion, the quality circle. Considering the historical Japanese culture, it is little wonder that the outcome of thousands of fact-finding visits to Japan and thousands of presentations by the Japanese have led to a false understanding of the reasons for their rapid rise to world leaders in industry, and of the real techniques that all other companies can and must pursue in order to catch up and even to leave them in their dust. Almost every Japanese presentation describing the genesis of superior product design and process operations has started with the milestone visit of Dr. W. Edwards Deming, the statistician, in the 1950s. Indeed, the messages Dr. Deming delivered were of major

---

[5]Maryann Keller, *Rude Awakening: The Rise, Fall and Struggle for Recovery of General Motors* (New York: William Morrow & Company, 1989).

[6]David J. Lu, trans., *Kanban: Just-in-Time at Toyota:—Management Begins at the Workplace* (Stamford, Conn.: Productivity Press, 1985).

importance to the long subsequent pursuit of defect-free quality. However, forty years later an entirely new awareness of how to achieve perfect
quality has evolved. What folly it is, then, to set out on the road to
improvement back where leading Japanese companies began forty years
ago! It is infinitely better to recognize that the solutions to perfect quality
and to superior productivity result from designing better products, fail-
safe processes, and operations that are incapable of producing defective
products. In the instances where perfect quality cannot be guaranteed,
perfect quality can be achieved only through 100 percent inspection!

Western industrialists are not alone in falling into the trap of starting
their productivity and quality improvement projects based on the 1950s
concepts of quality management (meaning statistical quality/process control.) One of the most experienced Japanese consultants explains that he
wasted twenty-six years trying to apply statistical techniques before finally realizing that one does not need statistics to control quality.[7]
Whereas heeding Shingo's message can help to avoid reinventing the
wheel, there is a new danger that some companies could mistakenly start
to work on a project of such broad scope that it will be impossible to
achieve success. For example, the very latest in quality control catch
phrases is "total quality control."[8] The scope of total quality control is
breathtakingly global, encompassing an integrated network of a company's customers and factories, the factories of its suppliers, and even of
those of the supplier's vendors. The total quality control concept envi-
sions all of these working harmoniously on every aspect of quality. This
process would start with the definition of the customer's needs and his
special wishes and continue through the design of products to meet the
product definition and then through the production of the product in
company plants on equipment designed to produce defect-free quality
using components and materials produced by suppliers on their own fail-
safe equipment and tooling—all at the lowest possible cost. Even after
production is completed, the integrated network continues through the
distribution channels and through the entire productive life of the product, encompassing field service, warranty, and spare parts distribution.
What an impressive vision of an integrated quality network!

In a few instances, mainly the largest export-oriented Japanese companies, most of the links of the network have been joined. Few, if any, have

[7]Shigeo Shingo, *Zero Quality Control: Source Inspection and the Poka-Yoke System* (Stamford, Conn.: Productivity Press, 1986).
[8]Armand V. Feigenbaum, *Total Quality Control* (New York: McGraw-Hill Book Company, 1983).

yet achieved the near-ultimate, total integration. Few are likely to come close to this exalted target in the next two decades because of the magnitude of the envisioned scope and the impracticality of direct, ongoing, simultaneous communication with all links. There is a distinct and ominous danger that a company might unrealistically charge operating personnel of all of the links with the responsibility for short-term achievement of total quality control, not comprehending that the resources required to do so might be hundreds or even thousands of man-years. Since operating personnel in the most productive organizations work full-time on necessary tasks, how can they be expected to implement sweeping companywide reforms, solving, in the process, serious problems that heretofore had been deemed unresolvable? Radical improvement requires a major investment of the time of creative people to design and implement the required changes.

The almost universal solution to the dilemma of working aggressively against an ambitious schedule while limiting the scope to a reasonable number of man-years is either to focus on a limited number of links in the chain or to pick a single product or product family on which to concentrate on the vertical integration of the most important total quality control links. Subsequently, step by step, the network can be as smoothly expanded as is feasible with the resources available and the experience gained in the initial links. The logical step-by-step process also helps to avoid failures attributable to trying to do too much without adequate resources. Many companies, after initial failures, hesitate for years before trying again, having been convinced by an inadequately funded first attempt that the concept rather than the implementation approach was at fault.

MACHINE BREAKDOWN: BUSINESS BREAKDOWN

Machines and other factory equipment can be manufactured, modified, and maintained in such a way that they can operate almost infinitely without loss of time due to unplanned breakdown. However, when machines are not properly maintained, no matter how well designed and constructed, they will frequently be out of commission. Breakdowns disrupt the entire manufacturing process and are one of the most common reasons for failure to meet production schedules. Large inventories are an inevitable result of poor machine reliability. Companies with a history of frequent downtime eventually resort to maintaining higher than necessary stock balances in an effort (typically unsuccessful) to minimize production disruption. And downtime is not the only dolorous aftermath of inadequate maintenance. Quality suffers, and rework and scrap costs rise when wear on a machine's components renders it unable to hold the tolerances for which it was designed. Shifting the costs of carrying inventory into improved preventive maintenance and permanent maintenance improvements is a sound tactic that often has fast benefits. Unfortunately, it is not always practical to calculate and predict scientifically the specific cost savings that will be achieved. Perhaps this is one of the reasons that maintenance improvement is often tackled long after other aspects of superior manufacturing have been implemented and have become an integral part of routine operations.

The new methods of performing maintenance, whether repair or preventive, should permit most companies to achieve more at lower cost. Amazing as it sounds, it is really very basic. All that is required to lower maintenance cost is a lot of common sense, hard work, and dedication to drastic improvements in maintenance productivity. Further, by decentralizing maintenance people and responsibility, and through simplification of maintenance accounting and scheduling procedures and systems (possible only by focusing the maintenance responsibility in the factory-within-a-factory), companies can minimize maintenance overhead costs and control real repair priorities based on current production schedules.

Finally, improved maintenance requires very little capital investment. Since more maintenance can be performed with fewer, lower cost employee hours, the pilot maintenance productivity improvement project can contribute to increased profitability right from the start.

COMPUTER INANE MANUFACTURING: CIM

Twenty-first-century computer systems hold the potential for finally delivering on their promise of increasing people productivity and improving operating results. Neither of these potentials has been the hallmark of the continuous expansion of computer usage in either manufacturing or other industries. Only a few leading-edge systems are starting to provide some of the new management information needs of the modern, focused factory-within-a-factory. Past misconceptions of the way executives and their managers operated their businesses led to an overwhelming avalanche of information. In fact, many speak of the information explosion age in awed terms, deeming the sea of data delivered to the hands and computer displays of executives and managers to be somehow beneficial. Somewhere along the line we seem to have overlooked the simple fact that if we choose to have our computer systems know everything about every business event, it is necessary for *people* to feed in the information. Once captured, the resulting massive amounts of information require additional armies of people who must review it if the intended purpose is to initiate some important reaction.

The capture and use of computer data can be of tremendous value when the pitfalls that have led to the costly misuse of data are avoided. For decades, for example, many computer technicians have extolled the advantages of the massive, centralized data base to which everyone in the organization has access and with which staff employees can police operations from their ivory towers. In the new world in which small, focused factories-within-a-factory are treated as entrepreneurial business units, the business manager is his own policeman. His detailed personal knowledge of the operations of his business come not from a written report but from direct observation and involvement in daily operations. These focused factory mangers need small, local computer system support. *They do not need, and should not be burdened with, permanent systems that perpetually require input information in order to report on operations that never vary significantly from year to year.* Relatively few have grasped the manager's true information needs. First, the average manager uses relatively few types of information in his daily job, and second, his needs vary from period to period. Managers should be able to initiate data capture, processing, and reporting when a problem first surfaces or when an opportunity triggers the launching of an improvement project. This is not to say that there is no need for a limited number of computer systems spanning the operations of all focused factories and extending out to the pipeline of supply. In fact, the clusters of customer and supplier factories described in Chapter 2 can achieve optimum competitiveness only when they are supported by systems that can instantaneously broadcast the latest production rates throughout the pipeline.

In a handful of leading edge companies, direct computer data transmission links between customers and suppliers are already becoming precursors of the future. However, far too few manufacturers have realized that these systems not only speed the flow of requirement information but also provide customers and suppliers with services that can significantly differentiate the company from its competitors. Imagine, for example, the tremendous promotional value of a superior inventory and material requirements planning system given gratis to a customer. The end objective of the system would be to transmit requirements and shipping authorizations automatically to the manufacturer that provided the system. Realistically, this would be of major interest to smaller customers who do not yet have, and otherwise could not afford, computer systems. However, larger customers would already have their own systems and would naturally prefer to continue to use them. Thus, a concerted effort to work with them to develop interfaces for automatic transmission of requirements and shipping authorizations would (for a while) be an important differentiating factor. After a while, all suppliers would be offering similar systems and interfaces since all would shortly learn the competitive advantage of being the supplier with the fastest linkage to the customer. When designed to be the best, such systems and interfaces have the potential for virtually eliminating entire order entry and purchasing order placement departments with automated data transmission.

Too few businessmen recognize just how much information is reported, processed, and distributed in the normal organization. As a consultant, the author has come to grips with systematic cataloging of the staggering volume. Project teams have collected *samples* of various data forms, reports, and displays in the process of reviewing operations. The typical results fill project team file cabinets. But, viewed objectively, the vast majority of data falls into one of two categories: either it is of use only to the operation at which it originates, or (2) the volume of data is so overwhelming that it precludes any meaningful use by staff or executives in higher tiers. Nevertheless, the thundering cry for improved reporting continues to be heard—interestingly, for data that is often already available. (This occurs for two reasons: first, many people do not consider information to exist unless it is in computer files and second, there is too much data available for most people to master knowing what it is and how to find it). As Davidow and Uttal point out, "Over time, the number and variety of quality measures tend to mushroom close to the point of unmanageability."[9] The same applies to every other form of performance measurement.

The pursuit of computer integrated manufacturing, in the context of elaborate computer systems, is all too often the errant focus of management attention intended to improve operations. Certainly no evidence supports the notion that computer integrated manufacturing systems have played any major role in the success of Japanese companies. As Sakurai points out, only 4 percent of these companies have such sys-

---

[9]William H. Davidow and Bro Uttal, *Total Customer Service: The Ultimate Weapon* (New York: Harper & Row, 1989), p. 202.

tems.[10] Our best computer specialists understand that business first needs to simplify and improve operations—and *then* begin the process of computer systems integration.

FINANCIAL AND ACCOUNTING SYSTEMS: COUNT BUSHELS, NOT BEANS

Manufacturing should be standing on the verge of an exciting new world of accounting practices designed to produce simple, practical results with a modicum of effort and cost. There should be a dawning recognition that precision in numbers is impractical when one product's actual results and costs are influenced by fluctuating demands and investments that routinely benefit other products' sales and production. On any one day, some good business decisions are made and some bad business decisions are made—both based on relatively inaccurate cost information. However, no decisions will be as far from hitting the mark as those based on the assumption that a forecast level of sales and production will prove accurate. Unfortunately, the volume forecast, at the level of individual products, is universally found to be the least accurate number of all of the components of accounting calculations.

The hard truth is that some things are terribly wrong with generally accepted financial and accounting practices. But the good news is that a lot more is terribly right. When the author reads the annual report of an audited manufacturing company, he usually feels quite confident that it reflects the earnings and stockholder equity as accurately as possible. However, arriving at the reported results involves an archaic set of procedures and systems that demand extremely precise calculations of product costs and allocations of overhead to products that have no chance of either representing real product costs or providing a sound basis for decision making that is *based on the assumption that the numbers are or will be accurate reflections of reality.* While sweeping changes are revolutionizing the way in which products are manufactured, relatively few advocates have applied comparable changes to accounting practices. Many of the contemplated changes are merely repetitions or increased detailing of practices that have been advocated for many decades—almost all of which

[10]Michiharu Sakurai, "The Influence of Factory Automation Management Accounting Practices: A Study of Japanese Companies," in Robert S. Kaplan, *Measures for Manufacturing Excellence* (Boston: Harvard Business School Press, 1990), p. 40.

involve a quest for precision that cannot help but will add to existing complexity and cost.

The author is one of many who have not yet been able to describe or find a model new system; thus there is no point in trying to set forth a detailed approach here. The author's comments on the need for new, productive practices and systems are therefore intended as an exhortation to chief financial officers and chief accountants to throw off the restrictive bonds of tradition and to start developing the radical improvement needed if accounting is to keep pace with developments in the new, focused factory-within-a-factory.

PERFORMANCE MEASUREMENTS: MEASURE MONEY, PROBLEMS, AND OPPORTUNITIES

The universal complaints about performance measures arise mainly because some of the information routinely provided by financial and cost systems indicates past performance in an inaccurate light or points to decisions about future operations that are wrong in terms of the real profit impact. The result has been an army of advocates demanding ties (integration) of financial and cost reporting with nonfinancial reporting and "cost generating activities." In reality, all but the least competent managers, or those in the most bureaucratic companies, do what is necessary and most profitable for the company. They and their bosses, if capable and experienced, understand the real meaning of the numbers. The vast majority of managers and executives who complain, although doing what is right, resent the fact that the financial and cost system shortcomings often force them to contravene policies and procedures in order to do what must be done. For those few others who blindly "manage by the numbers," the author has little sympathy.

Being of relatively advanced age, the author can see that most of the latest thinking on performance measuring systems has changed not one iota from what it has been for the past thirty years. And the manufacturers that have worked continuously on expanding performance measuring systems have not, for the most part, wrought any enduring improvements. What those who advocate a performance measurement approach fail to see is simply that the person responsible for operations is the same person who routinely sees problems and opportunities in his bailiwick as they occur (in real time) and goes to work on improvements at once. In those instances where the individual does not manage in this way he has probably not yet been adequately trained in the science of management or provided with the resources and authority necessary to do so. It is vitally important for companies to start spending their resources immediately on improving manager skills and production operations rather than invest in reporting systems designed to force people to action by policing their operations. Solving the operating problems and capitalizing on opportunities for improvement will eliminate the need for most of the numerous performance measures that have always been advocated by those who prefer policing operations rather than go to work on improving them.

Although much has been said about performance measures, the most vital features of effective reporting are probably different from those most frequently extolled by the measurement gurus. The author's list of measurement zingers includes the following:

1. The purpose of being in business is to make money for the business owners. Therefore, the profitability of operations is the single most important measure of success.

2. Performance measures should serve the person or organization (team) being measured. If they coincidentally inform superiors, good. But these same superiors must not view the measures as policing tools. If superiors do not know the performance of subordinates without resorting to formal measurement systems, they are simply failing to perform their own jobs. As Sink and Tuttle so aptly implied, performance measures must not be permitted to become "hammers looking for a nail to pound."[11]

3. Replacing conventional budgeting (responsibility reporting) systems with new measurement tools is unnecessary. There is, however, an urgent need to get the reports into the hands of the individuals and teams who can, should, or do control the budgeted costs. This is not to say that these systems cannot be improved. Cross and Lynch said it best: "Feedback has been too aggregated, too late, too one-dimensional, or too irrelevant to be useful to operating managers."[12]

4. Effective performance measuring systems must be simple and

---

[11]D. Scott Sink and Thomas C. Tuttle, *Planning and Measurements in Your Organization of the Future* (Norcross, Ga: Industrial Engineering and Management Press, 1989), p. 251.

[12]Kelvin F. Cross and Richard L. Lynch, *Measure Up! Yardsticks for Continuous Improvement* (Cambridge, Mass.: Blackwell, 1991), pp. 159–60.

must be limited to the smallest possible universe. The measures that the person being measured considers to be most critical are the ones of real importance. They must be useful in helping him to do his job.

5. It would unnecessarily complicate budgeting and cost and financial reporting systems to integrate them with quantitative reporting of related performance such as customer service, defects, employee grievances, ad infinitum.

6. Perpetually measuring an element of performance that never changes is nonsensical. When an operation is totally under control (well managed), the only activities warranting measurement are those on which improvement studies or implementation is under way.

In summary, performance measures will never be eliminated. As long as problems and opportunities for improvement arise, measurement will be necessary. But it should be limited to the periods when someone is actively working to design improvements. A handful of measurements will still be appropriate even when operations are improved to the point where improvements no longer address problems, only opportunities. The very best measures of a business's success are those that report costs and profits. Product costs are more efficiently measured by totaling estimated labor and actual material cost plus overhead. Other expenses are best planned by simple budget systems that systematically establish improvement targets.

FAD OF THE MONTH: AN EXECUTIVE PITFALL

The author can reflect on decades of fads that have burst on the industrial scene—all with a short-lived blaze of universal acclaim. The recent preoccupation with the word *paradigm* is a case in point. Its use has unaccountably spread like wildfire, sending most of us scurrying to our dictionaries. (Webster lists the following synonyms: archetype, example, exemplar, framework, ideal, *model*, original, pattern, and prototype.)[13] J. A. Barker, the fad originator, had a more complex definition, as reported

[13]Iseabail MacLeod and Mary Pauson, *Webster's New Dictionary and Thesaurus* (New York: Windsor Court, 1989).

by Bane and Garwood.[14] The author will not use the word paradigm again, preferring to use more commonly familiar words and to avoid furthering the cause of fadism.

What is the appeal of most fads? They either appear to get the job done with little effort on the part of responsible management (zero defects and quality circles, for example) or else offer an approach seemingly (but mistakenly) rooted in a logical methodology (benchmarking and value analysis, for example). While few fads have had universal or even notable success, most have a solid business basis, and most companies study (benchmark) competitors and their products as they should and as Camp so aptly advocates.[15] Therefore, even after the intense initial interest fades away, some new practices remain in operation in perpetuity. And although the author detests the "Just-in-Time" label as inadequate and misleading, the label might just have helped to establish the initial impetus and subsequent dedication to permanent pursuit of superior manufacturing practices. In the author's mind, contrary to McGill's opinion,[16] just-in-time will prove to be more than just one more fad of the month. When one reads about the simple techniques for the reorganized factory layout, the machine and tooling modifications, the low cost automation principles, and the personnel organization structures one cannot help but wonder why every enterprise in every country is not working at breakneck speed to implement one of these elements of the new industrial revolution. The fact is that there are numerous roadblocks barring the path toward superior manufacturing. Take misconceptions, for example. In the early years of the phenomena then commonly thought of as the Japanese methods, executives in every country found it convenient to view Japan's success as uniquely culture-based. In the intervening ten to fifteen years, we have been able to adopt and to improve upon the original ideas—on every continent and in almost every free country with a manufacturing industry. Thus the issue of cultural differences is being laid to rest. After all, if Indonesians, Brazilians in Manaus, and even justifiably proud Germans can benefit from simple, low cost but powerful new methods, why shouldn't the rest of the world roll up its sleeves and get to work?

---

[14]Michael Bane and Dave Garwood, *Shifting Paradigms: Reshaping the Future of Industry* (Atlanta: Dogwood Publishing, 1990), p. 115.
[15]Robert C. Camp, *Benchmarking: The Search for Industry's Best Practices That Lead to Superior Performance* (Milwaukee: ASQC Quality Press, 1989).
[16]Michael E. McGill, *American Business and the Quick Fix* (New York: Henry Holt, 1988), p. 25

MANUFACTURING VISION: A SYNOPSIS

The vice president of manufacturing must have his own future vision. His vision must be interwoven with the overall business strategy, but it is *his* prime responsibility since he must plan and execute the implementation of manufacturing's new methods. The author, whose experience lies in manufacturing process and product engineering, is equipped to contribute food for thought in these areas. Other authors can better address marketing, distribution, and high finance issues. The chapters of this book, in concert with the author's previous book,[17] parallel the areas in which executives should focus improvement efforts in preparation for the twenty-first-century competitive race. Following is a brief synopsis of the key issues that must be included in manufacturing's vision and reference to the relevant chapter in which they are discussed.

The opportunities of the future lie in optimizing the cost effectiveness .and responsiveness to customer needs of the entire manufacturing network of company and vendor factories. Thus, planning for the future operation of the network is the subject of Chapter 2, "Strategic Planning: The Manufacturing Network." The new mode of operating the network puts both responsibility and authority for the performance into the hands of those operating a company's new small, focused factories-within-the-factory. The bureaucratic overhead that is so symptomatic of companies that have become too big to control by direct meaningful involvement of corporate executives needs to give way to the empowerment of entrepreneurs of small businesses within the big company. Training in the new concepts of management and supervision *is* important, but on-the-job experience in the modern, reorganized plant is by far the more effective way to learn. Since new organizations and methods can be speedily adopted in the first focused factories, training can start almost immediately. Chapter 3, "Managing and Supervising the Focused Factory," deals with the issues of the management skills that must be cultivated in order to master the new science of management.

Far too little has been done to weld customer and vendor interests into a powerful competitive force, concerned with expanding the market share of both, in a partnership in profit, to improve the value of their products to the ultimate customer. The chief executive officer has a vital role to play in cementing this new spirit of long-term cooperation, as detailed in Chapter 4, "Supplier Network: Pipeline to Profit." However, neither

---

[17]Roy L. Harmon and Leroy D. Peterson, *Reinventing the Factory: Productivity Breakthroughs in Manufacturing Today* (New York: Free Press, 1990).

an end product manufacturer nor its vendors will be successful if their products are inferior in design to those of competitors, or are well-designed but prohibitively expensive. Further, many companies make the mistake of trying to offer something for everyone. Too many products cause control of operations to be vastly more complex than it need be. Those companies need to concentrate on improving product design, with an eye toward "design for manufacturability." Product and product line are the subjects of Chapter 5, "Faster, Better Product Design: The Second Wave."

The traditional solution to quality production has been to detect defects by inspection, with recent fads involving new forms of statistical sampling. Pursuing these types of defect control channels resources away from the read need: fail-safe manufacturing equipment and methods that make it impossible to produce defects, and product designs that are of inherently better quality. These objectives can be met only when quality has been engineered into the product during its inception. These issues are discussed in greater depth in Chapter 6, "Quality Engineering: Replacement for Quality Control."

The systems with which today's executives control operating costs run on high-powered computers. However, these computers could well be characterized as being perched on tall stools and wearing green eyeshades and sleeve garters. Cost management systems and their underlying theory have not progressed in the past century, except perhaps to become more complex, more theoretical, and less meaningful.[18] An immutable fact of business operations that is often forgotten is that all business decisions are and must be firmly founded on forecasts and predictions of highly questionable accuracy. Executives need to awake to this fact when they say they must make decisions contrary to and in spite of accounting systems. It has always been necessary for executives to apply their experience (often mistakenly called gut judgment) and business acumen to the imponderable future, to gamble regularly with the odds, and to make the bold, tough decisions on which business success depends. The fact that cost accounting relies on forecasts and predictions of the future is one of the important messages of Chapter 7, "Cost Management for Focused Subplants."

The most basic issue of manufacturing strategy is how much capacity should be provided, of what type, and when it should be acquired. High

---

[18]H. Thomas Johnson and Robert S. Kaplan, *Relevance Lost: The Rise and Fall of Management Accounting* (Boston, Harvard Business School Press, 1987).

cost automation is rarely economical[19] when all related costs are accounted for and when automation is applied to operations and products that are much more complex than they need to be. Further, most factories have a great untapped source of additional capacity—*the equipment already in operation.* Additional capacity can be squeezed from existing equipment by upgrading it and cutting the hours lost to repair and maintenance downtime. These related issues are discussed in Chapter 8, "Capacity: Constraint or Opportunity?" and Chapter 9, "Instant, Free Machine Maintenance and Repair."

SUMMARY

Executives, managers, and their employees need not wait to manage the factory of the twenty-first century. They can start today using the new management techniques appropriate to the factory of the future. The author hopes to debunk many highly touted (appealing but unrealistic) techniques that seem to relieve executives of the unavoidable, monumental task only they can spearhead. Examples of these "sacred cows" include quality circles, statistical quality control, computer integrated manufacturing, strategic planning, and total quality control. Full integration of all aspects of a business can only increase its complexity, whereas the urgent business need is to simplify. Simplification requires endowment and empowerment of the factory-in-a-factory team with the resources and authority needed to guarantee both successful operations and continuing improvement. Above all, factories must be geared to producing high value (versus high quality) products on fail-safe processes designed to produce defect-free output. To do so economically requires quantum improvements in equipment reliability at minimal preventive maintenance cost. It demands that improved product designs be developed at a faster tempo. And the entire supply pipeline must be able to slash the time required to fill the end customer's orders. Further, a new generation of accounting practices and systems must replace today's woefully outdated counterparts with capabilities designed to be as productive as the new factories on which they report. These new systems must start

[19]Buehler and Shetty put the issue like this: "There is a growing concern over the fact that American manufacturers have been plowing billions into high-tech equipment and automation without paying off in higher productivity." Vernon M. Buehler and Y. K. Shetty, *Competing Through Productivity and Quality* (Cambridge, Mass.: Productivity Press, 1988), p. 10.

to account meaningfully for the costs of new, improved products and the composite profitability of *all* products.

Investment in new and improved capacity is one of the most important manufacturing-related strategic issues. A wellspring of additional capacity may already be available in existing factory equipment. However, the tendency of most companies to add capacity too late can allow the competition to steal a march in the war to gain market share.

The author is neither theorist nor reporter. The practical, proven techniques in the book, gleaned from his and Andersen Consulting's more than two thousand factory and product improvement projects on six continents, are intended to help both companies just starting on the road to superior manufacturing and those advanced factories already looking for the next challenge. Every factory improvement project should achieve astounding improvements in operating costs, quality, and delivery timeliness. Improved, superior performance is a practical objective for any operation. Although the boilerplate list of keys to success (applicable to any major project) must be part of the approach, only executive management can empower and organize the project team and the entire enterprise in a manner consistent with optimum success. Ultimately, cross-training of all managers and their employees will produce an organization that will perpetuate the process of continuous improvement. The education and training of managers and employees in new modes of management will unleash an unprecedented force for creating change. What is needed to achieve major continuous improvement is an unending amount of hard work, especially on the part of executives and managers.

2

□□□

Strategic Planning:
The Manufacturing Network

UNTOLD BILLIONS OF DOLLARS are available for more productive investment if industry would merely reduce the necessary distances and inventory between supplier and user factories. Further billions are tied up in the distribution pipelines between factories and their ultimate customers. The complex network of a company's own plants and those of its vendors is thus a potential gold mine of untapped resources, waiting to be discovered by those executives eager to reap the benefits from compressing distance, inventory investment, and time in their pipelines. And while relocating factories, eliminating warehouses, and developing local sources all entail a giant initial infusion of capital, the recurring savings gained by cutting transport costs and trimming overhead costs incurred for controlling movement in the pipeline will permit superior manufacturers to lower their prices and thus steal a march against their competitors.

For some companies the location of facilities is the most important strategic issue. But in the long term *every* company will benefit from developing capacity strategies that will lower the investment required to meet market demands. Both plant and equipment are almost universally under utilized in all except process manufacturing factories. Therefore, learning to design plants and equipment that almost immediately operate near maximum will lower the investment required. This in turn will either increase return on investment or, alternatively, permit the manufacturer to lower his prices, thus providing an opportunity to increase market share vis-à-vis less aggressive competitors.

Vendors of materials and components serve many different masters and are inclined to skip to the tune of their largest customers or the customers who are currently most vocal in their threats to take their business elsewhere. Close-knit relationships and interlinking data systems are much rarer that necessary for most companies to qualify for entry into the ranks of superior manufacturers. Therefore, radically new vendor strategies that weld permanent links between customer and supplier are imperatives of great import.

The most exciting potentials for new strategic direction lie primarily in growth through acquisition or through the development of new product lines, the facilities for making them, and the distribution channels with which to bring them to market. For two reasons, these opportunities are not the primary focus of this chapter. First, others, such as Porter, have written extensively on these subjects,[1] and second, many companies have not had much success with their acquisitions and new product line introductions. Both avenues entail risk. In fact, to the author, the long-term failure rate of companies that have grown aggressively through merger and acquisition seems to be higher than the rate of success. He who is more conservative and less a gambler should prefer to work on the core business opportunities, where success is virtually guaranteed. However, be warned that the author holds some rather radical views on strategic planning. Chief among these is an experienced-based conviction that most successful businesses have achieved their positions not from pursuing a glamorous, earthshaking strategy, but rather from exceptional pursuit of continuous improvement in every detail of operations. Bhide said it best, "It is questionable whether this proposition [that strategy is about big plays that yield a sustainable advantage] is itself sustainable. The competitive scriptures almost systematically ignore the importance of hustle and energy."[2]

The opportunities in and controlled by manufacturing are quite different from those in such other functional areas as product design, sales, and marketing. The author's purpose is to focus mainly on strategies within manufacturing. After all, manufacturing's primary purpose, as reflected in its strategies, must simply be to obtain or construct the best practical network of company and vendor facilities and equipment and

---

[1]Michael E. Porter *Competitive Advantage: Creating and Sustaining Superior Performance* (New York: Free Press, 1985).
[2]Amar Bhide, "Hustle as Strategy," *Harvard Business Review,* September–October 1986, pp. 59–65.

to hire and keep the people best qualified to meet the technological and volume demands of the market. This assumption greatly narrows the otherwise complex universe of strategies. Second, the author has a deeply held, experience-based conviction that important, radical changes in strategic direction are (and should be) rare. Strategic changes in the *manufacturing* jurisdiction are even rarer than in the company as a whole. Thus, the importance of strategic manufacturing planning is often oversold. Further, although continuous change *is* necessary, most business changes are tactical—not strategic—in nature.

The process of formally developing a strategic plan is invaluable, when needed. However, the need for periodic, systematic formal planning stems from two shortcomings. One is the lack of adequate training, especially cross-training, of executives. Executives and managers with well-rounded experience and training in several different functional areas of the company will know how to plan continuously with a minimum of bureaucratic proceduralization. The other shortcoming surfaces when companies grow too big and forget how to give small business units the responsibility and authority for controlling their own destinies. In these companies, the first strategic plan should be built around decentralization. The best strategic plan is one that originates in the focused factory, not in the corporate offices. Thus, a successful plan will take most centralized participation out of the planning loop.

Day-to-day and year-to-year tactical decisions, although perhaps less glamorous sounding than strategic planning, are really at the core of operating a successful business. Further, the borderline between tactic and strategy is hard to define. For example, many might view the decision to pursue becoming a "just-in-time" or "total quality control" producer as a strategic decision. This is not the author's viewpoint. The improvements that are required to achieve these vaguely defined objectives are vast in number and in category. Continuous improvement is not a strategy. It is a vital necessity for survival in business! Therefore, this chapter will cover not only manufacturing strategy but also some of the most important tactical issues that are vital to becoming a superior manufacturer in the twenty-first century.

This chapter will begin by identifying some of the important strategic and tactical issues on which manufacturing executives should focus. It will then clarify the author's position concerning practical ways to conduct strategic planning and the shift from periodic to ongoing consideration of strategic alternatives. Be warned, however, that the author has rather radical, unconventional views. for example, he wholeheartedly concurs with Tom Peters's "first steps," including, "Scrap your current strategic planning process—now."[3]

CHECKLIST: STRATEGIC AND TACTICAL ZINGERS

A relatively brief list of strategies and tactics summarizes the most important keys to superior manufacturing status. Many of these will require several years to implement. In fact, the continuous improvement process in each strategic and tactical issue may never stop. Executives and managers can easily forget some of the broad array of opportunities for improvement and thus switch from one hot fad to another as the focus of their companies' annual strategies and goals. The race will not be won by companies with a narrow or frequently changed focus. Being the best, unfortunately, is hard and requires continuous work in every conceivable facet of the business. The eventual winners are using and will continue to use the following list (which they should continuously expand) as their perpetual program in the pursuit of excellence.

Strategic Issues

1. Aggressively develop clusters of assembly and component factories, including supplier plants. This should be one of the highest priority strategies.
2. Understand that the issue of where to locate capacity is far more important than the make or buy decision.
3. Limit vertical integration to those processes with the highest value of output per investment dollar.
4. Exchange equity with the suppliers destined to be long-term suppliers. This is an easy way to improve supplier control without having to vertically integrate or invest capital.
5. Strategize ways to escape being a niche supplier. Alternatively, plan to expand from being a high volume supplier to a combination high volume and niche supplier.
6. Boldly add production capacity earlier than competitors.[4] Once a customer is won over by a manufacturer with the capacity to meet

[3]Tom Peters, *Thriving on Chaos: Handbook for a Management Revolution* (New York: Knopf, 1988), pp. 505–11.
[4]Michael E. Porter, *Competitive Strategy: Techniques for Analyzing Industries and Competitors* (New York: Free Press, 1980), p. 329.

his needs, a competitor has virtually no chance to win him back. Further, the competitor with the biggest market share can afford the best, most productive tools and equipment, so the ultimate winner will be the company with the largest share of market.

7. Demand is flexible and always will be. Therefore, factories must develop flexible people, equipment, and practices capable of varying the rate of production to meet the current rate of demand. This ability will eliminate costly inventory buildup in slow periods and late shipments in others.

8. The ultimate in people flexibility will be new labor laws and agreements that permit wages to be fixed but working hours per week and by day to vary, within reason, as market and customer demand vary. Pioneers in adopting revolutionary new work scheduling practices will steal an important march on their competition.

Capacity analysis and planning are perhaps the most important parts of strategic planning unique to the manufacturing organization. The topic is important enough to warrant its own chapter, Chapter 8. Two key issues relate to strategic capacity planning. First, a factory's maximum practical capacity is usually more than is commonly presumed. Further, every company's plan for capacity expansion should be bolder than that of its competitors. The company that successfully adds capacity earlier than its competitors has a chance to win new business. If it works hard to retain the business gained, competitors may never be able to wrest it away.

Tactical Issues

1. Develop or strengthen the company's own tool and machine design and manufacturing skills. Recognize that being the best manufacturer requires using the most productive equipment.

2. Cross-training at all levels of an enterprise greatly enhances the worth of employees to themselves and to their companies. Meaningful cross-training is not achieved by several brief assignments in different departments at the beginning of a career. It should include longer-term assignments in multiple functional disciplines.

3. Companies today are drowning in a sea of computer inputs and outputs. The primary focus of future computer projects must be to cut computer operations drastically by developing improvements that eliminate their real or perceived need.

4. Today's computer systems still take much too long to communi-

cate the latest market demand (reflecting today's sales) to the entire pipeline of supply. Rapid, system-to-system transfer of today's needs will be characteristic of twenty-first-century systems.

5. Manufacturers will use a vastly reduced, permanent group of vendors. Working with a continuously shifting base of suppliers, in the perpetual pursuit of lower prices, has greatly complicated the manufacturing network and lowered quality.

6. The transport of components and materials in the network of suppliers and users is incredibly more expensive and slower than it should be. Leading companies will operate their own transport systems and will use trucks and docks of new, superior design.

7. Design and manufacturing engineering organizations will be combined, and engineers will be cross-trained in both disciplines. As a result, products will be designed for manufacturability.

8. Commercially available materials and components standardization will be greatly improved. Factories use an incredibly diverse array of similar but different items because of the scarcity of really effective design standardization tools.

9. Licensing of product and of tooling and machine technology must become a much greater source for acquiring such technology. For dozens of different companies around the world to invent or reinvent the same things simultaneously does not make sense, especially when many companies in different areas of the world are not competing with one another.

10. Quality can be achieved only by designing it into the product and into the tools, machines, and methods used to produce it. Notions of quality control through any form of inspection are obsolete, and most quality control organizations must be eliminated. They typically add to product cost by identifying defects, not by eliminating them altogether.

Each of these strategies and tactics are discussed briefly in this chapter. They are discussed in much greater detail in later chapters that cover the broader array of tactical subjects. The tactical items listed above are by no means a comprehensive catalog. Rather, they are an important sampling of a much larger universe of opportunity.

MULTIPLANT CLUSTERS: THE ULTIMATE PIPELINE

Seldom recognized advantages of the Japanese automotive manufacturers are factors that might be viewed as disadvantages: the terrain of the island nation, which limits fast practical transportation between different areas of the country and almost total dependence on imported raw materials. These conditions have forced the Japanese to focus clusters of customer and supplier factories in close proximity to a few major port cities, as shown in Exhibit 2-1. By contrast, U.S. automotive manufacturers have been at a disadvantage due to the great distances between assembly factories and the main concentration of suppliers located in Northeastern United States. With assembly plants scattered around the country, some components are produced more than 1,000 miles away. The importance of clustering has not gone unnoticed. For example, Jones, Roos, and Womack write: "This mode of production achieves the highest efficiency, quality and flexibility when all activities from design to assembly occur in the same place."[5]

Geographically close clusters of supplier and user factories yield three major benefits. The first is the reduced amount of inventory in the pipeline, and the second is the speed with which products flow through and out of it. The third benefit, often the only one recognized, is the lower cost of transport. And while transport cost is an important consideration, many companies could drastically reduce it by simply developing radically new transport methods as described in Chapter 4. After all, the

FOCUSED LOCAL SOURCES

Hiroshima

Nagoya

Tokyo

★ Assembly Plant

◯ Suppliers

EXHIBIT 2-1

[5]Daniel T. Jones, Daniel Roos, and James P. Womack, *The Machine That Changed the World* (New York: Macmillan, 1990), p. 200.

Japanese have mastered efficient transport techniques that make it possible to import raw materials and energy from halfway around the world, and still export competitive finished products across the same vast distances.

When organizing factories and clusters of factories, it is vitally important to understand that inventory tends to increase exponentially in relation to the distances between the supplier of a component and its user, the assembly factory. The top line of Exhibit 2-2 illustrates the ideal minimum inventory required when an engine block machining line is directly linked to engine assembly by a very short conveyor with capacity for only one engine block between the last machining and first assembly stations.

Traditional manufacturing lore presumes it to be necessary to use fleets of forklift trucks, which whiz up and down wide aisles with large containers of components, endangering the lives and limbs of the pedestrians who share the aisles' use. As a result, most factories are designed with wide aisles between machining and assembly, as illustrated by the second example on the exhibit. Because of the aisle separating the two departments, the engine blocks must be stacked on pallets at the end of the machining line to await conveyance by lift truck from one side of the wide aisle to the other. Typically, one or more pallets of blocks are found on both sides of the aisle. Thus, increasing the distance between the

DISTANCE INCREASES INVENTORY

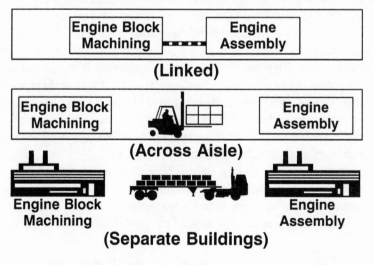

EXHIBIT 2-2

supplier and user causes the inventory of blocks to increase to ten, twenty, or more. In the third example in Exhibit 2–2, the machining and assembly lines are in separate buildings, perhaps only 100 meters apart. It now appears that the only economical way to transport blocks is on pallets on a flatbed truck. Thus, each building has a half-truckload of blocks, or more. A slight additional increase in the distance between supplier and user pushes the inventory of blocks to well over a hundred. The distances between supplier and user impose penalties of *both* excessive inventory and unreasonable transport costs. Experience has taught us that improved factory layout and transport design can and should reduce the number of lift trucks in a factory by as much as 90 percent.[6]

Using conveyors instead of lift trucks or flatbed trucks has not been an economical or timely alternative form of transport for reducing both inventory and transport costs. Often conveyors installed to reduce transport costs have had the capacity for even more units of inventory than the containers previously used between the two points. The charges for conveyor depreciation have rarely been less than the cost of the drivers and the vehicles. Nor are the penalties of excessive inventory limited to the value of the inventory, its carrying cost, and the transport cost. For example, the factory with near optimal inventory investment will be at least 50 percent smaller than the typical factory. Regardless of the unit of measure—feet, yards, or miles, the phenomenon of the expotential relationship between distance and inventory investment applies. The producer with a network of factories and supplier factories clustered in close proximity will have a competitive advantage over another with remote plants and suppliers. Not the least of the advantages is the speed with which the cluster can respond to customer needs.

Porter makes much of the national importance of *industry* clusters to the global competitive race.[7] This author's opinion is similar, if not as grand in scope. After all, while the national movers and shakers work on grandiose strategies at the national and industry levels, executives in *every* company must immediately start the process of building competitiveness in their own limited, fledgling clusters. None can afford to wait for the results of national or industry programs.

Many manufacturers should be working aggressively to develop local clusters of component suppliers, their minimum objective being the establishment of at least a few new local sources of supply each year as a not-so-long-term strategy. This applies to their own remote factories and

[6]See Appendix 2.
[7]Michael E. Porter, *The Competitive Advantage of Nations* (New York: Free Press, 1990), pp. 148–54.

to those of vendors. At one time, both user factories and their vendors guffawed at the idea that important component manufacturers could or should establish new, smaller factories in the vicinity of customers in remote areas of the country. Nissan, while building its first assembly plant in Tennessee, faced just such a situation, although it quickly made believers of the automotive suppliers that failed to win its business. Many major firms found the notion of small, competitive local factories absurd. While they were laughing at the notion of small factories in Tennessee versus giant factories in and around Detroit, Nissan simply encouraged its Japanese suppliers to come to the United States to build a focused factory near Nissan. It proved not only that the small, focused factories could be competitive but also that their size was instrumental in making them superior to the mammoth plants that supplied most of the domestic factories of American auto manufacturers. At the time, Western executives were still laboring under the delusion of economies of scale, not yet having learned that carefully designed, compact, focused factories can be developed with break-even points far below those of the giant out-of-focus plant. Now, not only Japanese–American businesses but also numerous local enterprises have learned of the magnificent benefits of small local factories to both customers and suppliers and are busily adapting to the lessons of focus. The companies that pursue local clusters most aggressively will undoubtedly be the superior manufacturers of the future.

PRODUCT OR PROCESS FACTORY CLUSTERS?

Leading edge multiplant companies are finding that the improvements in their individual factories are forcing them to reexamine the reasons for the locations and the very existence of their various factories. The main impetus for this reassessment is that their improved factories are found to use one-half or less of the space previously occupied. It is painfully clear, therefore, that only one-half of all existing factories are needed. Although there once were seemingly logical bases for specialization, today the rationale on which many enterprises based the operation of far-flung networks of plants with component and process specialization appears to defy reason. One such network of questionable logic (in retrospect) is the hypothetical RLH Corporation, Exhibit 2-3. In this example, one factory extrudes and cuts a bar to length, a second turns the bar, producing a shaft, and a third subassembles it into a housing and shaft assembly. Finally, a fourth factory assembles the end product,

MULTIPLE DEPENDENT PLANTS

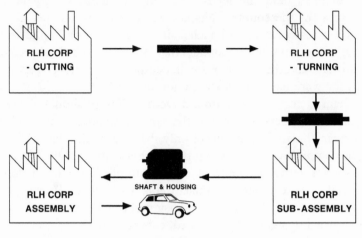

EXHIBIT 2-3

a finished automobile. Often, in real world cases like this, the basic material, steel, will have traveled thousands and even tens of thousands of miles before it finally becomes a component of the automobile. Some manufacturing networks that have evolved are even as complex as the multiple interdependent plants in Exhibit 2-4. In this example, three plants assemble automobiles, but each also specializes in other process types.

Considering the predilection companies have had for process specialization, it is really not too surprising that these types of factories have evolved. When the original small factory outgrew its site or the available workforce in the factory's vicinity, it seemed most natural to pick up a type of process—turning of shafts, for example—and move it to another location. The prevailing "conventional wisdom" was that the larger factory specializing in shaft machining had to be the most economical in the world because of economies of scale, and it would also have a corner on the world's shaft machining experts. The serious impact on the pipeline inventory and manufacturing lead time has seldom been recognized, and when it has, erroneous assumptions have been made regarding economies of scale.

A look inside most such monster, specialized component factories will reveal that specialization of the plant has not led to the theoretically expounded economies of scale. The shaft machining plant, for example, does not consist of a single manufacturing cell with the world's biggest, fastest machines. Instead, there are numerous cells, mainly because it is

MULTIPLE INTERDEPENDENT PLANTS

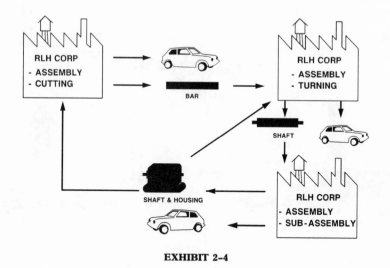

EXHIBIT 2-4

not economical to produce the smallest of shafts on equipment suitable for the largest. Nor is it possible to produce large shafts on machines suitable for small ones. In some instances, even though the volume of one size of shaft (or even a single type of shaft) is extremely high, there is more than one cell to produce it. The reason? Machines simply cannot be designed to cut shafts at the speeds that would be necessary to operate a single cell. What this implies is simply that it appears entirely feasible to move parts of the shaft machining factory into or nearer the assembly plants that use the shafts.

One actual case example involved the three factories in Exhibit 2–5. One of the factories assembled only the lowest volume products, while a second factory assembled both high and low volume products as well as machining components for use in both assembly plants. A third factory was dedicated to machining operations and machined components for both assembly plants. The volume of shipments, illustrated by the truck sizes, was very high between the machining plant and high volume plant, and lower in components traveling to the low volume assembly plant from the other two factories.

The long-term plan proposed to the company was complicated slightly by the fact that the specialized machining plant was not only the company's newest but also the apple of the chief executive officer's eye. (Almost no one in the company thought it worth the risk to suggest to the boss that the new factory be emptied). Further, there was too little factory

SPECIALIZED MACHINING/ASSEMBLY

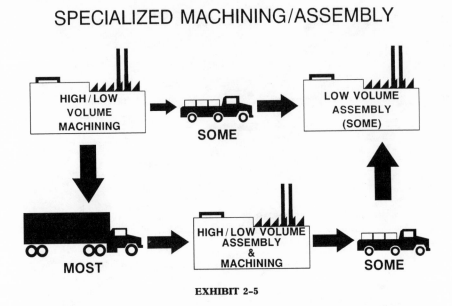

EXHIBIT 2-5

space and land on the site of the low-volume factory for both *all* low-volume product assembly and for the related machining. However, superior methods of process design and implementation were planned that would subsequently reduce factory space enough to eliminate one of the three factories. Exhibit 2–6 shows the long-range plan recommended and adopted by the company. It included moving all low-volume assembly and as much related component machining possible to the low-volume plant. All other machining was left in or moved to the high-volume assembly plant, and the specialized machining plant was emptied. This left a minimal amount of transport, trimmed tens of millions of dollars from the costs of operations and slashed inventories by several tens of millions more. No wonder the chief executive officer found it so natural to accept abandoning the new factory! And when the factory is sold or leased, adding to cash flow, the moves will look even better.

CURBING THE INTERPLANT
INVENTORY INVESTMENT

Few companies with multiplant networks have bothered to calculate the additional inventory investment caused by the remoteness of some of their plants that supply components to the other plants. Perhaps one reason for not doing so is the apparent difficulty of determining what

ASSEMBLY/MACHINING INTEGRATION

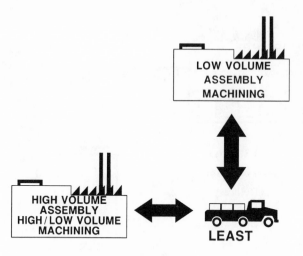

EXHIBIT 2-6

that investment is. The author has always found it relatively easy to determine a rough but reasonable estimate. Such an estimate is invaluable when decisions must be made concerning the locations of factories and the products and processes assigned to those plants. Following is an overview of some of the factors involved in determining the elusive value of inventory in the multiplant pipeline.

The frequency of shipments between remote plants, the size of the truckloads, and the hours in transit all have a predictable impact on the minimum amount of inventory in the pipeline. As Exhibit 2-7 shows, a fourth element of the aggregate inventory in the pipeline is the just-in-case safety stocks that both user and supplier build into their systems. These safety stocks may be formally recognized as such or might be built into earlier-than-necessary scheduled completion at the supplier plant, or the earlier-than-necessary scheduled receipt at the user plant, whether formal or informal. Their purpose is to protect against all the uncertainties of performance, including late delivery from the supplier's factory process, late shipment or arrival of a truck, the inaccuracy of requirements caused by fluctuation of demand, and the possibility of finding defective parts at either end of the pipeline. Such safety stocks are usually the largest and the least formally controlled element of inventory in the network. Often, inventory control clerks add their own quantities and early delivery days to each receipt. Since there are often no policies governing such informal safety stocks, the amount or days added to the pure

INTERPLANT INVENTORY

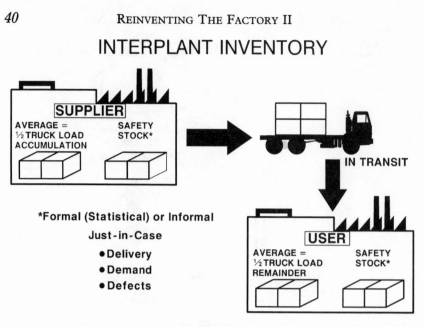

EXHIBIT 2-7

requirement varies from delivery to delivery. Some might view this practice as unwarranted, but if the clerks did not add the informal safety stock, there would be far more business interruptions, because there is so much uncertainty in delivery. Where there is no formal set of safety stock rules, it is not difficult to see that a company's actual inventory aggregate value can be used as a basis for estimating the value of the informal safety stock. The aggregate safety stock resulting from the inventory clerk's informal and variable decisions is the difference between the theoretical interplant inventory, calculated as indicated below, and the actual aggregate inventory of interplant components. Understanding the simple ingredients of multiplant inventory, Exhibit 2-7, makes it relatively easy to calculate the aggregate minimum investment that the network causes. The dollar value of the average truckload divided by the truckload delivery frequency is the theoretical minimum inventory illustrated on the graph, Exhibit 2-8. This inventory, in dollars, plus the average value of inventory in transit, plus safety stock is the inventory attributable to interplant shipment. All factors in the equation are fairly readily obtained from accounting and traffic records. For example, costed interplant transfers for a month, divided by the number of truckloads shipped, is the average value of a truckload.

Short-term reductions of the interplant inventory might well be achievable immediately, while decisions to relocate factory processes might take

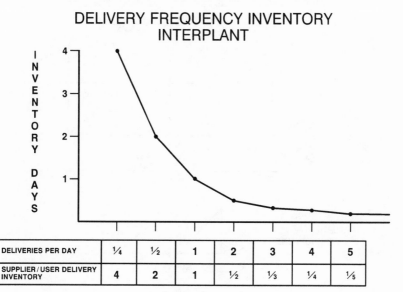

DELIVERY FREQUENCY INVENTORY INTERPLANT

DELIVERIES PER DAY	¼	½	1	2	3	4	5
SUPPLIER / USER DELIVERY INVENTORY	4	2	1	½	⅓	¼	⅕

EXHIBIT 2-8

months or years to implement. Increasing the frequency of deliveries is one way that inventory can be cut, as is seen in Exhibit 2-8. It may be less obvious that safety stocks should logically be cut in the same ratio as delivery frequency inventories. Exhibit 2-9 contains the classic "sawtooth" graph of inventory elements, and how they change over time. The total inventory peaks each time a truckload is received and declines steadily as inventory is used in operation, until the next truckload arrives. The lower, smaller graph depicts more frequent receipt of smaller truckloads and correspondingly smaller safety stocks. Management should ensure that interim inventory reduction programs include steps for shrinking the safety stock, not just the changes to the transport system outlined in Chapter 4.

When importation of materials and components from overseas is reduced by developing local sources and adding them to the manufacturing cluster, inventory reduction is not the only benefit. Importation is infinitely more complex than local procurement. It entails a large array of additional forms and procedures. And with wild or even moderate fluctuations of currency, international sourcing forces companies to become expert in the field of international currency management.[8] These factors, combined with the advantages of rapid response to market trends made

[8]Gregory J. Millman, *The Floating Battlefield: Corporate Strategies in the Currency Wars* (New York: ANACOM, 1990).

DELIVERY FREQUENCY

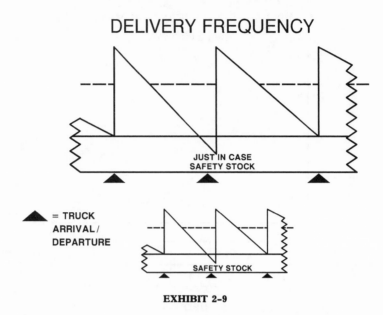

EXHIBIT 2-9

possible by local clusters, should encourage companies to work hard to reduce reliance on foreign suppliers.

MULTIPLANT SYSTEMS: FUEL FOR FEUDS

Amazingly, picking up a component manufacturing process and moving it into a factory of its own changes its relationship from one of a family of departments to much more like that of traditional customers and vendor. Components once flowed between supplier to user departments with a minimum of bureaucratic intervention when they were under the same roof. But as soon as the department becomes a separate plant, the customer plant starts to mistrust the quality and quantities sent from the sister plants and initiates policies and procedures for counting and inspecting incoming receipts. This is obviously nonsense. Executives of the superior enterprises of the twenty-first century will direct factories to act again like members of the same corporate family, using simpler interplant shipment scheduling and tracking systems. For example:

1. Sister plants are sometimes permitted to accept or alter requested shipment dates if they perceive that the request is scheduled too soon to provide adequate time to procure materials and to manufacture the item on schedule. This should not be permitted. If

every end product master schedule depended on winning the concurrence of every supplier, nothing would ever be produced. Every supplier in the network, including vendors, should understand that its responsibility is to do whatever is necessary to support the company's production plan, not to search for reasons, legitimate or not, for delay. Thus, the real mission of suppliers must continue to be finding ways to meet "impossible" schedules. Fortunately, most manufacturing people have always responded to the challenge; thus, they already know how to do so.

2. The number and frequency of "impossible" schedules can be sharply reduced by lowering the lead time and inventory in the pipeline and by frequently broadcasting timely, up-to-date schedules to every factory in the pipeline. Short lead times also make it practical to freeze a portion of the schedule. Frozen schedules help to cut the instances of surprise schedule changes that are already too late to meet.

3. The interplant requirements of the user plant should automatically become the shipping requirement for the supplier plant. Wherever practical, a single scheduling system should be used for both plants.

4. Counting and inspecting interplant receipts should not be permitted; thus, new systems need not accommodate changes to quantities reported as shipped by supplying plants. Every factory has internal procedures for handling inventory discrepancies and defective parts found in the routine course of operations. These same systems should be used to handle interplant parts.

The author's prior book outlined some thoughts on planning systems for the supplier network that emphasizes vendors.[9] These comments are equally applicable to sister plants. It should even be easier and faster to improve systems between factories of the same company than between customer and vendor.

MAKE OR BUY: THE IMPORTANT CRITERIA

Whether or not to vertically integrate the manufacturing processes of all components of a product is often deemed to be an important facet of strategic planning. "Make or buy" is a less esoteric term for the same

[9]See Appendix 2.

thing. Others have expounded at great length on numerous factors to consider when formulating a make or buy strategy, as if these decisions were a routine, integral part of managing a manufacturing enterprise. However, seasoned industry veterans readily agree that such decisions are rare and seldom of monumental importance to increased success or survival. They know that the practical realities of the existing company's factories and of its present and potential suppliers have at some time in the past been considered in determining whether to purchase or manufacture components. And in the majority of instances nothing has occurred to change the validity of the decision. Neither the academician nor the businessman has seen that the most important issue is not who should own and operate the component factory but rather where to locate it. The most efficiently manufactured products are produced in geographically compact clusters of a producer's factories and those of its suppliers.

Economic evaluation of the alternative costs of manufacturing versus purchasing have rarely been useful. Typically, they have been based on a company's current facilities and methods and those of its suppliers. The fallacy of a decision based on today's equipment and methods is that the productivity and quality of either or both can be drastically improved. Such improvement should be of higher priority than a make or buy decision. Further, whenever a factory out-sources items previously manufactured, the change almost always shifts fixed overhead costs to other manufactured items, lowering the factory's presumed profitability on other items manufactured. Nor is it often practical to lower the fixed expenses of the portion of the factory vacated. Thus, although the price paid to vendors can be lower than apparent internal cost, the real result may be to break even or even to suffer a loss.

Many other criteria could be considered when deciding to make or to buy. Porter, for example, lists several.[10] While these are not unimportant, some new, simple, yet powerful business objectives should drive the make or buy strategy. Two of the new objectives are:

1. Develop unique, patented in-house designed and manufactured machines, tooling, and processes with innovative features to provide a competitive edge over companies that use conventional machines supplied by machine tool manufacturers. Alternatively, make unique modifications to conventional machines to make their performance superior to the same machines used by competitors.

2. Maximize return on investment by giving priority to expenditures

---

[10]Porter, *Competitive Strategy*, Chapter 14.

for machines and processes with the lowest investment per dollar value of output.

During decades of working in factories around the globe, the author has seen a common factor differentiating the most productive factories from others. Today's superior manufacturers all have machine and tool designers and skilled machine manufacturing and toolmaking craftsmen who are trained and experienced in producing custom designed machines and tools unique to their products. The custom machines and tooling are distinctly of higher productivity and produce higher quality products for their applications than do the generic and modified-generic machines produced by the machine tool industry. Companies with insufficient or nonexistent machine design and craftsman skills must begin to acquire and develop them if they ever expect to survive long enough to achieve superiority. As Dertouzos and his co-authors point out, "the American tool machine industry is dissolving."[11] However, it is not only the industry but also the shortage of tool and machine designers in *every* company that threatens their ability to compete with enterprises that nurture and maintain these skills.

Once tactical programs for achieving the required capabilities are in place, a strategic plan for developing and manufacturing custom-designed machines becomes vital. The selection of which new equipment to develop should be based on the families of machined components that have the highest dollar volume and that competitors usually use generic machines to produce. Whether the company or its competitors currently purchase the component families is irrelevant, because when the new machines become available they certainly must be installed in the company's own factory to delay the competition's learning about the new techniques.

Focusing in-house skills on designing new machines and processes for the products of highest dollar output per dollar of investment is the powerful, simplifying strategy that mirrors the natural evolution of most businesses. Since assembly facilities are relatively inexpensive, and since the value of the output of final assembly is the largest of all processes, almost every company assembles its own products. At the other extreme, off-the-shelf hardware is almost always purchased from the major hardware suppliers. It is not a coincidence that the value of the hardware is rarely more than a few percentage points of the total product cost, thus a company's toolmakers and designers should focus their efforts on costlier

[11]Michael L. Dertouzos, Richard K. Lester, and Robert M. Solow, *Made in America: Regaining the Productive Edge* (Cambridge, Mass.: MIT Press, 1989), pp. 20–21.

items, leaving process design for hardware to the hardware specialists. Further, the cost of equipment designed to make such low cost items as hardware, while not astronomical, is quite high compared to the value of its output. In the middle ground, higher cost, machined, proprietary design items are most often manufactured in-house rather than purchased. Considering the impact of distance on the size of the inventory investment, if the items produced in the factory are the highest cost items, it follows that the required inventory investment will be the lowest possible. While the cost of machines to process these items may be expensive, the value of the material used in these items is also high. Thus, the output per dollar of capital investment is usually impressive.

One of the Japanese juggernauts' greatest strengths is that users and suppliers have a strong bond fostered by unilateral and mutual positions of equity. It is amazing that so few Western enterprises have caught on and so many have failed to avail themselves of the opportunity to exchange equity as a preliminary step toward establishing formal bonds. The earliest companies to institute these bonds will be the ones to enjoy the greatest loyalty and mutuality of interest in joint promotion of productivity and quality.

THE STRATEGIC ARENA

First and foremost, responsibility for strategic planning needs to be shifted from the corporate level to the level of the managers responsible for new, focused subplants. This is important to remember whenever one reads "executive" in the following explanation of strategic planning alternatives. Executives and their consultants have long been enamored of strategic planning, often out of proportion to its importance in their companies. The term "strategic planning" connotes everyone's ideal of executive suite strategists making brilliant, inventive business decisions and piloting their companies through the maze of innovative changes required to trigger quantum increases in growth and profitability. Every businessman knows about the industry giants who, at least for a time, have had the bold inspiration to make changes that have revolutionized their companies' competitive stance.

When a company lacks executives of superstar strategist category, and when it does not decentralize the strategic planning process, it must alternatively and logically look for a structured approach to ensure that its management considers all options that could lead to superstar-caliber successes, sans superstars. Fortunately, strategic planning can be proceduralized to guide executives through the steps of considering a checklist of strategic options for the enterprise's future direction. This is especially easy because the practical strategic alternatives to the status quo for an existing factory are limited to a few key issues. This fact may be a disappointing revelation to the theorist, but it is logical to the pragmatic businessman. He knows that generations of executives have successfully managed the company by studying and learning it well. At various times in the past they have made the right decisions concerning the company's core strategies; thus, he can conclude that the company is doing most things the way it should.

Executives who undertake the formal, proceduralized process of strategic planning for the first time wax most enthusiastic. The process provides them with a profound learning experience—one always finds assimilating new facts and new ideas exhilarating. It follows that the excitement level soars when the strategic formulation includes consideration of acquisitions and new product development. Sadly, many executives are also excited when introduced to strategic options for the existing business during the planning process. The lamentable reason for this excitement is that the executives of engineering, manufacturing, finance, and sales and marketing learn more about the other functions than they ever knew. Unfortunately, executives have not been adequately cross-trained throughout their careers to prepare them for executive status. Better functional cross-training of executives is a fundamental need for many companies. For example, Matsushita's cross-training program moves 5 percent of all employees from one division to another each year.[12] Since management and supervisory personnel account for the biggest percentage of those moved, the frequency of change for fast-track individuals falls in the two-to-four-year range. The largely false mystique surrounding the difficulty in mastering other functional specialties arises from the fact that specialists overplay the need for long technical training. They think extensive, specialized education, training, and job experience are needed to function in the various disciplines of engineering, production, finance, marketing, and even data processing. In reality, industrious people with executive and managerial abilities are able to acquire prodigious amounts of knowledge in other disciplines when given longer-term, temporary assignments in these areas. Meanwhile, in the short term, given the lack of adequate cross-training, executives should be vitally interested in the systematic planning process, since it helps to fill a void in their universe of business knowledge.

[12]Anthony C. Athos, and Richard Tanner Pascale, *The Art of Japanese Management: Applications for American Executives* (New York: Simon & Schuster, 1981), p. 53.

A few words of warning are appropriate. First, one must not be misled to believe that the strategic planning process will inevitably uncover new strategic imperatives of magnificent scope and assured success. Finding revolutionary new avenues to pursue will be the exception rather than the rule. However, the planning process inevitably leads to the identification of countless opportunities for *tactical*, not strategic, improvements. Second, institutionalization of the planning process as a periodic event may be a mistake. The primary value of an effective initial effort is that it provides a checklist of the major options to be considered. Once all people involved have been educated and trained, and have completed one planning cycle, mentally reviewing the checklist should become part of the executive's daily routine. Thus, he should habitually reconsider the options and recast his plans whenever opportune, not just during an annual planning process. Annual processes are necessary only when one fails to discharge the ongoing daily responsibilities of management.

Lastly, as with most aspects of business management, formalization and documentation of the details of strategic planning may lead to increased bureaucracy and complexity rather than simplification. After all, the procedure is really a substitute for the personal traits, experience, and dynamism of the super strategist. Its most important element is the checklist. All other formal documentation is superfluous. And, although top executives may be an important source of strategic ideas, the real power of the entire organization will best be unleashed by decentralizing and operating a bottom-up planning process as described by Tom Peters.[13]

Others have written at length on manufacturing strategy in the broadest sense, as a companywide strategy. The global company strategy, however, consists of multiple interdependent strategies, each of which falls under the jurisdiction of one of the individual executives responsible for product design, manufacturing, sales, and marketing. It should be no surprise that the product line and marketing issues are of overriding strategic importance. Manufacturing strategies must logically support them in the sense of ensuring that they will be within the technical capabilities of manufacturing's available and planned equipment and the practical constraints of its people, plants, and processes.

STRATEGY, TACTIC, OR GOAL?

In the rush to find glittering examples of manufacturing strategies, theorists manage to blur the issue by throwing in everything, including tac-

[13]Peters, *Thriving on Chaos*, pp. 510–11.

tics, goals, and the kitchen sink. (Maskell, for example, makes the common mistake of using goals as examples of strategies—such goals as inventory and lead time reduction.)[14] The author's definition of strategy is:

> Major changes of companywide scope. These usually require large expenditures and new and revised organization structures. They require more than a year to implement.

The valuable time of top management strategic planners can be protected by recognizing early that cross-functional participation of the planners is vital only when the strategy has major companywide (cross-functional) implications. This can be contrasted to the minor strategies and tactics of individual organizations that do not have complex interrelationships with other organizations.

For example, if a company makes a strategic decision to design and produce a new line of products, the ripples of the decisions quickly reach tsunami proportions, necessitating major efforts in engineering, finance, manufacturing, sales, and marketing, among others. By contrast, a decision by manufacturing to replace an old paint line with a new one with essentially the same capabilities has little if any impact on functional areas other than manufacturing. (However, if a new paint line were capable of higher quality or more attractive finishes, it might trigger intensive design and marketing efforts to capitalize on the new capability).

A manufacturing company has only a few strategic options in its global operations. Far fewer fall within the jurisdiction of manufacturing, and they can all be classified into one of two major categories:

1. Location in the manufacturing–vendor network
2. Manufacturing method

Several readers will be shocked at the apparent omissions in this extremely brief and simple classification. For example, some will have thought that the vertical integration (make or buy) strategy might have been excluded. However, the author's definition of manufacturing location encompasses the location in a building, the factory site location (company *and* vendor), and the city, state, and country. Thus, the decision to make or to buy is just another form of manufacturing location

---

[14]Brian H. Maskell, *Just-in-Time: Implementing the New Strategy* (Carol Stream, Ill.: Hitchcock Publishing, 1989), p. 25.

decision. Other readers might cite flexibility[15] and automation or even technology as overlooked strategic areas. The author, however, views these nebulous generalities to be mere details of the more significant whole, the entire manufacturing process. Yet others will ask themselves why the author overlooked the importance of the organization structure and workforce issues. The fact is that the author views the organization structure, including all support functions, as part and parcel of the global manufacturing method, while such people issues as training and compensation are viewed as tactical or policy matters, not strategies.

Finally, other critics will be shocked that quality and cost goals have not been defined as major strategic issues. Gunn, for one, treats strategy and objectives (goals) almost synonymously,[16] perhaps because it is so difficult to develop an impressive list of important management strategies. (Hall correctly identifies quality, reliability, product and volume flexibility, delivery dependability, asset and people utilization, and cost minimization as goals, not strategies.)[17] The author holds that every company must have the same goal categories, although the short-term quantification of different companies will be different based on how well they are currently doing. For instance, there can be but one long-term quality goal (not strategy). That goal is quality (number of defects) measured in parts per million. Further, quality is a direct result of the manufacturing methods employed (including the vendor's methods), as is the product's cost. Those who deem it appropriate to differentiate between low and high quality or low and high cost production as a strategy are undoubtedly confusing value and quality. Customers identify products of higher value as such primarily because the materials used to make them are inherently more valuable and/or of higher strength of performance characteristics. Products that are defective may be either high or low value products that have flaws due to errors in the manufacturing process.

Now that goals, tactics, and strategies have been defined, and differences between the strategies that are manufacturing's prime responsibility and those of other organizations have been clarified, a few words concerning product strategies are in order.

---

[15]Patricia E. Moody, ed., and Sara B. Bechman, *Strategic Manufacturing: Dynamic New Directions for the 1990s* (Homewood, Ill.: Dow Jones–Irwin, 1990), Chapter 6.
[16]Thomas G. Gunn, *Manufacturing for Competitive Advantage: Becoming a World Class Manufacturer* (Cambridge, Mass.: Ballinger Publishing, 1987).
[17] Robert W. Hall, *Zero Inventories* (Homewood, Ill.: Dow Jones–Irwin, 1983), pp. 302–8.

PRODUCT STRATEGIES

Since others have more than adequately covered product and marketing strategies, this chapter emphasizes manufacturing strategy. However, a few points pertaining to product strategy warrant further discussion before proceeding to manufacturing. One point concerns the concept of market niche. As will be seen, the author believes that being a niche manufacturer will ultimately mean that a company will not be among the survivors. Yet a company with a strategy designed to predominate in a market niche and with a plan to expand rapidly outside that niche can advance to the ranks of superior manufacturers, especially when the perceived niche supplier provides highly engineered, high cost, low volume products that compete with products of high volume producers. A case example in which two competing companies manufacture air conditioners will best illustrate the point. Each of the competing companies had radically different catalog sizes. One made hundreds of discrete products, the other thousands. The manufacturer of thousands of products was the smaller of the two and competed directly with every product sold by the larger, higher volume producer. The stylized drawing in Exhibit 2–10 highlights the main differences. The smaller of the two companies had accepted its role as a supplier to a small, special segment of the market (in other words, a niche). The pertinent strategic planning ques-

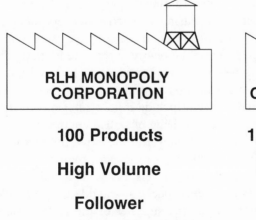

NICHE MANUFACTURER TODAY

RLH MONOPOLY CORPORATION	NICHE CORPORATION
100 Products	1,000 Products
High Volume	Low Volume
Follower	Innovator

EXHIBIT 2-10

tion was whether its future role should be that of a niche producer. For manufacturing personnel, the folly of offering thousands of low volume products versus a few hundred high volume products was (or appeared to be) crystal clear. They understood that costs, and therefore prices, of low volume products must be high. So they concluded that they would never successfully compete with the high volume producer on price as long as they remained low volume producers.

Sales, marketing, and engineering management of the low volume manufacturer were always convinced that they should continue to maintain a significant but small (proportional) presence in the marketplace. They felt that it was not only important to continue to offer thousands of product but also to expand the number of products and their variations as dynamically as possible. Their rationale was that many buyers, presented with a small and a large catalog, would automatically pick up the larger first, since it would be more likely to contain an air conditioner precisely matching the customer's perception of his need. Second, management perceived the company's strength as lying in its history of innovative engineering, having led the field in new technology for decades. Thus, they felt that buyers wanting products on the leading edge of technology would continue to buy from them rather than from lower cost, higher volume producers.

For which of the two companies should any executive prefer to work? The higher volume, large company. Although the smaller company's management recognized this, their dilemma was the extreme difficulty, costs, and risks of changing from niche producer to high volume producer. Unfortunately, some theorists view the role of niche supplier as a necessary, viable position in which to operate perpetually. But it is the author's belief that it must be the business objective of every niche company to drive continuously to expand from niche supplier to combination niche and high volume producer. The reality is that the large producer will and should inevitably begin to covet the niche market and move to take it over. If a niche must exist, in terms of the uniqueness of its products, the high volume producer will include in its strategic plan the acquisition of a niche producer or the hiring of skilled engineers, if necessary, to begin to take over the leadership in innovative product design. It might even build new state-of-the-art factories for producing the niche products at record low cost and price levels. As seen in Exhibit 2–11, the RLH Corporation, with its deep pockets, should easily be able to displace the Niche Corporation as the supplier of the niche products. For example, the real-life Niche Corporation offered many thousands more products than should have been necessary. As a result, its highly

NICHE CORPORATION TOMORROW

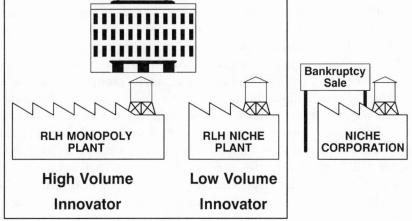

EXHIBIT 2-11

innovative engineers were unable to keep up with either new product innovation or incorporation of new technology into older products. Further, they had little time for adequate engineering of small incremental improvements into the entire range of products.

The air conditioning niche manufacturer needed to pattern itself after the RLH Corporation, which could achieve better engineered products with fewer, more qualified engineers by initially controlling the breadth of its new niche product line. It would offer a fairly high variety of customized products by improving the modularity of its design features, thus giving customers a range of highly standardized options from which to choose. Its sales and marketing organization had a long, successful history of channeling customer needs into sales of air conditioners slightly different from the customer's original perception of his need. Thus, sales could be channeled into what the company prefers to sell, usually to the customer's advantage since the produce he is persuaded to buy almost always costs less while being better suited to his application. By applying the skills of the high volume organization to the niche product line, the RLH Corporation could keep the number of products much lower than that of the Niche Corporation.

The manufacturing division of TTI, Inc., of Fort Worth, Texas, is an excellent example of a niche producer that successfully entered a fiercely competitive market (AMP/Matrix, Berg, Cannon, Cinch, and Molex are in the same field). It captured and subsequently expanded an important niche. In this case, a setup reduction program was one vital element of a project to help TTI master production of small lot sizes. With close-to-zero changeover cost, pricing of small lot sizes can be in the same ballpark as pricing by producers of lot sizes in the thousands. However, TTI's objective is to capitalize on its innovative methods in order to grow rapidly, thus making itself one of the biggest suppliers.

The long-term strategy of every company must be to become or continue to be the superior producer, excellent in product performance, quality, and cost. Ultimately only the best survive. Lesser companies fall by the wayside sooner or later. A company's market share is, therefore, one of the most important measures of its success or failure. For the confident company that now has too many products in its line, but knows that it will be able to channel sales to a far fewer, higher volume, lower cost line, there is great hope! Chapter 5 outlines practical methods for achieving product line rationalization and product standardization, both ingredients of the formula for increasing sales volume and lowering product cost.

COMPETITIVE BENCHMARK: PREREQUISITE OR PROCRASTINATION?

The words "competitive benchmarking" are almost guaranteed to raise the author's temper to near the boiling point. In the early days when Western industries were rapidly losing market share and even dropping from the competitive race entirely, numerous companies undertook lengthy projects to develop benchmarks as a prerequisite to planning improvements to keep or to regain a competitive edge. Never mind the fact that the keys to success were obvious and simple and that improvements could be started immediately. Some felt that systematic setting of quantified, justifiable goals was the only way to get into action. When one is bleeding profusely, one does not tolerate waiting for a doctor to chart a complete recovery plan. Nor, while continuing to bleed, does one send the doctor out to study the methods used on other patients. Even competitive industry leaders cannot afford to take the slow road when they are aware that they have opportunities for becoming even better. The quest for continuous, revolutionary improvement is the only sure way to keep ahead of the pack. And the stakes are too high to delay beginning the quest.

Nevertheless, while benchmarking should not be considered a prerequisite to beginning improvement projects, the author does not argue that knowledge of competitors is unimportant. It *is* argued that knowledge of methods is substantially more important than advance quantification of their results. For example, virtual elimination of setup (changeover) costs has tremendous benefits that should be obvious to every manufacturing executive. Should one wait to quantify the financial results of a competitor before getting work on setup reduction under way? Definitely not. The author further argues that to focus study only on *competitors* would be a most grievous mistake! Thousands of factories, with entirely different types of products and processes, have a wealth of generically similar circumstances. The relatively small number of competitors are unlikely to have the *best* ideas for such generically similar aspects of production and distribution. By contrast, the number of *all* companies that have ideas that could benefit factories in other industries is much higher. Almost every study group that goes to Japan tries to visit factories in its own industry. In Japan, any company study team wanting to see the very best will visit a Toyota factory. The team knows it will have to adapt what it learns to its own product and process, understanding that the basics of manufacturing are common to all factories. Therefore, the companies studied should not be limited to the best competitors, but should include the best companies regardless of industry.

Camp, whose entire book is dedicated to benchmarking,[18] quickly gets to the pith of the matter by explaining how U.S. manufacturers were caught off guard by the Japanese. He explains that "the Japanese did not accept the notion that goods and services could be competitive by simply mimicking the past." He goes on to say: "They recognized that new methods, processes and practices had to be uncovered, and more important . . . the best of these had to be combined." Thus, when outlining an approach to benchmarking, he clearly indicates that while the study of *practices* is of supreme importance, the study of quantified results is of considerably less importance.

Numerous companies have deemed benchmarking to have been of considerable value. For example, comparing the few defects in a competitor's product to the many defects in one's own products has been viewed as a powerful motivational tool in winning acceptance of rigorous new goals. The underlying assumption is that it is necessary to quantify the difference in order to convince the company's people that a difference exists. Simply to say that the competition is making giant inroads in market share as evidence that it is doing things better is considered not good

[18]Robert C. Camp, *Benchmarking: The Search for Industry Best Practices That Lead to Superior Performance* (Milwaukee, Wis.: ASQC Quality Press, 1989).

enough. In retrospect, it seems ludicrous that one could believe that the bureaucracy of an intelligence system like the one Porter illustrates[19] should have been necessary to alert automotive executives to the growing competitive threat of imports. The flood of vehicles across the docks was not enough to do the trick, nor was the wealth of statistical data available to the industry. What the responsible individuals at all levels failed to do was to be *directly* involved in keeping abreast of product and process technology. In retrospect, quite obviously, the industry had too much confidence based on past performance and thus failed to look outside its own environs and give credence to the powerful advantages of the Japanese success—low cost simplification of both product and process. While the author suspects that the largest companies will and must continue to employ the bureaucratic staff approach to competitor intelligence (benchmarking), the key to the most successful focused operations will be executives and managers who routinely stay abreast of developments in their industries and in manufacturing in general. Not only will they be aware of all important trends and developments, but they will also use their knowledge to spur their own organizations to be on the leading edge, not just followers. This is the way to become a superior manufacturer.

STEP-BY-STEP STRATEGIC PLANNING APPROACH

Strategic planning, as usually conducted, should involve virtually every function in the manufacturing enterprise. The planning chart overview, Exhibit 2-12, outlines the most important segments of strategic planning. The process starts with the organization of the strategic planning team and the review of any prior strategic plans, whether formal or informal. Paralleling this review, the team performs a financial analysis, with the objective of putting the financial facts into perspective. Having developed proforma financials helps the team define an aggressive plan of attack based on the strategic and tactical issues with the highest potential improvement, and to minimize the time spent on issues of lesser importance.

The strategic plan usually includes a few issues that cross several functional areas, as in the case of the addition of a new product family. Hence, the product planning team needs to understand the operations of each functional area. For that purpose, there are separate planning chart seg-

[19]Porter, *Competitive Strategy.*

PLANNING CHART OVERVIEW

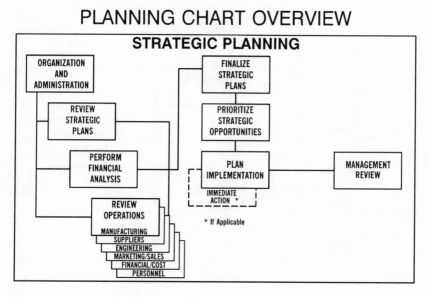

EXHIBIT 2-12

ments for reviewing the operations of each function. Since additional planning charts, at the next level of detail, are available for each functional area, strategic planning can easily be tailored to include as many functional areas as is practical. This book, given practical limits, could not possibly cover each segment of the overview planning chart, not to mention each of the steps within each segment. However, it will perhaps be informative to look into one segment, the one titled Finalize Strategic Plans. Exhibit 2–13 details the next level of detail within that segment. The major ingredients of the plan are represented by the steps for developing them. The various "chapters" of the plan include the product plan, the marketing/sales plan, the manufacturing plan, the supplier plan, and, very importantly, the strategy for the organization. The organization plan includes the strategies and tactics for both revising the organization and developing the education and training plans to prepare all of the organization's people for the new strategic direction.

The last "chapter" of the strategic plan is the financial plan, which should usually take the form of pro forma projected operating statements and balance sheets. Since strategies should usually be designed to improve the results of operations, the widest number of people will most readily understand them if they are expressed in terms of their financial impact on operations.

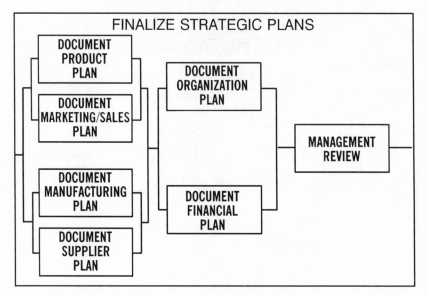

EXHIBIT 2–13

SUMMARY

Networks of plants in multiple-plant companies cause inventory investment and transportation costs to be more than those needed in self-contained factories. Since twenty-first-century factories will require one-half as much space as old-fashioned (and even recent) factories, it is imperative that enterprises with networks of dependant and interdependent factories reexamine plant operations with an eye toward consolidation into one-half as many facilities. Nor is it necessary to wait until factory consolidation is complete to reduce inventories, pipeline lead time, and transport costs. Major short-term opportunities for improvement in interplant systems, inventory policies, and transport operations can help pay for the longer-range reorganization and relocation of manufacturing operations.

3

□□□

Managing and Supervising
the Focused Factory

EXECUTIVES OF COMPANIES on the leading edge of organizing focused
factories-within-factories ascribe a major share of their new subplants'
success to employee empowerment: delegation of significant new authority and responsibility to managers, supervisors, and cell and line operators. They understand that individuals entrusted with the responsibility
and authority for operating a small business (or factory-within-a-factory)
will immediately start to manage that business with all of the dedication
of an entrepreneur. The original entrepreneur is often one of the first to
recognize when his business has grown to the point of not being manageable by a single individual.[1]

As the factory undergoes the revolutionary changes that yield major
continuous improvements in productivity, the roles of managers, supervisors, and employees require modification. To realize the maximum benefits of the superior factory, people must understand new ways of managing and operating the focused subplants. The best executives prepare
their organizations not only for the factory changes but also for the new
employee roles. Operators of cells and lines learn that their teams will

---

[1]For example, one of the author's earliest clients, Bill Sauey, the founder of Flambeau
Corporation, has been quoted as saying, in effect, that if he did not decentralize the
management of an acquisition, he himself would "screw it up." Michael E. McGill,
American Business and the Quick Fix (New York, Henry Holt, 1988), p. 67.

be largely self-supervised, with authority and responsibility delegated to the team as rapidly as it can assimilate them. Supervisors learn that they are to become business managers, and managers learn that they will become the visionary planners who propel their operations into the age of superior manufacturing. All learn that they must begin to obtain more knowledge, and thus value, by gaining wider experience in several departments of the organization through on-the-job cross-training.

It may surprise some readers to know that the main emphasis of this chapter is *not* the trite, commonplace exhortation to executive management to turn the responsibility for reinventing the workplace over to the entire workforce. Indeed, chaos may well have originally been invented through design by a committee. The perceived panacea of delegating the awesome task of reinventing the factory to all employees is popular in some academic circles. It has had some success in a limited number of companies but was never the most important ingredient in the success of the Japanese or their successors in either the West or the Pacific Basin.[2] The author contends that factories must be designed by engineers who follow a master plan, which, when implemented, will thrust the factory into the forefront of productivity leaders. However, to take maximum advantage of the resulting factory equipment and layout improvements requires marshaling the involvement of all of a company's people, not just it's managers and supervisors. All must be trained in work methods and management practices suited to effective operation in the new environment. They must be enlisted in cow-kicking programs that help people discard the erroneous premises on which factory operations have been based in the past. Among the plethora of sacred cows that must be booted out are the following:

1. Large factories are better than small factories.
2. The practice and concepts of time and motion studies are passé.
3. Pay incentives are necessary prerequisites to gaining employee cooperation and satisfaction.
4. Machinists and assemblers must be specialists in the operation of a single machine or work station in order to be optimally productive.
5. The scope of job tasks must be increased substantially to reduce boredom and stress.

[2]See the "Achievers" appendix of the author's book, *Reinventing the Factory: Breakthroughs in Manufacturing Today* (New York: Free Press, 1990), pp. 273–87. More than a hundred companies listed are working on factory improvements comparable to and, in some instances, better than Japanese factories. Appendix 1 of this book lists additional achiever factories.

Executive management must bear the responsibility for directing the destinies of its companies, leading the charge to discard the excess baggage of accepted manufacturing dogma and to adopt the new concepts of superior manufacturing. One of its first challenges will be to prepare its organization for new roles and new modes of operation. This will involve extensive educational programs and participation of all management and labor personnel at each stage of the change process.

CHECKLIST: MANAGING AND SUPERVISING ZINGERS

Following is a short list of the key ingredients of the new working environment. Only executive management can instill the acceptance of and enthusiastic support for these objectives in its employees and their unions. Thus, management itself must understand and adopt the principles it wholeheartedly supports, as a prerequisite to its organization's doing so.

1. Supervisors will no longer be required in superior factories. They must, therefore, prepare to become the managers of focused factories-within-a-factory.
2. Cell and line teams will be largely self-supervising.
3. Manufacturing engineers will design from 75 to 90 percent of the improvements necessary for their factories to become superior manufacturers. The number of manufacturing engineers employed must increase sharply.
4. The cross-training of workers for multiple operations will not only provide them with greater satisfaction but also give the company greater flexibility of capacity. As the mix of demand in the market changes, employees will be able to move from cell to cell and line to line with ease. Since the value of employees to the business is thus enhanced, and since productivity gains are expected, management must be committed to apportioning a fair share of the financial rewards to all workers.
5. Drastic reductions in the number of job classifications, made possible through cross-training, will greatly simplify personnel administration.
6. Cycle times of jobs will be shortened to make jobs more productive. Job enrichment will be provided by cross-training employees and frequently rotating the jobs within a work team.

7. Every company will establish guidelines for sharing revenues (less payments to suppliers and depreciation) equitably between the shareholders and the employees. Agreement with these guidelines, by management and union, will help reduce the complexities of future contract negotiations.

8. Piecework pay, based on the volume of production, will disappear.

9. Education will be expanded and, rather than generic, will be oriented to the company. Real education will come more from on-the-job training than from lectures.

10. Interpersonal skills will be ingrained in all, so that everyone will command the skills necessary to make group activities such as quality circles really work. This will involve learning how to accept almost 100 percent of employees' suggestions.[3]

11. Cross-training will create better executives by broadening their perspective. Executives will not have to job-hop in order to attain personal satisfaction and advancement. Career-long diversity of assignments will present new challenges and opportunities and will increase the value of the executive to his company.

12. Computer systems, like the factory, will be designed to work smarter, not harder.

13. Tons of bureaucratic procedures and paperwork will be eliminated by giving focused factory-in-a-factory managers the authority and the responsibility for their operations.

14. People will learn to simplify their work languages, thus making it easier for others to be educated and trained in various functional disciplines.

The remainder of the chapter will focus on these and other points.

LARGE FACTORY/BUREAUCRATIC FACTORY

Small, entrepreneur-operated factories have almost always outperformed larger businesses that produce the same products, using the same processes.[4] Most recently, leading-edge manufacturers have been reorganizing

[3]For example, in Yasuda's table we see that of more than 2 million Toyota suggestions each year, 96 percent are adopted. Yuzo Yasuda, *40 Years, 20 Million Ideas: The Toyota Suggestion System* (Cambridge, Mass.: Productivity Press, 1991), pp. 70–75.

[4]Wickham Skinner, "The Focused Factory," *Harvard Business Review,* May–June 1974, pp. 113–21.

their plants into multiple smaller factories, called subplants, within existing facilities.[5] The primary objective of reorganization is to reestablish the entrepreneurial management style in each small subplant, through physical changes in factory layout and equipment and decentralization of office and support functions. The best location for the latter is in the subplants they serve. The most progressive companies are not only delegating the responsibility for all aspects of factory management to operating personnel but also expanding their authority, empowering them to routinely make the types of operating decisions that ultimately determine the productivity and the profitability of their operations. Exhibit 3–1 shows an example of the organization structures evolving in leading-edge enterprises. The manager of Sargent-Essex's mortise lock subplant in New Haven, Connecticut, has been identified as the person who will be responsible for staff and support functions, such as materials management and maintenance. However, an immediate leap from one organization form to the other is neither prudent or practical. Thus, the team developed a two-year transition plan (as indicated by the dotted lines and boxes). Although the plan is still in transition as of this writing, it has already boosted production by 20 percent in its first year. Incidentally, delegated responsibility and authority produce the best results when as-

SUB-PLANT ORGANIZATION

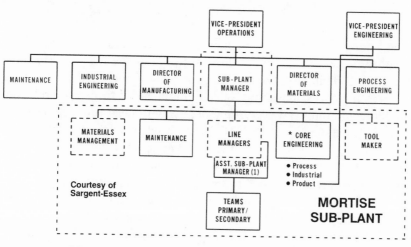

Courtesy of
Sargent-Essex

* Product Engineer Rotates Periodically

EXHIBIT 3–1

[5]See Appendix 2.

signed to producers, namely machinists and assemblers. Delegating authority is one way to curb the need for initiative-stifling rules and regulations. As Reid mentions in his book chronicling the Harley-Davidson success story, one sure way to kill employee participation is to flood the factory with rigid rules, regulations, and directives.[6]

The processes of reorganizing into small factories-within-the-factory and delegating responsibility can start immediately. Every manager and supervisor needs to learn that his future performance evaluation will depend to a large degree on how well he trains his subordinates to assume new responsibilities and decision-making authority, rather than on how well he personally controls every aspect of his realm of responsibility. At the same time, he must start to learn and take responsibility for functions historically belonging to his superior. Since one objective of the new organization is to reduce reporting levels, it is most likely that a supervisor will eventually take over most or all of his boss's functions. However, education and training alone are not enough. Management at all levels must immediately start to delegate additional authority and responsibility and to move staff and support functions directly into the organization of the factory-within-the-factory. Cross-training at all levels of the enterprise is also something that can be organized and started almost immediately.

THE NEW SUPERVISOR: SUBPLANT MANAGER

Chief among the radically new concepts of supervision is the virtual elimination of supervisors. The traditional image of the ideal supervisor is that of an individual who spends most of his time on the shop floor training employees, observing operations in order to detect problems, and doing anything and everything necessary to meet production schedules. Taylor and, subsequently, Gilbreth originally fostered this notion of specialized "functional foremen."[7] They specifically decided that it would make sense to divide what had previously been the foreman's responsibilities into eight separate specialties. In the process, they reduced the role from that of small business operator to that of technician. They perceived this as unavoidable in that the universal image of the working man and his supervisors was that they were of inferior intellect and thus

---

[6] Peter C. Reid, *Well Made in America: Lessons From Harley-Davidson on Being the Best* (New York: Mcgraw-Hill, 1990), p. 164.

[7] Frank B. Gilbreth, *Primer of Scientific Management* (Easton, Pa.: Hive Publishing, 1985), pp. 10–11. (Originally published by D. Van Nostrands, 1914).

incapable of learning any but the simplest tasks. Since manufacturing requires performing a wide variety of ever changing tasks, it was deemed necessary for the supervisor (one of the "functional foremen") to control closely each worker's operations. In pioneering projects in hundreds of Western companies, supervisor responsibilities have changed substantially. Emphasis has shifted from activities that focus on coping with recurring problems to those that will permanently solve them. A 1990 Andersen Consulting survey of supervisors working in new focused subplants shows how dramatic the initial shifts are. As Exhibit 3-2 indicates, for any single supervisor, the average number of employees supervised rose by 76 percent when manufacturing was changed from traditional to focused plant layout and methods. At the same time, the hours spent on traditional supervision and employee training dropped by 73 percent per employee (52 percent fewer hours were spent for 76 percent more employees). As previously noted,[8] the reason for the reduced need for traditional activities is that jobs and processes have been simplified to the point where the lack of complexity not only reduces the training required but also eliminates most of the potential for making quality mistakes. The most important aspect of superior factory management in the new focused subplants has been that supervisors have been able to shift their efforts toward process and product improvement. Exhibit 3-2 shows the extent of these increases—twenty-four times as much work on product

BETTER TIME UTILIZATION

	% Change
Employees Supervised	76 +
Supervision/Training Per Employee	73 –
Product Improvement	2,424 +
Process Improvement	250 +
Overtime Worked	28 –

EXHIBIT 3-2

[8]See Appendix 2.

improvement and $2\frac{1}{2}$ times as much on process betterment. It is especially significant that, although the number of employees increased substantially, supervisors found themselves working 28 percent less overtime hours.

SPEED OR JOB ENRICHMENT?

Management, more than employees, must revitalize industry by developing low cost factory automation techniques and employee work methods that exploit our inherent work ethic in tomorrow's factories. Revitalization of the work ethic is a vital component of transforming the manufacturing industry to a position of world leadership. Not that the work ethic is entirely dead or even seriously ill in all factories. To the contrary, movershakers understand the value of work. One, the General Director of Operations of a division of General Motors, when asked what was the most important lesson of their improvement project, answered, "Work is what it is all about." Further, it is rare to encounter an individual who does not take pride in the work and games in which he participates. Most people want their performance at work and games to be of superior quality and speed. Although a few businesses and/or their unions have fostered work habits that have led to blatantly less than a full day's work for a full day's pay, in our experience they are, fortunately, in the small minority—fewer than 5 percent of all factories. All such factories with work ethic problems have one or both of the following characteristics:

1. In doing their jobs, people move so slowly, compared to the speed of the average person, that even an untrained eye can see that they are working far below their potential.

2. Work in the factory begins to wind down and finally even comes to a standstill long before the end of a shift.

The work pace in these extreme cases can easily be contrasted with that of private entrepreneurs. For example, in a one-man painting business, the painter paints each house as quickly as possible so he can move on to the next house. Some would contend that money is the sole reason for his fast pace. However, monetary reward does not account for the fact that the painter does household chores at the same rapid pace, whether performing them at home or when visiting a friend. Further, when friends work together, both inevitably make a contest of the work, thus driving at a pace even faster than usual. The reason for this faster pace is obviously the satisfaction that comes when one produces more or better work than expected. It is equivalent to winning the game. These examples point out that the desire to perform (or the work ethic) is an innate quality of most people. The ultimate winners of the competitive race will be those companies, unions, and employees who best unleash the latent capacity of all people to enjoy the satisfaction of performing to their practical potential. As Sandy wrote, "There is a vast untapped energy in work force that lies dormant because people do not feel their contributions will make a difference."[9]

However, the main burden of pace improvement must fall on management. Not surprisingly, owners, executives, supervisors, and employees of medium to high volume factories agree on one aspect of manufacturing. They all agree that factory operations that are short, simple, repetitive, and rapidly performed achieve the highest rates of productivity. But these same tasks may, for some, also make work a boring drudgery and might therefore fail to utilize the full physical and mental capacities of the workforce. Incidentally, Ohno refutes the argument that repetitive work must be boring. His workers found it exciting and rewarding to discover that they were more productive when working this way.[10] Not that there are no risks associated with short-cycle production. Greg Socks, Vice President of Briggs & Stratton's Large Engine Division, recently told the author that he sees two areas in which an overly short cycle time might adversely affect performance. The first of two issues involves assemblers. Under the pressure of a very short cycle time the assembler may knowingly or inadvertently pass defective production on to the next operation. The operator makes this choice because there is not enough time in the incentive pay standard to take corrective action without reducing the amount earned. Or, the numbing fatigue assumed to be an automatic by-product of short-cycle production might cause the workers to overlook defects. The second issue addresses continuous improvement. When each worker's job on a long assembly line is only a few seconds, it is difficult to envision how to make improvements. If you cut one second from one assembler's job, what benefit can result when the other hundred assemblers' jobs, being longer, still pace the line?

The author has found little documented proof that cycle times and defect rates are correlated. Nevertheless, like most practitioners, he be-

---

[9]William Sandy, *Forging the Productivity Partnership: The Path-breaking Blueprint for a High-performance, Lightning-reflex, Smooth-running Business Force* (New York: McGraw-Hill, 1990), p. 63.
[10]Taiichi Ohno, *Workplace Management* (Cambridge, Mass.: Productivity Press, 1988), pp. 8–9.

lieves that the danger is real and that the short cycle cannot be permitted to increase passage of defects down the line. The superior manufacturer solves the problem by empowering every assembler with the authority and responsibility to stop the line until a temporary fix is developed. To give this authority mechanical teeth, every assembler has a button[11] with which to summon help and stop the line (Toyota calls this method "Andon"). It is also vitally important for executives and managers to be committed to encouraging line stops, especially with the constant pressure to meet schedules pushing workers to compromise quality for the sake of on-time production. Further, line stops must trigger putting staff to work on permanent solutions.

The second potential problem, difficulty in identifying and benefiting from continuous improvement activities, warrants additional discussion. The author has previously described the primary shortcomings of standards for assemblers: (1) standards are inaccurate, and (2) people are not standard.[12] Thus, the actual speed of an assembly line will be paced by a combination of the longest actual (accurate) operation and the slowest assembler. For this reason, the author designs the longest assembly lines with small buffers (preferably one or two units) between assembly teams (assembly teams should range from five to ten people). These buffers draw attention to points on the line at which there should be improvement opportunities. Teams that usually have units in incoming buffer positions either have too much work or might be naturally slower, on the average, than other teams. As discussed in the previous book, team members find it comparatively easy to identify the balance of work and speed in their own teams and should have the authority and duty to apportion work accordingly (the author defines this methodology as "cooperative recovery").[13] *The ultimate objective of improving work on an assembly line is not to reduce the already short cycle time by a second or two for each assembler but, rather, to cut enough seconds to eliminate one assembler!* This is perhaps the most important key to continuous improvement on long assembly lines.

Low volume manufacturers and their workforces see and envy the superior productivity of higher volume companies. Most recognize that their characteristically long, complex operations are frustrating to management and employees alike. Both see that mastering complex operations takes a long time. Thus, once a trained individual masters an operation, neither the trained individual nor his management will think it

[11]See Appendix 2.
[12]See Appendix 2.
[13]See Appendix 2.

practical to transfer him dynamically from one operation to another. During the time required to learn the new operation, the trainee's work pace would be slower than normal, and the potential for production errors (quality defects) would be higher.

At one time, Henry Ford's factory was organized as a low volume plant that, by definition, penalized both Ford's customers and his employees. In 1915, when Ford changed from numerous small teams, each assembling an entire automobile, to assembly lines, productivity increased dramatically.[14] This enabled Ford to more than double his worker's pay. Part of the savings from increased productivity was passed on to the customer as lower prices. This spurred sales to such an extent that, for decades, Ford was the biggest, privately-owned car manufacturer in the world. The remarkable improvement not only did not cause rampant unemployment, but allowed Ford to expand his workforce and improve the life-style of all employees.

Undoubtedly, some of Ford's workers recognized that the new assembly line removed most of the challenge of the previous complex operations and, theoretically, added the stress of maintaining a pace equal to the speed of the moving assembly line. Nevertheless, the rewards to employee and customer alike were so great that a return to complex, low productivity operations would be unacceptable in factories of the future. Incidentally, one should wonder whether the stress is greater when one is required to master an infrequently repeated, extremely complex task or one that is quite simple and frequently repeated.

In recent years, social scientists have deplored the lot of our workers, based on their belief that the jobs must be boring and stressful because of their fast-paced repetition. Clear-eyed realists among them, however, realize that both work and home life involve myriad boring and stressful social responsibilities, household chores, and work tasks that are highly unlikely to disappear in our or our children's lifetimes. Like Tom Juravich (who gained his insight into factory conditions by working in one),[15] the author believes that almost any effort to improve the factory environment will be beneficial but does not necessarily agree that job humanization programs address the basic problems of employee morale.

Lest we permit ourselves to lose perspective completely, we should review the working and living conditions prevalent in industry and the home until the early twentieth century (and still prevailing in almost all

[14]Henry Ford, *Today and Tomorrow* (Cambridge, Mass.: Productivity Press, 1988), p. 158.
[15]Tom Juravich, *Chaos on the Shop Floor: A Worker's View of Quality, Productivity and Management* (Philadelphia: Temple University Press, 1985), pp. 147–49.

Third World countries, which encompass most of the earth's population). The workday of the factory worker, the miner, and the farmer was seldom less than twelve hours, and the work week, six or seven days. Fringe benefits such as paid vacations, retirement programs, and health care were virtually nonexistent. Children made up a significant portion of the workforce. Few mechanical devices were available to reduce the backbreaking requirements of heavy physical labor in either the workplace or the home. The average worker's pay barely covered the minimum necessities of life. Only through rigorous saving could the typical worker occasionally afford items then viewed as luxuries and now commonly perceived to be staples of life.

Although life today is incredibly richer and longer than that of our predecessors, we do not need to settle for the status quo in terms of the satisfaction and challenge provided by our jobs. Methods of working *can* be improved continuously. The objectives should include the following:

1. Enhance every job by minimizing unreasonable physical demands, discomfort, and odious work conditions, such as temperature extremes and poor air quality and lighting.

2. Put enjoyment and satisfaction into jobs to the extent practical and consistent with the need to improve productivity continuously.

3. Reduce the man hours required to produce goods and services, thus increasing the return on investment in people, plant, and equipment.

4. As a result, further enrich life for current and future generations, by way of continuing to reduce the real cost of living and further increase our abilities to afford pleasant pastimes and healthier, longer lives.

How then can work methods be designed to improve the comfort and safety of jobs and increase the volume of production? Whether it be in the factory or the home, automation (including the adoption of the simplest, lowest cost mechanical devices) that replaces strenuous and odious work is one obvious and desirable avenue. Therefore, every design team should use checklists of the ergonomic aspects of the workplace layout and equipment, as in Gross's example.[16] Ways to put fun and satisfaction into jobs may not be as obvious and are therefore one of the foci of this chapter.

---

[16] Clifford Gross, in Klaus M. Blache, ed., *Success Factors for Implementing Change: A Manufacturing Viewpoint* (Dearborn, Mich.: Society of Manufacturing Engineers, 1988), pp. 184–89.

In 1911, Gilbreth advocated that every worker be trained in the funda-mentals of motion study.[17] Yet eighty years later factories are wasting billions of unnecessary motions. Somewhere along the way companies made the decision to train only industrial engineering specialists in the science of time and motion. These specialists have always been too few to accomplish both the study of time and motion in present operations and the reduction of waste by inventing new methods. In the vast major-ity of companies employing time standards, no one works routinely at reducing unnecessary motion. If Gilbreth's advice had been heeded, if education in motion study were universal, millions of employees would now be helping to minimize waste motions in their work. (Gilbreth's teachings are still honored in Japan, as can be seen in the English version of *Kaizen Teian Handobukko.*)[18] It is not too late to marshal the help of all employees by inaugurating the necessary time and motion education programs in factories and even in schools. The emphasis of these pro-grams must be upon improving efficiency and reducing fatigue, not es-tablishing work pacing standards. Since we conclude that productivity demands short, repetitive cycle times, companies must implement meth-ods that put satisfaction into short-cycle jobs. Fortunately, the solution is relatively simple. When accomplished, it greatly increases the the mo-bility of workers between various jobs. This brings greater flexibility to the entire factory in terms of the ability to respond rapidly to changes in the scheduled mix of products. This flexibility comes from workers' abil-ity to switch from one simple job to another with ease. What is this magic formula for such great simplicity and flexibility? Cross-training!

CROSS-TRAINING

A brief review of the evolution of work design practices will help to reinforce Leroy Peterson's message in the Foreword. The message, in summary, is that practices have now come full circle. Workers in small factories once learned to do everything. They operated a variety of ma-chines, stored the parts and materials they used, maintained and repaired their machines, and inspected the quality of their own work. As factories grew in size, it was deemed more efficient for the worker's job to be much more specialized. Thus, the machinist was trained on a single ma-

---

[17]Frank B. Gilbreth, *Motion Study: A Method for Increasing the Efficiency of the Workman* (Easton, Pa.: Hive, 1985; orig. 1911).
[18]Japan Human Relations Association, *The Idea Book: Improvement Through Total Em-ployee Involvement* (Cambridge, Mass.: Productivity Press, 1988), pp. 148–51.

chine, and his sole responsibility was to produce parts. In the new cells and focused factories-within-factories, it is again practical to broaden the responsibilities and authority of every worker. This requires that they be cross-trained in a variety of responsibilities. (Ouchi was one of the earliest to recognize the importance of "nonspecialized career paths" to Japanese success.)[19] The cross-trained worker has much greater value to the company in that the availability of versatile skills helps the company achieve superior delivery performance while minimizing required inventory investment. Executives, managers, and supervisors can start immediately to enhance their employees' value by beginning or accelerating their movement from job to job to gain training and knowledge spanning a wider range of responsibilities. As Maryann Keller has reported, the New United Motor Manufacturing factory, a joint venture of the Toyota Motor Company and General Motors, was able to cut the number of classifications in the plant to three, while as many as 183 can be found in some General Motor factories.[20] It is easy to see that this had tremendous benefits in terms of simplifying personnel administration. However, it is not enough simply to cut classifications. The ideal end result of cross-training is that cell and line team members routinely and frequently interchange positions. For example, in a Matsushita factory, workers rotate jobs every hour.[21] The rotation is controlled not by a supervisor but by the team members. The side benefit of rotation is the excellent job satisfaction fostered by encouraging employees to learn every aspect of work performed by the team. A further enhancement of the concept is to rotate teams among cells and sections of a line (although less frequently than rotation within the team's usual cell or line). Although job satisfaction is a side benefit that is important to every employee, the primary benefit to both employee and stockholder is the workforce's flexibility. When workers have widespread training, they have great mobility and can move from one cell or line to another, working on the products and customer orders most urgently required at the moment. This flexibility is one of the key factors in helping companies reduce the time needed to ship new customer requirements. Raychem Corporation's Circuit Protection Division in Menlo Park, California, provides special motivation to team members in the cell to achieve cross-training. They have three cell labor grades: one for new people, one for those certified in their primary opera-

---

[19]William Ouchi, *Theory Z: How American Business Can Meet the Japanese Challenge* (Reading, Mass.: Addison-Wesley, 1981), pp. 29–37.
[20]Maryann Keller, *Rude Awakening: The Rise, Fall, and Struggle for Recovery of General Motors* (New York: William Morrow, 1989), p. 131.
[21]David Hutchins, *Just in Time* (Aldershot, Eng.: Gower Technical Press, 1988), p. 15.

tions, and a third for those certified in all cell operations, including material handling, preventive maintenance, setup, and so on.

Considering all of the benefits of cross-training and the comparative ease with which it can be started in the ranks of middle management, if not in the factory, executive management should place its pursuit near the top of its "to-do list."

FAIR DAY'S WORK: FAIR DAY'S PAY

Working by himself and for himself, nothing motivates an individual to work harder and faster than money. In instances where there is an endless amount of work and no practical way in which an individual can work as a member of a harmonious team, an individual's pay should be based on the amount of work performed. In all other cases, performance-based pay (incentive pay) is not desirable, feasible, or necessary, assuming that all employees have a fair share of revenues. Nevertheless, other issues surrounding how and what to pay factory workers in the new cell and line organization occupy large amounts of management's time. The issue is especially important when the factory has historically based pay on production, but the nature of new facilities will make incentive pay completely impractical.

The eternal management–labor conflict revolves around the proportion of a company's revenues that goes to its employees as wages and benefits. Both parties should always agree on a common guiding principle, namely "a fair day's work for a fair day's pay." The tough part is the quantification of each side of the equation. Management's objective has always been to receive the highest possible amount of work for the least amount of pay, while labor's quite natural objective has been the opposite. From management's perspective, incentive pay (based on the volume of work produced) has had high appeal. Workers who produce more than the incentive standard lower the overhead costs per unit of production, which theoretically lowers the total unit cost of production. Unions, familiar with management's drive for faster production rates, must be concerned with the potential for creating unbearably difficult jobs. They therefore find it desirable to eliminate incentives in favor of day rates equal to or higher than those earned under piecework. Fortunately for both management and labor, the new physical layout and work methods of the factory of the future are not compatible with incentive labor.

Henry Ford could easily see that a variable rate of pay based on the volume of production (piecework) was not workable on his long automobile assembly line. Even if most people on the line were to work near their fastest practical and sustainable pace, the line would nonetheless move at a rate equal to the speed of the slowest person. Thus, individual workers are not able to cause an increase of output and, therefore, higher earnings. This eliminates the individual's motivation to work at a faster pace. On shorter assembly lines that have smaller, manageable crews, however, pay incentives quite naturally spur the team of workers to perform at a speed close to the fastest pace of its slowest worker. For example, while on an assignment for Briggs & Stratton in the 1960s, we saw assembly crews working closer to maximum sustainable speed than we had ever seen before (or since). Employees and managers both told us that they attributed the superior pace to the following factors.

1. The production standard, based on time and motion study, was relatively "tight." Thus, to earn extra pay for extra production required faster than average work.
2. Regardless of the relatively "tight" standard, when the team worked at high speed, it consistently earned a substantial bonus.
3. The assembly process was short enough for work accumulating at the slowest worker's station to be spotted easily. Since this person limited the earnings of the entire crew, the crew would bring incredible group pressure on the miscreant and, if necessary, would resort to harsh practical jokes to force this person to transfer or resign! Eventually, all members of the team would be capable of working and would routinely work at a pace acceptable to the team. While the pace was very close to 100 percent of the maximum practical on a sustained basis, it was still much less than what most assemblers could achieve in short spurts.

The fact was that the earnings of the Briggs & Stratton crews were still limited by the speed of the slowest crew member, which explains why some crews evolved in which the average speed of one line's crew was slower than that of others. A further incontestable fact is that each individual's speed varies because of many factors, including physical condition, size, training, and age. Only recently have some companies realized that shifting some of the slowest worker's work to the fastest worker unlocks a major new opportunity for improvement. Far too few factories are taking advantage of this simple but powerful lesson. Most fear that employees will reject this notion, based on the belief that the majority of a crew will wind up carrying the load that a few malingerers shirk. In our experience, seasoned crews want the increased earnings, and they understand how group discipline works to preclude intentional malingering. In factories with no comparable crew experience, it will pay to work on making this new idea successful!

At Briggs & Stratton, as is the case in most factories with incentive pay systems, an upper limit on earnings was virtually never exceeded. Most standards were "tight" enough so that actual production in excess of the standard by 50 percent (or more) would be unimaginable. However, an untold number of companies evaluate their standards as being "loose" overall. This usually means that actual performance might sometimes, or even often, exceed the standard by up to 50 percent. Industrial engineers in these factories acknowledge that in many cases the standard could easily be exceeded by as much as 100 percent. However, universally acknowledged (but unofficial) earnings limits usually deter employees who could work at a faster pace.

If workers were to produce frequently at rates much higher than the standard, it might trigger a management decision to review the methods and standards and to develop more demanding ones. For that reason, our workforces have long imposed informal earning limits on their peers to help disguise "loose" standards. A second substantial factor behind the informal earning limits is the socially disruptive effect on co-workers when a fellow employee perpetually earns notably more than the others. Co-workers inevitably become jealous, undermining morale and creating a hostile environment.

Whether assembly lines are long or short, companies should reconsider whether to base performance pay/measurement on a comparison of actual production with a predetermined standard. Some pertinent factors include the following:

1. The average worker's pace in factories using piecework pay is sharply higher than plants with hourly employees.

2. When standards are routinely used to measure individual performance but not to determine pay, productivity is higher than in plants that do not measure performance. But the factory that measures performance and yet does not pay according to output has lower performance than factories with incentive pay.

3. The costs of developing and administering individual performance measurement standards are substantial, and the cost associated with administering incentive pay is even higher.

4. In the best factories of the future, all manufacturing operations will be directly linked to the single synchronized network of all machine and assembly operations for a product family, including the operations of every part, every subassembly, and the final as-

sembly itself. Thus, using individual incentive systems will not be practical since no one worker will be able to relate his productivity to the entire network's output.

5. When incentive payment causes production in excess of requirements, the long-term result will be higher inventory and the related costs of its storage. Eventually, the buildup of slow-moving and obsolete inventory may necessitate major inventory write-downs (a major cause of management shakeups).

6. Incentive standards on some products are inevitably "looser" than on others. This invariably leads to a preference for producing the product that pays more and shows better productivity performance. As a result, some customer orders are delayed while products preferred because their production is easier go into the warehouse to gather dust.

Together, management and labor must start the process of eliminating individual incentive systems, one of the most challenging (difficult) steps on the path to the factory of the future. However, the next issue is whether or not to develop pay schemes that tie the production output of large groups to their pay, either period-by-period or for a longer period. Ishikawa has some interesting observations on this subject. He stresses the importance or nonmonetary reasons for motivation and specifically mentions joy, desire, and pleasure as even more important than monetary reward.[22] Work must be designed to supply these elements, which means it will no longer be acceptable to design jobs that make one man an island.

THE TECHNOLOGICAL TRAP

However vital the constant development of new technology is, it must not be allowed to become the tail that wags the dog. Too many companies are willing to make ill-advised investments in technology even though these investments end up increasing the total cost of manufacturing. For example, consider the manufacturing (industrial) engineering organization and the less than satisfactory job it is doing.[23] It rarely develops new designs for complete factory processes, concentrating more on designing

[22]Kaoru Ishikawa, trans. David J. Lu, *What Is Total Quality Control? The Japanese Way* (Englewood Cliffs, N.J.: Prentice-Hall, 1985), pp. 25–28.
[23]Alan D. Anderson and Ernest C. Huge, *The Spirit of Manufacturing Excellence: An Executive's Guide to the New Mind Set* (Homewood, Ill.: Dow Jones–Irwin, 1988), p. 73.

or selecting machines for a single operation. These engineers are and should be the group responsible for designing the processes and the associated people-oriented work of the whole factory (as contrasted to design done in quality circles discussed later). The engineer's attention is almost always focused on the automation or hardware aspect of the operation, to the point of virtually excluding low cost modifications of existing equipment and other cost-contributing facets of related support functions such as material storage and equipment maintenance. And when the engineer does take a look at material storage, he typically takes the automation route, selecting automated storage and retrieval as against lowering or eliminating the inventory or moving it to focused stores at the point of use. This explains how engineers as a group earned the label "catalog engineers." Their first reaction, presented with a request to improve operations, is to reach for a catalog containing the latest (and usually most expensive) equipment on the market. Subsequently, they must creatively prepare a cost justification for the required expenditure, because, in truth, automation rarely reduces the cost of manufacturing. The engineer rarely considers the principles of low cost automation in a procedure that considers every element of the operation, including people, materials, and systems. Thus he seldom considers the total cost impact of the combination. Incidentally, Taiichi Ohno has concluded that it *never* makes economic sense to *replace* a machine, versus maintaining it in perpetuity. He has written, "If adequate maintenance has been done, replacement with a new machine is never cheaper, even if maintaining the older one entails some expense."[24]

This discussion does not mean to imply that engineers do not want to do the job and do it well. If blame must be placed, it is more the fault of management for insisting on following cost justification procedures that are misleading and for failing to build an adequate engineering organization. The most vital manpower resource necessary for superior manufacturing and the one in shortest supply is the manufacturing engineer. The author rarely visits a company (except in Japan) where the number of engineers is even remotely close to the number required to improve systematically and continually tooling, machines, methods, and entire factories while applying the best of available affordable technology. As Melman wrote, "Almost all of depleted industries in the United States severely lack the engineering and allied skills needed to design products to world standards and to operate production systems at high technical

---

[24]Taiichi Ohno, *Toyota Production System: Beyond Large-Scale Production* (Cambridge, Mass.: Productivity Press, 1988), p. 64.

and economic competence."[25] Executives must start to address this issue by aggressively recruiting more engineers and by planning projects that will pay their salaries hundreds of times over. Incidentally, recognition of the engineer's importance has not escaped leading-edge project teams at General Motors. For example, the team at the Romulus Engine Plant took great pains to define the roles of manufacturing engineers vis-à-vis the team of production workers. The traditional responsibility for engineering tools and equipment continues to be one of the main specialized engineering functions. In addition, the engineer pays considerably more attention to working with and supporting the team.

In many companies, building a manufacturing organization of superior stature will be difficult unless something is done about the disparity of compensation and status between design and manufacturing engineers. Although the majority of an engineer's education can be usefully applied to either product or process design, most graduate engineers will continue to gravitate toward product engineering until pay and status are equalized. Also, the third type of engineer in the equation is the quality engineer. Both manufacturing engineers and quality assurance specialists suffer from a poor image, although somewhat more importance has recently been accorded to quality than in the past. Nevertheless, the quality specialist is still viewed as a shirt-sleeve factory type, Exhibit 3-3, as contrasted to the suave and prestigious product engineer. Even less stature is accorded to the lowly manufacturing engineer, who is viewed as a dirty-fingernail, blue collar, coveralls type.

As a short-term interim measure, combining product and process engineering organizations may be a step toward equalizing the status of the process engineer while providing a pool of engineers that, with little training, would be capable of working interchangeably on both product and process. In the long term, the engineering organization will perform all three types of design: product, process, and quality. The quality engineer's role will be to eliminate the need for quality control in the factory. He will do this by making sure that product designs embody the necessary level of quality and that process designs are fail-safe in terms of producing products that always conform to the product specifications. Thus, as indicated in Exhibit 3-4, the engineer may be a product designer today, a quality engineer tomorrow, and on yet another day, a process engineer. Cross-training of those specializing in the engineering disciplines is no less important than for the other disciplines. In fact,

---

[25]Seymour Melman, *Profits Without Production*, 2d ed. (New York: Alfred A. Knopf, 1988), p. 249.

THE STATURE PROBLEM

DESIGN ENGINEERING   **QUALITY ASSURANCE**   **MANUFACTURING ENGINEERING**

EXHIBIT 3-3

THE MULTIFUNCTIONAL TARGET

YESTERDAY   **TODAY**   **NEXT-1**   **NEXT-2**

DESIGN ENGINEERING   **QUALITY ENGINEERING**   **MANUFACTURING ENGINEERING**   **?**

EXHIBIT 3-4

engineers should also have meaningful experience in other functional areas to prepare the best of them for broader positions of responsibility. As a result, in the future a much higher percentage of chief executive officers will have started their careers in engineering.

Once a company hires the necessary engineers, it will need to educate and train them in the principles and techniques of designing low cost automation and highly productive labor operations. However, the best training material will come from examples developed during the company's own improvement projects, and the best training will be the on-the-job experience.

GOING AROUND IN CIRCLES

Some companies have found they have gone around in circles, instead of making giant strides, when starting to use the quality circle idea to solve all of their woes. The notion of people involvement is right! For example, my colleague Leroy Peterson wrote (in the Foreword to this book), "Marshaling the resources of every employee in a company has the potential for unleashing an unbeatable force for improvement." To unlock this potential will require managers, supervisors, and staff specialists to listen to their employees, to honor the value of their ideas, and to move rapidly to make the changes suggested. One-on-one communications between factory managers and all employees and between supervisors (until there are no more supervisors) and employees is among the best ways to operate. It has a double payoff. It rewards the employee when the boss acknowledges the value of his contribution, and it benefits the business's performance, which means that when the boss is evaluated by his boss, he will gain recognition for his success in drawing ideas for improvement from everybody.

However, contrary to popular belief, mobilization of the entire workforce to solve problems and design improvements was not the primary reason for the successes of leading companies. This is evidenced in the rapid decline of the number of quality circles after a meteoric rise in the late 1970s that peaked in 1980. The reason for the decline is clear: lack of results. To try to foist off the responsibility for plantwide change onto a workforce that is already burdened with full-time responsibility for meeting daily production schedules is simply unrealistic. Nor do many companies realize the massive investment needed to prepare the entire workforce to be self-directed teams (the epitome of circles). Moran and her colleagues note that teams take years to mature. Further, "the rewards of self-direction depend on massive planning, intensive training and retraining, prompt access to resources, and often the physical redesigning of plants and offices."[26]

A better approach is outlined by Dr. J. M. Juran. He points out that project teams are necessary for substantive improvement.[27] Perhaps he should have made it clearer that part-time teams are not a good alternative to those which work full-time. The biggest reason for management's disappointment at the pace of improvement is its expectation that improvements can be designed as a sideline of the normal job. Major progress is unlikely when improvement design and implementation are treated like a hobby, that is, when they have to be squeezed in amid normal business activities—as though people normally waste a lot of time and thus should have plenty of "extra" time to devote to special improvement projects.

Stressing the need for full-time teams and advocating that manufacturing engineers be the core of the factory improvement effort do not negate the desirability or the necessity of wider personnel involvement. As a matter of fact, in the area in which it is working, it is especially important for the project team to involve all personnel with related duties. This includes not only the machinists, the assemblers' and their bosses, but also indirect employees and staff members. Although changes in factory hardware (such as machines, tooling, and conveyors) and the organization of these into new plant layout configurations can always improve operating results, involving all appropriate personnel leads to even better results. Also, since properly managed circle activities can yield significant improvements in micro areas, there is every reason to encourage simultaneous use of both teams and circles. Realistic executives, however, will soon understand that about 85 to 90 percent of an organization's achievements come from the full-time project team and the normal engineering organization. This range, incidentally, corresponds to the author's Japanese experience, based on his informal survey of factories during first-time visits.

Nevertheless, quality circle activities provide several important lessons, gleaned from the more successful circles' experiences. The first is that every employee's suggestions are valuable. At an international conference in the early 1980s, a speaker from Hitachi told a mesmerized audience that during the previous year one employee had made more

[26]Linda Moran, Ed Musselwhite, Jack Orsburn, and John H. Zenger, *Self-Directed Teams: The New American Challenge* (Homewood, Ill.: Business One–Irwin, 1990), p. 24.
[27]J. M. Juran, *Juran on Leadership for Quality: An Executive Handbook* (New York: Free Press, 1989), p. 22.

than two thousand suggestions.[28] His suggestions were a tiny fraction of the total of more than 2 million suggestions from all employees. The 2 million suggestions had won the company the national award for most suggestions that year. As moderator of questions and answers, the author was disappointed that as many questions focused on how and why one employee could have made so many suggestions. (The answer, in part, was that he was a process engineer). Finally, I interjected by own question, the one I felt to be of overwhelming importance: "Of the 2 million suggestions, how many were rejected?" Having been a member of a circle in Japan for two years, the author was not surprised by the answer. It was "zero." How could every suggestion be found valuable? By recognizing that people are always right when they see a problem or an opportunity for improvement. In suggesting a specific method for achieving the improvement, any one employee's idea may be less than perfect. In rare cases it might even be a terrible idea. In other cases, even good ideas might prove too expensive. Hitachi recognized that the true value was not the suggestion itself but the identification of an opportunity for improvement. Thus, it credited the person suggesting it regardless of how the opportunity was eventually realized. Subsequently, the circle would work on and continuously reshape an idea until it might no longer bear any resemblance to the original suggestion. But the company still credited the adopted solution to the suggestion's originator.

It is human nature to want to be heard and to have one's thoughts and ideas accepted. After a few times of hearing one's suggestions torn apart, many people would stop trying to make suggestions. In most societies it seems that most people reviewing the ideas of others feel compelled to pile on negative criticism instead of purposely finding something to praise. In quality circles negative criticism should not be permitted. (Mizuno makes clear how important this is by listing it as the first "brainstorming" technique.)[29] Facilitators must teach circle leaders, and the leaders must teach the group, to stress the good points of every suggestion and to build solutions on those strengths. People who have had the experience of having their ideas savagely dissected sit silently at the outset of participation in circle activities but become fertile producers of ideas once they see that their thoughts are valued.

When any group meeting (not just quality circles) is dominated by one or a few speakers (who may or may not be the most brilliant of the atten-

[28]Robert W. Hall, *Driving the Productivity Machine: Production Planning and Control in Japan* (Falls Church, Va.: American Production and Inventory Control Society, 1981).
[29]Shigeru Mizuno, ed., *Management for Quality Improvement: The 7 New QC Tools* (Cambridge, Mass.: Productivity Press, 1988), p. 128.

dees), the potential contributions of the group are never heard. In Japan, the author observed that every executive listened with extreme patience to people's presentations of their viewpoints. Only at the end did they add their own comments. Many times the executive's decisions differed from those suggested. They frequently had ideas that were distinctly better than those of their subordinates. This results from the Japanese system, which is very good at helping the very best personnel gain wide experience through cross-training and then systematically promoting them. The end result is executives superbly capable, through wide experience, of contributing some of the most insightful ideas. In quality circle activities the supervisor and the circle leader must be taught to be quiet until after all circle members have made their contributions.

In companies where factory employees work eight hours a day on production, it would be painful to take them away from production work to participate in circle activities. The Japanese practice of expecting circles to meet on their own time after hours or on breaks may not fly too well in most of the rest of the world. But even if time is made available for circle meetings, a logical question would be "How long will it take to do all of the detail work necessary to implement a change?" In many Western companies the answer has been months. The circle, to be effective, needs someone to work continuously on its ideas. The logical candidates are the area supervisor and the manufacturing engineer responsible for the area. They should be an integral part of every circle, primarily to act as the circle's hands while the circle members are doing the most vital job, getting production out. However, because companies do not have enough engineers, the few they have are seldom able to spend time on both their normal jobs and on the suggestions of the circles.

The New United Motors Manufacturing, Inc. (NUMMI), a joint venture of Toyota and General Motors, managed in Japanese style, was a stunning success for years without quality circles. That is why no reference to quality circles is found in Sepehri's case study.[30] When one considers the nature of its process, a long, continuously flowing assembly line with thousands of workers, it was easy to see that it would have been difficult and costly to have relied on quality circles to produce the results that were achieved. How could the assembly line stop to accommodate circle meetings? If it did stop, where would thousands of workers hold their meetings? Although these may be interesting problems, the fact is that the mangers from Toyota already knew how to produce radically

---

[30]M. Sepehri, case author, and C. A. Voss, ed., *Just-in-Time Manufacture* (London: IFS Publications, 1986), pp. 281–90.

better results in the factory (which, incidentally, had previously been closed by General Motors because it was so unsuccessful). Why wait until quality circles invent improvements if you already know what the improvements should be? Just get right to work on designing the tasks of each worker and instruct them about what to do and how to do it. That's how NUMMI got the job done. The author contends that most companies can get the same major improvements, the same way, without even having to form joint ventures with the Japanese. We know what needs to be done in our factories and should get to work doing it!

THE "MOTHERHOOD" KEYS TO SUCCESS

For every company that has had magnificent success in lowering production costs and vastly improving product quality, another company has failed to accomplish similar objectives, even though both began with the same potential for improvement. The vast majority of successes center on equipment modifications and physical improvements in factory and office layout. These tangible alternations of plant and equipment are constantly becoming much better understood as the number of books and articles on the topic increases. Although most of these publications touch on "motherhood" success factors, most of them fail to identify the most serious roadblocks to progress and the ways to remove them. These less obvious, vitally important, truly unique success factors can pave the way for progressive companies to join the swelling ranks of superior manufacturers.

Any consultant (internal or external) worth a grain of salt will promote a standard list of "motherhood" keys to the success of any major factory improvement project. Some of the elements of the standard list include the following:

1. Setting specific, unusually high targets for improvement and striving to meet and exceed them (Some experts caution against setting goals too high. The author's view is that it is infinitely better to fall slightly short of a very challenging goal than to pursue a goal that does not stretch the project teams to the limits of their abilities.)

2. Top management that is fully committed to achieving the established goals, and meaningfully involved in the change process

3. Full-time teams responsible for designing and implementing changes

4. Maximum practical involvement of all people impacted by contemplated changes

5. Recognition that improved operations lower total cost (Thus, new methods must be invented to simplify operations, lowering the costs of those functions to which automation can then be applied. Many factories should attain superior performance using existing, modified equipment rather than jump immediately to expensive new automation. The author calls this "low cost automation".)

As important as these items are, none is as powerful as involved, enthusiastic people committed to high goals and new concepts. Such individuals, when empowered with the authority to implement change, are sometimes able to achieve faster improvements than can formal project teams. And they do so while continuing to manage ongoing operations. However, when the scope of desired improvements is plantwide (or even extended through the network of suppliers, through the distribution channels and into the operations of the end customer) no single individual will have the necessary authority and staff to do the job. Thus, a full-time team is usually vital to all projects other than those of the most limited scope.

Project failures have always been easy to predict, since the most vital success factors are commonly absent in all such unsuccessful endeavors. Conversely, the presence of these keys to success is the ingredient that sparks superior achievers' triumphs. Enthusiastic participation and buy-in of all the people involved is an extremely important success factor. However, employees and their unions are rarely roadblocks to progress. It is middle managers[31] in every functional discipline who are the most common culprits! Influential, seemingly irreplaceable managers are clearly all too often permitted openly or convertly to obstruct the path of progress. Addressing this very serious problem and removing the roadblock will open the flow of improvements to the epic proportions being experienced by the leading achievers of this age.

HOW TO PRODUCE RESULTS

Many companies have heeded the list of "motherhood" keys to success and have assigned full-time teams of committed individuals to work with

[31]Grazier cites a study in which middle management resistance was identified as a hindrance by 79 percent of the responding companies. Peter B. Grazier, *Before It's Too Late: Employee Involvement . . . An Idea Whose Time Has Come* (Chadds Ford, Pa.: Teambuilding Inc., 1989), p. 92.

enthusiastic middle managers, but *still* have had disappointing results compared to the best achievers. The most common reasons are the following.

1. People working on an area's redesign are too familiar with its present operations. They have a hard, almost impossible time seeing the potential for doing things differently. Some of them may have been the architects of present methods.

2. The highest degree of inventive design requires the input of inventive, creative people. The creative spark is the least commonly available asset of any project team. Lacking an adequate creative resource will lead to less than creative results. When shortage of creativity is a noticeable problem, the team must operate in a mode that provides a practical, result-producing alternative.

3. Project team members are chosen, as they should be, from among the best people in the company. As a result, the team consists mainly of bosses. If the bosses are unwilling to do the necessary work, little will be accomplished.

4. Team members do not always accept the radical new concepts of operations. Thus, too much time is spent fighting change and not enough creating and implementing it.

The careful selection and empowerment of a company's project manager is a success factor that is all too frequently overlooked. When his team fails to perform up to expectations, he must have the ability and the authority both to persuade and to order team members (if necessary) to perform the roles expected of them. They must be dedicated to the new concepts and willing to work as designers and workers (not as supervisors or managers). Above all, they must work with the various involved individuals (other than just other team members) and be able to accept and build on the ideas contributed by others. When it becomes clear that a project team member is incapable of performing as necessary, the project manager must be the dynamic individual who rapidly and tactfully arranges a replacement.

Design by committee, of sorts, is a reasonable alternative to brilliant, creative people. But only if most of the work is based on extensive groundwork by an individual with full-time responsibility for the design. The power of the group should routinely be used to enhance people's individual creative efforts, but it can be efficiently brought to bear only when the starting point is the comprehensive groundwork prepared in advance of review by the group. Incidentally, every group includes some who resist change. Resisters of change include both rational and ir-rational people, as do any other groups. Those who are rational can al-ways be convinced by logical and rational discussion, albeit with time-consuming effort and even by dictating cooperation (although this should be avoided except in instances where the urgency of change is critical). Irrational people are unlikely to be converted regardless of the effort spent to convert them. Thus, early identification of irrational people can present an opportunity to save time and money. In the case of managers and supervisors, management must take the action necessary to eliminate the possibility that these individuals will hamper progress. The humane way is to move them to other, parallel positions, although the company might be better off without them in some instances. Of the numerous interpersonal interaction techniques for converting resisters to involved supporters of change, a few easy and effective methods stand out. The first is simply to establish and enforce a rule that requires respecting the comments of each person in every meeting of two or more. Virtually every comment has some merit, though sometimes it is not readily appar-ent and thus requires time to search out this merit. Even when the lis-tener perceives the merit to be something different from what the speaker intended, the exchange serves to help convert potential adversaries to allies. For example:

Speaker 1: There is no way factory containers could be downsized without increasing the cost of moving them from operation to opera-tion.

Speaker 2: You're right. As long as operations are spread all over the factory and require long moves, and only one small container is moved at a time, costs would indeed increase. How could it then be possible to avoid these added costs?

Speaker 1: Obviously, moving related operations closer together would reduce the distance each container would need to travel. Fur-ther, it would be logical to move more than one container at a time, even if it means moving containers whose contents consist of more than one part number. Since two small containers might be the same size as one big one, the total movement cost will be lower. Come to think of it, if the operations are very close to one another, it may be possible to move them by short, gravity feed conveyors. This would completely eliminate human transport costs.

Embedded in Speaker 1's response is an example of a second important rule. This rule requires that the person identifying a problem with a suggestion provide at least one potential solution to the problem. Even if the solution is too costly or ultimately proves to be unworkable, starting to work together is a valuable step toward inventing the answer. And answers always evolve if the issue is pursued as long as it takes for the solution to emerge. Insisting that the resister make a contribution of at least one idea, no matter how practical, may generate some better ideas, but the more important side effect is that he will become involved. Involvement is the key to converting resisters into enthusiastic participants who help to guarantee success.

The third powerful rule and practice is absolutely to ban critical, negative responses to others' ideas. For centuries in Japan it has been socially unacceptable to make another lose face. Thus, when two opposing factions or individuals present alternative approaches to an executive for a decision, the executive always praises the losing proposal for its numerous merits before announcing selection of the other approach. The negative, critical individual must be politely but firmly reminded, each time, to rephrase his comment as a positive observation. Should the miscreant fail to get the message, the next step is to excuse him from attendance at the meeting. Few rational people are ever excused, even fewer are ever excused from meetings more than once. This new way to work is easy to learn and can be adopted in the short term.

The problem of czar-like managers would be minimized, if not eliminated, by a career-long process of cross-training. Cross-training may also help reduce the turnover of managers who have depended on changing jobs to find opportunities for new, broadening experience and promotion. Hutchins identified the transiency of executives as a significant deterrent to convincing middle management that top management is fully committed to continuous improvement through adopting superior manufacturing techniques.[32] Frequent changes in top executives in the past have resulted in correspondingly frequent changes in management's programs. Many new executives have their own pet fad of the moment and start their reign by canceling prior initiatives and introducing new ones of their own choosing. Improved executive education offers hope for changing this. Education is an important tool for cementing commitment to the program of improvement starting at the board of directors level. A large group of executives that are firmly committed will make midstream abandonment of superior manufacturing initiatives much less likely. Any single new executive would find it hard to induce the group to change the thrust of its strategic and tactical plans. Further, if every executive and board member in the world is well educated in the principles of

---

[32]Hutchins, *Just in Time,* p. 162.

superior manufacturing, project completion is likely to become a top manufacturing priority in the eyes of every executive in all companies, including the newly hired ones. Thus, changes in executives will be less likely to cause a cessation of the superior manufacturing projects. These avenues of minimizing the disruption caused by job-hopping are not enough. The fact is that a company's executives with long and varied experience are much more valuable than those visiting briefly while awaiting an outside job opportunity. Companies must work harder to retain experienced executives by making long tenure as attractive to the executive as it should be to the company. In the longer term, the cross-training concept is most likely to help stem the flow of managers from one company to another. It will do so by adding job satisfaction, opportunity for new challenges, and broadening experiences in a single company. However, in the short term one must heed the warning of Jones, Roos, and Womak. They advise that "a danger exists that employees who feel trapped in lean (superior) organizations will hold back their knowledge. . . . Western companies . . . will need to think far more carefully about personnel systems and career paths than we believe any have to date."[33]

THE MIDDLE MANAGEMENT ROADBLOCK

Skillful use of manager resources will be among the most critical elements supporting achievement of aggressive new goals. The best middle managers hold the keys to success or the seeds of failure in their hands. Conversely, a few obstructionist managers can doom or disrupt progress if they are not identified and neutralized. To fail to do so will slow a company's march into the world of the factory of the future. Although executive management and office and factory workers are always supportive of change, middle managers frequently resist it. This is a common, internationally recognized roadblock to progress. While executives universally recognize the problem and its reasons, they too often fail to place the responsibility for removing the roadblock where it belongs: at their own desk. As Ohno has said, "In rejuvenating a company, there are no easy methods. The extent to which we achieve success is dictated by the degree to which management is committed to innovative change, not making excuses."[34]

[33]Daniel T. Jones, Daniel Roos, and James P. Womack, *The Machine That Changed the World* (New York: Macmillan, 1990), p. 251.
[34]Taiichi Ohno with Setsuo Mito, *Just-in-Time: For Today and Tomorrow* (Cambridge, Mass.: Productivity Press, 1988), p. xii.

The characteristics of the recalcitrant middle manager needing management's attention are quite common. They are as follows:

1. Most of their careers have been spent in a single discipline, in a single department or section.

2. They have come to be considered indispensable (not necessarily because they are, but more because they have not even tried to train subordinates in their experience-based knowledge).

3. They operate as dictatorial rulers in their little empires, rejecting any but their own ideas for change. At times some even steal the ideas of others and claim them as their own.

4. They have often made valuable contributions to the successful operation of their areas of responsibility, in the context of the old way of operating. Thus, it is easy to understand why their managements are too often willing to empower them with the authority to veto proposals for improvement.

The myth of the indispensable individual is one of the most assailable reasons for permitting a tyrannical individual to interfere with executive management's desire to become a superior producer. And surely it is only a myth! For example, in several decades of work with hundreds of companies on six continents, the author has yet to encounter a single instance in which the sudden departure of an "irreplaceable" individual has seriously disrupted ongoing operations. In fact, in almost every such instance, within two weeks or so the replacement manager (or executive) is functioning so well that the difference is barely perceptible. For this reason, executive management would be well advised to solve the problem of active (overt or covert) resistance and obstruction by removing the offender from such a position to avoid disrupting progress. Fortunately, many executives take the drastic action when it is necessary. For example, Russell Eisenstat describes how the plant manager at Ashland Corporation's Fairfield Components Plant recognized this type of problem and solved it by reassigning the individual.[35] Not that this needs to involve unfair treatment of managers who in the past have made important contributions to their companies' success. On the contrary, transferring these individuals to another department, in a lateral move, will allow them once again to demonstrate their value by bringing their consider-

---

[35]Russell A. Eisenstat, "Compressor Team Startup," J. Richard Hackman, ed., *Groups That Work (and Those That Don't): Creating Conditions for Effective Teamwork* (San Francisco: Jossey-Bass, 1990), p. 415.

able experience and native skills to bear on the improvement of a different operation. It might also be a desirable, humbling experience for them to learn that they were not really the mainspring of the business, as proved by the replacement manager's mastery of the area's complexities in relatively short order. If executives recognize that any of their middle managers operate like little czars, they must take immediate corrective action. While some might prefer their improvement project teams to convert the manager into an advocate of change, this rarely works. Even when it does, it usually compromises the design of improved operations, lowering or even negating the opportunities for improvement and thus delaying the company's goal of becoming a superior producer. In a very few instances, such managers become converts without compromising operations design, but only at an enormous cost in terms of delaying progress. Because these types of managers *are* the sole authority in their departments, they are always exceptionally busy. Thus, getting enough of their time to sell them on new ideas or even to educate them in the tried and proven basics of superior factory design is often extremely difficult.

Another alternative is to start initial pilot projects in areas where other managers are eager advocates of change. Of course, this only defers the necessary corrective changes to a later date. Nevertheless, it is often necessary to get started as quickly as possible and as smoothly as practical. Personnel reassignments, no matter how well handled, are always distractingly difficult for co-workers and responsible executives. Terminations, when necessary, are usually much less disturbing.

Too many companies devote far too few resources to developing superior managers. It appears that responsible executives place far too much faith in the ability of their senior managers to teach the new generation by example. If, however, one takes the time to review all the criteria that go into successful management (as defined by Hatakayama, for example),[36] one can easily see that the average manager falls far short of the model. Nothing short of comprehensive new programs for the continuous, formal education and training of both senior and fledgling managers will close this gap between superior manufacturers and the also-rans.

The most effective form of managerial and executive business training is that of gaining experience in several different functional areas of the company. There is no real justification for limiting the horizons of the brightest managers by restricting their experience to engineering, ac-

---

[36]Yoshio Hatakeyama, *Manager Revolution: A Guide to Survival in Today's Changing Workplace* (Cambridge, Mass.: Productivity Press, 1985).

counting, sales and marketing, or any other discipline. Nor do "executive training programs" that shuffle the trainee from department to department every few weeks and only at outset of the executive's career fill the bill. Meaningful experience requires assignments of a few years. As Lu writes, "The almost certain job rotation coming within three or four years makes all management-bound employees give top priority to their company's overall interest rather than the parochial interest of their currently assigned section or division."[37] Managers should have a lifetime opportunity to expand their experience, and hence their value to the company. Every company can and should get its system of rotation started immediately.

FUTURE SYSTEMS: SUPPORT VERSUS ENFORCEMENT

The challenges and opportunities presented by ever increasing computer power are limitless but should not be squandered on wastefully processing and storing ever increasing amounts of data. In fact, the first order of business is to simplify the stupefying maze of interconnected computer systems, integrated data bases, and batteries of terminals manned by armies of white collar workers. The best of our system analysts are starting to develop radically improved systems, designed to work in harmony with the new simpler, focused factory and to achieve drastic reductions in their operating costs. However, the majority still do not grasp the concept of system simplification.

Stripped down, bare-bones, modern systems now being implemented will speed the very latest customer demands through the order entry and requirement planning process, out to the network of a company's own factories and to and through those of its vendors. The best of these systems communicate the rate of demand to every link in the chain. But electronic kanban is the system by which almost instantaneous resupply instructions are flashed to suppliers as consumption occurs. These systems make maximum use of simple but powerful data processing technology, such as bar coding, to minimize the costs of data acquisition, and on-line, real-time data entry that can virtually eliminate costly, complex

---

[37]David J. Lu, *Inside Corporate Japan: The Art of Fumble-Free Management* (Cambridge, Mass.: Productivity Press, 1987), p. 33.

error correction cycles. However, the most important aspect of these new systems is the emphasis on decentralization of authority (not just responsibility), which eliminates legions of bureaucratic performance monitors.

Big brother is watching you if you work for a company with a conventional management system. These systems were founded on the premise that business operations are too complex and too important to be managed by the oafs in the factory. However, the best possible way to manage operations is to give factory people entrepreneurial authority and responsibility for their parts of the enterprise and permit them to manage by eye and by walkabout. The best management style can be supported by gathering, processing, and reporting only a limited amount of data on the few key indicators that best show the *total* performance of the small factories-within-factories and of the business as a whole. However, most systems today operate on the assumption that businesses need to be controlled by policemen who monitor operations and enforce the taking of corrective action. As a result, executives and their policing staffs are awash in a sea of information too vast to review and understand, which certainly does not help in terms of review and understand, which certainly does not help in terms of making "management" decisions. The veritable ocean of information is created by placing a heavy data input burden on the backs of the organizations, which are then criticized for the unfavorable results they so honestly report. Worse, the reviewers of reports are never quite up to date since they depend on periodic reports, which are never completely current. Thus, even though corrective action is usually initiated by the factory oaf in real time because he is at the scene when problems arise, he must routinely respond to the policing staff's queries stemming from the reporting system, after the fact. Outmoded systems of the past have worked well to report on and to maintain the status quo and have had some success in highlighting problems reported by the people providing input. However, they have proved ineffective for fostering quantum improvements in the operations on which they report.

Most of today's computer systems are still best at massive data processing, producing mountains of output to be dispositioned by clerical and technical-level personnel. They provide relatively little that is useful for managers and executives. All but the best, leading edge computer technicians have a hard time grasping the new realities of "Just-in-Time." Thus, many continue to design systems that generate work for clerks that should be unnecessary in the new environment, if jobs are designed as they should be. For example, Hernandez explains a computer-generated shortage report in his just-in-time book[38] (although there should be no shortages in the successful company). In the new world of virtually no inventory, the computer system must find either that every component is in short supply (because the ideal delivery occurs at the moment that inventory drops to zero) or that none is. Shortage reports based on imminent stock outage would list every item. This could easily keep armies of expediters and clerks busy chasing shortages that evaporate just-in-time for production. Reports based on projected availability would list none since true just-in-time systems automatically make schedules equal to requirements. The shortage mentality has been one of the most persistent roadblocks between current practices and superior manufacturing. As the author has previously said,[39] the best way to cure shortage problems permanently is to *stop the line* whenever a *real* shortage occurs. Many companies have found that this practice suddenly forces internal and external suppliers to solve problems never before resolved. And it does not take long to make shortage-free operation the norm.

Some technicians spend disproportionate time on computer operating and application software issues but very little on inventing innovative application approaches. In some companies substantive improvements have been delayed for as much as five years while application software packages were evaluated. (Incidentally, Goddard highlights some of the important new software criteria).[40] And in the end, a decision had to be made regardless of the probability that a new package or package enhancements might be forthcoming in the coming months or years. The point is that action must be swift and sure. No package can be deemed to be the ultimate, or even reasonably close, if the premise of continuous improvement and past history are considered. (Companies that have replaced old systems with new ones every five or ten years understand that they will continue to do so in the future.) Technicians need to comprehend the astonishing new factory environment. To do so will require leaving the isolation of their little cubicles and spending time learning about the factory-within-a-factory. In the long term this will best be accomplished by career-long job rotation. Additionally, technicians must learn to pursue the new objectives our best designers are adopting for the systems on which they are working. The new challenges must be as aggressive as:

[38]Arnaldo Hernandez, *Just-in-Time: A Practical Approach* (Englewood Cliffs, N.J.: Prentice-Hall, 1989), pp. 47–49.
[39]See Appendix 2.
[40]Walter E. Goddard, *Just-in-Time: Surviving by Breaking Tradition* (Essex Junction, Vt.: Oliver Wight, 1986), pp. 159–64.

90% reduction in the volume of printed pages
80% reduction of computer code lines, compared to old
75% reduction in the number of input and output formats
90% reduction of the number of transactions processed
50% reduction of the data elements stored in the system
50% reduction in the user work
75% reduction in the user's transaction process time

These stringent standards of excellence will force a degree of simplicity and productivity into computer systems that is comparable to the standards used for factory improvement projects. Since integration has a long past track record of being counterproductive, the concepts of focus and simplicity (small and simple is best) must become fundamental characteristics of twenty-first-century computer operations.

Undue emphasis on technology tools is not unique to engineering. It is also a problem with many technicians responsible for developing computer systems. The siren song of technology is a constant temptation to some who mindlessly accept and pursue the ethereal "Computer Integrated Manufacturing" (CIM) system. In three decades of working on and with computer systems, the author has seen them become increasingly complex with each passing year. During these years, the cry for integration has been a constant goal of every system project. The cry has been heeded, and as a result most systems today are so highly integrated that even small improvements require further convoluting the logic and structure of innumerable computer programs. Major improvements usually take years and complete systems revision. The problem of the wrong sort of "integration" has led the author sometimes to suggest that the new Holy Grail should perhaps be "Computer Disintegrated Manufacturing." Clearly this tongue-in-cheek statement is not intended to belittle the need for new interfaced systems working in concert to "broadcast" the latest customer orders or schedules throughout the manufacturing network in the shortest possible time. New systems, however, must be simpler and less intertwined to support substantially lowering the cost penalty associated with changing a business organization's subsystem. For example (although perhaps a minor technical point), every data matrix that the author has ever seen clearly shows that a relatively low percentage of data elements are commonly used in more than one or two diverse organizations such as engineering and purchasing. Therefore, emphasis on common data bases may be considerably less important than data communication (interface). Thus, if different organizations' systems are designed to communicate through interfaces, each such system will be much less dependant on *integration* with the systems of other organizations. For example, a final demand forecast is developed from a vast amount of detail data and processing logic. The production organization needs a final sales forecast to drive production plans but has little routine need for the detail that went into its determination. When the sales forecasting system is conceived and constructed as a stand-alone system with one important interface (final forecast) to production, it can be changed or completely replaced without ever causing complications vis-à-vis the production system, as long as the interface itself does not change.

Decades of pursuing the Holy Grail of integration were inexorably accompanied by ever increasing costs of white collar overhead but were rarely accompanied by tangible, enduring improvements in operating costs. For example, in manufacturing companies, one of the largest benefit areas, which should be and has been the subject of most improvement projects, is inventory investment. However, with the exception of a few years of economic boom or bust, national and international business inventories have never ceased their inexorable climb. At the same time, increasing degrees of integration have continuously reduced our flexibility in terms of being able to easily revise systems to include improved, user-oriented techniques. Enhanced systems should simplify the user's operations, as opposed to simply automating previous manual operations. They should radically modify the way the enterprise works in order to improve operating results in the broadest sense.

The main reason that past systems have not yielded major tangible improvements is basic. Contrary to popular opinion, problems and opportunities are not automatically addressed merely because data are collected and scrutinized. They can be attacked only by changing and improving the operation at the source. For example, improved inventory systems are always justified by expectations of reductions in inventory investment. In the long run, however, most companies' inventories stay at the same levels or increase. Exhibit 3–5 points out the fallacy of the approach. Based on the opinions of hundreds of experienced professionals, of all of the potentials for improvement in manufacturing operations, including inventory levels, 90 percent of the potential can be realized *only* through operations improvements. That leaves 10 percent of all gains to be achieved by new or changed systems. (My esteemed colleague Leroy "Pete" Peterson believes these numbers are 80 percent and 20 percent, respectively, based on the large impact systems can have on the network of factories and vendors. Our friendly disagreement centers on how much can be accomplished in the short term with manual versus

MANUFACTURING
BENEFIT POTENTIAL

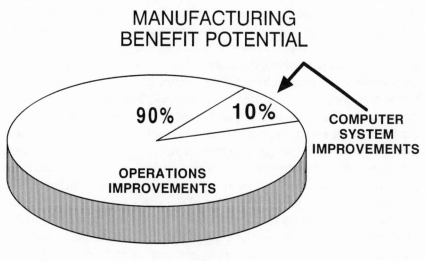

EXHIBIT 3-5

computer systems. However, we both agree on the urgent need for improvements.) This is not to say that the computer system is not an invaluable tool when used effectively and appropriately. For example, nonmanufacturing expenses and payrolls in most enterprises make up a much larger share of the total pie than do manufacturing costs, exclusive of purchased materials. As Exhibit 3-6 shows, general and administrative, engineering, and sales expenses often represent 80 percent of the pie. In these areas, potential benefits of improved procedures and systems can

BUSINESS BENEFIT POTENTIAL

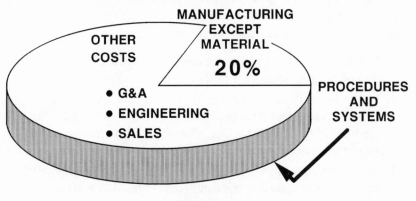

EXHIBIT 3-6

substantially increase the efficiency and profitability of operations. Incidentally, the science of designing manual procedures has almost vanished in the age of the computer (almost as though the pencil had never been invented). Today, anything documented is entered on the computer and then displayed or printed back for the person entering it. The first chapters of this book were produced the same way. The author drafted them by hand, then key-entered them on a word processing system. After editing the printed result, keying in changes, reediting, ad infinitum, it was finally completed, albeit at a higher than necessary cost. While these chapters were thus completed in less time than if the firm's formal word processing organization had been involved, the key entry person's (the author) cost was far greater than that of the specialist who can type several times faster. (Since then, the old dog has learned new tricks and is producing the remainder of the book directly on his personal computer, eliminating pencil draft). The results now appear to be more cost-effective than when using word processing, since the author writes and types at about the same speed. The point of this real-life exposé is that not all old habits die easily. Extensive training and on-the-job practice would have led the author to change earlier. The same attention to training is a vital ingredient of any improvement project. Incidentally, in Japan the manuscript would not have been typed at all since a practical typewriter with thousands of keys does not yet exist. This simple important "disadvantage" allows Japanese companies to operate without the seemingly unavoidable armies of typists required by most large Western companies. We tend to have anything we write typed. Fortunes could be saved if it were practical to uninvent typing devices and change the popular slogan "don't say it, write it" to "don't write it, say it."

The pervasive myth of the computer system's value in answering manager's questions is a dangerous misconception. Although it is frequently true that managers are often frustrated by the time and cost involved in obtaining special analyses, most would agree that:

1. Special analyses frequently are not really needed. Managers simply do not have enough time to digest more computer output.

2. In almost every case of information need, data are available—albeit in less-than-perfect form or degree of summary or detail. Managers are very adept at interpreting whatever information is available to meet their needs, whether in computer or manual form.

3. After special analyses are obtained, "managerial decisions" are rarely directly related to the data. Nor are the data a major decision-making factor in most instances.

4. The prime reason for managerial success is frequent direct interaction with the manager's network of interpersonal relationships. McGill writes: "Managing effectiveness depends upon building, maintaining and utilizing a complex network of relationships up, down, across and outside of an organization. Electronic interaction is no substitute for human interaction when it comes to getting managerial work done."[41]

The author recently saw a highly regarded computer expert on educational television. He was extolling the value of the computer to managers, commenting roughly as follows:

> Imagine how difficult it would be to perform an analysis of the effect on total sales of a 2.5 percent increase in sales by two hundred salespeople. The results would be of utmost importance in making a business decision. A computer could answer the question in ten seconds.

His statement is misleading and shows a naïveté regarding the information that is routinely available in business and the way in which good managers operate. Specifically,

1. Every business has *total* sales and other financial information readily available. Sales data are often updated as frequently as daily. The hypothetical question could be answered, in less than ten seconds and without using the computer, by adding 2.5 percent to the total sales amount.

2. Detail on two hundred salespeople is an example of data too voluminous for managers to use. Two or three such lengthy analyses would fill a manager's day, leaving no time to work with his network of business associates.

The speaker was a computer technician, not a business manager. Thus, although a leader in his field, he does not understand the realities of existing, noncomputer business information or of the everyday roles of business managers.

If based on how the individual does and should operate as a manager, information systems for executives and managers can only contribute to an enterprise's success. In most cases, managers need to improve their management methods, and these changes must also be reflected in the types of system support they use. Policing executive and manager performance will not necessarily cause them to pursue continuous improve-

[41]McGill, *American Business and Quick Fix*, p. 199.

ment. Systems that *support* the manager will be of much greater value. Cross-training and job rotation in both functions will eventually be the bridge between computer technician and business manager.

PAPERWORK: BOON OR BANE?

Paperwork can inhibit accomplishment, contrary to the popular belief that formally writing requests or instructions will help to ensure their successful completion. For example, while working on a setup reduction project on a complex machine line in West Germany in 1982, the author went to an executive committee meeting with unbridled exuberance. When starting to work on the first machine line, after opening the sound-proofing covers of the machines, the author and his team found hundreds of different sizes and types of fasteners, all of which were involved in changeover. Several sketches of standardized fasteners and fast-release alternatives were used to present methods for saving several hours of work at each changeover. At the start of the next executive meeting, one week later the author announced that the (German) factory would never compete with the Japanese. A somewhat stunned and insulted group then heard the author explain that on the way to the meeting he walked past the line, one of seventeen similar lines, and saw that not one of the fasteners on any line had been changed. In Japan, by contrast, whenever we saw a comparable opportunity, it was only a few hours at most before most of the changes were made. In Germany and in the rest of the Western world, secrets for reducing the amount of time required to make changes has eluded us until recently. It has taken weeks to accomplish things that should be possible to do in hours or days.

It did not take long to realize that the delay in Germany (and in most Western countries) was caused by overly bureaucratic systems requiring changes to go through the normal documentation procedures and approval processes (i.e. "red tape"). The usual procedures and documentation for authorizing and specifying a change are so intimidating and complex that they have always discouraged people with ideas from submitting them. Even after preparing the necessary change request documentation, a fairly high percentage of requests have always been rejected. A variety of reasons cause such rejections: The requested change is not considered detailed enough; the costs and benefits are not detailed enough; and the person approving the request was the original designer of the tooling or method, so he often feels that the improvement could not be as good as his design. (He rejects too many ideas without giving them due consideration.)

In Japan, the diversity of fastener types would have been reduced overnight. This would start by determining a standard fastener head configuration and by rushing to the maintenance storeroom or to the local commercial hardware store for the required replacement fasteners. In Germany (as in most Western countries), process engineers must prepare engineering drawings of the machine revisions, updating the drawing list of materials to reflect the new fasteners. Finally, upon completion of the specifications, it would be necessary to open a work order to be used by a tool and die maker to remove the old fasteners and install the new. In Japan, the team members from the area would decide which screws to use, would pick them up, and would install them.

Our project teams always develop fast track procedures for changes originated by the teams, thus substantially reducing the effort and time required to implement changes. This has been so successful that, in numerous instances, other people have brought their changes to our project teams for processing, in anticipation that their ideas will be acted on with dispatch. In the long run, documentation, if any, for this type of change should be owned by the focused factory-within-a-factory, which must have the authority to make the change either before or after completing the minimal documentation required. In many cases, a photo of the machine, after changes have been made, will be the easiest-to-understand, lowest cost form of documentation.[42] In others, the machine or tooling itself is more than adequate documentation. That a picture is worth a thousand words in constantly becoming clearer. Engineering drawings that are difficult for even the most experienced engineer to understand are seldom used on the floor of new focused factories. Instead, three-dimensional drawings (or sketches, preferably), which are much easier to understand, are used. For example, Utilimaster Corporation in Wakarusa, Indiana, has found that hanging simple drawings like Exhibit 3-7 in front of assemblers helps to reduce assembly errors sharply.

Sketches usually cost less to produce than formal drawings, while photographs and video tape may be even less expensive and can be produced more rapidly without using drafting or artist specialists. Fortunately, the latest and best computer-aided design and manufacturing software systems features make it easy to use computer data for both conventional and three-dimensional drawings. These are important options for reducing costs and increasing clarity in the factory of the twenty-first century.

[42]Tetsuichi Asaka and Kazuo Ozeki, eds., *Handbook of Quality Tools: The Japanese Approach* (Cambridge, Mass.: Productivity Press, 1990), p. 67.

SIMPLE ASSEMBLY INSTRUCTIONS

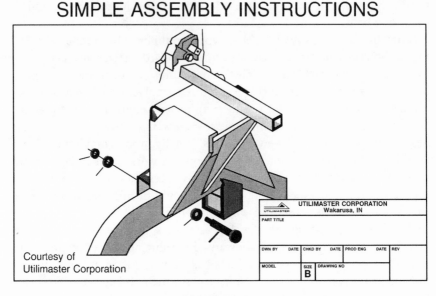

Courtesy of
Utilimaster Corporation

UTILIMASTER CORPORATION
Wakarusa, IN

PART TITLE

| DWN BY | DATE | CHKD BY | DATE | PROD ENG | DATE | REV |

| MODEL | SIZE | DRAWING NO |
| | B | |

EXHIBIT 3-7

EDUCATION: THE HOPE OF THE FUTURE

Very few of the superior manufacturing ideas are radically new. One of the most important is simply the application of time and motion study, the traditional industrial engineering practice that has been in limited use for close to a century. Fukuda, for example, has noted that two-thirds of improvements made by Japanese employee groups have resulted from applying traditional industrial engineering techniques.[43] However, this powerful tool has not been used as vigorously as its success warrants. One reason is that its use has been limited to a small group of specialists in the industrial engineering department. Furthermore, education and training in its concepts and techniques have generally been limited to this same small group. Schonberger pointed out that when people on the shop floor participate in industrial engineering, the amount of improvement work that can be done will multiply several times.[44]

Regardless of the fact that innumerable companies have availed themselves of the services of educators and their videotapes to educate hundreds of thousands of employees, progress in putting education to work

[43]Ryuji Fukuda, *Managerial Engineering: Techniques for Improving Quality and Productivity in the Workplace* (Cambridge, Mass: Productivity Press, 1983), p. 130.
[44]Richard J. Schonberger, *World Class Manufacturing: The Lessons of Simplicity Applied* (New York: Free Press, 1986), p. 46.

has been maddeningly slow. One reason has to be the quality of the education. As we all know from our own postuniversity experiences, we discover that we apply only a small percentage of what we have learned in school to the conduct of our jobs once we leave school. The commonly recognized reason for this is that the educators who develop courses have had limited, if any, practical experience in industry. As a result, they are unable to educate their audiences in the specific step-by-step process of designing and implementing improvements. To the extent that their courses draw upon real-life examples, they can hardly represent the thousands of types of companies that make up the manufacturing industry. Little wonder that after seeing people attend some of the most superb educational courses available, the most common critical comment is that while the course was very interesting, it had little, if any, applicability in the attendee's company.

The new wave of education must be a combination of generally applicable materials (developed by the educator) and company- and industry-specific material developed in the process of making improvements in actual operations. It will never suffice to conduct a one-time program of a few hours or even a few days, ending the education program there. Most people, after six months, forget as much as 90 percent of what they heard in formal educational programs. Periodic refresher course programs, at least annually, will be necessary until such time as the subject matter is routinely practiced as part of every employee's job. It is imperative that industry and educators must start drawing upon industry experience for the permanent programs that will equip our employees with the education needed for our companies to become the superior manufacturers of the future.

Companies in the United States are becoming more and more aware that the educational system is failing to equip students with the education and training necessary to become working cogs in a highly competitive, world class company. Nevertheless, industry and labor leaders are not making a substantial commitment to the intensive postschool education programs that are necessary to increase the value and performance of every working person in an enterprise or union. Although the author thinks that an average of two to four hours per week per employee (advocated by Gufreda, Lytle, and Maynard for these types of activities)[45] is too extreme, near zero is far from enough. Nor should industry be expected to carry the entire burden. Organized labor and each individual

---

[45]Joseph J. Gufreda, Lucy N. Lytle, and Larry A. Maynard, in Ernest C. Huge, ed. *Total Quality: An Executive's Guide for the 1990s* (Homewood, Ill.: Dow Jones–Irwin, 1990), p. 163.

must be dedicated to new lifetime programs of improvement. Volunteer employee programs sponsored by both labor and management could start to prepare every individual to be an important part of the international competitive race. It is time to get started!

TECHNICAL FOG: THE LANGUAGE OF TECHNICIANS

In every aspect of business, simplifying operations, products, and systems will do more to improve competitive advantage for the company than any of the more widely ballyhooed business improvement nostrums. However, computer system technicians lead the pack in adding to the ever increasing complexity of the world of business. Of the three languages of business, two are natural and vital to business communication. They are the languages of money and of things. Executives and managers must be fluent in the monetary language since the enterprise's fundamental purpose is to raise capital and invest it in equipment and facilities with which to earn profits for the owners and to meet the payroll and pay for the employees' fringe benefits.

Most office and factory workers and even supervisors have not yet been trained in the money language and perhaps need this language much less than the second language, the language of things. The things with which they deal *every* day include pieces of paper, components and materials they use and handle, and the machines and tools required to do their jobs. Systems must be designed to support both management and the working people and must be described in the two languages they understand best. However, more and more, technicians are introducing an entirely new third language into the business arena. This language is technical fog. (Charlotte Hofmann dubs it "techno-speak").[46]

After listening to a discussion among computer technicians for an hour or so, one might easily conclude that they are the most intelligent people in the world—a unique, elite group. The reason: the entire conversation to the lay person is as incomprehensible as Esperanto to the average person. However, the technicians are able to understand each other perfectly. The roots of technical fog are alphabet soup (Fox and Goldratt also point out the need to sort out the alphabet soup)[47] and numbers. The alphabet soup comprises of an endless array of acronyms, most of

[46]Charlotte Cook Hofmann, "Hidden Costs of Computing," in Vernon M. Buehler and Y. K. Shetty, eds., *Competing Through Quality* (Cambridge, Mass.: Productivity Press, 1988), p. 373.

[47]Robert E. Fox and Eliyahu M. Goldratt, *The Race* (Croton-on-Hudson, N.Y.: North River Press, 1986), p. 16.

which describe computer operating systems, application software, and various functions and features thereof. Further, the alphabet soup is applied even to the smallest and most mundane of the data elements. Numbers, somewhat less prevalent in the misty language, are used as identifiers of computer and telecommunication hardware. The point is, in summary, that the trend in business has been to permit computer technicians to complicate the world by forcing businessmen to be trilingual. The computer technicians need to learn and use the real languages of business so as to serve better the people who use their systems.

Although today's hardware and software are infinitely better than in past decades, the use of these tools is seriously limited by the inability of the technicians to communicate information about their features and operating instructions. The technician speaks his specialized language so incessantly that he loses the ability to communicate with the rest of the world in an intelligible tongue. If the trend continues, the profession of technical fog translator is bound to become one of the future's most vital and best-paid jobs. The challenge implicit in this discussion of languages is clear. Those guilty of its use should strive to be as fluent in their native languages as they are in that of their colleagues. Better still, they would contribute mightily to the simplification process if they would stamp out the creation of technical fog at the source.

Lest the computer technician feel picked on, the author readily admits that technical fog abounds in every field of specialization. However, data processing and defense industry specialists would probably win the prize for the amount of obfuscation. (General Kelly was elected to be the Pentagon spokesman during the recent Desert Storm war because he was one of the very few military men capable of discussing military operations in English rather than defense-ese.)

SUMMARY

Although people who go to work in the newly rearranged factory, using new tooling and modified machines, will automatically produce better quality with higher productivity, the job won't be done until supervisors and managers are also performing their *new* roles as well as their employees are doing theirs. Further, no company can afford to accept the status quo as its goal. Everyone must realize that exciting new and improved methods are just around the corner. Therefore, every employee must be educated and trained in the techniques of turning those corners. Although the hardware side of the business is important, nothing will ever be as important as the men and women who make the factory run.

4

□□□

Supplier Network:
Pipeline to Profits

PURCHASES CONSTITUTE THE SINGLE GREATEST POTENTIAL for improving the quality of our manufactured products while reducing their costs and, consequently, their prices. Materials and purchased components account for 60 to 70 percent of the cost of goods manufactured in almost every company. Each manufacturer's inventory investment and customer service level are thus controlled less by its own processing time than by its suppliers' lead times and delivery reliability. For example, the supplier's ability to deliver in rapid response to the latest schedule, to deliver the exact quantity required, and to deliver materials and components of perfect quality is critical to the customer's ability to respond to the needs of its own market. Yet, shockingly, those responsible for purchasing have been slow to adopt radically new ways of dealing with suppliers. The old ways and the old paperwork and computer systems still dominate the everyday practices of both the purchasing organization and the supplier's order entry and billing operations. The result? Suppliers are forced to continue running their end of the pipeline in the business-as-usual mode. Worse, most purchasing organizations have no long-range plan for working toward the elimination of the institutionalized practices that put barriers between the purchaser and the supplier instead of uniting them in the pursuit of common goals.

When a purchasing department follows the traditional purchasing strategy, the roles of customer and vendor are essentially adversarial. Exhibit 4–1 shows a customer and a vendor with very different sets of priorities. The customer's purchase agreements are based on price, delivery, and quality. Price has always been the primary vendor selection decision criterion, although sometimes overridden by an urgent need for delivery. Where delivery speed is of the essence, the vendor able to deliver fastest gets the order. Quality, as a criterion for vendor selection, has historically been considered but usually with much less weight than price. At the other end of the telephone line, in Exhibit 4–1, sits the vendor with his criteria for accepting new orders. The vendor knows that the higher the volume of products he can sell, the greater the fixed overhead absorption, a combination that maximizes his profitability. For this reason, few suppliers reject any orders—even when extremely high order backlogs almost guarantee missing requested delivery dates. Despite having completely oversold their capacity, they will nevertheless promise on-time delivery, hoping that their capacity log jam will break, making the impossible possible. The vendor plans his manufacturing operations to minimize cost and also orders from the lowest cost suppliers to further minimize his costs. These vendor habits are not always consistent with delivering quality products.

In the traditional adversarial customer—supplier relationship it is virtually impossible to work toward the common good of both. Each adversary is actually doing its best to put the other out of business, although neither realizes this. The customer, by obtaining competitive quotations,

VENDOR RELATIONSHIPS

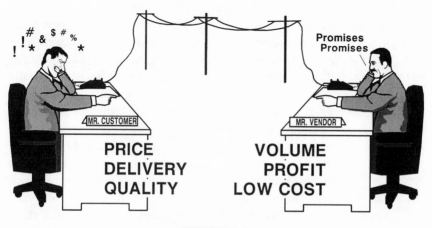

EXHIBIT 4-1

does his best to force vendor prices so low as to preclude the supplier from earning a reasonable profit. At the same time, the supplier pushes in the opposite direction, trying his best to get the highest possible price while supplying products of less than ideal quality or value. The path suppliers must follow to become the best in business is clear. A supplier must make investments in process improvement to produce near perfect quality at the lowest cost; he should produce in small lot sizes while still minimizing his cost and maintaining a reasonable profit margin. He should use materials of value so his products will have value. (Chapter 6 discusses the confusion between quality and value. Often the products thought of as being of poor quality are actually produced to [and meet] very exact specifications—the real problem is they are made of cheap materials. This can be improved only by engineering changes to the material specifications.)

In the supplier's factory the U-form cell is usually the way to produce the highest quality, lowest cost products, while setup reduction improvements are the key to enabling him to deliver frequently and in small lots. Most suppliers would be reluctant to make investments in cells or setup reduction for the benefit of any single customer. Vendors know that the moment a competitor offers the products for a slightly lower price, the customer is likely to shift its business to the lower priced source. Loyalty to the dollar rather than loyalty between customer and supplier can no longer be permitted. Superior manufacturers have a new way of working with suppliers, which is vital to fostering incredibly improved relationships through a new "partnership in profit," Exhibit 4-2. The customer cannot expect the supplier to cooperate in making the improvements necessary to lower both his and the supplier's costs and inventories unless there is commitment on both sides to forming a permanent linkage. The fruits of the improvements made practical by permanent linkage are better quality and price of the customer's products, which increases its sales and market share. With increased volume thanks to improved absorption of fixed overhead, both supplier and user will increase profits. Radically new procedures and systems for purchasing must go hand in hand with the new customer-supplier relationships. When a company adopts the new methods of vendor negotiation and schedule communication, numerous forms and related procedures and systems used for hundreds of years become obsolete. Among them are purchase orders, purchase order change notices, blanket purchase orders, quotation requests, supplier certification, inspection report, and quality auditing, to name a few. Yet, sadly, even some recent books on the subject continue to espouse these

PARTNERS IN PROFIT

CUSTOMER   SUPPLIER

EXHIBIT 4-2

archaic practices, which should long since have been recognized as failing to help companies achieve the degree of success needed in today's world.[1]

CHECKLIST: SUPPLIER NETWORK ZINGERS

Reaping the benefits of vendor improvements will entail both short- and long-term efforts. Short-term goals must focus on simple, fast, common-sense improvements that will almost immediately start to yield improved operating results. However, the ultimate superior vendor will attain its goals only by making revolutionary changes in the customer—supplier relationship and the methods that encourage working together in closer harmony. It might take years of unparalleled cooperation to find ways to overcome the traditional roadblocks to becoming partners in profit. Following is a checklist of some of the key steps on the journey toward such a goal:

1. The vendor program is of such importance to both vendor and customer that it should involve the chief executive officers of both companies.

[1]See, for example, Jerry W. Claunch, Michael W. Gozzo, and Peter L. Grieco, Jr., *Supplier Certification: Achieving Excellence* (Plantsville, Conn.: PT Publications, 1988).

2. The most competitive vendors will establish small focused factories, each dedicated to a single customer. Because the capacity of each focused factory or cell will belong to one customer, the problem of juggling the competing priorities of various customers will disappear. Superior customers will beat their competitors to the punch by purchasing the capacity of vendors' cells and subplants dedicated to their components.

3. Vendor and multitiered distribution warehousing increases the cost of business and should be discontinued. The perceived business advantages of warehouses are better provided by improved transportation methods and rapid shipment of customer orders through faster order-processing systems and speedy order-filling operations.

4. Vendor agreements will encompass commodities, not just individual purchased items. This will cut the time spent in price negotiation and will give the customer additional purchase leverage with which to interest suppliers in beginning improvement programs.

5. Multiple, simultaneous suppliers of a single item will cease to be used since this lowers the potential volume of any one supplier, cutting what he can afford to spend on better tooling. Reduction of active vendors by 80 to 90 percent should be a fundamental goal of the vendor improvement program.

6. Single source suppliers of "critical" purchases will be expected to have plans and provisions for disaster contingencies to ensure that the customer's business disruption, if any, would be minimal. Deming ranks the concept of single sources as number 4 of his "fourteen points," a reflection of the great importance that he attaches to it.[2]

7. Improvements in the speed with which requirements are updated and communicated to the vendor will sharply reduce the radical surges and drops in demand that are one of its biggest headaches.

8. Drastic cuts in the vendor–customer manufacturing pipeline lead time will further minimize wild swings in the vendor's schedule.

9. New computer generated schedules, transferred electronically to the supplier's computer, will eliminate purchase orders and purchase order change notices. By bypassing intervening manual steps, the computer-to-computer transfer of requirements will also

---

[2]W. Edwards Deming. *Out of Crisis* (Cambridge, Mass.: MIT Center for Advanced Engineering Study, 1986), pp. 35–38.

be one of the keys to reducing swings in requirements and increasing speed of delivery by reducing the time required to communicate the latest requirements.

10. Trucks, trailers, and loading dock facilities will be constructed to permit loading and unloading from any point around their perimeter. This will drastically reduce the load-unload time, reduce the number of docks needed, and simplify the loading-unloading sequence problem. As a result of faster turnaround, fewer trucks and trailers will be needed.

DEALING AT THE TOP

Although a company's buyers are the front-line troops who deal with the intricacies of the vendor program, top level executive involvement of both customer and supplier enterprises is the most important key to success. One of the best ways to get the ball rolling is to conduct a meeting involving the Chief Executive Officers, Presidents, and Manufacturing Vice Presidents of both companies. Vaughn Beals, former Chairman of the Board, and Tom Gelb, Vice President—Operations and Engineering, have said that a large measure of the success of their vendor program at Harley-Davidson was a direct result of their personal, active participation in customer–vendor executive meetings. Incidentally, the author considers supplier certification to be an anachronism unsuitable for twenty-first-century superior manufacturers.[3] The rote checklists usually use excessive, detailed operations evaluations as a substitute for executive judgment. Checklists were necessary when a company had thousands of suppliers. With a few hundred at most, it becomes practical for executives and their top managers to visit and thus actually get to know their most important suppliers in the best way possible, by direct observation and conversation.

No wonder executive level discussions are the best catalysts. After all, the buyer's normal contact in the supplier organization is the customer service representative or even the sales vice president, in exceptional situations. The customer service representative simply does not have the authority or even the interest required to trigger the initiation of factory and product improvement projects. The most important aspects of improving the vendor's quality, delivery, and productivity involve its man-

[3]Jerry W. Claunch, Michael W. Gozzo, and Peter L. Grieco, Jr., *Just-in-Time Purchasing: In Pursuit of Excellence* (Plantsville, Conn.: PT Publications, 1988), pp. 55–59.

ufacturing and engineering organizations and require executive approval of the vital ingredients of the program (reorganization of the factory into customer-oriented cells, for example). Underlings simply will not be able to commit their companies to undertaking improvements. Vendor personnel at the customer service representative level will rarely have the vision to grasp the fact that two companies can work together as partners in profit, especially when the supplier company is large and important. By contrast, the chief executive officer who does not become enthusiastic when presented with the future vision of working with customers in long-term relationships for the benefit and profit of each is rare indeed.

Japanese supplier–customer relationships are bound not solely by tradition but also by practical business ties. Commonly, major manufacturers own at least a little stock of both small and large subcontractors and have cross-ownership ties with important vendors. Too few Western enterprises have taken advantage of this way of bonding the customer with the supplier. They should begin to investigate the possibility of at least a nominal exchange of equity with suppliers. For the supplier it is one way to ensure that the customer will do its best to do business with it rather than its competitors. As one of the shareholders of the company, the customer will benefit from the priority assigned to its needs. The improved willingness of the supplier to make investments in improving the cost, quality, and speed of delivery will also benefit the customer. The possibility of equity swap is one of the subjects that could be discussed only at the executive-to-executive level.

The vendor's development of cells and subplants dedicated to producing a customer's components and materials is another executive-to-executive issue. The supplier president should be enthused at the prospect of increased productivity and reduced delivery lead time. He should understand the potential of the dedicated facility as a powerful sales tool. To retain his customers requires a vendor not only to reduce delivery lead time and inventory but also to make the quantum improvements in quality that are usually free by-products of cell and focused subplant production.

The prospect of radical improvements in a vendor's productivity, quality, and delivery should be exciting to its executives. It should be even more exciting to learn that the customer is planning to buy every item in the commodity (or commodities) they supply from a single source. If they can master the technique of marketing entire commodities rather than individual items to *all* of their customers, they will undoubtedly see an opportunity for quantum market share gains. For its part, the customer's purchase of all items in a commodity or multiple commodities from a single source should be an exciting way to increase its purchase leverage with the vendor selected. So, both customer and supplier will benefit from this new practice.

The executive(s) responsible for initial meetings with vendor counterparts must be equipped with a discussion agenda, supported by presentation material, and have an in-depth grasp of the subject. Mastery of the subjects of discussion is the surest key to convincing their counterpart executives of the benefits and the urgency of the vendor program. A summary list of some of the key topics follows.

1. Vendor cells or subplants dedicated to the customer's requirements
2. Purchasing of a specific vendor capacity, where appropriate, rather than only individual items or commodities (Capacity purchases help the vendor keep his capacity loaded. The customer also benefits from purchasing capacity because it eliminates jockeying for priority with the vendor's other customers. The company, as "owner" of the capacity, can continuously schedule its production sequence, considering only *its* priorities.)
3. Single-source purchase agreements for entire commodities
4. Rapid requirement communication systems to reduce vendor response time and to lower the incidence of radical, surprise swings in the volume of demand
5. Improving vendor operations to increase productivity while simultaneously providing higher quality and better on-time delivery, through use of a structured vendor program
6. Possibilities of new, focused local factories and exchanges of equity

CUSTOMER SUBPLANTS: THE ULTIMATE SOLUTION

Supply problems that have perpetually plagued manufacturers and have appeared to be unsolvable will finally be cured when customers start to purchase vendors' subplant or cell capacity and when those subplants or cells are dedicated to production of the single customer's products. Further, the company that presents a plan for new cells and subplants dedicated to a customer's products will have a tremendous competitive advantage over other suppliers who plan to continue to operate old-fashioned, giant job shops. In the job shop every other customer's order competes for available machines. Suppliers try to be fair in deciding priorities. Thus, they plan to produce their customers' order requirements on a first-come, first-served basis. Since customer order backlogs are often equal to weeks or months of available capacity, the next order received will normally be scheduled and promised that far in the future. When unexpected changes in demand occur (always), the supplier cannot possibly recast his entire schedule to the latest requirements of every customer. Worse, when supplier backlogs are high, customers start to order more and earlier to allow for longer delivery lead time. This causes the backlog to increase further and delivery lead times to lengthen even more. Thus, a very high percentage of backlogs, in times of strong market demand, consists of customer orders that are not really required but are created solely as a safety measure to "reserve" capacity before other customers do so. Paradoxically, the net effect of all of the safety stock orders is a sharp reduction in the vendors' delivery performance, decreasing rather than increasing the safety level attained.

The customer lucky enough to have placed his orders first is not really so lucky after all. For one thing, if he receives everything he has ordered, his inventory investment will soar. Further, his forecast needs, used to launch orders weeks or months in advance, are always inaccurate. Therefore, even with inventories up to the ceiling, the customer experiences numerous shortages that restrict production, causing it to fall far short of actual customer orders. While working with an outdoor furniture manufacturer on a vendor program in the early 1980s, the author had an early opportunity to see the radical impact of establishing customer subplants in a fabric supplier's factory. The custom fabrics used for outdoor furniture were much like designer fabrics in the fashion industry. The real demand was impossible to forecast with any degree of accuracy before the start of a brief season of peak sales. Thus, the inventory of fabrics at the furniture factory was always chaotically different from actual requirements. Some fabrics had actual inventories far in excess of any future demand while others were out of stock for extended periods of time. When all of the fabric orders (previously ordered from numerous vendors) were placed with a single supplier, the combined requirements were roughly enough to fill the twenty-four-hour capacity of four out of one hundred looms at the mill. Previously, the furniture manufacturer's fabric orders were produced on any of the hundred available looms. Once scheduled, orders could rarely be rescheduled since doing so would normally cause the capacity to be reassigned to another vendor. After negotiating a deal to buy the capacity of four specific machines, the customer found it easy to update the vendor's fabric schedule continuously according to the customer's latest needs. What made it easy was that there were no other customers vying for the capacity of the machines. Thus, the time interval between notifying the supplier of the next fabric required and the date when it was completed and shipped was sharply reduced. Part of the process of negotiation for machine capacity involved developing the terms under which relatively small amounts of excess capacity could routinely be "sold" back to the fabric vendor.

Not all items will be as suitable for dedicated vendor capacity as the fabric in this example. Items produced to the customer's unique specification and produced in high volume are most suitable, while low volume, standard stock items are less so. However, where dedicated capacity applies, the links between supplier and customer can be forged so strongly that shortages will disappear and lead time will shrink by 90 percent or more.

COMMUNICATIONS: KEY TO RESPONSIVENESS AND COOPERATION

For years the author has painted a word picture of the incredible difficulty that rigid, bureaucratic organizations have placed on communications between the factory people who use purchased components and materials and the people who make them in vendors' factories. The scenario described below is repeated thousands, perhaps millions, of times every day in factories all over the world. The chain of events is as follows: (1) A production worker notices that a purchased component (or material) that he uses is defective and brings it to the attention of his supervisor. (2) The supervisor agrees that there is a defect and fills out the appropriate defective material form. Since a high percentage of the stock on the floor is visibly defective, resolution of the problem is obviously urgent. The supervisor, therefore, calls in the quality control person to verify the defect. (3) The quality control person verifies the defect and fills out appropriate forms to report the defect officially to the production control organization. (4) Production control immediately processes paperwork to instruct the central storeroom to withdraw all inventory of the item and to return it to quality control to determine how much of the inventory is defective. (5) The quality control section sorts the item into good and defective material and finds that most of the material is defective. They prepare paperwork to report their findings to the production control organization. (6) Since the situation is now quite obviously critical, the production control organization fills out the paperwork necessary to notify purchasing to request immediate replacement of the material and to return or rework the defective stock. (7) The purchasing department almost immediately calls the supplier service representative and describes the circumstances. To abbreviate the message, subsequent communication steps in the supplier organization are (8) production control, (9) quality control, (10) supervisor, and (11) production worker who is busily producing more of the part. Imagine what happens next, when it becomes clear that the nature of the defect reported has been lost or garbled in the process, and it is necessary to go back and forth between these channels once or twice before a reasonable approach is developed for refilling the pipeline with defect-free production.

It is shocking that the classic response to this dilemma has mainly been to add computer inputs and communications to each of these steps, which only adds still more steps and complexities to the problem. To the author, it is glaringly clear that the real problem is the neat compartmentalization of specialized functions. For example, purchasing, and only purchasing, is permitted to contact the supplier. The traditional, ostensible rationale is that only purchasing has the experience to deal with suppliers. Besides, too many people dealing with the vendor could only lead to confusion! The probable reality is that each functional area, including purchasing, fiercely protects its "turf" from invasion from the outside. After all, if others start to take over traditional responsibilities, will it not lead to diminished importance for the function?

Logical simplification of the process, supported by the best possible electronic tools, is a much more fruitful avenue. For example, consider the following scenario. (1) A cell or line team member notices that a component is defective. (2) One team member checks the team's focused storage area to determine the quantity of the defective material while other members quickly sort out good parts and keep production rolling. (3) The team lead person telephones the lead person of the vendor cell or line and they discuss the nature of the problem and the steps they will take to rework and/or replace quickly all of the defects in the very short pipeline. The supplier team at General Motors' Delco Moraine NDH Plant recognized the power of direct communication from the outset of their program when it empowered every team member to call any vendor about any quality problem.[4] One of the industry's most crying needs today is to simplify communications and to reestablish direct, person-to-person relationships as the foundation of new, cooperative teamwork between both internal and external people and organizations.

[4]Charles R. Birkholz, and Jim Villella, *The Battle to Stay Competitive: Changing the Traditional Workplace* (Cambridge, Mass. Productivity Press, 1990), pp. 13–15.

VENDOR AND DISTRIBUTION WAREHOUSING: A TERRIBLE STRATEGY

When companies in the West first heard that Japanese manufacturers were operating with virtually no inventories and saw that suppliers were making daily and even hourly deliveries, they erroneously drew the conclusion that the suppliers were required to maintain huge inventories to support this. Accordingly, quite a few enterprises diligently started making arrangements with their suppliers to stock the materials and components supplied in their factory warehouses and even in warehouses near the customer's factories. It would appear that the companies that made these deals naïvely presumed that suppliers would absorb the cost of inventory and warehousing out of supreme kindness, since the supplier could pay the added cost only out of profits or by increasing prices. Before too long, it became evident that the supplier started to increase prices as soon as the next contract negotiations came due.

Prior to these types of arrangements, delivery quantities requested from a supplier were often based on the historical practice of scheduling once-a-month delivery of all but the most expensive items. In some instances, the vendor's machines and tools were of speed (capacity) that required that the items be in production continuously in order to meet the customer's once-a-month delivery requirement. Exhibit 4–3 indicates

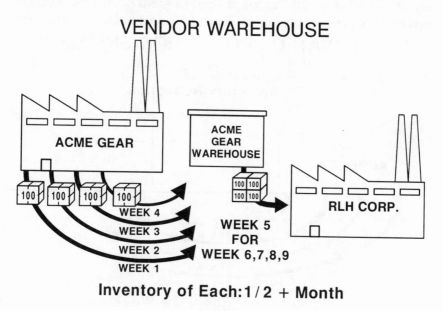

VENDOR WAREHOUSE

Inventory of Each: 1 / 2 + Month

EXHIBIT 4-3

the inventories that would result from Acme Gear producing gears for the RLH Corporation each week, storing them in its own warehouse, and holding them for the once-a-month delivery requested by RLH Corporation. If Acme produces and RLH uses the gear daily, the average inventory of each would be one-half month (assuming no safety stock, production precisely to schedule, and delivery precisely on the required date). The author has found that the total inventories in the vendor–customer pipeline can often be dramatically reduced even before the vendor goes to work on setup cost reduction. For example, after simply discussing Acme's situation with its executives, it would quickly become obvious that if Acme were to ship gears directly to the RLH Corporation weekly, at the time they are produced, both would experience big benefits in inventory reduction. As Exhibit 4-4 shows, the resulting inventories of each will be a one-half-week supply, a reduction of 75 percent as compared to monthly shipments. In company after company, the author has found major opportunities for fast and permanent inventory reductions by simply determining how to match the vendor's production frequency with the scheduled deliveries. However, this requires understanding how to avoid increasing other costs as a result of shipping and receiving more purchased lots.

Warehousing of materials and components in the global vendor and manufacturing network ties up billions of dollars in unnecessarily large inventories. However, the excess of finished goods in distribution channels is of even greater magnitude. Executive management's programs for

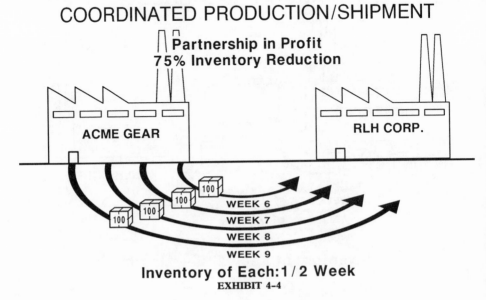

COORDINATED PRODUCTION/SHIPMENT

Partnership in Profit
75% Inventory Reduction

ACME GEAR

RLH CORP.

100 100 100 100 100

WEEK 6
WEEK 7
WEEK 8
WEEK 9

Inventory of Each:1/2 Week
EXHIBIT 4-4

streamlining manufacturing operations, reducing operating inventories, and decreasing the amount of time required to ship customer orders must also target drastic reductions of distribution inventories as an ultimate objective. While manufacturing's cost of setup or changeover is continuously being lowered, it becomes increasingly practical to respond immediately to new and changed customer requirements. As soon as the cost penalty of changeover is reduced to insignificance, production can be switched from one job in process to a new, more urgent item. Further, factories with cross-trained workers and flexible machining and assembly equipment capacity will add to a vendor's rapid response capability. Rapid response capability of the end producer, made possible by rapid response of its suppliers, will win more business for the supplier if his competitors are slow to respond. The increased sales volume should usually benefit the suppliers as much as the end producer.

A factory does not need to attain utopian levels of flexibility before beginning to enjoy the benefits of lower distribution inventories. The fact is that multiple tiers of finished goods warehousing, common throughout the world, hold vastly greater amounts of inventory than are necessary to provide competitive customer service. For example, a machine tool insert company had just completed a major expansion of its multitier distribution warehousing network, only to find that inventory investment had skyrocketed and customer service had not improved appreciably. In fact, the total time between production at the factory and delivery to the ultimate customer had increased many fold. Accurate forecasting of any item's demand at the regional level was even more impossible than accurately forecasting the item's total sales. Therefore, when large, unexpected customer orders could be met only by new production back at the factory, such customer-order-driven warehouse replenishments had to compete for production capacity and priority with all other replenishment orders, including those which still had stock balances on hand. However, the clinching argument for abandoning the multitier distribution system was a competitor's recent rapid increase in market share. The competitor had geared up to make air express deliveries from its European factory, guaranteeing twenty-four-hour delivery service. The keys to success for this competitor were the facsimile order procedure, the same-day order-filling warehouse operations, and an instantaneous order-processing system.

Transport costs are often used to justify establishing a network of distribution warehouses. Subsequently, the warehouses are usually replenished by infrequent truckload shipments as opposed to the prior frequent (but less-than-truckload) deliveries from a central warehouse direct to customers. The combination (of the cost of truckload deliveries to the new local warehouses and the short-route delivery from the new warehouses to customers) is typically, although erroneously, presumed to be less costly than direct delivery from the central warehouse. An additional and often even more important justification for the warehouse network is the long delivery time from central warehouse to customer. Shipment by truck from the East to the West Coast of the United States takes several days, as do those from Northern to Southern Europe. The fallacies of a warehousing network are as follows:

1. The real costs of warehousing, including both its operating costs and inventory costs, are rarely projected realistically.

2. Many local warehouses do not have enough sales volume to warrant daily truckload deliveries. Therefore, out-of-stock items may delay the shipment of customer orders by several days, caused by waiting for the next full truckload of replenishments. This aspect of local warehousing is often overlooked. Therefore, learning that local warehousing fails to eliminate slow delivery is often a nasty shock.

3. Although radically different transport-related methods could sharply improve the timeliness and cost of delivery, companies do not adequately explore these alternatives. Typically, they bring little ingenuity to the exploration of radical, pioneering transportation methods.

Improvements in the costs and time required for transportation will be one of the keys to joining, or staying in, the ranks of superior suppliers. Accordingly, executive management should charge the traffic organization and productivity improvement project teams with responsibility for inventing new modes of transportation. Managers of existing central warehouses must also play a role in developing ways to vary order-filling volumes flexibly to meet peak order volumes while achieving same-day shipment performance.

LOCAL SOURCES OF SUPPLY

Conscientious buyers and their bosses routinely consider freight cost differences when deciding which supplier to use. However, virtually none have adequately understood the principle described in Chapter 2—inventory increases in exponential relationship to increases in distance between the supplier and user factories. Because of the huge impact of distance on inventory investment and the effects of easy local communication on the smoothness of business operations,[5] local sources of supply will easily prove far superior to remote sources. In some instances, offshore procurement has reduced direct material cost, but this can be quite misleading. It tends to increase the pipeline lead time, inventory investment, and overhead costs in the materials organization.

In Exhibit 4-5, the large Acme factory from which RLH Corporation has always bought gears is located in the East, about 1,000 miles from the RLH factory in the Chicago area. The questions that the exhibit addresses are twofold: (1) whether it would be best for both companies if Acme were to locate a warehouse or a factory in the Chicago area, and (2) the advantages of one over the other. The answer to the desirability of the local *warehouse* is no, while the answer regarding a local *factory* is often yes! Regardless of whether the customer or the vendor warehouses the gears, the costs of warehousing, including the inventory carrying costs, should be comparable. Some people might be naïve enough to believe that the supplier will not eventually act to recoup the costs of warehousing. They can be assured that these costs must eventually be included in the price of the items if the supplier is to earn a reasonable

LOCAL PLANT ADVANTAGES

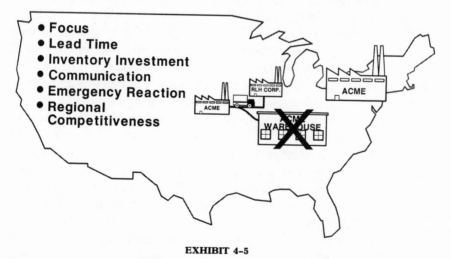

- Focus
- Lead Time
- Inventory Investment
- Communication
- Emergency Reaction
- Regional Competitiveness

EXHIBIT 4-5

[5]Richard J. Schonberger, *Japanese Manufacturing Techniques: Nine Hidden Lessons in Simplicity* (New York: Free Press, 1982), pp. 171-72.

return on his investment. In fact, the additional handling of receipts into and shipments out of the supplier's own warehouse should increase the total amount of labor and overhead in the pipeline. Thus, the total costs of adding an Acme local warehouse must be higher than those of storing them in RLH's storeroom.

As to point (2), RLH executives can use several arguments to help their Acme counterparts understand the advantages to Acme of a small, focused local Acme factory. The first of these is the focus argument. As discussed in Chapter 3, the small, focused factory can be expected to outperform the large factory. Thus, the new small factory will most assuredly improve profitability. It is equally clear that lead time and inventory in the pipeline will decrease as a result of the local plant. Because shipments from the East Coast are likely to be truckload lots, once or twice a month, even Acme's inventory will be reduced by shipping small daily lots from the new local factory. The improvement in communications between the vendor and customer factories is remarkable when they are in the same area. Frequent plant visits and local phone calls become not only quite feasible but probable. Finally, RLH is not likely to be Acme's only customer or potential customer in the Chicago area. Thus, establishment of a local factory will help Acme increase its regional competitiveness and market share.

All of the preceding examples presumed that Acme's processes are such that it would be feasible to construct a small focused factory. Some processes are so capital-intensive that this would not be the case. It would be unlikely, for example, that a steel mill could be located in the center of Nevada to serve the needs of a small customer factory that needs only a few tons of steel a month. However, in those instances where a small focused factory is feasible, the executives of a customer company should be aggressively discussing it with their supplier counterparts and should not drop the discussion until the local factory is a *fait accompli.*

In many cases the existing local source of supply does not appear to be a likely first choice to fill the role of long-term supplier. If so, the underlying reasons must logically be that it is not competitive in cost, quality, or delivery. It would be to the advantage of the customer company executives to hold discussions with the executives of the local source to identify its shortcomings and to help them identify the changes that would bring them to superior manufacturing status. This is often the fastest way to develop a local source of supply without having to persuade a competitor of the local vendor to locate a factory in the area. The fact that the local supplier has plans to upgrade his facilities, and hence his price, quality, and delivery, may also help to induce other suppliers (not its competitors) to relocate in the area.

SINGLE SOURCES OF SUPPLY:
ALL EGGS IN ONE BASKET

In 1977 the author was in Japan reviewing purchasing procedures and systems as part of a companywide improvement project at Yamaha. One important computer system issue was how to handle items purchased simultaneously from more than one supplier. After having been told that this was not an issue because almost no such cases existed, the author asked for a computer list of the items with more than one supplier. The list contained thirty part numbers. (Yamaha's operations included more than 300,000 part numbers.) Nevertheless, whether one or one thousand items had more than one supplier, the computer processing logic required to handle them would be the same. The only way to eliminate the logic (one of the most difficult, complex business problems to handle in the purchasing arena) would be to eliminate completely all instances of multiple suppliers. The issue was discussed at length at the next weekly meeting with the responsible vice president, since the project's objective was to simplify the system greatly, not to complicate it. The executive's decision not only was fast but also got to the heart of the problem with the most obvious solution. He turned to the purchasing representative in attendance and told him to change all thirty parts from multiple- to single-source suppliers. In less than one month, no multiple-source items remained. Incidentally, Jones, Roos, and Womack disagree with the notion that Japanese *automobile assemblers* have only single sources of supply for any item.[6] They contend that Toyota uses two (simultaneous) suppliers of *small* parts and, further, that Nissan and Honda, while using only one supplier per item, might shift parts to a different supplier if one fails to deliver quality on time. (Since late delivery and defective quality are virtually nonexistent, these instances must be extremely rare.) Jones and his co-authors might have been misinformed concerning Toyota's practice, as some of their own statistics would seem to indicate (very high purchased item content, very low number of suppliers compared to other assemblers). Further arguments against the position that any single

[6]Daniel T. Jones, Daniel Roos, and James P. Womack, *The Machine That Changed the World* (New York: Macmillan, 1990), pp. 154–55 and 286, note 16.

Toyota assembly plant uses multiple simultaneous suppliers of small items are as follows:

1. Virtually all other information sources, including the author, have not found individual Toyota assembly plants to operate this way. (Hay describes sole sources as the "logical *extreme*.")[7]
2. Maintaining two sources would make controlling quality more difficult than necessary. One supplier might make parts at one end of the tolerance limits, the other at the other extreme.
3. Two sets of tooling would be twice as expensive.
4. Administrative costs (for example, price negotiation and delivery coordination) would be twice as much as necessary.

Although the Jones book is one of the best on its subject, the author found it necessary to take exception with this single point. He (and many others) believe single sources are a key ingredient of superior manufacturing. Far too many traditional purchasing advocates will seize upon any excuse to avoid single sourcing, to the detriment of their companies. This being the case, it is important to stress that some do not agree on this point.

Among the great strengths of the best Japanese manufacturers is their recognition of the vital importance of economies of scale—that the enterprise that produces more of a given item than any other will be able to afford to spend more on tooling than its competitors. Better tooling will yield lower costs and better quality. Therefore, these manufacturers do as much as possible to help their suppliers become or remain among the highest volume producers in the world. The more than 33 million videotape recorders manufactured in Japan in 1986[8] are a good example of the economies of scale. At this level of production, the Japanese manufacturers have no competitors of note, other than Japanese companies.

Realistically, however, those relying on single sources are really putting all of their eggs in a single basket. Since Japan has a history of continuous natural disasters—fires, earthquakes, tidal waves, and volcanic eruptions, to name a few—this practice must really jeopardize the enterprise's continued existence. And natural disasters are not the only dangers. Obviously the supplier, being a single source, might choose to take advantage of the situation by demanding exorbitant prices compared with those of

---

[7]Edward J. Hay, *The Just-in-Time Breakthrough: Implementing the New Manufacturing Basics* (New York: John Wiley, 1988), pp. 125–27.
[8]Karel van Wolferen, *The Enigma of Japanese Power* (New York: Alfred Knopf, 1989), p. 398.

its competitors. Further, the failure of the supplier's business or such interruptions as strikes could imperil the smooth continuance of operations. Any of these things could happen. Or a meteor might even demolish the supplier's factory. (Notice the tongue in cheek.)

Regardless of the risk of any of these events, Western purchasing practice is much too strongly entrenched in the just-in-case philosophy. As a result, it has become an accepted (albeit expensive) tenet that buyers must continuously work on the development of new alternative sources. They are also expected to purchase some "critical" items from two different suppliers simultaneously, just in case one should suffer a catastrophe or simply fail to meet its commitment. Several logical arguments should be considered, not the least of which is how frequently is a disaster *likely* to occur? And *if* one should occur, the probable duration of disaster recovery should be of equal or greater importance. The answer to the first question is usually seldom, if ever. The answer to the second question should be that it should not take too long, especially if a contingency plan is prepared by the single-source supplier. Few customer–supplier relationships exist anywhere in the world where the customer uses anywhere close to the capacity of the supplier's industry to make the item in question. Therefore, in most cases of disaster, the supplier's industry will be able to provide the capacity to fill the gap. Further, World War II has shown that even after intensive bombing raids, many Axis factories were able to salvage equipment from the rubble and continue operations almost immediately. Faced with a major catastrophe, mankind responds with exceptional efforts. If catastrophe recovery plans are prepared in advance, these exceptional efforts can come to fruition even faster.

In order to consider seriously placing all of its eggs in one supplier's basket, a company must be prepared to deal with the issue of how to be assured that the chosen supplier will work on continuous improvement and thus price its commodities competitively. Also of concern are the unscrupulous suppliers that might take advantage of the opportunity (as the single source) to push prices even higher than its competitors. As Sandras notes, sample auditing of competitors' prices is one tool that will help monitor the competitiveness of a single-source supplier's prices.[9] The honesty of these prices can be checked periodically as part of the semiformal agreement on which the customer–supplier business relationship is founded. Both parties should agree to share in the benefits of improved productivity and quality and increased volume. An indepen-

[9]William A. Sandras, Jr., *Just-in-Time: Making it Happen—Unleashing the Power of Continuous Improvement* (Essex Junction, Vt.: Oliver Wight Limited Publications, 1989), p. 152.

dent auditor should periodically sample the supplier's cost versus price to provide the necessary assurance of compliance with this informal but important agreement.

Leading edge Western companies are blazing a trail of successful programs to reduce radically the number of active suppliers. In the first year of its program, one 3M factory in New Ulm, Minnesota, trimmed the active vendor list from 2,800 to 600, and in the second year to 300. Once again, one of the superior manufacturers of the West has proved that no "Japanese" business techniques are beyond the reach of superior manufacturers—regardless of cultural differences.

RAPID REQUIREMENTS COMMUNICATION

Vendors are constantly being whipsawed by their customers' radical schedule changes. Customers, after long periods of demanding deliveries ·at or exceeding the supplier's output capacity, have been known to cut order quantities suddenly by amounts equal to several weeks of demand, and to wipe out the immediate delivery schedule while drastically reducing schedules in later periods. Often after long periods of producing at relatively low rates, the customer will suddenly raise his schedules by large amounts. These radical changes in delivery schedules, up and down, are one of the most difficult problems facing suppliers. Minimization of radical changes is, therefore, the area in which a customer can do the most to make improvements that will greatly benefit the vendor.

At the end of the distribution chain, the peaks and valleys in consumer demand will continue to occur, because national and international economic cycles will continue, as will numerous other factors that effect a manufacturer's sales volume. Vendors understand this but do not as readily understand why the shifts are so often sudden and drastic. Both customer and vendor would prefer to see more gradual adjustments as downturns or increases in demand start to become apparent. After all, consumer demand rarely plummets or skyrockets as radically as the demand of vendors at the start of the supply chain. Part of the reason for radical changes in supplier demand is the excessive lead time in the pipeline of supply from the start of the manufacturing process in the vendor factory through the customer's factory and into the distribution channels. The pipeline for many products is often weeks or months. If the pipeline lead time is four months and requirements drop by 25 percent, the pipeline supply will suddenly jump to five months at the new rate of demand. Therefore, the vendor at the start of the pipeline is expected to stop production completely for one month until the pipeline inventory is reduced to the four-month level. Amazing as it may sound, the pipeline lead time can be slashed by as much as 90 percent or more! Part of this, perhaps the most important part, becomes possible when a manufacturer and its vendors reduce machine, process, and assembly setup times and costs to the point where they can make and ship every material, component, and product every day. Lowering the just-in-case lead time and inventory throughout the pipeline is the next most important part of the companywide reduction program. Hout and Stalk explain this point in their example in which buffer stocks are planned at both ends of the vendor–customer pipeline.[10] When one stops to think of it, it seems obvious that one of the reasons that pipeline lead time is so long is that our systems are supplied with manually determined lead time factors that control the throughput time. Thus the lead times turn out to be approximately the same. Most of the lead time factors are just-in-case provisions. For example, most manufacturing people accepted the fact that actual operation time is typically 20 percent or less of the total lead time. When an understanding that lead times are unnecessarily inflated and with a certain degree of courage and conviction, the best executives can be persuaded to reduce lead times in the pipeline somewhat as arbitrarily as the lead times were originally inflated. The results can be extremely good, especially when problems that subsequently arise (and they will arise) are permanently solved, not just handled with temporary, jury-rigged solutions. Unfortunately, many companies have tried reducing lead times only to revert back to longer lead times as soon as problems start to arise.

Factory processes are not the only component of pipeline lead time. The author's prior book described the traditional manual procedure for reviewing and updating computer suggested orders and reschedules.[11] The author has visited hundreds of factories in which offices full of analysts and buyers work weeks to translate computer suggestions into purchase orders and order revisions. These days or weeks of office processing time are an important part of the total pipeline lead time. Drastic reduction of the clerical lead time is neither new nor unique to Japan, although some of the best Japanese manufacturers have gone farther than most other companies in the world in their efforts to eliminate this waste. For example, in the early 1960s the author worked on the design and operation of one of the earliest multiplant computer systems at Outboard Marine Corporation. The system eliminated the use of purchase orders

---

[10]Thomas M. Hout, and George Stalk, Jr., *Competing Against Time: How Time-Based Competition Is Reshaping Global Markets* (New York: Free Press, 1990), p. 241.
[11]See Appendix 2.

for thousands of parts supplied by one of the company's factories for use by other factories around the world. The author's project at Yamaha in Iwata, Japan, used the concepts of the Outboard Marine system but included schedules for suppliers (and even their suppliers). As seen in Exhibit 4–6, Yamaha's network of its own factories and those of its vendors and subcontractors included 640 entities (focused factories). The material requirement planning system developed during the Yamaha project delivered shipping and production schedules to each entity in the network in the afternoon of the day on which a "black box" computer system generated final assembly schedules and planned requirements of all pipeline entities.

In 1981, as expected, our project team at Harley-Davidson found that it would take months, even years, to modify its computer system to produce vendor schedules. Prior to that time, the company had always used purchase orders, not schedules. In the meantime, inventory analysts spent weeks reviewing computer-suggested action and generating the new and revised purchase orders to match requirements. Even after the purchase orders were updated, they were based on computer logic that maintained a safety stock in excess of actual requirements and lot-sizing logic that lumped several periods of requirements into a single order. As a result, the order schedules did not accurately communicate real needs and priorities to the vendor. Therefore, a great deal of the purchasing organiza-

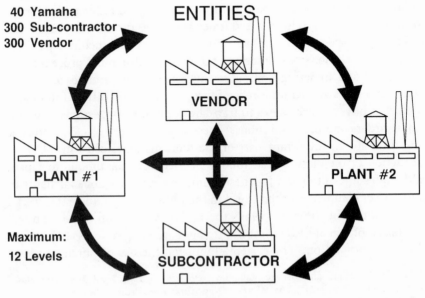

EXHIBIT 4–6

tion's time was spent in communications with vendors, trying to convey the real priorities. The interim, noncomputer solution was simply to copy actual requirements (before safety stock and lot sizing) onto a simple manual vendor schedule. This was actually faster and cheaper than analyzing and changing the suggested order action. And it put accurate information into the vendors' hands days and weeks earlier. The new master schedule fed into the old computer system was relatively frozen in early weeks. This helped to minimize erratic swings in the vendor's delivery requirements.

In the early 1980s it was truly discouraging to hear time and time again (even from some of the best Western executives) that adopting the use of vendor schedules in the West would be impossible. This uncharacteristic pessimism is no longer all-pervasive. The author believes that superior manufacturers must already have their system analysts and purchasing organizations hard at work developing these rapid requirement communication systems.

LONG-TERM VENDOR AGREEMENTS

In Japan, two companies that have a customer–supplier relationship will ordinarily continue to work together in that harmonious affiliation virtually forever. They do so with a minimum of formal documentation and virtually without legal contracts. By contrast, Western purchasing systems have always been founded on legalese. (Note the terms and conditions in microscopic print on the reverse sides of purchase orders and blanket purchase orders.) Early attempts at documenting long-term relationships between supplier and customer centered on a Western-style compromise, the development of a contract. However, it did not take long to discover that it would take months or even years for both companies' legal departments to come to agreement on the wording of such a contract. More important, the spirit of the new relationship must be one of mutual interest and trust. If the parties to the agreement are not presumed to be honorable and trustworthy, prospects for success are dismal. If this is the case, it is probably best to seek out a different partner in profit. A legally nonbinding agreement, by contrast, can formalize the understanding of how the new relationship will operate.

PURCHASE COMMODITIES, NOT ITEMS

The amount of work that goes into the purchasing process and the volume of paperwork are mind-boggling. The bundles of specifications sent to each supplier asked to submit a quotation create the need for a veritable small printing business as a part of the purchasing function. Reviewing every price quotation returned by numerous vendors of a single item is a daunting task, especially when part of the buyer's performance evaluation criteria is how many different suppliers submitted quotations. By contrast, when every item in a commodity is purchased from a single long-term supplier, only a small fraction of the buyer's time and that of the paperwork factory is required.

Getting started on implementing new purchasing practices can appear to be an awesome task. Many medium-size companies routinely place orders for production material and components with as many as three thousand vendors annually. However, the job is greatly simplified when management decides to reduce the number of active suppliers by 80 to 90 percent, a reasonable target. By reducing the number of active suppliers, the customer can greatly increase its leverage with the single remaining supplier of a commodity. For example, if in the past a customer ordered small aluminum castings from six active suppliers and large aluminum castings from four others and is now able to buy both small and large castings from one supplier, the amount of work from that supplier will obviously be much greater, as will the potential for lower prices.

The simplified example of a preliminary package of items in one commodity, rubber components, Exhibit 4–7, is a tool that the author has

PRELIMINARY VENDOR PACKAGES

ITEM		VENDORS					PACKAGE	
NO.	DESCRIPT.	1	2	3	4	5	NO.	
12345	O-Ring	X	X	X	X	X	1234	●
12347	O-Ring	X	X	X			1235	
23456	Gasket	X			X	X	1234	●
24567	Seal	X			X	X	1234	●
34568	O-Ring	X	X	X			1235	
35678	Seal	X			X	X	1234	●

1 = A011-RLH Corp.   4 = F456-Whammy Co.

2 = B124-ACME Inc.   5 = H079-Blotto Ltd.

3 = C321-U.S. Seals

EXHIBIT 4-7

found to be helpful in initial negotiations with potential suppliers. For example, jmh Bostrom Europe, an early (1984) supplier program client, used this type of computer report to identify opportunities to reduce the number of suppliers. Colin Howell, Director, and Don Lorraine, Works Manager, report reducing suppliers of stampings from eleven to two, one for large, another for small parts.[12]

In Exhibit 4-7, not all suppliers are capable of supplying all items, and the final decision as to which items should be included in which commodity package is left to the responsible buyer. When a company plans to have a kickoff meeting with a group of vendors, giving each attending company a list of the items in the commodity(ies) for which they will be competing seems to heighten their interest in pursuing the opportunity to become the partner-in-profit.

TRANSPORT ECONOMY: STRATEGIC DESIGN

As superb as Western manufacturers are in designing mechanical transport mechanisms, it is baffling that they have not done a much better job of minimizing some obvious elements of waste. For example, I have often watched truck traffic entering and leaving automotive assembly plants and have been appalled at the scandalous waste of transport resources. Trucks arrive with full loads of components and materials and depart empty. At the same time, specially constructed automobile transport vehicles are continuously arriving empty and departing full. Imagine the gains in a company's economies of transport if it designed automobile trailers as turnaround vehicles, capable of returning with loads of components and materials. When the automobile industry designed "optimum" single-purpose transport vehicles, it fell far short of optimization, considering the universe of strategic opportunities. As a result, current trailer designs optimize the number of automobiles transported, considering the maximum possible vehicles that fit into the legally permissible trailer height and length. A vehicle designed for two types of cargo would certainly have less automobile carrying capacity, but its ability to haul return loads would more than offset this disadvantage. It would also serve to regulate the flow of material by keeping inbound and outbound loads in balance.

[12]Colin Howell and Don Lorraine, "The Implementation of Just-in-Time Techniques and its Impact on jmh Bostrom Europe," in John Mortimer, ed., *Just-in-time: An Executive Briefing* (Bedford, Eng.: IFS Ltd., 1986), pp. 75–80.

American industry suffers from another poorly designed transport mechanism that most European and Japanese manufacturers avoid. Highway and rail vehicles and their dock facilities have been constructed to be loaded and unloaded from only one door. This makes loading and unloading painfully slow, which has forced the number of docks to be much higher than otherwise necessary. Also, scheduling the sequence of loading and unloading is unduly complicated. The side-loading trailer, Exhibit 4–8, commonly used in Japan (as reported by Hall)[13] and in Europe, allows loading and unloading around the entire trailer perimeter. It can turn any driveway or parking lot into a loading dock, since lift trucks have access to all sides of the truck as opposed to just the back door. In planning new factories of the future, careful consideration must be given to receiving and shipping dock alternatives, and how they will work with the trucks and trailers of the future. Exhibit 4–9 is an example of an ideal design that is most suitable when exposure to severe cold weather is not a problem for receiving personnel. (That is, when the weather is never unreasonably cold). In this example, docks surround the perimeter of the factory, enabling deliveries to be made at entrances convenient to each subplant. Conventional trucks would be able to back up to these docks to load or unload, but with considerably less speed and

SIDE-LOADING TRUCK

EXHIBIT 4–8

[13]Robert W. Hall, *Zero Inventories* (Homewood, Ill.: Dow Jones–Irwin, 1983), p. 209.

PERIMETER DOCKS

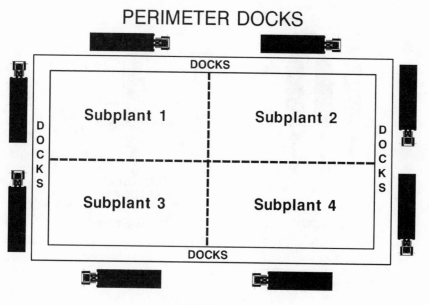

EXHIBIT 4-9

efficiency than rigs with open sides. The open-sided trucks can drive from one dock to another, unloading deliveries at each dock, without the difficulty of having to back up to a dock. Large crews would make rapid work of any inbound or outbound load at each dock. Incidentally, these types of docks are favored by many of the most successful Japanese manufacturers. At dock locations where entire truckloads of large items are frequently received or shipped, it would make sense to mechanize the combination of trailer bed and dock, to transfer loads automatically from trailer to dock and vice versa. It should be obvious, for most factories, that this design would completely eliminate the delay most trucks experience when waiting for dock availability or for a truck to be loaded or unloaded. To minimize idle tractor time, many factories park trailers at the docks, then disconnect them and drive the tractor away to work with another trailer. The very fast load and unload times at the new docks will eliminate this waste.

Where inclement weather is a serious problem and parallel parking at perimeter docks is not a reasonable method, companies should consider the new high-speed, back-in dock, Exhibit 4–10, if it is practical to convert to the use of side-loading trailers and trucks. On the left side of the exhibit is an example of a drive-in dock that accommodates several trucks side by side. As indicated, since conventional trucks and trailers can be entered only through the rear door, the raised dock is needed only at the

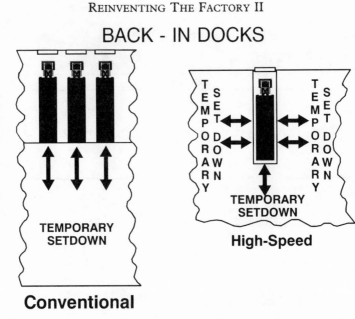

EXHIBIT 4-10

rear of each trailer. Only one lift truck can feasibly work on one trailer at a time. Also, the temporary setdown area where skids and containers are placed until the loading or unloading is completed is long and narrow. This causes the average distance from where a load is picked up to where it can be put down to be farther than it need be, lengthening the time it takes to load and unload. With the high-speed dock of the future, which works with side-loading trailers, the area of the dock that is level with the trailer floor surrounds the tractor and trailer. Thus, the temporary setdown area is always much closer to the truck. With this layout, several lift trucks can work simultaneously on the same load, reducing the total load/unload time to a fraction of that required at conventional docks.

Far too few Westerners have realized the radical difference between the typical ownership of Japanese and Western transport systems—just one more important link in the chain of practices that differentiate the front runners from the pack. In Japan, over-the-road traffic of manufactured components and materials is almost exclusively carried out by the trucks of the vendor and the customer. By contrast, independent common carriers perform the vast majority of movement in the United States. The notable exceptions, like Caterpillar, have almost always turned out to be the superior enterprises in their product lines. Caterpillar, incidentally, operates one of the largest trucking businesses in Illinois. Keeping the trucking business in the company family eliminates most of the difficulties of communication with outsiders and increases the manufacturer's control over transport scheduling. However, many companies have purposely avoided the trucking business because they perceive the trucker's union of the past to have been a quagmire of illegal and shady officers. Few companies have been willing to grapple with and solve this problem through the logical process of negotiating with the unions to determine if there is really reason for concern. In the next decade or two, company trucking fleets should proliferate. The average vehicle size and investment should simultaneously shrink. With fewer active vendors and more local sources of supply, smaller trucks that can dash between vendor and customer and load and unload in minutes or seconds will be much more economical than large, conventional rigs.

The Leather Center, a Carrollton, Texas, manufacturer of high quality, custom-manufactured, fast-delivery leather furniture, is another company that uses its own (leased) fleet of tractors and trailers to speed its products to the home or office of its customers. A recent multifaceted productivity improvement project included a review of delivery operations. Before improvement, large tractors were used to transport finished furniture from the factory to warehouses in the customer's vicinity. Later, furniture was again loaded on smaller trucks better suited for delivery to the customer's home. The company found that this double handling and storage caused many problems and added cost to the product distribution process. For example, although the furniture was very well protected by factory-applied packaging and loaded on trucks with extreme care at the factory, the furniture often arrived damaged at the customer's premises. The damage obviously occurred during unloading, storing, and reloading at the warehouses. In addition, the warehouses were expensive to lease and operate even when costs were held to a practical minimum. Further, the warehouses always contained some inventory, including customer rejections that were often stored and forgotten. The Leather Center switched from using single long trailers for shipments from the factory, to two tandem trailers, loaded to facilitate direct delivery to the customer. Now the two trailers are dropped in the local showroom lot, and then, without reloading, each is attached to a tractor and delivered directly to the retail customer. Imaginative approaches like this make the Leather Center a formidable competitor.

Opportunities for speeding smaller component and material shipments between supplier and user factories do not depend only on company-owned transport. Improved, judicious contracting of transport services can also substantially reduce the time and inventory in transit and at the same time reduce the actual cost of transport. Elimination of stops at terminals and transfers from one carrier or truck to another via a terminal are important keys to savings. Each stop and each shipment transfer from truck to terminal to truck entails penalties in terms of both delay and added labor and overhead costs. For example, shipments to General Motors' Allison Transmission Division, located in Indianapolis, from a supplier plant in Cookeville, Tennessee (340 miles), at one point had a transit time of four days, as illustrated in Exhibit 4–11. Each shipment previously traveled through four terminals on four different trucks operated by two different carriers. After Allison contracted with a single carrier to make direct dock-to-dock deliveries (from the supplier to Allison) the time in transit shrank to less than one day. In another situation in the author's previous book,[14] shipments had once gone directly from a particular vendor's factory to a General Motors factory without stopping at terminals or changing carriers. It had previously been felt that the only practical schedule for shipments would be once a week, in order to accumulate enough for economic (truckload) shipments. However, weekly direct shipments from a single supplier were changed to daily "milk run" stops at several supplier factories. This and other changes drastically slashed inventories at both ends while cutting transport costs by 67 percent.

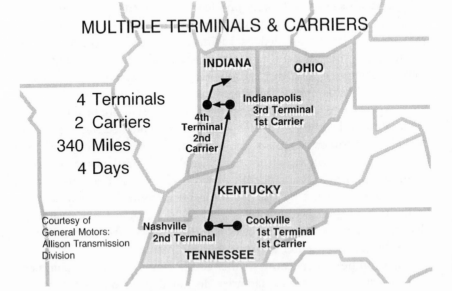

EXHIBIT 4–11

[14]See Appendix 2.

THE BEST PACKAGE: NO PACKAGING

The United States undoubtedly spends more on packaging materials than any other country. Packaging of end products and their components, such as instruction manuals, to hold them together, protect them, and make them attractive to the consumer are perhaps unavoidable requirements. However, as most visitors to some of the best companies in Japan have seen, packaging of components that travel from vendor to customer *is* avoidable. At these companies it is virtually impossible to find components packaged in cardboard. As Wantuck points out, cardboard is not inexpensive.[15] The Japanese understand this very well and, as a nation of manufacturers, save hundreds of millions of dollars each year by using permanent turnaround containers. Western companies can also save not only cardboard costs but also numerous costs of packaging and unpacking. Exhibit 4–12 schematically shows the added costs of packaging within a supplier's factory, starting at the machine that produces an item and continuing through shipment to a customer. The machine operator usually "packages" the components he makes, in the sense that he puts cardboard sheets between layers of the completed items to protect them

SUPPLIER PACKAGING - CARDBOARD

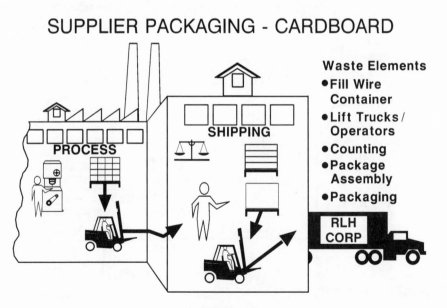

Waste Elements
- Fill Wire Container
- Lift Trucks / Operators
- Counting
- Package Assembly
- Packaging

EXHIBIT 4-12

[15]Kenneth A. Wantuck, *Just-in-Time for America: A Common Sense Production Strategy* (Milwaukee: The Forum, Ltd., 1989), pp. 321–22.

from damage due to jostling back and forth while being moved. He usually puts completed parts in giant shop containers, and in so doing spends hundreds of hours a year stooping into and rising out of the container and occasionally inserting protective cardboard. Each time he fills one of the giant containers, he loses some productive time while waiting for a lift truck to come (from wherever it is in the factory) to move the full container and replace it with one that is empty. The lift truck operator then transports the container the great distance to the shipping department. The shipping department will usually remove the components from the shop container, count them, and repackage them into cardboard containers. Often the containers include cardboard components, like dividers, which require assembly before they are ready for use. The use of cardboard, which is rarely returned and reused, adds cost but not value to the delivered product. It also adds hundreds more hours of packaging labor. Finally, lift trucks must load packaged products onto the truck that will deliver them to the customer.

Packaging waste does not end in the supplier factory. Exhibit 4–13 shows how the waste continues on the user's end of the pipeline. It starts with the lift truck moving parts from the truck to the receiving area, where receipts are again counted and parts are sometimes repacked in the factory's own containers. From there the containers are taken by forklift truck to storage and sometime later are transported the great distance

USER UNPACKING - CARDBOARD

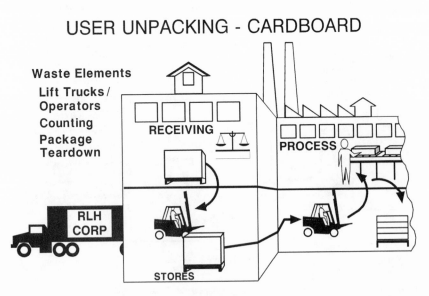

EXHIBIT 4-13

to the assembly area. The assembler spends a significant portion of each assembly cycle bending and reaching into large containers, straightening up, and moving parts from the container to the line. In cases where the container must be opened and disassembled, even more time is wasted on activities that do not add value to the product. The entire process harbors waste: packaging material costs, packaging labor and equipment cost, forklift labor and equipment, and counting.

Permanent, self-packaging, returnable containers on wheels that re-place cardboard packaging can cut major portions of packaging costs. Exhibit 4–14 shows how to simplify the process. First, the person man-ufacturing the item puts it into a much smaller container. Many con-tainers are constructed like single-layer egg crates. The individual com-partments of the egg crate container protect each part from damage caused by contact with other parts. The container's smaller size reduces the time and motion required to put completed parts into the container. Permanent containers eliminate the time required to construct the con-tainer and the cardboard packaging cost. The containers, with their own wheels or mounted on wheeled dollies, can be pushed away from the machine without requiring a lift truck. In ideally designed factories, the shipping dock is immediately adjacent to the final operation. Thus, the wheeled containers or dollies can be pushed a very short distance onto the truck. The wheels and the short distances virtually eliminate the lift

SUPPLIER PACKAGING ELIMINATED

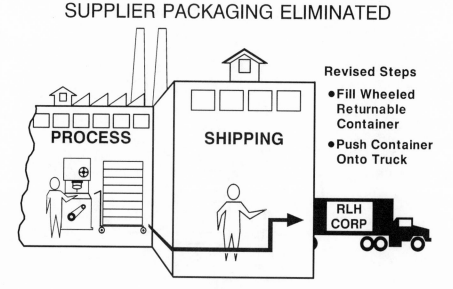

Revised Steps

- Fill Wheeled Returnable Container
- Push Container Onto Truck

EXHIBIT 4-14

truck and its operator. Since all containers hold a uniform quantity of items, weight counting before shipment is reduced or eliminated. A single glance at the "egg crate" container is usually all that is necessary to verify that it is full.

The savings attributable to improved container design and practices continue in the customer organization that receives the "egg crate" containers on wheels. As Exhibit 4–15 shows, the superior customer's combination receiving dock–storage area is adjacent to the focused factory where the components are assembled. The wheeled containers are wheeled off the truck into the receiving–storage area and, a short time later, to the nearby assembly station. Counting, if any, involves simply verifying the number of full containers. The assembler needs only minimum time to retrieve components from the containers since the containers are small and do not require disassembly. They fit conveniently into a space very near the point where they are assembled. Again, the lift truck has been virtually eliminated.

Considering the advantages of small containers, it is hard to grasp why so many companies use such large containers. There are several reasons, none of which withstands the test of logic. One such reason is undue emphasis on transport costs. Because the factory layout has always been so poor, it has been necessary to transport things over much longer than ideal distances. Even the stretches from factory to factory have been per-

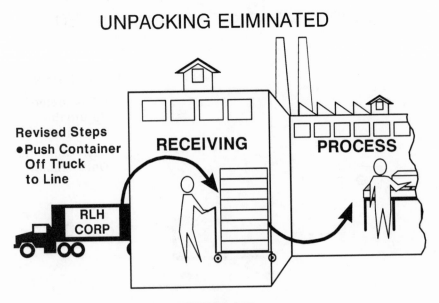

UNPACKING ELIMINATED

Revised Steps
- **Push Container Off Truck to Line**

RECEIVING

PROCESS

RLH CORP

EXHIBIT 4–15

mitted to be too great. Large containers have proliferated because companies have focused on the symptoms rather than the problem. Cutting the transport distance is a giant step toward enabling a company to cut container sizes. However, even with long transport distances a large size overpack that holds smaller containers (illustrated on the left side of Exhibit 4–16) will provide economies of movement of large containers while still providing small containers for use at the supplier's operation and at the customer's assembly operation. Thus, both will minimize the wasted time and motion caused by large container sizes. However, if each small container in the overpack were equal to one or more day's supply, a larger-than-necessary inventory would result. Thus, an overpack of numerous different components, as shown on the right side of Exhibit 4–16, would be preferable.

RETURNABLE CONTAINERS: STRATEGIC DESIGN

Why do Western manufacturers typically use cardboard packaging to ship components and materials? The chief reason is that it has always been viewed as economically impractical to use permanent, returnable containers. It would involve an added freight cost to return empty containers and, perhaps, an extremely large investment to establish a supply of the containers equal to the amount of inventory in the pipeline. Fortunately, with superior manufacturing practices slashing the cubic volume

OVERPACK - INNERPACK

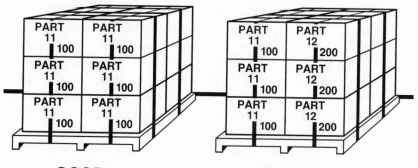

EXHIBIT 4–16

142   REINVENTING THE FACTORY II

of inventory by as much as 90 percent, almost everyone now understands that the number of containers needed will be much less significant. And if some of the newly emptied small containers can be used for items previously stored in large containers, no new containers would be necessary. However, finding imaginative solutions that will make new containers economically advantageous (when new containers *must* be purchased) is an interesting challenge. It is usually easy to do so, since the inventory reduction easily covers the container cost. The distance between customer and vendor is often another seemingly insurmountable barrier to the use of returnable containers. For example, Paul Tompson reported that New United Motors Manufacturing, Inc. (NUMMI), found it necessary to use disposable packaging for the majority of their purchases.[16] The reason was that California, where the factory is located, is too far from the factories of many of its suppliers. However, when NUMMI attracts more suppliers to the local area, the number of returnable containers will undoubtedly increase correspondingly.

Switching from multiple suppliers to a single vendor of an entire commodity will often greatly increase the volume purchased from the vendor selected. This higher level of purchase volume should help motivate suppliers to work aggressively to help the customer switch to returnable containers in both of their factories. After all, the savings related to reduced production costs can be approximately the same for both vendor and customer. A vendor who is the customer's sole source for an entire fastener commodity will be much more likely to be excited over switching to returnable containers than would a vendor who is one of many suppliers. One should keep in mind that the supplier of standard products usually uses the same types of containers as its customers. It uses cardboard packages to ship products and shop containers (usually plastic, metal, and wood) for work-in-process in its factory. With a factory and a finished goods warehouse full of existing containers, switching containers for the small requirements of a single customer would be highly impractical. This would be especially true for suppliers of standard items produced for finished goods inventory. Most suppliers fill all customer orders from finished goods in the same standard, labeled cartons. Asking the supplier to repackage the inventory for just one customer would add to total cost, not reduce it. Nor would it be very feasible to ask him to package the single customer's needs when they are produced. It would force the supplier to change (complicate) his production flow (unless the

[16]Paul R. Tompson, "The NUMMI Production System," in Yasuhiro Monden, *Applying Just-in-Time in America: The Japanese-American Experience* (Atlanta: Industrial Engineering and Management Press, 1986), p. 97.

supplier produces the product in a cell or a focused subplant dedicated to production for the single customer). Further, it would force the customer to order from the next production run rather than off the shelf. This would lengthen lead time—directly the opposite of the main objective. The supplier might more readily revise his flow (to stock completed items in their shop containers and to package them to every customer's specifications immediately prior to shipment) if most customers started to specify packaging.

The day is bound to come when more countries reach the point at which Japan finds itself now. All vendors and customers will use the same small, standard plastic containers for small parts. When visiting competing automotive plants in Australia, for example, the author learned that the automotive industry had already resolved to standardize containers for the benefit of the entire industry and its customers. In the future, some containers will be labeled with the name of the company to which they belong and will be expected to travel continuously between supplier and customer with nothing more than the identification on the container to ensure that it will eventually get back to its owner. Unlabeled containers will most often be used only in the factory in which they are found. In some countries, however, unlabeled containers could be billed to the recipient whenever they travel from one company to another. These containers would not need to be turned around, at least not in the usual sense. They could be sent empty to the closest supplier, thus minimizing the return freight cost.

Just as every long journey starts with one step, the road to becoming a superior manufacturer is a long journey of an almost countless number of small steps. One of the less glamorous but fundamental steps is the strategic plan for the transition from using throwaway cardboard packaging to permanent containers. Therefore, container design is an important ongoing task.

VENDOR PRODUCT DESIGN IMPROVEMENT SOURCE

The author has rarely worked with a factory in which people on the plant floor have not had valuable ideas for improving the design of the components and products they produce. People in supplier factories also have valuable ideas. Design engineers have not always been keen to accept suggestions for design improvements from the shop floor and have been even less receptive to suppliers' suggestions. Unlocking the wealth of ideas originating from both the shop floor and the supplier's factory is comparatively easy once the mechanisms are in place to process suggestions promptly and objectively. Vendor and shop personnel have often reached the point of discouragement at which they do not bother to report their ideas. Past experience has shown them that their ideas have been rejected in almost rubber-stamp fashion. Fortunately, as soon as the company starts to heed and implement their suggestions, it releases a pent-up flood of ideas.

Vendor participation in design improvement, especially as it relates to those ideas that help him reduce his own manufacturing cost, is a simple but powerful element of the complete vendor program. Procedures can be developed and engineers trained to value and give priority to the suggestions of others quite easily. This relative ease should make the vendor participation aspect of the program a high priority objective for early implementation. The resulting benefits will provide savings that can help finance the rest of the program. For example, one part of an automotive project involved a three-party review of the flow of door insulation through three factories. As Exhibit 4–17 shows, insulation fabricated by a vendor was assembled into a door panel by a subassembly plant, then shipped to the final assembly factory for ultimate use in automobile assembly. The project team and the supplier representatives found that the supplier specifications called for perforating (but not removing) all door insulation. The perforation made it possible to remove a cutout needed for the electrical controls for only those automobiles with power windows. Although every piece of insulation was perforated, the automobile assembly plant removed the small perforated portion only for cars with power windows. One full-time person worked at this operation. The team

MULTIPLANT MANUFACTURABILITY

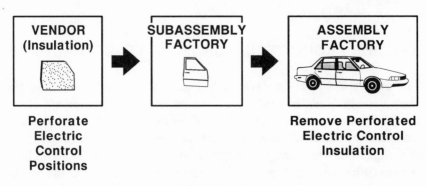

EXHIBIT 4-17

quickly concluded that it was preferable to cut and remove the insulation (instead of perforating it) at the supplier factory. This automated process would not add labor or machine time at the supplier factory and would eliminate the labor operation in the final assembly plant. The small reduction of insulating material in cars without electric windows made no discernable difference in noise level. Further, the insulation previously removed in final assembly had always been scrapped. Removing it at the supplier factory would allow the factory to reprocess the material, thus lowering material costs by the amount of material saved.

The world of manufacturing abounds with these types of improvement opportunities. Capitalizing on them usually requires no more than a cooperative effort by a team empowered to identify the opportunities and implement the required changes with the least amount of bureaucratic red tape.

PAPERLESS SUPPLIER COMMUNICATIONS

An army of white collar workers prepare, process, or file the paperwork associated with vendor communications. The supplier schedule, as previously noted, replaces purchase orders and purchase order change notices. When carried to the ultimate conclusion, vendor schedules can be transferred from a customer's computer system directly to that of the supplier, eliminating a major portion of the purchasing department's white collar work. It will also virtually eliminate the supplier's customer order processing department. These cuts will contribute drastically to reductions in total overhead payroll and expenses.

Superior manufacturers and their vendors, while striving to achieve daily or more frequent delivery of every component, recognize that when the frequency of deliveries increases from monthly to daily, the number of accounts payable (for the customer) and accounts receivable (for the supplier) increases twentyfold. Unless radical changes to accounting procedures and systems have been made, this will cause an explosion in the costs of accounting for transactions. Therefore, the need for new approaches is of paramount importance. However, these new approaches must also provide the accounting checks that virtually preclude inaccuracy and fraud.

The dishonesty and errors in every culture and society have long dictated that financial transactions be carefully audited to ensure honest and accurate books of account. Although none of the somewhat standard accounting systems completely eliminates the potential for fraud and error, such systems add immeasurably to the bureaucracy of business. For example, the international model of accounts receivable and payable, outlined in Exhibit 4–18, includes checks and cross-checks of each shipment/receipt transaction by both vendor and customer. Acme, at the time of shipment, prepares duplicate copies of the invoice, sending one to the customer for payment and one to its own accounts receivable department or system. In the meantime, the shipment of parts is accompanied by a packing list of all items included in the shipment. Upon receipt, the RLH Corporation receiving department checks all items against the packing list and prepares receiving reports for the items and quantities actually received. (If the items and/or amounts received are different from the packing list, additional paperwork, the discrepancy report, is required.) Receiving reports are then sent to accounts payable for matching and reconciling to the vendor's invoice and the original purchase order. The purpose of matching to the invoice is to make sure that the invoice is honest, as evidenced by the fact that a receiving report has been prepared. The validity of the receiving report is verified by checking it against the vendor's invoice and against the authorizing purchase order. In addition, the prices on the vendor's invoice are validated against the prices on the authorizing purchase order.

When everything checks, the accounts payable department or system prepares a check for one or more items and invoices and a remittance

TWENTIETH-CENTURY ACCOUNTING

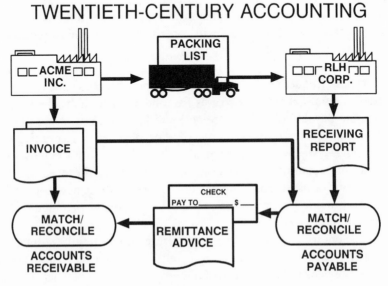

EXHIBIT 4-18

advice document, which details the invoices/items for which the check is being remitted. The vendor, upon receipt of the payment, matches it to his own copy of the invoice, reconciling any differences with discrepancy reports and notices of rejected material.

By the twenty-first century, the superior manufacturers of the world will have taken full advantage of new approaches to accounting, utilizing state-of-the-art computer technology and automatic fund transfer systems like the one depicted in Exhibit 4–19. Shipments from Acme to the RLH corporation will be accompanied by bar-coded kanban cards. These cards, electronically transmitted from the RLH Corporation to Acme (no less frequently than daily) will authorize Acme to ship a replenishment on the same day. As the shipment and its kanban cards are received, the bar-coded cards will be scanned electronically to record the receipt on inventory balance records and to inventory accounts. The computer system will check the receipt of each item against a single record for the item (maintained once or twice a year) to obtain the authorized price and to transmit an electronic transaction to the bank for automatic transfer from the account of the customer to that of the supplier. The electronic statements of the customer's and vendor's account balances, generated by the bank's computer system, will then be transmitted to the account

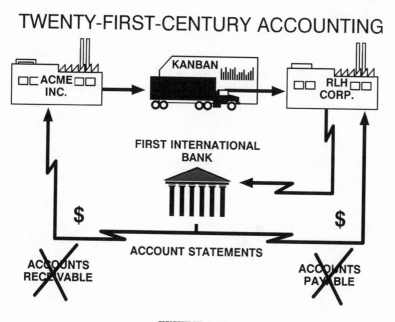

EXHIBIT 4-19

holders. Incidentally, unlike McNair,[17] the author believes that this system can operate *without purchase orders*. Elimination of purchase orders (and production orders) is an important factor in speedy, paperless communications between customers and vendors.[18]

The accounting systems described above would not be feasible in the factory and vendor networks of the past. Frequent changes in suppliers and the inventory bloat in the network would make it virtually impossible to detect either sophisticated fraud or simple inaccuracy until long after the fact. In superior networks, the environment will be very different, as the following points illustrate:

1. Single sources for virtually all items or even commodities will isolate mysterious inventory losses and gains as being attributable to a single vendor. Put simply, there are only two parties involved. Thus, if the customer does not have it, it must not have been received. Conversely, if the customer was able to meet the production schedule, he must have received and used the material.

2. Inventory remaining in the network will be minimal. Thus, if shipments are billed but not delivered they will be detectable by virtue of production stoppages.

3. Inventory will be kept in many focused subplants rather than in one giant controlled storeroom. It will be quite easy in the small, focused storage area to scan inventory records frequently and detect differences between records and actual amounts.

4. The computer record of the annual or semiannual price agreement with the single supplier of an item can be audited and otherwise controlled with much less cost than auditing and controlling the price of every receipt.

5. Computer bills of material and/or computer-generated kanban cards will be the only sources of shipment authorization. Auditing and control of master records used to authorize shipment will also greatly reduce the cost of the control effort.

Since it may take some time to organize and coordinate paperless payables and account receivables among vendor, bank, and internal procedures and systems, a company must consider interim half-measures that provide some of the benefits of the ultimate system, as illustrated in

---

[17]Carol J. McNair, William Mosconi, and Thomas F. Norris, *Beyond the Bottom Line: Measuring World Class Performance* (Homewood, Ill.: Dow Jones–Irwin, 1989), p. 156.
[18]See Appendix 2.

Exhibit 4-20. In this interim system, the RLH Corporation produces computer-generated checks and remittance advices directly from kanban cards for items received, without referencing either vendor invoices or authorizing purchase orders. The vendor can be advised that the customer will no longer use his invoices in the payment process. Thus, the vendor has two choices: he can continue to create invoices for use in his own reconciliation process or modify his system to accommodate the new mode of payment.

VENDOR KICKOFF MEETING

Many of the author's clients have kicked off the vendor participation program with one or more mass supplier meetings to explain the company's plan. Many buyers and even purchasing agents and materials vice presidents have been amazed by the turnout at most such meetings. Almost every company with which the author has worked believes that it represents too small a percentage of the vendor's sales volume to have any leverage. For years the author has heard, "We are not as big as General Motors, so we do not have enough influence to receive attention." Even at the first General Motors plant in which I worked, protests were raised that the plant represented too small a percentage of the supplier's

INTERIM ACCOUNTING

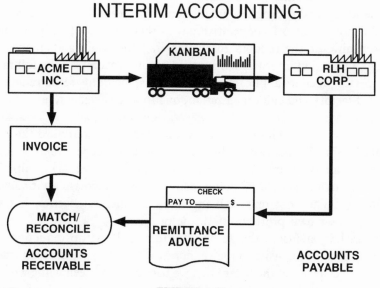

EXHIBIT 4-20

volume to command special attention. However, in the *suppliers'* factories in which I work, even small customers are given lots of attention. When it comes to the potential for losing any small customer's business, it is always evident that a small percentage of sales can have a big impact on profitability. The last few sales are those which over-absorb overhead and therefore contribute most to profit. For this reason, when suppliers are asked to send executives, not just sales representatives, to these meetings, the turnout is usually surprisingly good.

In several such kickoff meetings, the first agenda item was to ask the participants to look around the room, then full of active suppliers, and to anticipate coming to another meeting in a year or two, only to discover that nine out of ten suppliers would no longer be present! They would no longer be active sources, thus would not be invited to a vendor conference. What this means to the suppliers that survive is that they will have a bigger piece of the company's purchase pie. This is powerful incentive to work hard to be among next year's survivors. Incidentally, my colleague Leroy Peterson, when reviewing the above scenario, considered it too negative a way to put it to the vendors. He believes it would have been preferable to be more diplomatic. However, the companies that have used such shock tactics have had successful programs. Perhaps our suppliers need a dash of cold water in the face to get their attention. However, I agree with Pete that one needs the carrot more than the stick. The prospect of winning 100 percent of the customer's purchases for all items in a commodity is the carrot!

The ideal vendor program entails sending a team to the selected vendors' factories to work cooperatively with them to identify improvement opportunities in the vendors' (or customers') operations and engineering design. Operation improvements would usually encompass the full range of superior practices applicable to all factories, including setup reduction, focused factory and cell organization, quality improvement, and systems and procedure simplification. However, a customer company's resources are not usually enough to pay for visiting every supplier unless the visits would be spread over two or three years. What is needed, then, is to get vendors started on implementing improvements on their own initiative. Vendors can and should be doing many things to increase their value to customers. They not only will increase customer satisfaction but will improve their own profitability in the process.

At Harley-Davidson, the author considered the setup reduction program to be a prerequisite to the vendor program. At that time, educators were not yet aware of the things that we had done and seen while working in Japan, so they were unprepared to provide meaningful education.

(Shingo's comprehensive book first became available four years later.[19] Even then, all too many manufacturing managers could not rapidly grasp how the ideas applied to their own machines.) It was necessary to develop Western case examples to show Harley-Davidson's vendors that what the Japanese were doing was also possible in the West. The setup reduction presentation, based on changes made on Harley-Davidson machines, became one of the most important features of the vendor kickoff meeting. The vendors needed fast, error-free setup in order to improve their quality and deliver small lot sizes daily. Today, with a wealth of educational material available, vendors can get started more easily. For example, suppliers might wish to take any of a number of recommended courses if they have not already done so.

Internal productivity improvement programs should precede or parallel vendor programs in most companies. It just does not seem logical to demand (or request) that vendors reduce setup costs and improve productivity and quality when the customer's factory itself has no track record of similar improvement. However, in situations like that of Zebco, defective vendor-supplied parts can be such a major problem that the correction of vendor problems will be the single most important need. Jim Dawson, vice president of manufacturing at Zebco, in Tulsa, Oklahoma (one of the author's first post-Japan clients in 1980), found that 85 percent of all problems were "rooted in bad parts from suppliers" as reported by Waterman.[20]

It is reasonable to ask suppliers to develop an improvement program for the products they supply to the customer in preparation for the selection of the single vendor. Although a vendor improvement team might not be able to visit the vendor for some months, there is no reason that the supplier should not start work on improvements in the interim. The quality of the program for improvement and the aggressiveness with which the vendor works to achieve it should be important factors in selecting a long-term partner-in-profit. Some of the exciting opportunities include such mundane things as reducing the size of containers. At one of the author's client projects, management agreed that big savings potentials could be realized simply by downsizing the containers. However, they did not have enough staff to analyze container needs and to negotiate changes with all suppliers in less than a few years. Therefore, all vendors were asked immediately to consider container size improvements, to pres-

---

[19]Shigeo Shingo, *A Revolution in Manufacturing: The SMED System* (Stamford, Conn.: Productivity Press, 1985).
[20]Robert H. Waterman, Jr., *The Renewal Factor: How the Best Get and Keep the Competitive Edge* (New York: Bantam Books, 1987), pp. 295–97.

ent their designs to the customer, and to implement their use as soon as possible.

Although quality improvement is one aspect of improvement in every vendor program, it is certainly not the only one or the one most sorely needed. Many companies have oriented their vendor programs exclusively to quality, confusing suppliers who have had no quality problems yet have often been forced to start charting quality statistics in order to continue to be "certified." The quality messages of Chapter 6 are as applicable to vendors as they are to the customer factory. The main message is that quality improvement should be a by-product of improving factory layout, tooling and machines, and the organization of teams of employees. Every vendor program should therefore focus on improvements in the supplier's factory and in the factories of the vendor's suppliers.

THE STEP-BY-STEP VENDOR PROGRAM APPROACH

Vendor program activities fall into two major categories. The first, procedures and systems, involves the design and implementation of new and changed paperwork. It is supported by standard methodology for procedures and systems. The primary applications to which the methodology is applied in the vendor program are:

1. Supplier schedules
2. Kanban/electronic kanban
3. Product design improvement
4. Paperless payables (and receivables)
5. Annual/semiannual commodity price agreements

The second type of vendor program activity, to which a different methodology applies, is that of new and changed operating practices. These include:

1. Dedicated vendor cells or subplants development
2. Temporary vendor (versus customer) inspection and test
3. Poka-yoke (fail-safe) vendor process design
4. Improved transport and containers

The planning charts and methodology applicable to most of the vendor improvements is no different from that used for a company's own operations. The author's previous book outlined this methodology.[21] A key feature of the methodology, applicable to both customer and vendor factories, is the pilot project approach. Pilot projects, limited to a fraction of a factory but very broad in scope within that area, serve to convince skeptics that they too can do what thousands of others are doing. As Peters and Waterman wrote, "when 'touch it,' 'taste it,' 'smell it' become the watchwords, the results are most often extraordinary."[22]

SUMMARY

Improvements in the vendor network are likely to have even greater financial benefits than those in a company's own operations. Very few companies are taking the aggressive steps necessary to vault into the radically improved twenty-first-century system for vendor networks. Accordingly, companies starting late on improving their own factory's operations may benefit from starting far-sighted vendor network projects, expecting to leapfrog past their competitors into the ranks of superior manufacturers. However, future-oriented objectives should not be permitted to delay the short-term benefits that can be realized by the easy implementation of the simple ideas presented in this chapter. The front-line troops in the vendor campaign, the company's buyers, are the organization's most valuable resource for initiating new practices with the hundreds of vendors who will become permanent single sources of a commodity in the next century.

[21]See Appendix 2.
[22]Thomas J. Peters and Robert H. Waterman, *In Search of Excellence: Lessons from America's Best Run Companies* (New York: Warner Books, 1984), p. 140.

5

□□□

Faster, Better Product Design:
The Second Wave

SUPERIOR MANUFACTURERS ARE TURNING the product planning and design engineering world on its ear! Those who thought the results of manufacturers' first response to the Japanese competitive threat, radical factory improvements, has been exciting haven't seen anything yet! They will be awed by the second, more important wave (Exhibit 5–1), giant strides in product improvement. Delivery of completed product designs to the factory in 75 percent less time is now possible.[1] But reduced lead time is only one of the benefits. New designs require far fewer engineering changes after they are released to production. These changes, necessitated by design oversights and required to improve manufacturability, can be reduced by as much as 80 percent. As a result, engineers will have more time to develop new products and rationalize existing product lines. Not only will they reduce the large backlog on management's product plan wish list, but they will also speed a greater number of new and improved products to the market with the potential of gaining market share vis-à-vis competitors who are unable to match the pace. Management should not cut the engineering staff in response to the 50 percent savings achieved by reducing engineering and design correction work.

---

[1]James A. Tompkins is credited with predicting typical reduction by two-thirds. See Klaus M. Blache, ed., *Success Factors for Implementing Change: A Manufacturing Viewpoint* (Dearborn, Mich.: Society of Manufacturing Engineers, 1988), p. 368.

THE SECOND WAVE

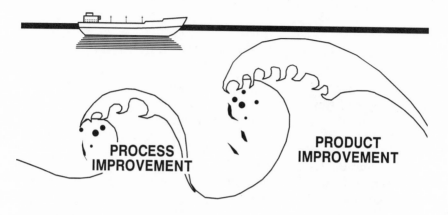

Instead, they should use the extra capacity to double the amount of new and improved product design output.

The ultimate objective of the engineering improvement effort is to design and produce products that best meet the expectations of their customers. This goal requires that a company's products have greater inherent value to their customers than competitors' products. This means not only that they should cost less but that the value–cost relationship should also be better than that of competing products. Product costs can be reduced in several ways. For example, the amount of material cost in the product can be reduced by using less material or an alternative material that performs equally well, or better, but costs less. Even if alternative materials cost slightly more, they may reduce total cost by improving the ease of manufacturability and lowering scrap and rework rates. Products designed to be more producible can also drive down factory labor and overhead costs. Simplification and standardization of products and component designs must not only reduce cost but, more important, enhance the products' performance and make them easier to service. Management can feel comfortable setting objectives for improving standardization of basic materials and commercially available components by as much as 50 percent (reducing the number of items used and stocked by one-half). Design simplification, mainly through reduction of the number of product components, should be expected to contribute up to a 30 percent cost reduction.

Finally, improved product design must be expected to reduce the dollar value of component and product inventory investment. The reduction of material and component costs, in tandem with lower factory costs, are factors that contribute most to the reduction of investment.

CHECKLIST: PRODUCT DESIGN ZINGERS

The following list, extracted and summarized from the more detailed later sections of this chapter, encapsulates some of the most important features of the new engineering design methods:

1. Design cells, like factory cells, should include an engineering team responsible for all design tasks. Designs should flow from operation to operation, hand to hand, to eliminate large queues between operations.

2. Design, manufacturing and quality engineers should be cross-trained so that any one of them can work interchangeably on the current highest priority design aspect (product, process, or quality). Further, manpower can then be shifted to the design function with the highest backlog of work.

3. Engineering personnel should be cross-trained not only for design, quality, and manufacturing engineering functions but also in various other specialties of each discipline.

4. Decentralized, focused maintenance of engineering drawings and specifications has several benefits. First, it helps avoid reinventing already designed items, because existing designs are easier to find. Also, it increases chances of standardizing components of similar products.

5. Fewer engineering projects should be in process at any time. As a result, more people can be assigned to each project, cutting the elapsed time of each.

6. The number of products sold or offered for sale can be cut sharply by revising catalogs and sales techniques. Customers need information on which catalog products and options have high demand and thus are not only more readily available but also less costly.

7. Standardization of raw materials will have the greatest, fastest cost reduction potential for most companies. Most companies spend proportionately more for custom-manufactured items than for commercially available purchased components. Although proprietary design items are seldom suitable candidates for standardization, their components and materials are.

8. One key to standardizing materials and commercially available components is to prioritize items based on the number of different subassemblies and end products on which they are used. The objective is to find and to use a similar item that is used on even more products and subassemblies, thus increasing the volume required, and achieving better economies of scale.

9. Matrix bills of material that display similar components of similar products side by side are a powerful component standardization tool. They make standardization (or lack thereof) easily visible.

10. Engineering departments need to reduce time wasted in reinventing existing products and components by improving the study of competitors' products. While products manufactured in other countries are seldom analyzed, they are often valuable sources of revolutionary ideas. Thus, engineers must broaden the scope of competitive product analysis to include more foreign products.

11. Manufacturing methods should be based on inflated estimates of the company's future share of market. Only by using machines and tooling suitable for higher volume production can costs be lowered to the point of being competitive with the highest volume producer. Using methods suitable for higher volume production will lead to achieving that end.

12. Producing engineering drawings or specifications for commercially available components is a waste of time. Companies that do so can save drafting and engineering effort by adopting a simple system for cross-referencing a company part number to that of a standard commercial, government, or vendor number.

13. Engineers need a new standardization tool to help them make the right decisions when they select commercially available components for new and changed products. The tool should include purchase prices and should show the quantity currently purchased. The tool should be of utmost simplicity.

14. Engineers need a fast way to access specifications of commercially available components. The payoff will be in increased standardization. Commodity coding schemes are a poor substitute for a simple, flexible, low cost cross-reference system.

15. Engineering test equipment and model shop machines should be as simple and low cost as possible to perform the necessary operations. Small, simple machines may be inexpensive enough to be put into each engineering cell that needs them. Compared to a single piece of test equipment (a major bottleneck in the flow of

every component that requires testing) numerous small, simple machines will reduce reliance on test specialists, cut lost time while waiting for test results, and greatly increase the engineering organization's flexibility.

16. License agreements are one low cost way to acquire product designs at a fraction of the cost of do-it-yourself design.

REDUCING DESIGN TIME: FASTER TO MARKET

Purchasers of custom-designed products often select a supplier based on the time it takes various competing suppliers to design and produce them. They often buy from the vendor able to make the speediest delivery, although the vendor with the lowest price is also often the winner. When all suppliers are considered to be about equal in price, value, and quality, the one that delivers fastest is bound to get the business (as long as the price is reasonable). However, even the company that sells standard products from stock can usually benefit from faster engineering. Sometimes basic research yields superior new materials that become available to all competitors simultaneously. The supplier that first brings new or revised products containing the new material to the market is the one most likely to become accepted as the market leader. For all of the above reasons, both low volume, custom-design producers and those that manufacture standard, high volume products should be excited at the prospect of quantum improvements in product design time. For example, James Treece has noted how important it is for General Motors to be working on reducing new product development time, because other auto manufacturers "enjoy dramatically speedier product-development cycles."[2] As noted in this chapter, General Motors *is* making seven-league steps in this regard.

The reasons that design engineering factories (*paperwork* factories) have such great potential for improvement are identical to those of conventional, functionally organized manufacturing plants. Jobs travel long distances in the engineering factory, from project engineer to model shop and back. Next they travel to test and back, followed by drafting, design checking, and so on, until released to production. Each step in the process is plagued by big queues of work in containers that are too large (in- and out-baskets). The result is excessive amounts of work-in-process and

[2]James B. Treece, "The Corporation: War, Recession, Gas Hikes . . . GM's Turnaround Will Have to Wait," *Business Week*, February 4, 1991, pp. 94–96.

correspondingly long times between the first and last operations. Since employees are not cross-trained, bottlenecks shift back and forth from one type of operation to another, leaving some people idle while others are swamped and work long overtime hours to catch up. Some of the bottlenecks are machines (test equipment and model shop). Monstrously large and complex test equipment is used to perform tests on not only very complex items but also on many other simpler items that could just as well be tested on simpler, lower cost equipment. Since the equipment is very expensive, engineering usually has only one of each type. Not surprisingly, since it is the worst sort of bottleneck, it operates around the clock. Incidentally, the changeover for testing different items carries a high price tag—in both time and cost. When equipment is inoperative because of changeover (of both hardware and software), the time loss cuts into the equipment's potential productive capacity. Setup (changeover) reduction techniques can and should be used to reduce this time by 75 percent or more, just as is done with any factory machine with long changeover time.[3] For example, in Carrollton, Texas, the Lennox Industries air conditioner test room project cut setup time from five hours to forty-five minutes. So far, this and other improvements have helped reduce the development cycle by 50 to 70 percent, depending on product complexity. The time saved has helped avoid adding a new quarter-million-dollar test room.

While designs of higher quality and reliability and lower production costs must be the principal targets of improved engineering methods, these objectives can be met at the same time as the engineer's productivity is boosted. Exhibit 5–2 shows the potential for productivity increase, another vital component in the drive to reduce the time required to deliver new products to the market. The exhibit depicts the average daily activity of the typical design engineer. This example was developed by a research and development project team that was responsible for compressing engineering time. It shows that, prior to the project, the typical engineer spent 11 percent of his time putting new designs on paper. While this may at first seem shockingly low, the author finds it representative of most large companies that produce complex products and outclass the competition in technological development but not in speedy delivery. Engineers, like executives and managers in other functional areas, spend approximately one-third of their time originating, receiving, and processing various communications. On one typical design project, more than eight hundred memos were created and distributed. (Of these,

[3]See Appendix 2.

ENGINEERING TASK CLASSIFICATION

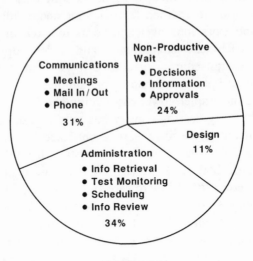

EXHIBIT 5-2

93 percent were conventional and 7 percent were electronic mail.) Administrative tasks consumed another one-third of engineers' workdays. For example, all people in the engineering organization (not just the engineers) must normally report their "production" and, after the data reported have been processed, must monitor such things as schedule and budget status and test results. Another major time consumer in the administrative time category is the retrieval of engineering data needed to respond to inquiries (communications). Unfortunately, primarily because of delays (in decisions, approvals, and receiving information from other sources), 24 percent more of the engineers' day was nonproductive.

Modern computer-based engineering systems are one key for converting wasteful, nonproductive activity to time available for design development and improvement. Andersen Consulting's leading-edge Engineering Connection Demonstration at the Infomart Center in Dallas is a perfect example of the integration of numerous computers and hundreds of software programs that process the information used by design and manufacturing engineers, as Exhibit 5-3 shows. The workbench can put the power of all the computers and programs into the hands of every engineer. It eliminates the need to create engineering and communications documentation since other users can access the data through their own workstations. Two important tools of the workbench, word processing and electronic mail, sharply reduce the burden of written communi-

ENGINEERING WORKBENCH

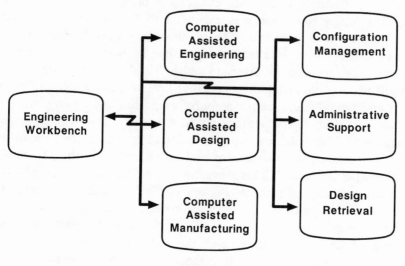

EXHIBIT 5-3

cation. Messages can be forwarded electronically, as can approvals. And secretaries, who would otherwise type messages and other forms of communication, can be cut from the message loop, reducing operating costs and speeding the communication process. Thus electronic mail will be one of the tools of the reinvented engineering "factory" of the future.

In summary, "speed to market" will be one of the most important differentiating factors in the twenty-first century. As Alan Magazine has said, "nimble and fast-moving market staffs must prepare to seed markets with new products even while the product is still in the conceptual stage. Without speedy product development, companies quickly become technological laggards."[4]

REINVENTING THE WHEEL VERSUS FILCHING IDEAS

At this very moment, at least one engineer, somewhere in the world, is busily "inventing" a new component for a product that has been marketed in similar versions by companies all over the globe. Chances are that the resulting design will be better in some respects than existing

[4]Alan H. Magazine, "Competitiveness in Today's Global Economy," in Ross E. Robson, ed., *The Quality and Productivity Equation: American Corporate Strategies for the 1990s* (Cambridge, Mass.: Productivity Press, 1990), p. 23.

designs, and not as good in others. Before beginning any discussion of other opportunities for lowering the costs of bringing better, lower cost product designs to market, it is imperative that engineers face one fact. The author sees too many engineers reinventing wheels, while too few are looking at the wheels already in operation. In short, they are spending much more time than necessary to get the job done. Every engineering department should maintain an extensive inventory of competitors' products and should study them closely before putting their own pencils to paper. The study of competitors' products must not stop with an understanding of their design structure and materials. Juran wrote: "For many product features, the competitive analysis should go further. It should evaluate performance."[5] This is especially important when a competitive product performs better and lasts longer. Such products are bound to gain market share if they are also price-worthy. Life and performance tests of competitors' products will help engineers understand better just how good their designs are vis-à-vis those of their competitors.

Companies that do not study competitors' products are rare. Those that study all of them in the detail necessary to avoid reinvention are even rarer. For example, few companies bother routinely to search out products not marketed in their own countries or regions. The author was recently struck by the difference between Scandinavian urinals and those manufactured in the United States. The traditional (not modern) Scandinavian model is ultramodern in appearance, with its streamlined, thin design. By contrast, all models in the United States are massive. Since raw material and finish make up most of the urinal cost, the Scandinavian product should cost a fraction of its American counterparts. The first American company to market the new design might save the country billions by reducing not only the product's cost but also the size of the room in which it is installed.

Incidentally, the company that rushes the new urinal to market would be wise to negotiate a license deal with the premier Scandinavian producer for product and process specifications. Use of such specifications could lower engineering costs significantly. More important, it could substantially slash the time-to-market and help the company steal a march on its domestic competitors. The Japanese and, later, the Koreans experienced a tremendous leap forward by licensing technology from the United States and Europe. That so many companies are missing the opportunity to pursue similar strategies avidly is a puzzle. Karatsu, for one, noticed the Western reluctance to imitate foreign producers. He wrote,

[5] J. M. Juran, *Juran on Planning for Quality* (New York: Free Press, 1988), p. 119.

"Contrary to American thinking, technological innovation does not preclude imitation. People in the United States [say] that there is no point in producing a product that was not invented in your own country."[6]

In view of its great importance, in addition to being a routine function of ongoing engineering operations, the study (and acquisition, if necessary) of competitors' products must become one of the earliest steps of the methodology we use for every product improvement project.

DO IT RIGHT THE FIRST TIME

Curt Morris, then Corporate Vice President—Manufacturing at Outboard Marine Corporation and my boss at the time, gave me a lesson that will stay with me all my life. I had just discovered a simple engineering change that saved tens of thousands of dollars per year in machining operations. I was understandably jubilant when the opportunity arose to tell Curt about this cost reduction. After Curt listened to the enthusiastic explanation, he said: "Please understand that what you have done is not a cost reduction, it is an error correction." It was his way of saying that no amount of "cost reduction" changes would approach the value of doing the job right the first time. Thereafter, I concentrated on getting closer to design engineering at the time of engineering release. This drastically reduced the amount of savings that could be claimed because opportunities for improvement were incorporated before starting mass production. It did not take long to discover that much greater effort was required to make changes in products once they were in production. To this day I remain convinced that cost reduction projects will seldom have the cost-benefit impact of working on a new product. However, when all new products are engineered with minimal errors, the time needed to correct errors in the rest of the pipeline will drop dramatically over the long term.

Even the best quality control experts recognize that more than just statistical methods are needed to achieve near-perfect quality. Kane writes, "Many people have been mistakenly led to believe that the use of SPC (Statistical Process Control) charts is the key element needed for improved quality." He goes on to say that a defect prevention system is needed.[7] However, his system definition does not get to the heart of the

---

[6]Hajime Karatsu, *Tough Words for America* (Cambridge, Mass.: Productivity Press, 1987), p. 129.
[7]Victor E. Kane, *Defect Prevention: Use of Simple Statistical Tools* (New York: Marcel Dekker, 1989), p. 585.

real problem: original product and process design. Many manufacturers erroneously think they have quality problems when what they really have is product design flaws. When this is the case, no amount of statistical control or factory improvement will help.

PRODUCT DEFINITION: NOT A HOBBY

Most large companies, like Lennox Industries, need the input and guidance of marketing, sales, accounting, design and process engineering, manufacturing, purchasing, and service to develop feasible new product plans and preliminary specifications. Many, however, manage the new product planning process as if it were a sideline (hobby) for the product planning people who represent their organizations' viewpoints and search out the information upon which to base product decisions. Often the first tentative product ideas take several months to be developed to the point of being well-defined product design projects. Each person participating in the planning process usually has his normal full-time job in addition to his product planning assignment and thus can spend only minutes, now and then, on new product development. As a result, relatively few hours or days of work are spread over several months. In the meantime, it is entirely likely that competitors with faster product planning and engineering processes are stealing a march on the company.

Lennox found that the best solution was to detach the major product planning people from their everyday jobs in their normal organizations for a brief intensive period, in which they would work together full-time on the new product. Lennox christened the planning team "Scope Team" and identified design and manufacturing engineers, marketing, service, and manufacturing personnel as the primary full-time team. Other support personnel, called on an as-required basis, include accounting, purchasing, dealer representatives, and vendor representatives, to name a few. As a result, Lennox found itself able to cut product planning time to a mere fraction of its former length. A fast, efficient organization and methodology for product planning are vital prerequisites for faster delivery of new products to market. Once the new product and process have been defined, a much more efficient, focused organization is needed to complete the detailed design. The product/process design cell is an organization that fills this need.

PRODUCT/PROCESS DESIGN CELLS

Some systems and engineering technicians may be disappointed that the main thrust of this chapter is not computer aided design and computer aided manufacturing (CAD and CAM). However, the rush to use automation to solve engineering bottlenecks has failed to provide cost-effective results routinely. In fact, the majority of such systems have added cost to the engineering process. The reason is clear. Too many companies are automating engineering without first simplifying. The NavCom experience in the 1970s *did* include some simplification (using two drawings, one for each side of an integrated circuit board, rather than a single drawing in two colors as in the past).[8] In going right from a bad manual system to a better computer system, NavCom robbed itself of a chance to know what economies might have been achieved by simplifying without automating. Certainly this was the reason for its difficulties in converting to the new system. Since design process simplification is the key to tapping into mammoth productivity improvement, the first priority of any engineering organization must be to rationalize the process, starting with the development of a superior design organization.

A component plant of a major U.S. automotive company and its customers, the automobile assembly plants, as part of a major project to speed new products to their customers, found that communications concerning the design of new and revised products were complex and time-consuming. The reasons were that the fragmented responsibilities of the conventional functional organization (and its people), Exhibit 5–4, were scattered over numerous offices and buildings. Recognition of this communication nightmare led to wide-ranging improvements, including the development of a new customer-oriented design organization, Exhibit 5–5. The component factory's products were unique to the specifications of each customer plant. Therefore, teams were organized for each customer and the customer's products. The makeup of each team included full-time and part-time people from all of the functional specialties.

Since the engineering office and conventional factory processes share the same characteristics, it follows that similar improvements should apply to each. The first and fundamental improvement involves establishing an organization of engineering design cells that go far beyond

---

[8]Daniel Pereira, Appendix 2, in Robert E. Blauth and Carl Machover, eds., *The CAD/CAM Handbook* (Bedford, Mass.: Computervision, 1980).

FUNCTIONAL ORGANIZATION - BEFORE

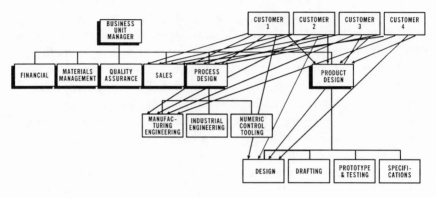

EXHIBIT 5-4

CUSTOMER PRODUCT FOCUS

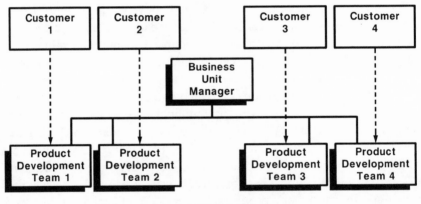

EXHIBIT 5-5

simple team effort Gozzo and Grieco describe.[9] The design cell should permanently bring together the various specialists from three different predecessor organizations: design engineering, manufacturing engineering, and quality control (the quality engineers in the engineering cells of the twenty-first century will be specialists in designing fail-safe quality into manufacturing operations and products and will be responsible for

[9]Michael W. Gozzo and Peter L. Grieco, Jr., *Made in America: The Total Business Concept* (Plantsville, Conn.: PT Publications, 1987), p. 57.

designing test equipment). Various specialties have always been part of each of the three organizations. (For example, design engineering comprises product and project engineering, drafting, data control, configuration control, model shop, and testing). In the new cell, all of the team members should be able to work interchangeably on any of these specialty tasks.

Cross-training within and between the three engineering specialties will make the cell team extremely flexible in terms of ability to move from one specialty operation to another. Movement from an operation at which there is momentarily no work to an overloaded (bottleneck) operation can virtually eliminate delays between operations. Thus, a design project should take no longer to get through the cell than the sum of the hours of work required divided by the number of engineering personnel in the cell. The small new cell, like the small factory-in-a-factory, should be managed like a small entrepreneurial business. The cell head should manage by walkabout. He will not need a project control system to keep track of the design status. After all, in his small factory he should have no more than two product designs in process at a time—one starting into the first operations while a second is being completed.

The deplorable effect of working on multiple design projects can not be overemphasized. When multiple simultaneous projects are combined with inflexible specialists and workloads that vary dynamically from operation to operation, the results are similar to those illustrated in Exhibit 5–6. The bars in the exhibit represent the actual work performed by one

LEAD TIME - BEFORE

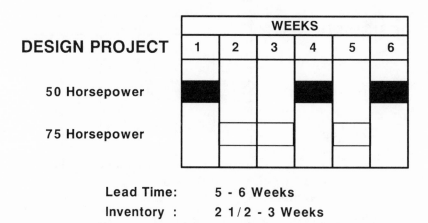

DESIGN PROJECT	WEEKS					
	1	2	3	4	5	6
50 Horsepower						
75 Horsepower						

Lead Time: 5 - 6 Weeks

Inventory :   2 1/2 - 3 Weeks

EXHIBIT 5-6

engineer on two projects over a six-week period. After working on one aspect of the 50-horsepower project for one week, he did some work on the 75-horsepower job, perhaps because it was the only work in his in-basket at the start of Week 2. Note that by the time he had an opportunity to work on the 50 again, he had lost two weeks during which he might have kept the 50 in motion. In the example, the average elapsed time for him to complete operations on both projects was in the range of five to six weeks. Later a rule was mandated that allowed only one project to be released at a time, and not until any in-process work was completed. The result? The average lead time of the two projects was halved, as shown in Exhibit 5–7. However, this was not the end of the lead time reduction. By assigning various design modules in the 50-horsepower project to different individuals, as opposed to just one, the company was able to reduce elapsed time further, from three weeks to one.

The number of products, components, and materials in the average company's file of drawings and specifications is typically in the range of tens of thousands or more. Their sheer number complicates the engineer's objectives of design standardization and reuse of existing designs. Indeed, it complicates the job so much that engineers fall far short of achieving these goals. Product coding has long been viewed as one method by which engineers could more easily access prior designs. But most code systems have failed as a consequence of the complexity of assigning codes to such a profusion of items. From the author's point of

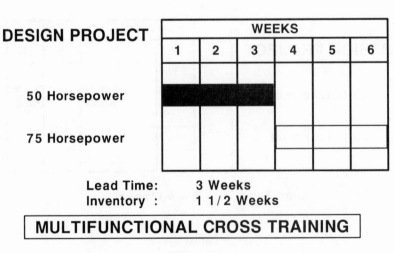

LEAD TIME - AFTER

DESIGN PROJECT

WEEKS					
1	2	3	4	5	6

50 Horsepower

75 Horsepower

Lead Time: 3 Weeks
Inventory : 1 1 / 2 Weeks

MULTIFUNCTIONAL CROSS TRAINING

EXHIBIT 5–7

view, adding a complex code (or even a simple one) only undermines the challenge: to simplify rather than add complexity to an environment that is already too intricate. In the author's experience, most companies that use elaborate codes have had to add more staff to handle the coding and to try to locate existing similar designs before starting to develop new ones. When only the code specialists can master the code scheme, engineers must come to them to have new designs or requests for previous designs encoded. While they are thus requesting codes, they are losing time that would be much more productively spent at their drawing boards. Thus, the code systems not only have failed to do the job but have unfortunately added to engineering costs. The real underlying problem of design filing and retrieval is lack of focus!

When factories become too large and complex, the solution is to break them into smaller factories-within-the-factory. Exactly the same solution applies to design drawings and specifications. Instead of monstrous central design files (either paper files or magnetic media in companies using computer added design (CAD), files should be split into numerous smaller files. When the drawing files are organized according to the design teams that use them, the team's job of filing and accessing designs becomes much simpler. Designers that are still dependent on a central data control department (or section) waste substantial time going to (or ordering from) them to retrieve drawings and specifications. Often the engineer needs to review a large number of drawings in order to select the one on which a new design might be based. If he does not know which to ask for, the situation is infinitely worse. He usually does not attempt to locate them, concluding that he would rather create a new drawing than waste time trying to find one that may or may not already exist. Exhibit 5–8 shows how files of drawings and specifications have been broken into smaller files (by the horsepower of the product) and further subdivided into functional families of parts (gears, pistons, shafts, and blocks). Note, in this example, that these files are located beside the responsible designers' desks. In the small design team "factory," every file is in easy reach of every team member. The gear designer will now be able to riffle quickly through the relatively small gear file when he needs to see if a gear of the type identical or similar to his needs already exists. The concept of the file subdivision applies to both manual drawings and designs that are maintained *only* on a computer file. It will still drastically reduce the time it takes the designer to find the drawing he needs. Exhibit 5–8 also reinforces the importance of cross-training of the design team members. Since different teams and different specialists within them will have varying workloads, cross-training will be vital to

DESIGN TEAM FILES

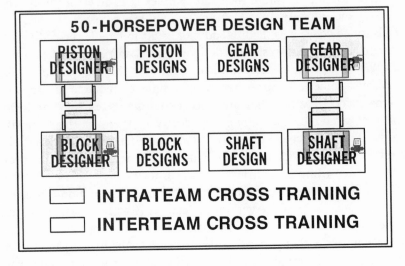

EXHIBIT 5-8

enabling each to move routinely to where the work is, whether in another design cell or in another specialized job within the cell.

Incidentally, the most innovative engineering organizations will go beyond the point of instituting design cells in the context of implementing their organization charts and cross-training programs. For example, Japanese style open-office desk clusters would foster quantum improvements in communications and cooperation. The Fucinis describe an alternative, employed by Mazda's Flat Rock, Michigan, factory, that is a minor compromise with the Japanese model.[10]

DESIGN STANDARDIZATION: SIMPLIFICATION AND COST REDUCTION

As previously mentioned, few companies that manufacture a wide range of products have managed to achieve near-perfect standardization of components and materials across the entire spectrum of products. Therefore, these companies still have plenty of opportunity to lower product costs by increasing levels of standardization. One obvious benefit of increased

[10]Joseph J. Fucini and Suzy Fucini, *Working for the Japanese: Inside Mazda's American Auto Plant* (New York: Free Press, 1990), p. 43.

standardization is that the resulting usage volume increase will often push the item into a lower price break range. In addition to the price break, additional factory savings will result from reducing the number of items used. Some of these are listed below:

1. Simpler, lower cost storage due to a reduction in the number of stockkeeping units in focused stores

2. Reduction of changeover cost (When changing from assembly of one product to another, standardization minimizes the number of components on the line that requires changing.)

3. Reductions of the number of people required to order, receive, and account for the reduced number of components

4. Reduction of the number of machines, tools, dies, and fixtures

Standardization of existing product components, like every improvement project, should get under way only after aggressive targets have been set. Since many people know that goals of 20 and 30 percent product cost reduction are feasible,[11] superior manufacturers should set their targets even higher. These aggressive goals will be achieved only if the project team reduces the number of components and material in the range of 50 to 60 percent and the number of production processes by 30 percent or more.

Unfortunately, the costliest components are not often the components that have the highest potential for increased standardization. In fact, the opposite situation is more prevalent. For example, opportunities to standardize the large components of an automatic washer and dryer are rare, while their hardware and wires are much easier to standardize. Nevertheless, most companies will enjoy savings in the range of six- or seven-digit numbers by improving standardization. Unfortunately, many companies waste time looking for ways to improve high value items that do not lend themselves well to product standardization. Instead, companies must understand which types of components are readily standardized and should use a methodology that will concentrate their efforts on the items in the categories (commodities) that will have the highest, fastest payback.

Two of the three functional component and product types are quite likely to be used in more than one product. The three types are:

[11]Toshio Suzue and Akira Kohdate, *Variety Reduction Program: A Production Strategy for Product Diversification* (Cambridge, Mass.: Productivity Press, 1990), pp. 73–76.

1. Proprietary designs
2. Commercially available components
3. Raw material

Methods for standardizing each of these categories follow.

MATRIX BILLS OF MATERIAL: PRODUCT STANDARDIZATION TOOL

Proprietary designs are developed by a company's own engineers (or, rarely, by vendors whose designs are then owned by the customer) and are ordinarily the only items for which design drawings should be produced. The subdivision of proprietary design drawing files by product, as previously illustrated in Exhibit 5–8, might be viewed by some as having serious drawbacks related to items that have, or should have, commonality (standardization) across several product lines. However, in the author's experience proprietary designs can seldom be used in more than one product family. For example, logical engine families are horsepower-oriented. Most of the proprietary design components of 25-horsepower engines will be radically different in size from those of the 50-horsepower engine and therefore will not have standardization potential. (For example, muffler, tailpipe, carburetor, spark plug). However, given a family of motors that are all the same horsepower, it would be quite difficult to comprehend why these types of components should not be standardized.

A case example will show one way in which the standardization of proprietary design components was simplified. In the 1970s, Yamaha asked the author to move to Japan and help on a companywide improvement project. Its tremendous success and growth had left it with thousands of discrete products in hundreds of models. With this goldmine opportunity to standardize, Yamaha's initial sole interest in the author's experience lay in design standardization. The sheer mass of component bill of material data was so overwhelming that it seemed to defy analysis. Today, Yamaha is benefiting from the "Grupo Listo" system, which has reduced data analysis to manageable proportions. It does this by making standardization opportunities readily visible and by helping control the proliferation of component differences in new versus prior models.

Yamaha's previous bills of material, essentially one list per product, were rather conventional. Their thousands of products, each containing hundreds of components, made it impossible to imagine being able to compare, side by side, all of the bills of material of similar products. The length of each bill, by itself, made it extremely difficult to search through two lists to find, for example, two different headlight part numbers. The solution was clear. Find a practical way to do the following:

1. Subdivide bills of material into small, manageable groups.
2. Array similar product-subdivided bills of material side by side. The short lists, side by side, would make similarities and differences easily identifiable.

The author recommended that bills of material be organized by the types of assembly groups illustrated in Exhibit 5–9. He usually finds that any type of component (wheel, for example) would always be assembled at the same assembly station even though many different products might be assembled on the one line. Since different families of similar products are usually assembled on different lines, the product-to-line relationship was helpful in identifying similar products. The thirty to forty logical component groups per line at Yamaha cut the number of components on each group list bill of material to ten or less. Exhibit 5–10 illustrates four of Yamaha's forty group list bills of material: chassis/engine, rear fender, handlebar, and headlight. The computer-prepared group lists, Exhibit 5–10, list up to twenty-five products in matrix form. The Xs in columns indicate the products in which each component is used. In the example, the screw is standardized, as seen by the fact that it is used on all of the

ASSEMBLY LINE GROUPS

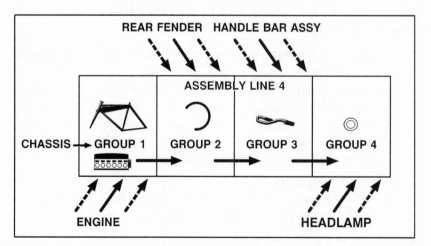

EXHIBIT 5–9

GROUP LIST BILLS OF MATERIAL

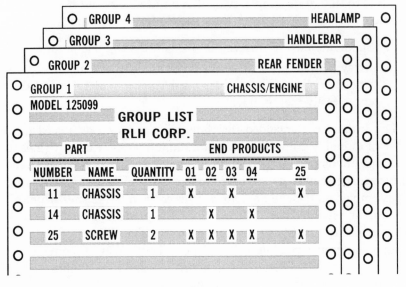

EXHIBIT 5-10

products. However, the fact that there are two different chassis assemblies indicates an opportunity to increase chassis standardization by designing one to fit all products.

Incidentally, as Hall reported, foremen resisted the new idea (for good reason): A component type was *not* always assembled at or near the same assembly station.[12] All assembly lines had to be reorganized in order to make the system work. Subsequently, all lines were reorganized (standardized) for the following reasons:

1. Standardization was a necessary prerequisite to automating assembly operations.
2. Assembling one component type at different assembly work stations for different products increased the operation's complexity. This made the job more complex for the assembler and the material handler, who needed to deliver the component to different places on the line for different products.
3. Kanban cards (called Synchro cards at Yamaha) required assembly line delivery location. The group list system made the determination of delivery location almost automatic.

[12]Robert W. Hall, *Driving the Productivity Machine: Production Planning and Control in Japan* (Falls Church, Va.: American Inventory Control Society, 1981), pp. 54–56.

COMMERCIALLY AVAILABLE COMPONENTS: INFINITE VARIETY

Commercially available, off-the-shelf components used on two or more product families are much more likely to have the potential for commonality and standardization than are proprietary designs. The reasons for such great potential become apparent when one reviews the decisions an engineer may face. When he must decide on the screws to fasten the fuel filter housing and cover, Exhibit 5–11, the engineer obviously has wide latitude, from a structural standpoint. The combinations of different diameters and lengths that will meet the structural needs is almost infinite. In reality, engineers rarely take the time to calculate this value. Instead, they employ their common sense and use components that far exceed the maximum stresses to which they will be subjected. There is logic in this process! The required calculations would be prohibitively complex, time-consuming, and expensive; in the end, the resulting number would nevertheless be increased by a factor of two, three, or even more to provide a maximum safety factor. Diameter and length are only two of a number of variables. Among others are head types (including slot, Phillips, Allen, square, and hexagonal), thread sizes, and washer types. To complicate matters further, each of these comes in a variety of alloys and hardnesses. The vast array of screw possibilities inevitably results in a company's using and stocking many more than are really needed, which

HARDWARE SELECTION VARIABLES

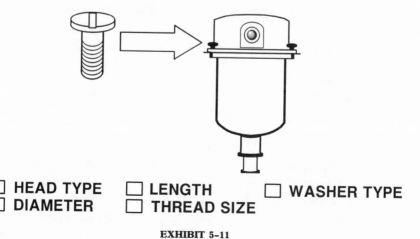

☐ **HEAD TYPE**   ☐ **LENGTH**   ☐ **WASHER TYPE**
☐ **DIAMETER**   ☐ **THREAD SIZE**

EXHIBIT 5-11

precludes it from buying a smaller variety in larger volumes at lower cost.

The best way to pursue the standardization potential of commercially available items is, first, to rank commodities based on the dollars spent per year. Working on the highest purchase value commodities first makes the items of highest saving potential top priority. Next, a decision must be made about the item on which to standardize in each category. The primary factor for making this decision should be the unit price of each item in the category. To be valid, this comparison must compare the unit price of each item using the same price break volume. The final step is to analyze the tentatively chosen item in all applications in which slightly different components are used. The purpose of the analysis is to determine if the standard item meets the structural and functional needs of the products on which it will be used. It is then possible to prepare change specifications for any affected mating components as well as those authorizing the change to the standard item.

A fast, shortcut way to channel engineers' selections of commercially available components is to provide them with information about the existing usage of these types of items. Thirty years ago, the author found Briggs & Stratton to be one of the best in the world at standardizing engine components. All it took to achieve this was an index card file for each active item. After searching through the cards to find the item used most widely, every engineer posted the products on which he used the item on the cards. At that time the business was not too complex, so engineers knew all products and roughly what their sales volumes were. Thus, the engineers understood roughly how to translate model-used-on information into the quantity used. In today's more complex businesses, engineers need a component standardization aid like the one illustrated in Exhibit 5–12. As could be expected, in this example a direct correlation exists between the size of the screws and their purchase price (based on the 10,000 price break for any of the screws). This would be expected, because 50 to 70 percent of the vendor's cost is raw materials. Thus, larger screws cost more. Since the engineer could use any of several screws in a size range, he should continue to attempt to use the smallest (lowest cost) possible. However, the design aid (report or display) alerts him to the fact that he might be selecting an item with very low usage. This is a virtual guarantee that the price break range for his application will be higher than the highest usage item. This is illustrated by the differences between the present prices (based on present volumes) and the price based on a 10,000 purchase. In this specific example, it is clear that to use the third screw will clearly be the most economical decision.

COMPONENT STANDARDIZATION AID*

Commodity: Common Screw: Slot Head: 1/4 Inch Diameter				
PART NUMBER	LENGTH	PRESENT PRICE	PRICE/10 THOUSAND	PRESENT USAGE
12345	16/64	10.00	10.00	10,000
21354	17/64	10.00	11.00	100,000
05432	18/64	9.00	12.00	1,000,000
36549	19/64	25.00	13.00	500
25416	20/64	20.00	14.00	5,000

* Computer Report or Display

EXHIBIT 5-12

The component design aid, Exhibit 5-12, can be made available only if structured around a cross-reference system that makes it simple, and thus fast, for an engineer to access the items that are candidates for use in his current product. The author has little respect for most of the commodity code schemes that have been touted as tools for standardization. Most are so complex that specialists are needed to translate the engineer's inquiries into code. The author prefers to help clients develop their own customized, simple cross-reference systems. These systems, in various forms, have been used for decades. The basics are illustrated in Exhibits 5-13 and 5-14. In the examples, an engineer, needing a hose for his application, starts the search by looking in an alphabetic index book, which is the first book in the complete set of cross-reference books, Exhibit 5-13. In the user-friendly index, he finds that hoses have been assigned cross-reference number 123. Note that the search begins with the most natural of search keys, the *functional* description of the item. Most commodity code schemes, by contrast, start with either material or shape. The index number, 123, leads the searcher into the cross-reference volume for item numbers 100 through 199. Matrices that describe the specifications of indexed items are of such great variety that they must fit the specific needs. Thus, the system involves the use of free-form matrices. Incidentally, a company does not need to produce its own engineering specifications and drawings for these types of items. The best

ALPHABETICAL INDEX

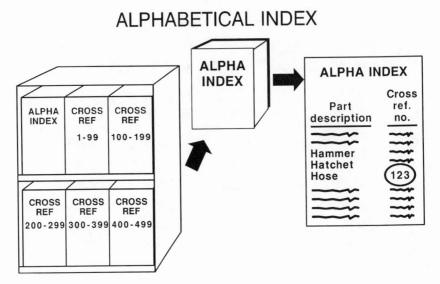

EXHIBIT 5–13

way to document them is simply to cross-reference the company's own part numbers to the commercial or government specification or the vendors' part numbers, and to use those specifications.

The engineer next finds the page series of matrices for hoses, numbered 123, and searches to find the half-inch hose he needs, Exhibit 5–14. The matrix that contains hoses best suited to his purpose shows a variety of lengths and colors that are available. Since the engineer is indifferent to the color but needs a 10-foot length, he selects the only hose of that length that was previously assigned a part number (the white hose, which is company part number 214 and vendor part number W10).

The cross-reference system exhibits were originally used on a project for MTS Corporation and were based on a similar system the author used earlier at the Guidance and Control Systems Division of Litton Industries. The MTS project charter at the time was to design computer systems, but urgent business problems required immediate solution. Thus, it was necessary to develop rapidly a practical and flexible interim system. The speed with which the system was devised and actual matrices were developed, item by item, disproved the notion that everything must be mechanized. Even today, cutting and pasting of various government and vendor specifications will be the fastest and lowest cost way to get started.

FREE-FORM MATRICES

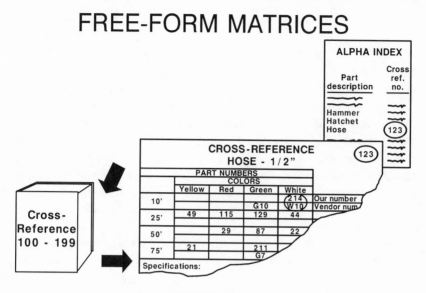

EXHIBIT 5-14

RAW MATERIAL: THE STANDARDIZATION GOLDMINE

The average expenditure per raw material item is usually much greater than for purchased components. Thus, improving the cost of one raw material often yields as much benefit as improving the designs of dozens of purchased components. The same type of analysis that is used for purchased component standardization, as illustrated in Exhibit 5–10, can be applied to raw materials. The main difference will be that analysis of raw materials will be much simpler since far fewer items need analysis.

The complexity of today's products and factories often masks the fact that the lack of standardization of raw material is causing product and operating costs to be much higher than necessary. For example, while working with a South American plant of an international earthmoving equipment producer recently, the author had occasion to study the raw materials used in one machine. He was startled to learn that more than two hundred different steel plate specifications were stocked. The original project charter involved improving the scheduling of plate cutting to reduce inventories. This was to be done by reducing the lot sizes of components cut from each large plate as indicated by improved lot-sizing algorithms. Since usage of some small components of each plate type was very low, substantially more was cut than required for immediate purposes. Even then it was necessary to combine more than one item on a plate with other items used on other products. This was necessary to fill up a large plate in such a way as to minimize the amount of "skeleton" (waste material after cutting the components out of the plate). Because of variability in the production schedules of different machines and the different lot sizes of various components, the components combined for a cutting pattern were different for every plate layout. Variations in the schedules of different products, and thus in their component requirements, made it impractical to minimize the amount of "skeleton." More material was wasted than should have been. When one conjures up a vision of hundreds of bulldozer components, each being stored in multiples of several machines' worth of usage, one begins to envision the look of the factory—giant piles of components in formal stores and scattered all around the factory.

Besides the "skeleton" waste, one saw storage space waste, large fleets of transport equipment to move the components into and out of storage, and large inventory investment. Clearly, any scheme to improve the scheduling of plate-cutting and lot-sizing algorithms would only increase the complexity of the operation and offered little hope of substantially lowering operating costs.

Radical reduction of the number of raw materials, however, offered a new spectrum of possibilities. For example, standardizing and thus drastically cutting the number of raw materials would make it practical to design preplanned plates. Each plate could be patterned to hold the components of just one machine with minimum skeleton. The cut components could be moved to fabrication just as they were required, virtually eliminating excess inventory, formal stores, and handling. Further, permanent plate cutting patterns could cut "skeleton" waste to the bone (pun intended).

Paradoxically, a value engineering or value analysis program usually expands the number of raw materials if a limited number of standard materials have previously been selected. Those who practice value analysis have often seen that some components are made from material slightly stronger than required, and so have changed the material specifications, expecting the material cost to drop, as well it might. The problem is that this decision added innumerable overhead costs, which are rarely practical to understand and calculate for each component. Suzue and Kohdate discuss the costs[13] but perhaps fail to offer a practical solution. The author believes that most decisions, without too much additional thought,

---

[13]Toshio Suzue and Akira Kohdate, *Variety Reduction Program: A Production Strategy for Product Diversification* (Cambridge, Mass.: Productivity Press, 1990), pp. 29–36.

should be to use the standard materials. This follows from his fervent belief that the huge benefits of standardization make any decision to the contrary nonsensical. The instances in which the lower cost material will be justified will usually be very apparent. The primary reason for changing is that a high volume of material will be required, making the best price break available to the customer. As always, commonsense judgment, supported by practical experience, is the most valuable asset for balancing fast delivery of engineering designs against detail analysis of every design cost impact.

FOCUS ON PROFIT: PARETO ANALYSIS FOR DESIGN IMPROVEMENT

Engineers face a daunting task when they embark on a project to improve even a single product's design. For many companies the universe of products and their components is so big that it would take years to revise every product and each product's components. Therefore, it usually makes sense to have separate subprojects working on commercially available components and material while others are working on entire products. The author previously described an approach based on annual purchases for selecting the items of highest potential payback. However, the ultimate savings come from experience: engineers who have already revised major parts of at least one product (however, using the new "do-it-right-the-first-time" project organization and methodology). A successful pilot experience will lay the groundwork for applying the same methodology to everyday operations. Thus, every subsequent new or changed product has a chance of being designed right the first time.

However, some companies have products that are so extremely large and complex that the cost of completely revising their designs would be too time-consuming. These companies should, instead, select a few items from each of four categories on which to perform analysis and design improvements. Pareto analysis of the four component categories (assemblies, manufactured parts, purchased parts, and raw materials) should be used to select the items of highest savings potential. Exhibit 5–15 shows a useful report form for selecting these items. The report lists the pilot product's components (in a separate report for each category) in descending sequence by annual usage value. Two annual usage figures are used to help in the selection. The first is the usage in only the pilot product. The second is the total usage. Some components might have little usage on the pilot product but much higher usage when considering all other

COMPONENT COST ANALYSIS

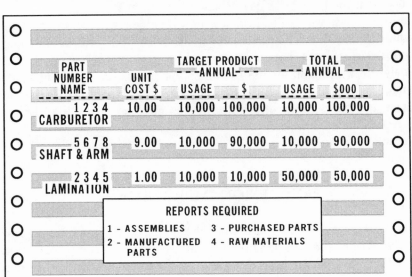

PART NUMBER NAME	UNIT COST $	TARGET PRODUCT ANNUAL USAGE	$	TOTAL ANNUAL USAGE	$000
1 2 3 4 CARBURETOR	10.00	10,000	100,000	10,000	100,000
5 6 7 8 SHAFT & ARM	9.00	10,000	90,000	10,000	90,000
2 3 4 5 LAMINATION	1.00	10,000	10,000	50,000	50,000

REPORTS REQUIRED

1 - ASSEMBLIES   3 - PURCHASED PARTS
2 - MANUFACTURED   4 - RAW MATERIALS
    PARTS

EXHIBIT 5–15

products. In Exhibit 5–15 the first two items on the sample report, the carburetor and the shaft and arm assembly, are used only on the pilot product (as seen by the fact that the target product and total annual usage amounts are the same). However, the third item, the lamination, has $10,000 usage on the pilot product and $50,000 total usage on the pilot and all other products. If the lamination design is improved, the engineer will need to consider not only the pilot product but all other places where it is used. The option to select high value items based on *total* usage enables the engineer to generate the highest possible savings and to avoid reduction of common component usage (standardization).

PRODUCT LINE RATIONALIZATION

Different companies have various product line problems. Some have too many products, others too few, and still others a mixture of both. Although the company that successfully compresses its product line can reap major benefits in reduced operating costs and investment requirements, the real beneficiary should properly be the customer. In truth, the customer does not always benefit from a reduction in the variety of products offered. Product lines must be based on best serving the customer's needs. In the long term, companies should expect their product lines to expand continuously, not only in response to customers' needs and wants but also in response to perceptions (sometimes erroneous) of what the market might want. Rather than permit product lines to grow continuously through all eternity, every company should periodically analyze the line and cut it back. Three examples will help the reader understand the different types of products to which product line compression and diversification are most suitable.

A project to standardize engines at Briggs & Stratton in which the author took part illustrates the first situation. Prior to this project, the company's catalog offered a wide range of options on each major size and type of engine. For example, the customer could specify almost any configuration of crankshaft end. (The crankshaft end is what interfaces with the customer's application. For example, on a power lawnmower the blade is attached to the crankshaft end.) Examples of different ends included threads (in a wide variety of sizes), key slot, cotter pin, and combinations of all of these. When the project team met with several customers' engineers to discuss specifications, they expected to hear what the engineers in fact told them. The engineers, given no criteria to lead them to the most desirable configurations, wound up selecting such design features as crankshaft end more or less at random. Almost all agreed that, given a standard, they could easily adapt their product interface to it. By doing so, they could change their specifications from a custom engine to those of a "stock" (standard) engine. Since the standard engine had high demand, it would be easier to get, even on short notice. Fast, reliable delivery is so important that customers' top managements were usually eager to jump at the chance to change to the standard engine. The important message here is that catering to each customer's wants is not always necessary and may not be the best way to offer fast service. Rather, selling the customer the product that best satisfies his needs and wants is often better. This is of special importance when doing so will both lower the cost and improve the speed of responding to the customer's needs.

The second example, *necessary* product proliferation, is based on heavy duty trucks, which are manufactured for operation in a wide variety of applications and operating conditions. Thus, an important part of the process of ordering and engineering a truck is defining the operating conditions in which the truck will be expected to perform and then selecting the components designed to perform within those parameters. (Three important examples of operating conditions are predominant grade, load weight, and altitude.) The actual variety of conditions and other options that customers need and want is so great that to imagine two identical customer orders is impossible. Therefore, if the bill of material and engineering drawings for a truck were to include *all* components, custom engineering every order would be extremely expensive and take inordinate amounts of time. In addition, controlling the proliferation of component designs would be extremely difficult. When the author worked with Bill Smythe, then Vice President–Engineering at White Truck, the project charter was to develop *modular* bills of material and index systems to match previously engineered modules rapidly with customer truck order specifications. The payoffs included lower engineering costs, better and more standard designs, and faster processing of customer orders into engineered specifications.

The third example cites a case in which product line reduction is most applicable because the number of products had obviously proliferated to the company's detriment. A manufacturer of automatic washers and dryers should logically be able to limit its line of products to only a few basic models, based primarily on size and features. For example, it might have a very small model washer for use in recreational vehicles, a larger one for apartments, a still bigger one for conventional homes, a supersized for the largest families, and a rugged coin-operated machine for do-it-yourself laundries. In each size a company would typically offer both a basic, no-frills model and an all-feature model. Most would agree that this list would encompass almost all conceivable customer *needs* but that different colors and perhaps different styling would be necessary to meet the variety of customer *wants*. In fact, at one time, in an attempt to increase their market share, appliance manufacturers offered a very wide variety of colors selected to match more closely customers' interior decorating schemes. The fad, however, did not last. It proved impractical to stock such large items in many different colors in showrooms or even in local warehouses. In addition, "in style" colors change relatively frequently, leaving an inventory of old colors that are almost impossible to sell. Since washer and dryer products will be inclined to proliferate as new models, options, and combinations of each multiply, it makes sense periodically to pare back the number of products.

Today, few companies have only a single product family. Therefore, if management decides either to rationalize product lines or to improve their design, the starting point will be to prioritize product families in the sequence in which they will be worked. Exhibit 5–16 is a Pareto analysis report for product families (in this case, various horsepower products). The report highlights the material cost of the families since material is the biggest element of total cost and has the biggest savings

PRODUCT SELECTION ANALYSIS

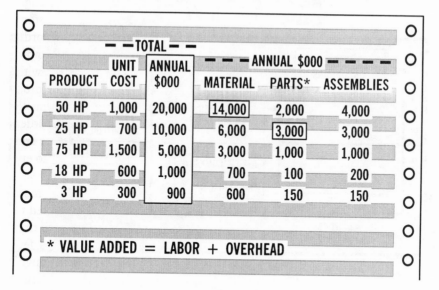

PRODUCT	UNIT COST	TOTAL ANNUAL $000	MATERIAL	PARTS*	ASSEMBLIES
50 HP	1,000	20,000	14,000	2,000	4,000
25 HP	700	10,000	6,000	3,000	3,000
75 HP	1,500	5,000	3,000	1,000	1,000
18 HP	600	1,000	700	100	200
3 HP	300	900	600	150	150

* VALUE ADDED = LABOR + OVERHEAD

EXHIBIT 5-16

potential. Additional cost elements are part and assembly labor. Reporting on the breakdown of cost focuses priorities on reducing those of highest potential. In the exhibit, the 50-horsepower has the highest material and assembly costs, but the 25-horsepower has the highest manufactured component costs. Accordingly, the priorities for improvement might be:

1. 50-horsepower material
2. 50-horsepower assembly
3. 25-horsepower manufactured parts

Having selected the family on which to begin product line rationalization, the company should next analyze which products with which features to offer and, conversely, which to drop. The main steps in product line rationalization are outlined in the planning chart, Exhibit 5-17. (The later section titled "Step-by-Step Approach" shows the relationship of these activities to the entire design improvement project.) Surveying the customer's product expectations is a critically important step in the product rationalization process. After all, the strategy must be to use change to gain sales, not to lose them. Therefore, the marketing and sales organization must know how to channel a customer's orders into products and options that would not necessarily match the customer's past

PRODUCT LINE REVIEW

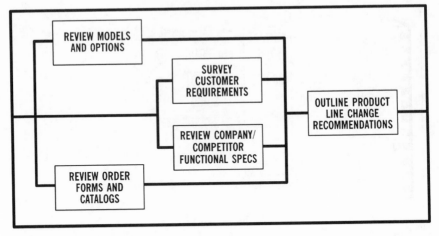

EXHIBIT 5-17

perceptions of what he needed or wanted. To meet the objective of holding or increasing market share, a company must also know which new features and options the customer *must* have.

Part of the process of product line review involves the review of standard order forms (if any) and catalogs. This step, Exhibit 5–17, not only is intended to help the team learn more about the product but also is a vital prerequisite to improving the forms and catalogs as part of the overall project's scope. Further, when designed properly, catalogs and standard order forms can be one or the best and least expensive tools for channeling sales into the products and options the manufacturer *wants to sell.*

Since the history of customers' orders often represents a superb expression of the market's needs and wants, customer surveys are not always necessary. Exhibit 5–18 illustrates a situation where an Easy Ryder automobile model is offered in Basic, Custom, Deluxe, Super Deluxe, and Luxury variations. Further, the Easy Ryder option catalog permits and even encourages the customer to order almost any option for any model variation. In this catalog, the bench seat is identified as standard; thus, the buyer of the luxury variation will need to order the power seat as an exception (option) to the standard, even though almost every luxury buyer prefers the power seat. Because of the additional seat-related options, the variety of possible seat configurations is much larger than is prudent.

VARIATION PROLIFERATION

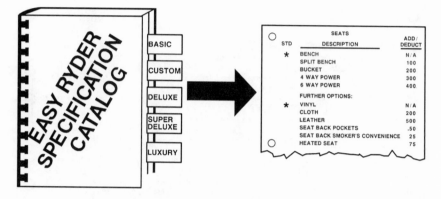

EXHIBIT 5-18

The model/option analysis report, Exhibit 5–19, contains sales histories for the same model variations and options. The matrix format makes it easy to spot customer preferences, and these patterns of preference can be the basis for configuring fewer model variations. For example, based on the great similarities of pattern for Super Deluxe and Luxury, a single offering would appear to meet the majority of customers' wishes. Further, since all customers of these products have always ordered the six-way power seat, that seat should be standard on the new luxury variation. Exhibit 5–20, part of the new standard order form for the Custom and Luxury variations (the Basic, Deluxe, and Super Deluxe have been dropped), indicates that some previous independent options (pockets, seat heater, and smoker's conveniences) have been made part of the standard seats.

The author has found this type of analysis useful in rationalizing product lines for companies with relatively high volume products, such as Briggs & Stratton and Harley-Davidson. However, the same type of analysis has been useful in lower volume, custom-engineered product companies such as White Motors.

FEWER COMPONENTS: IMPROVED COST AND PERFORMANCE

My colleague, Bob Halverson, while Vice President of Manufacturing at Bell & Howell some years ago, spearheaded the design of a new projector.

MODEL/OPTION ANALYSIS

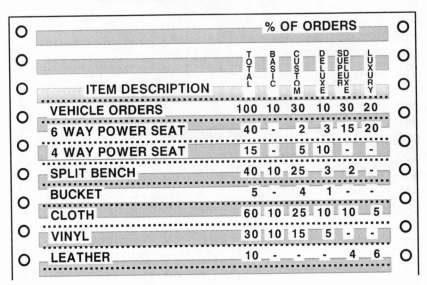

ITEM DESCRIPTION	% OF ORDERS					
	TOTAL	BASIC	CUSTOM	DELUXE	SD UE PL RE XE	LUXURY
VEHICLE ORDERS	100	10	30	10	30	20
6 WAY POWER SEAT	40	-	2	3	15	20
4 WAY POWER SEAT	15	-	5	10	-	-
SPLIT BENCH	40	10	25	3	2	-
BUCKET	5	-	4	1	-	-
CLOTH	60	10	25	10	10	5
VINYL	30	10	15	5	-	-
LEATHER	10	-	-	-	4	6

EXHIBIT 5-19

VARIATION LIMITATION

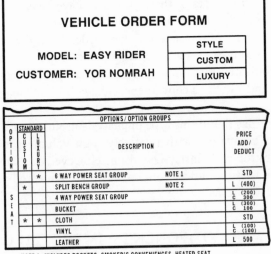

VEHICLE ORDER FORM

MODEL: EASY RIDER

CUSTOMER: YOR NOMRAH

STYLE
CUSTOM
LUXURY

OPTIONS / OPTION GROUPS

OPTION	STANDARD CUSTOM	LUXURY	DESCRIPTION		PRICE ADD/ DEDUCT
SEAT		*	6 WAY POWER SEAT GROUP	NOTE 1	STD
	*		SPLIT BENCH GROUP	NOTE 2	L (400)
			4 WAY POWER SEAT GROUP		L (200) C 300
			BUCKET		L (300) C 100
	*	*	CLOTH		STD
			VINYL		L (100) C (100)
			LEATHER		L 500

NOTE 1 INCLUDES POCKETS, SMOKER'S CONVENIENCES, HEATED SEAT
NOTE 2 INCLUDES POCKETS

EXHIBIT 5-20

A major goal was to reduce the number of components as compared to those found in previous models. Bob believed that this would substantially reduce the projector's costs. One new component, a molded plastic housing, cut the number of metal components used in the previous housing assembly from more than a hundred down to six. This success story is but one of hundreds of similar occurrences in recent years that point out how dramatic the results can be. In each case, management identified component reduction as one of the most important goals for the design team. The radical reduction of components reduces the number of manufacturing operations required (labor), the number of purchases, and the quantity of tools, fixtures, and machines required. It also sharply reduces the frequency of failure in the field and the cost of remedying it, as noted by Hayes, Wheelwright, and Clark.[14] Given improvements of this scope and magnitude, every assembly company should include component reduction as a design team objective. Minimizing the number of a product's components applies not only to assemblers but also to part producers. For example, a Lennox Industries project team at the Columbus, Ohio, plant was able to reduce the number of slit coil widths stocked by more than 55 percent. This improvement, one of many, helped Lennox double the output of its factory while reducing the number of required people.

DESIGN FOR MANUFACTURABILITY

Whenever the author looks at a product or component that costs more to manufacture than it should, he expects to find (and usually does) that the greatest opportunities for reducing its cost (and increasing its quality) lie in the possibility of changing its design. Although there are also major opportunities for improving manufacturing methods, machines, and tools, product design changes will produce improvements of much greater magnitude. Bralla has had the same experience. He says that "the most significant manufacturing-cost reductions and cost avoidances are those that result from changes in product design rather than changes in manufacturing methods or systems."[15] Therefore, the best product strategy is to design manufacturable products right from the start. This is easy to say but harder to do.

[14]Robert H. Hayes, Steven C. Wheelwright, and Kim B. Clark, *Dynamic Manufacturing: Creating the Learning Organization* (New York: Free Press, 1988), p. 174.
[15]James G. Bralla, ed., *Handbook of Product Design for Manufacturing: A Practical Guide to Low Cost Production* (New York: McGraw-Hill, 1986), p. xiii.

When a designer systematically pursues two broad design objectives, he achieves manufacturable designs. The first objective is to know the best applicable machines, tooling, processes, and assembly methods, and to design products and components to optimize the efficiency of the ideal process. The designer's second objective must be to use materials and design or select existing components that lend themselves to low cost, high quality production.

Separation and specialization of design and manufacturing engineers is one reason why product designs are so frequently far from ideally manufacturable. After all, if the design engineer has only scant knowledge of factory operations, he cannot be expected to produce designs ideally suited to the factory's capabilities. The best way a company can work itself out of this dilemma is to combine product and process engineering and to start designing manufacturability into the initial drawings and specifications. Eventually, the engineering workload stemming from original design errors will be sharply reduced. In the interim, maintenance (error correction) engineering change procedures can be streamlined to enable engineers to process more of these types of changes without hiring more engineers.

The cross-trained engineers in the new combined engineering organization will solve most of the manufacturability problem in the long term. However, even when the engineer is cross-trained, he will need to use a manufacturability checklist to ensure adequate attention to the most important factors. Following is a brief list of some of these factors.

1. General purpose machines. Items designed should not require unique or seldom-used machines. Cell design is much more difficult when a few items require operations by seldom-used machines. Use of special purpose machines should be limited to items of very high usage volume.

2. Machine and tooling tolerances. Machines and tooling have very specific capabilities in terms of the best tolerances they can achieve. Different types of machines can do the same type of work but with big differences in precision. The machining cost per unit produced is always higher when the machine precision is higher. As Bandyopadhyay recently pointed out, "Unnecessary burden on production processes for precision can increase the production cost significantly."[16]

[16]Jayanta K. Bandyopadhyay, "Product Design to Facilitate JIT Production," *Production and Inventory Management Journal* (American Production and Inventory Control Society), Fourth Quarter, 1990.

3. Material workability. Some materials are more difficult to work with than other similar materials. If a more workable alternative material is a satisfactory replacement, it should be used.

4. Assembly stack and direction. The best assembly design is one that permits components to be added one on top of (following) another. When one component must be inserted between or behind another, it adds cost to the process. If assemblies are designed so that parts can all be assembled from a single side, costs will be held down. (Trucks points out that assemblies must be designed for the assembly method to exploit best either manual or automated methods.)[17]

5. Stretch life-use estimates. Tooling design and type of process are radically different for very low volume and high volume items. Tooling designed for low volume production condemns the company owning it to the role of low volume producer. More aggressive companies can increase market share by underpricing competitors too timid to make or buy tooling suitable for higher volume production. The lower costs of the producer with superior tooling will almost automatically win additional market share.

The author has never been in a factory where people on the shop floor were not aware of innumerable manufactured components that could be more economically produced if design engineers would only agree to modify a design or loosen a tolerance. All too often the responsible engineer just does not have the time to investigate the possibility of change, since he always has a backlog of high priority work.

An engineering change involving two Harley-Davidson crankshafts is an excellent example of how to improve producibility. Exhibit 5–21 shows the crankshafts before and after an engineering change. An oil access hole in the two shafts had always been drilled at two different angles relative to a line perpendicular to the shafts' centerlines. This simply resulted from two different engineers independently designing the shafts for use in two different models. In the exhibit, the angles before engineering change were zero and 15 degrees. The engineering change, requested and approved, made the angle of both shafts zero degrees.

Prior to the change, the two different shafts had required two different fixtures, Exhibit 5–22. The changeover of fixtures from one crankshaft

[17]H. E. Trucks, *Designing for Economical Production* (Dearborn, Mich.: Society of Manufacturing Engineers, 1987), p. 313.

SHAFT DESIGN CHANGE

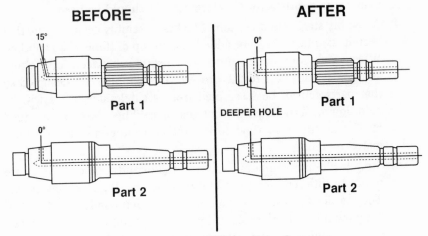

BEFORE   **AFTER**

15°   0°

Part 1   DEEPER HOLE   **Part 1**

0°

Part 2   **Part 2**

Courtesy of Harley - Davidson Motor Company

EXHIBIT 5-21

DESIGN CHANGE: GEARSHAFT FIXTURES - BEFORE

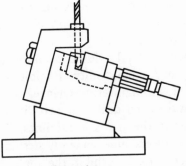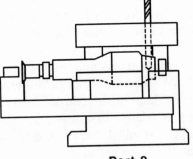

Part 1   **Part 2**

114 Minutes

Courtesy of Harley - Davidson Motor Company

EXHIBIT 5-22

to the other required 114 minutes; thus, the lot sizes and inventories of crankshafts were excessive. Once the engineering change was approved, modifying one of the fixtures (as shown in Exhibit 5–23) to accommodate both parts was a relatively easy matter. The changeover time was consequently reduced from 114 to twelve minutes.

Since the design team is responsible for both product and process design, it must also work on the simplification of the process. Carelessness in designing products can make them more difficult to produce, especially if the product design is more complex than it could be. It is always possible to find high cost methods of solving product design problems. For example, cooling components heated by tempering operations and welding could be done by running a conveyor line through a refrigerated tunnel or a cold bath. Much simpler, low cost alternatives, however, are easy to find. Following is an example of one practical application of a cooling improvement.

COOLING PROCESS IMPROVEMENT

Many project teams have encountered situations in which items being produced cannot flow directly from one operation to another because they require cooling between operations. In some instances, the cooling

DESIGN CHANGE: GEARSHAFT
COMMON FIXTURE - AFTER

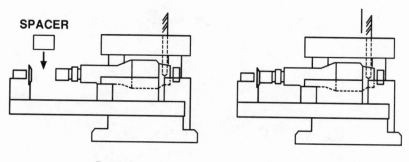

SPACER

Part 1   Part 2

12 Minutes

Courtesy of Harley - Davidson Motor Company

EXHIBIT 5-23

process between the operations injects extra time and considerable inventory investment into the process. In addition, the cooling process often precludes using a single person to perform the operations before *and* after cooling, and therefore doubles the labor cost. In one cooling example, from the Allison Transmission Division of General Motors in Indianapolis, Indiana, torque converter pump bodies were stacked for cooling after welding a metal shroud to the aluminum pump body casting. Before improvement, the hot bodies, expanded as a result of the heat generated by welding, were placed in stacks on a 25-foot conveyor between the welding operation and the next operation, boring and turning (Exhibit 5–24). The long conveyor was presumed to be necessary to provide enough time for the expanded body to return to its original dimensions, which prevented distortion of machined dimensions at the next operation. Because of the large mass created by stacking, the cooling time was much longer than necessary. On average, the project team found 240 bodies (eight hours of production) on the conveyor. The long conveyor separating the two operations made it impossible to foster teamwork between the two workers, and the eight hours of cooling time made fast response to schedule changes impractical.

By using a new open-sided cooling rack, Exhibit 5–25, and placing welded bodies on wire shelves, the project team helped the operators reduce the cooling time to one hour. The smaller new rack permits air to circulate around the bodies. The new mass to be cooled is only one

PUMP COOLING - BEFORE

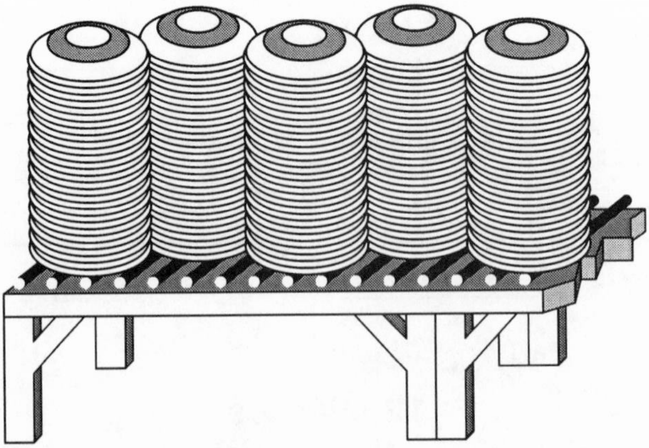

Courtesy of General Motors: Allison Transmission Division

EXHIBIT 5–24

PUMP COOLING - AFTER

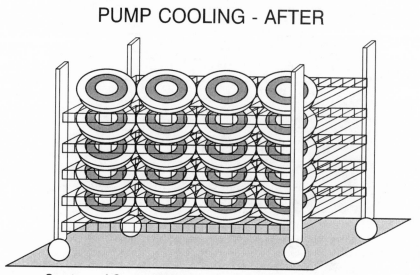

Courtesy of General Motors: Allison Transmission Division

EXHIBIT 5-25

body. The rack also brings the two operations into proximity, about 5 feet apart. The two operators now function as a team and have reduced the average quantity of bodies between their operations to twenty-eight pieces, a reduction of work-in-process (in these operations) of almost 90 percent!

MATERIAL COST CONSERVATION

At all levels in the manufacturing pipeline, starting with converters of basic raw materials and ending at the factories of finished product customers, purchases average up to 70 percent of the manufacturing cost. Therefore, conservation of material use is of vital importance in the global race to become low cost producers. Material usage conservation can be achieved in three ways: (1) improving process yield, (2) reducing material used in the product, and (3) using alternative, lower cost materials.

The end product in Exhibit 5-26 could be produced in one of two ways. One way would be to turn it on a lathe, the second to forge it to approximate shape and size, then finish machine it to its final, precise dimensions. The top figure in Exhibit 5-26 shows that when the part is produced from a rod, the lathe removes roughly one-half of the original

TURN VERSUS FORGE

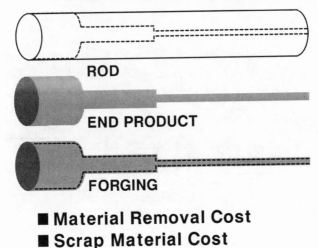

ROD

END PRODUCT

FORGING

- ■ **Material Removal Cost**
- ■ **Scrap Material Cost**

EXHIBIT 5-26

material. Although the chips created by the lathe can be sold to a scrap dealer, the material loses up to 90 percent of its value when it is converted from rod to chips. The forged product, being much closer to the size and shape of the finished product, requires much less turning and produces a negligible amount of chips. The material cost of producing a rod in the turning operation is nearly twice that of forging. Several other considerations go into the decision to turn or to forge, including the strength and hardness of the resulting product and tooling and energy costs. In this specific example, however, the difference in material cost is most likely to have the biggest impact on the decision.

Several processes have always been designed to use less than 100 percent of the material fed into the process. For example, cast and molded parts, made of both metal and plastic, are usually produced with more material than the part itself needs, because the process requires gates and risers. Plastic gates and risers can usually be snapped off immediately, reground, and reused. Few manufacturing managers recognize gates and risers as yield loss. Rather, they tend to accept them as inevitable and sometimes state specifically that no loss has occurred because the material can be reused. But, for that very reason, most gates and risers are much larger than necessary. Paying closer attention to using the minimum amount of material for gates and risers can substantially reduce the energy cost that goes into the melting and remelting processes and can even reduce evaporation losses.

The easiest way to design cast and molded parts is to use much more material than needed so that calculations of the part's strength become unnecessary. Because this is the easiest way, it is no surprise that it is also the practice of most engineers. Therefore, most companies stand to make major material cost gains by doing a better job of designing parts that minimize the material used. Stampings and parts cut from plate stock also have great savings potential, for the same reasons. Typically, the standards used to determine the minimum skeleton wall size are very liberal, providing enough material to cover the worst contingency. In many cases, improving machine and tool control to narrow the range of skeleton wall thickness variation will reduce the amount of material required. In other cases, long experience with specific part types has shown that the standards for their skeletons can easily be reduced, since the thinnest part of the skeleton is often at least twice as wide as necessary.

STEP-BY-STEP APPROACH

A planning chart is a road map that guides the improvement project team through a time-tested, established route to simpler, better, lower cost product designs. The author's prior book included a chapter on the step-by-step approach used for designing improved processes.[18] Therefore, he will not discuss process improvement planning charts here. However, the best method by which to improve product design is to work simultaneously on both product and process designs. The schematic in Exhibit 5–27 depicts the combination of planning charts for product and process into a single, unified effort. The construction of separate methodologies for each not only makes the charts useful for the ideal, combined project but also supports specialized projects where the scope is primarily limited to one of the two areas.

The typical combined project team is often best subdivided into smaller, focused specialty teams, as illustrated in Exhibit 5–28. The process side of the product and process project, by itself, is a major undertaking, so most projects teams should have a separate, focused group dedicated to process improvement. Later, after team members are cross-trained in both product and process disciplines, the goal should be to work on both aspects simultaneously. In Exhibit 5–28, the purchase team works on purchases, in the sequence of each item's annual budget (purchased materials and commercially available items), as previously dis-

[18]See Appendix 2.

PRODUCT/PROCESS METHODOLOGY

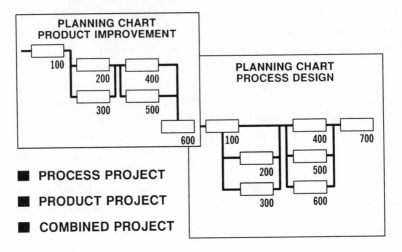

EXHIBIT 5-27

TYPICAL PROJECT ORGANIZATION

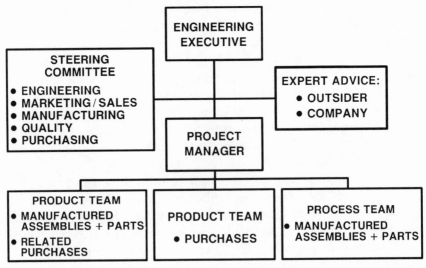

EXHIBIT 5-28

cussed. The purchase team works with purchases that are often common to several different products and product lines. This approach achieves improvements more rapidly than the third focused team that works on manufactured parts and assemblies, one product or product line at a time. This typical project organization chart does not include a subproject to rationalize the product line, although some projects should include such an objective in their scope. When that is desirable, another dedicated team would focus on that effort.

The engineering executive in Exhibit 5–28 is charged with the responsibility for the project's success. In companies that still have separate design and manufacturing engineering organizations, a combined team may not be practical. In these cases two project teams, each spending substantial time coordinating its work with that of the other, is usually needed. Although this alternative is a compromise, it may be the only expedient way to guarantee progress until the engineering organizations are carefully prepared for merger. The detail product improvement methodology is, by itself, so extensive that it requires several documentation binders. However, the following brief excerpts provide some valuable insight into a methodical, step-by-step, uniform approach to achieving superior product and process engineering status.

The highlights of the planning chart for the first phase of product design improvement, Exhibit 5–29, are as follows:

1. Selection of the product and components on which to work. The usual objective is to focus on items expected to have the highest, quickest payback.

DESIGN FOR MANUFACTURABILITY

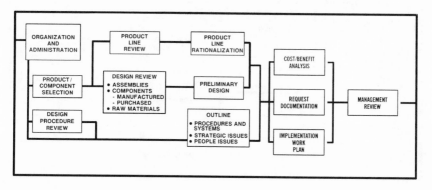

EXHIBIT 5–29

2. A separate, parallel activity to rationalize the produce line. Some companies will come to an early conclusion that they do not need to be concerned with rationalizing the line and thus can forgo these activities. Others will deem it to be of overriding importance and will structure their projects for product line rationalization and forgo design improvement activities.

3. The design improvement activities, review and design. These will be explained later. They are the main focus of most projects.

4. The review and design of engineering procedures. This is a third, parallel activity usually included in the scope of product design improvement projects. But it can also be the main thrust of a project to streamline the routine flow through engineering.

5. Request documentation preparation. This step uses the company's own engineering change and release paperwork, systems, and procedures to document and drive the implementation of improvements developed in this phase of the project.

The design review activity, like all activities on Exhibit 5–29, is supported by its own planning charts. Separate but similar design review charts exist for manufactured assemblies and components and purchased components and raw materials. Following are some of the highlights of the manufactured component review chart, Exhibit 5–30.

MANUFACTURED ASSEMBLY REVIEW

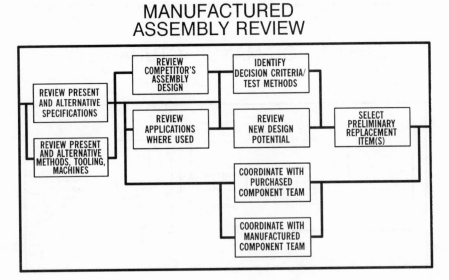

EXHIBIT 5-30

1. The review of process alternatives may mean coordination with another subproject team. Optimally, it would be a function of the person responsible for product design improvement.

2. Reviewing competitors' designs helps to ensure that new, improved designs will be neither inferior to those of the competitors nor reinvention of the wheel. The resulting design must be better than that of competitors to become or to remain the superior manufacturer. Schonberger's case example of the small, average supplier (disguised as Toyonda Company)[19] shows the importance of "tear down labs" even in small, simple businesses.

3. An improved design must fit and function not only in the product on which the design project is focusing. It must also fit and function in every other product in which it is a component. Therefore, all other applications must be reviewed to maintain design standardization.

4. Many proposed design changes cannot be accepted until they are tested and proved. The engineer working on the design needs to know if approval depends on testing. If so, he needs to plan and execute the required test.

5. Where there are separate subproject teams coincidentally working on the same purchased and manufactured components, coordination of efforts must be routine and efficient.

Paperwork (including the electronic variety) can become a bureaucratic nightmare in every methodology, including product design. Technicians always seem to create mountains of paperwork, thus bringing the appearance and fact of methodology to their ideas for accomplishing complex tasks. Just how voluminous the paperwork mountain can become is illustrated in King's book. It contains a complete set of documents for use in product design (all documentation illustrations use a pencil as the product illustrated—King encourages readers to use only those documents that help with their real problem.)[20] No amount of paperwork can substitute for testing prototypes and the first products made with production tooling. Testing the actual hardware and electronics is one of the easiest ways to determine if they function and perform as intended. Therefore, such testing is a key step in product design methodology.

---

[19]Richard J. Schonberger, *World Class Manufacturing Casebook: Implementing JIT and TQC* (New York: Free Press, 1987), p. 52.
[20]Bob King. *Better Designs in Half the Time: Quality Function Deployment in America* (Methuen, Mass.: GOAL/QPC, 1989).

SUMMARY

Improving product designs while lowering costs is the next frontier for many companies. Engineers know all too well that management pressure is forcing them to churn out new products at a rate too fast to do the job right the first time. However, engineers also produce less than ideal designs because they lack the necessary process knowledge. In addition, releasing inferior designs to production results in a flood of redesign effort after the new product goes into pilot or mass production using production tooling and equipment for the first time. Paradoxically, engineers will find additional time to do the job right by starting to do so for new products. Fixing problems after products are in production takes more of the engineer's time than doing it before release. Further, the cumbersome flow and methods of product design reduce the engineer's efficiency. Improvements in this area will also contribute to increasing the amount of time engineers can spend on design.

The improved efficiency and quality of design, the new, focused engineering organization, and streamlining of parallel design activities all combine to enable leading-edge companies to achieve unprecedented speed in designing new and improved products. This will permit them to put these superior products into their customers' hands weeks or even months earlier than competitors who have failed to recognize the competitive advantage of drastic improvement in methods for speeding designs to market. The potential for improvement is enormous, but full realization will require a radical departure from past practices. Progressive enterprises must accelerate progress just to stay abreast of the world's superior manufacturers.

6

□□□

Quality Engineering:
Replacement for Quality Control

QUALITY IS NOT JOB ONE! To thousands of executives who have heard myriad presentations on quality, this may sound like heresy. Nevertheless, it is true. For example, innumerable companies are mystified by overemphasis on quality, because their customers are thoroughly content with the appearance, performance, and reliability of their products. Further, their products are produced with insignificant amounts of quality control, scrap, and rework costs, or customer returns and warranty claims. Notable examples of these types of factories are food processors, chemical product manufacturers, and a host of companies producing mundane high volume, low cost products such as staples, pencils, matches, nails, and so on.

However, for every company without materially important quality problems or opportunities, hundreds of others have opportunities to reduce manufacturing costs substantially, increase market share, or both through quality improvements. Should quality be job one for them? The answer is still a resounding *no!* Process design, not quality, should be job one. Why? Operation improvements to increase productivity are almost always of greater importance than quality control improvements. Further, *improved quality is an automatic byproduct of superior process improvement.* A. F. Giacco, Chief Executive Officer of Hercules Incorpo-

rated has declared, "Productivity and quality are inseparable concepts."[1]
It is an incontestable fact that manufacturing operations can be designed
either to produce perfect dimensional and functional quality or to detect
automatically and instantly when a defective item is produced[2]—and then
either to adjust the operation automatically or stop the machine. Alter-
nately, the defective part might be mechanically ejected from the process
while the process continues. Notice that this statement is made with respect to the quality of the item's dimensional and functional properties.
Some other aspects of quality that are less readily machine-detectable
include aesthetic qualities, perceptions, durability, reliability, serviceabil-
ity, and conformance to specifications.

Creating and maintaining a separate organization of quality specialists
has proved to be an ineffective way to improve quality, although it has
served to cull out defects. Real improvement must put the required tools,
machines, and organization into the hands of the person responsible for
production. In the future, the need for quality specialists will be limited
to quality engineers, and quality engineering skills will be only one of
the roles of the new multifunctional engineer. However, even in Japan,
as evidenced in Shiguru Mizuno's explanation of quality engineering,
some academicians are continuing to encourage an unnatural separation
of the two engineering specialties responsible for quality measurement
and process design,[3] the latter of which ultimately determines the quality
level achieved. In the future, the design, process, and quality engineering
functions must be interchangeable parts of a single engineer's job if a
company ever expects to design products to make the best use of the
factory's machine and process capabilities for producing perfect quality.
Therefore, the most progressive companies must start cross-training engineers in all three disciplines (process, product, and quality engineering)
and developing the new multifunctional engineering organization.

CHECKLIST: QUALITY IMPROVEMENT ZINGERS

Until quality has reached the parts-per-million level, survival depends
on programs for continuous improvement. Here is a summary list of

[1]John G. Belcher, Jr., *Productivity Plus: How Today's Best Run Companies Are Gaining
the Competitive Edge* (Houston: Gulf Publishing, 1987), pp. 146–47.
[2]Robert N. Stauffer, "In-Process Gaging for Real Time Quality Control," *Manufacturing
Engineering* (Society of Manufacturing Engineers, Dearborn, Mich.), April 1990, pp. 40–
43.
[3]Shiguru, Mizuno. *Company-Wide Total Quality Control* (Tokyo: Asian Productivity Organization, 1984), pp. 134–37.

several key methods for improving quality while reducing quality control costs:

1. Rank the various aspects of quality by their importance to the success of the enterprise and the seriousness of the quality problem. The fast, formal evaluation will be used to focus projects on the best opportunities for high and fast payback.

2. Reorganize engineering skills so that engineers can interchangeably produce the product and process designs necessary to achieve perfect quality. As an interim step, quality engineering should be established as a function responsible for building quality guarantees into product and process designs before releasing them to production.

3. Move successive operations into closer proximity to facilitate instant verbal communication of quality problems between them. This will speed up and simplify feedback and eliminate bundles of quality paperwork.

4. Cross-train production, test, and repair people and make them all members of a common team. Production operators will be able to control quality in production better by virtue of their broadened horizons. At the same time, test and repair personnel can bring their knowledge of past problems to bear on the causing operations, thus accelerating the implementation of improvements in tooling and methods.

5. Cut back and/or discontinue inspection of items that are seldom, if ever, produced with defects. This would include items with superb quality histories and items that have no critical quality criteria.

6. Establish an almost permanent, full-time team to design quality improvement solutions. Establish the team's priorities based on Pareto analysis of the processes that produce the most defects and/or have the lowest yield.

7. Aggressively eliminate operator and inspector measuring, gauging, and visual inspection and replace them with free and low cost inspection at the subsequent operation.

8. Set aggressive goals for improvement (higher than deemed feasible) and challenge the full-time team to exceed the targets.

9. Involve people in the improvement process. If the company can afford small group activities (quality circles) and if the company culture is right, use this technique in addition to one or more full-time teams.

10. Establish a full-time team to work on vendor improvement activities and have them develop a program for working with vendors to improve their tools, machines, layout, and methods with the goal of eventually eliminating all manual inspection.

11. Move all responsibility for inspection and test back in the network, to the vendor. Use a single, agreed-upon inspection and test procedure. This eliminates the conflicts that arise when supplier and customer each develop valid but different inspection and test procedures and equipment with two different sets of quality readings.

12. Change the product design wherever tolerances are unreasonably tighter than required. Unnecessarily tight tolerances complicate the flow of production, adding to product costs. If tight tolerances are necessary, go to work on improving machine and tool capabilities.

13. Formally and permanently differentiate between those specifications critical to customer expectations and product performance and those where minor deviation will not cause customer dissatisfaction or failure to function.

14. Use charts sparingly—only as problem analysis tools for specific difficult problems, never as permanent control tools.

TOTAL QUALITY CONTROL: THEORY OR PRACTICE?

At a recent national conference on quality and productivity in Colombia, I was preceded on the program by several speakers whose presentations extolled the benefits of total quality control (TQC). When my turn came, I began by telling the audience of seven hundred chief executive officers and presidents that the single most important thing they could do when they went back to their companies would be to forget what they had heard about total quality control! I then explained this radical, tongue-in-cheek shocker as follows. First, every preceding speaker had painted grandiose pictures of the total integration of the quality function throughout the entire company. Schematic diagrams depicting the interrelationships between the various functions defied mere mortals to understand their completely integrated but mind-boggling, complex splendor. My point was that we need simplicity in everything we undertake. An executive returning from the conference will not want to tackle a program of companywide quality awareness and integration. He might worry about whether or not he would still be around to enjoy the fruits of significantly improved quality and productivity since it might just take too long. What he wants from a conference is a few new ideas about how immediately to identify and go to work on a limited number of improvements that will have fast and impressive payback. Once he has seen his organization achieve those improvements, he will be ready to launch the next few projects of highest priority and payback for the company.

Total companywide awareness and participation in quality improvement is not unimportant, but the knowledge needs and the potential contributions of different functions vary within the company; relatively few specific quality improvement and control methods apply across every function. For example, statistical quality control techniques do not have much relevance to the routine operations of the marketing and sales organizations. In fact, the greatest proportion of the body of knowledge that exists today is focused on improving the quality of manufactured items. Far less published knowledge exists concerning how to design quality into the product, although this is the area that would be of greatest benefit to the largest number of companies. People in engineering will continue to design the product, either successfully or unsuccessfully designing quality into it. Although people in other functional areas will occasionally have worthy product improvement ideas, they will not work full-time on product design. Only the full-time design engineer can be expected to have the time necessary to design near-perfect quality into the product.

The quality improvement roles of marketing and sales people should revolve around learning the customer's perceptions of his quality requirements and of their own companies' performance in meeting the customers' expectations. Engineering and manufacturing people will seldom, if ever, play this same role and thus have little need to learn the details of marketing and sales quality procedures and systems.

In summary, it is best to think of total quality control as a slogan rather than a technique or collection of techniques. Ishikawa defines it as involving everyone in every division (department or function) in studying, practicing, and participating in quality control. The only unique, method-related feature of his total quality control is the use of a cross-functional committee that directs the organization to the areas requiring improvement.[4] The management-by-committee approach should probably be considered suspect since it conflicts directly with the concept of giving every manager complete authority and responsibility for the successful operation of his focused business.

[4]Kaoru Ishikawa, *What Is Total Quality Control? The Japanese Way* (Englewood Cliffs, N.J.: Prentice-Hall, 1985), p. 91.

Philosophy? Yes. Theory? No. The loose collection of thoughts on the subject of total quality control do not form a coherent theory. Practice? No. The meaning of total quality control is so vague that to evaluate what exactly would be required to qualify as practicing it is neither practical nor possible.

RUSH TO MARKET: DEFECTIVE DESIGN

Rushing to market with defective, untested, and unproven product designs is one of the common reasons for "quality problems." Aerospace and electronic manufacturers are notably guilty of creating and releasing designs to production that should really be considered experimental rather than production-ready. (Not that automobile manufacturers, machine tool producers, and others are not also culpable. They are.) The military tends to be in the forefront of those demanding more than what is reasonably achievable—the development and production of weapon systems and support equipment with performance specifications far in advance of state-of-the-art technology. These manufacturers and their customers are shooting themselves in the foot by deluding themselves that it is reasonable to put experimental designs into production. After the start of production, the inevitable and repeatedly seen result is a flood of (1) engineering changes and (2) changes to changes to fix design flaws that make the product inoperable, unsafe, and inferior in performance. These design changes often go down to the level of raw material and purchased components, making entire warehouses of these items obsolete. Worse, untold millions of hours are spent reworking products in various production stages to comply with emergency changes. The epidemic rate of recall and retrofitting of products in the field is even more serious. The end result can be disastrous, sometimes culminating in loss of life as in the case of aircraft, space vehicle, and even automobile crashes.

As a first step in bringing order to this realm of chaos, what is needed is a hard-nosed appraisal of each design purported to be ready for production. When a company's operating officers repeatedly refuse to face reality, it behooves the board of directors to get in touch with the problem and demand improvement. Independent outsider appraisal will be invaluable in these cases. In the long term, slashing the time it takes to design, test, redesign, retest, and run pilot production is the best solution to the problem. Better methods and organization are proven ways to reduce the lead time to market by as much as 90 percent.

In summary, defective design costs and problems are all too often mistakenly viewed as poor quality issues. A forceful management can easily rectify these self-inflicted injuries with product design changes. Careful attention must be paid to separating easily addressed design improvement opportunities from factory quality betterment opportunities that often require widespread tooling and methods changes and even new machines.

FAIL-SAFE PROCESS DESIGN

The advent of increasingly accurate, low cost, computer-controlled measuring devices such as linear variable differential transformers has made it increasingly feasible to install these devices in machines to achieve control of the process quality through automated and instantaneous inspection. The Society of Manufacturing Engineers' handbook contains a simple, effective example of such a device that is used to control the grinding of the diameter of a workpiece.[5] These types of devices are especially suited to such conventional machines as grinders, lathes, mills, and broaches, to name a few. They are even more valuable when used on transfer lines and computer-controlled machine centers because of their high cost and long cycle times. The complexity and long cycle times of these equipment types make it probable that production delays will occur when defective production causes shortages. Together, shortages and production delays raise product costs to levels at which market share may be lost. A better direction in the battle to become the superior manufacturer is to get rolling on the design of low cost modifications to thousands of existing machines of various ages and in different stages of disrepair. Considering the benefits of such changes, progress has been distressingly slow. Incidentally, the benefits are not limited to improved quality control alone. For example, the same devices can also serve to reduce the time and cost of changing over (setting up) from one job to another. On the bright side, lack of progress to date means that superior manufacturers can still capitalize on gigantic improvement opportunities.

For every off-the-shelf device for controlling the quality of a process, an almost infinite variety of simple, new custom devices are waiting to be invented. One such device was used to improve the productivity of the gear blank lathe operation illustrated in Exhibit 6-1. Prior to im-

[5]Charles Wick, editor-in-chief, *Tool and Manufacturing Engineers Handbook, Vol. 3,* (Dearborn, Mich. Society of Manufacturing Engineers, 1987), Chapter 3.

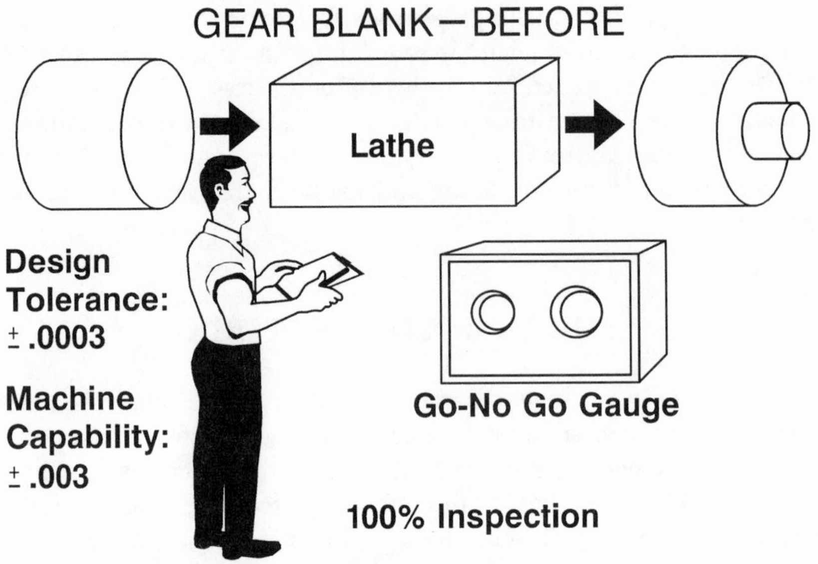

GEAR BLANK—BEFORE

Lathe

Design Tolerance: ±.0003

Machine Capability: ±.003

Go-No Go Gauge

100% Inspection

EXHIBIT 6–1

provement, the lathe operator was tied to a single machine, since it was deemed necessary for him to check every single gear blank using a go/no-go gauge. Given the machine's long cycle time, the operator had more than enough time to gauge each part but not enough time to operate more than one machine simultaneously. Because the design tolerance (±.0003mm) was tighter than the machine capability (±.003mm), 100 percent gauging was necessary. One might wonder why design engineers are allowed to produce specifications that are incongruous with the capabilities of the factory's machines. Perhaps it is because of the ivory tower syndrome; engineers are often too remote from the factory to be familiar with the its machines and their capabilities. If the machine capability were equal to or better than that required by the design tolerance, and if the process were perfectly controlled, no inspection would be required. Exhibit 6–2 demonstrates how a simple, low cost exit slide can inspect every gear blank and eject the defective ones. Pulled by gravity, every finished blank rolls down the chute on a rail to the point where two stops impede movement if the blank is too large or too small. If a gear blank comes in contact with either the upper or lower stop, the stop activates a rejection mechanism that causes the blank to drop out of the process. In the factory where this device was used, the stops performed 100 percent inspection at zero payroll cost. This freed the operator to tend several

GEAR BLANK—AFTER

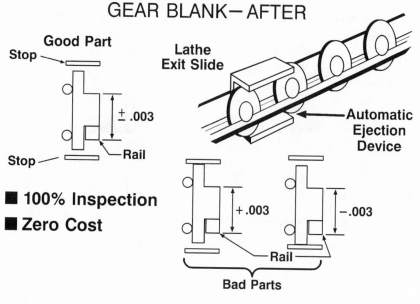

Good Part

Stop

Lathe
Exit Slide

± .003

Rail

Stop

Automatic
Ejection
Device

■ **100% Inspection**
■ **Zero Cost**

+.003

−.003

Rail

Bad Parts

EXHIBIT 6–2

similarly equipped machines at the same time. It did not eliminate defects requiring rework or scrapping, but it detected them automatically.

The Japanese have documented hundreds of similar examples involving manufacturers of a diverse variety of products and processes.[6] Encouragingly, factories outside Japan are producing an ever increasing number of their own fail-safe quality improvement examples. One such example, from an automotive project, involved the design of fixtures for two operations used in the production of a ball joint assembly. The two operations, pressing a rubber sleeve onto the ball joint stud and pressing the ball and sleeve into a liner, were both subject to quality problems. In high speed, high volume operations it was possible inadvertently to press the rubber sleeve on backward or to miss it altogether. Further, units with missing or backward sleeves could sometimes be pressed into the liner, compounding the quality defect. Although such occurrences were rare and were detected later in the process, when they did occur, they often caused costly production disruptions. Exhibit 6–3 shows what would happen if the sleeve were to be inserted backward. In the cylinder of the fixture used to press the stud into the sleeve, a stop made it impossible to complete the press operation. In addition, the inside diameter of

[6]NKS/Factory Magazine, ed., introduction by Shigeo Shingo, *Poka-Yoke: Improving Product Quality by Preventing Defects* (Cambridge, Mass.: Productivity Press, 1988).

FAIL-SAFE SLEEVE INSTALLATION

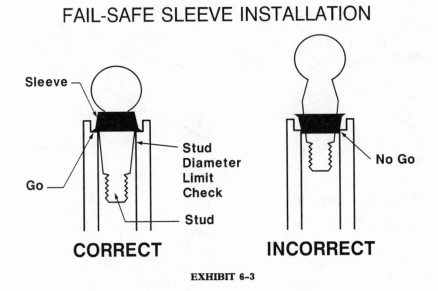

EXHIBIT 6-3

the cylinder used to hold the sleeve was equal to the maximum permissible stud diameter. Thus, if any stud were oversized, it would not be possible to insert it and complete the press operation. The new fixture for pressing the ball end of the stud into the liner, Exhibit 6-4, uses a stop to limit the travel of the handle. When the sleeve is missing, the stop prevents the ball from being pressed into the liner.

FAIL-SAFE STUD INSERTION

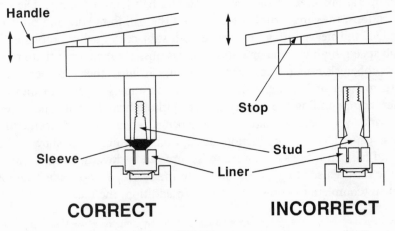

EXHIBIT 6-4

Another example of failsafe quality control techniques, taken from the Utilimaster Corporation of Waukarusa, Indiana, is based on color coding. Utilimaster has color-coded the torque guns dedicated to tightening specific components and the corresponding part trays used in assembly, as illustrated in Exhibit 6-5. Switching quality control from inspection-orientation to control by tools has simplified process quality control for Utilimaster. It no longer needs to inspect each unit produced to determine if fasteners are tightened to the proper torque. By calibrating guns and adjusting the torque settings daily, the company ensures perfect control of fastener tightening quality.

Low cost fail-safe devices are not only applicable to machining and simple assembly operations but also to long, complex assembly lines. The Holiday Rambler Corporation in Wakarusa, Indiana, provided one such example of color coding for quality control and productivity on a complex assembly. Exhibit 6-6 illustrates one technique that precludes assembly errors while increasing productivity and reducing inventory investment. Holiday's new cart on wheels organizes all of the metal structural components for one recreational vehicle floor assembly into a transport vehicle that can carry the components from the chop saw to the floor welding operation. Since each vehicle model requires a different set of components, the face plate of the cart is color-coded, with a different color for each model. Each "slot" of the cart is coded with the letter of

DEDICATED TORQUE GUNS

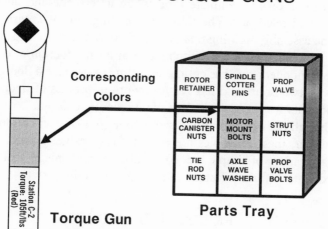

Courtesy of Utilimaster Corporation

EXHIBIT 6-5

QUALITY CONTROL BY COLOR

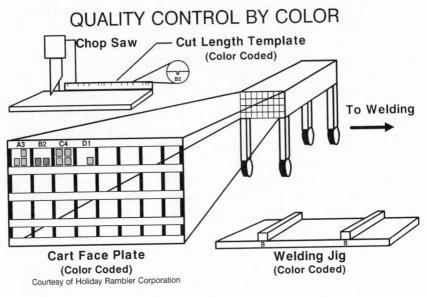

Courtesy of Holiday Rambler Corporation

EXHIBIT 6-6

the component that should be cut and placed there, and a number to indicate how many pieces are required per vehicle. The cart is used like a kanban card. It authorizes production of a *set* of components every time a cart is emptied at the assembly line and returned to the chop saw. The cut length template used to control cutting to the precise length required (fail-safe quality) is also color-coded with the matching color, and the length mark on the template repeats the letter code and quantity code from the wheeled cart. The color/letter coding scheme is carried forward into the assembly/welding operation, where the fixtures and jigs are also the same color and code. Switching from lot production of components to the component cart has cut the lead time to produce a floor from three weeks to two hours and has reduced work-in-process of floors and their components from the equivalent of 117 floors to seven.

Although the exact solution used by one company will seldom, if ever, fit another, these examples are of significant value to help understand the vast variety of simple low cost, fail-safe mechanisms that can be invented to transform a factory into defect-per-million status.

FREEZE THE PROCESS

Supervisors and foremen have always loved long production runs. Although costly in terms of increasing inventory investment, a job that is set up and run as long as possible requires fewer changeovers and involves much less work and bother for the supervisor. Further, after changing setup from one operation to another, many operations require several hours or even days to reach peak efficiency and quality. The longer and more complex the changeover, the more tweaking it takes to stabilize the process, eliminate defects, and reach maximum speed. This being the case, once peak quality and efficiency are achieved, continuing the run as long as possible will increase the average production rate and decrease the average defect rate. Factory supervisors have been doing their best to take advantage of the principle of freezing a process once it is under control, by producing the longest possible production run. However, the process of freezing the process by producing a long production run has a harsh penalty—increased inventory. Further, each new run requires entirely new machine and tool settings and a long period of transition from slow, defect-ridden production to fast, high quality output. This is definitely not the way to run the show!

It is now an established fact that any setup can be radically improved and simplified. Eliminating wasteful trial and error is a key ingredient in achieving fast changeover.[7] Long tweaking periods should be completely eliminated. This is achieved by determining the ideal setting or position of each adjustable tool or machine element, and then designing equipment and tool modifications that enable the setup person to adjust machines and tools directly to the correct settings without tweaking. (Examples will follow). Incidentally, "tweaking" is one topic in Robertson's book. For those who are not strong in mathematics or statistics, his book is both simple and easy to understand.[8] Ross's book is more suited to those with strong mathematical background.[9]

The factory alchemist would like to believe that every changeover requires different settings and that only an extremely experienced person could achieve the unique, magical blend of required settings. In fact, every process the author has ever worked on has been suitable for standard settings. Even in the worst cases, establishing standard settings has been possible for all but a few most variable elements. Changeover then entails automatic setting of most settings and tweaking of few. By contrast, before improvement, when every single adjustable setting of a process is considered to be not only variable, but variable in relation to the

[7]See Appendix 2.
[8]Gordon H. Robertson, *Quality Through Statistical Thinking: Improving Process Control and Capability* (Dearborn, Mich.: ASI Press, 1989), pp. 305–7.
[9]Philip J. Ross, *Taguchi Techniques for Quality Engineering* (New York: McGraw-Hill, 1987).

unique combination of all other settings, finding the right combination should be nearly impossible. In fact, processes with settings that are treated this way have some of the longest changeover times and produce some of the highest levels of defective material in the transition period. However, even these complex changeovers can be improved.

For example, an Armstrong project team working on process quality noticed that the amount of defective floor covering usually increased at the changing of shifts, even though the machine was in continuous production on the same product both before and after the shift change. Subsequent investigation revealed that each new shift crew immediately started to tweak the machine's adjustments, thus routinely throwing a process that had been in control out of control. Then, of course, it took some time to tweak all of the adjustable variables to bring the process back into control. Each crew sincerely believed that it alone was uniquely qualified to determine the various settings. This is a most vivid example of the need to freeze the process.

Armstrong's fierce dedication to superior quality required that all defective production be culled out by 100 percent inspection and scrapped. Thus, although the customer never suffered from defective production, Armstrong's costs of production were higher than necessary until it started to eliminate defects. It's ultimate solution was to develop standard settings for each product and eliminate trial-and-error tweaking.

NEXT OPERATOR VERSUS SELF-INSPECTION

Although it is technically feasible to design every process to produce and/or pass on only perfect quality, it is not always economical to do so. Some operations or processes are better suited to flaw-proof design than others. Flaw-proofing should focus on processes that produce the highest volume products, since the costs of improvements can have faster payback. Manufacturers of lower volume and custom products are less likely to be able to afford designing and fabricating the tooling and equipment modifications required to control automatically the production of perfect quality.[10] Even for high volume producers, certain manual assembly operations are prohibitively expensive to control by device. Since every business should have perfect quality as its goal, the processes and manual assembly operations that are too expensive to control by device will re-

---

[10]Robert W. Hall, *Attaining Manufacturing Excellence* (Homewood, Ill.: Dow Jones–Irwin, 1987), p. 71.

quire 100 percent inspection and/or functional testing if the target of perfect quality is ever to be achieved. This being the case, the question that must then be answered is, "Who should perform the inspections?" The almost universally accepted answer is that the machinists and assemblers who perform the operation should inspect their own work. Unfortunately, this answer is wrong in most cases. In the first place, the person doing the work cannot be completely objective about the quality of his own work. Second, operator inspection is just not the most economical approach in many instances.

Zero-defect programs of the past that emphasized placing the responsibility for quality at the source encouraged the practice of inspection by responsible operators. The results were to lower source defects somewhat at best, but not enough to achieve perfect quality. Therefore, inspectors at the end of the line continued to be necessary. Why? Mainly because humans err. When they perform repetitive tasks at high speeds, their minds become fatigued, and they lose their ability to maintain the concentration necessary to see what they are looking at. Thus, defective items are sometimes passed from the operation as good production. These problems are not limited to only high speed, short operations. In fact, infrequent, long, and complex tasks are even more subject to human error. Chief among these is the very human error of oversight—forgetting to perform some task, even one explicitly listed on the operation instruction sheet. The most difficult aspect of these human errors is the extremely low frequency of their occurrence. Inattention and oversight may occur only once in a thousand operations. However, if the end product consists of hundreds of components, and thousands of operations are performed on the components themselves, and thousands more on the end product during assembly, the odds are that every product will have one or more defects. Nevertheless, operator inspection, while not the perfect quality solution, should be one way to begin to reduce drastically the defects that flow through several operations before detection. For example, in Brunswick Corporation's Muskegon, Michigan, Ball Plant, new focused factories feature the placement of inspection and repair facilities in each cell, as seen in Exhibit 6–7. Cell operators inspect and repair their own work. This improvement, among others, rapidly slashed defects passed on to final inspection by well over 90 percent and the quantity of scrapped balls by 70 percent.

Even if defect rates of each component are low, statistical techniques based on sampling simply won't work to find every defect or to reduce their rate to the zero-defect level, because perfect final assembly quality can be accomplished only if all components are perfect. Final inspection

SELF INSPECTION & REPAIR

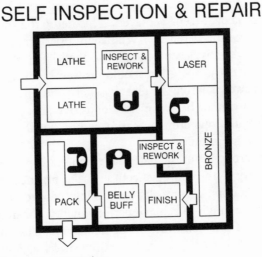

Courtesy of Brunswick Corporation:
Muskegon Ball Plant

EXHIBIT 6-7

of the product is even less effective because of the vast array of components and operations that might be defective. Many of the components are even hidden from the inspector's view, inside the assembled product, making it impractical to inspect them without disassembly. Further, inspection at the end of the line is too remote from the responsible operator. Too much time passes before the responsible person learns of the problem and can take corrective action. In the meantime, the operator may have produced large additional amounts of defective products that will require rework. Finally, even if final inspectors could completely inspect every detail, it would add immeasurably to the cost of production. This is counterproductive since the alternative could be inspections that are virtually free.

In 1960, Shigeo Shingo was one of the first gurus to realize that the best answer was to perform most inspections at the *next* operation.[11] The reasons that this approach works so well and costs so little include the following:

1. In many cases, inspection by both the first and the second operator is automatic and free. For example, some defects are readily detected just by looking at the item. It is almost impossible to work

[11]Shigeo Shingo, *Zero Quality Control: Source Inspection and the Poka-yoke System* (Cambridge, Mass.: Productivity Press, 1986), p. 67.

on or to assemble an item without looking at it in the process. If the same glance required to pick the item up is all that is required to note some critical defect, the inspection is free.

2. Complete (100 percent) inspection by the next person to handle the item sharply reduces undetected defects. If the defect rate is one in 1,000 and is due to operator inattention or oversight, and if the same rate of fatigue and error is applicable to the second operator, the possibility of the error going past the second person is 1/1,000 × 1/1,000, or one in a million.

3. If the next operator must assemble the item into the product or place it into a fixture, and it does not fit, a free quality check has been performed. Many assembly fixtures and tools can be designed or modified to increase the number of such free inspections.

4. The second person can inspect the work of the first more objectively.

Next operator inspection yields fantastic results when operations are designed for superior manufacturing. However, it may not be at all practical until machines have been arranged into cells or semicells, and until the distance, time, and work-in-process between machining and assembly have been reduced to minimal levels. In the functionally organized factory of the past, illustrated in Exhibit 6-8, large distances, inventories,

FUNCTIONAL FACTORY LAYOUT

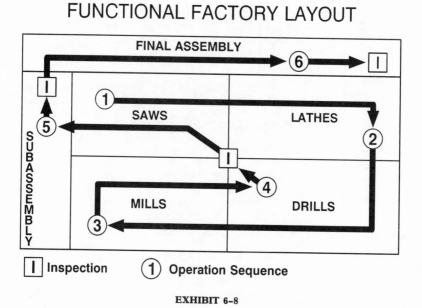

EXHIBIT 6-8

and time separate machining operations and inspection. Typically, large lots of machined parts sit in stores before they are used in subassembly. Similarly, long intervals and big inventories of subassemblies accumulate dust in storage between the subassembly line and the final assembly line. Further, assembly and test are at the end of long lines, and when defects are finally found there, they may be rampant all through the pipeline.

The time lapse between the first operation and the detection of a defect at the second operation must be limited to seconds or minutes to minimize the possibility of mountains of inventory between two operations or between machining and assembly. Any such inventory would require rework if a defect is detected much later than when the condition that caused it came into existence. In the new, superior factory of the future, as depicted in Exhibit 6-9, the end of the machining cell would be close to the start of the new, much shorter subassembly line. The subassembly line would also be as close as possible to the subassembly's point of use on the serpentine-shaped final assembly line.[12] This layout, in conjunction with the reduction of changeover cost to minimal levels, makes it possible to operate with negligible time and inventory between operations. In the ideal factory, units in machining cells travel from hand to hand and pass from the cell to the assembly line the same way.

SUPERIOR FACTORY LAYOUT

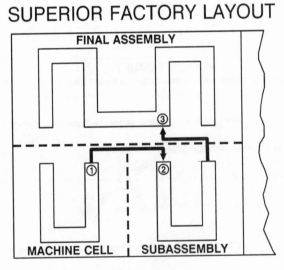

EXHIBIT 6-9

[12]See Appendix 2.

TWO DIFFERENT INSPECTION/TEST PROCEDURES

Parts from perfectly honest suppliers, inspected and tested by the vendors before shipping, are repeatedly found to be defective when they are again inspected and tested in the customer's receiving process. Most often, the underlying problem is that the vendor and customer are using two separately developed, slightly different sets of inspection and test procedures. And, of course, each uses its own different measuring tools and test equipment. Customers commonly supply engineering drawings and specifications to the vendor, relying on the vendor to develop its own inspection and test methods and to use and even design and manufacture its own test equipment. At the same time, the customer's quality engineering organization develops the procedures and tools for receiving inspection. That the design work is duplicated in both organizations is bad enough. Far worse, the duplicate but different procedures and equipment will be the source of ongoing disagreements between vendor and customer, because they will indicate different quality and performance information.

Just as it is impossible to make any two products that are exact duplicates, it is also impossible to make any two measurement or test equipment devices that will duplicate the test or measurement results of the other, down to the last decimal point. For this reason, measurement results from two different sources are bound to be minutely different at the boundaries of the acceptable tolerance range. Thus, to inspect and test twice is not only economically unjustifiable but also bound to cause suspicion and distrust between customer and supplier. Since, in some cases, parts perceived to be defective are at the boundaries of tolerance limits, as often as not the rejected items will function perfectly well in the product (if the material review board decides to accept the deviant material). This happens so often that the approval of deviation usually becomes routine, although it adds work to the processing of each receipt.

Since duplicate inspection and testing have so many disadvantages, quality improvement projects need to make a single set of quality control design specifications available to the supplier and then eliminate similar but different inspection and test procedures. Nor is it necessary to wait for a project team to initiate changes, since this is the type of improvement that many companies can put into effect immediately!

RECEIVING INSPECTION: A WASTEFUL BOTTLENECK

Receiving inspection ranks among the most wasteful manufacturing costs, particularly when one considers the alternatives, which include inspection at the source by the supplier and, ultimately, the complete elimination of inspection. Better inspection by the supplier[13] is *not* a satisfactory solution to quality problems. Complete elimination of inspection must be the ultimate goal. The obvious waste of inspecting incoming materials is that the supplier has already inspected the same items. Since the supplier does not do this out of kindness, he includes inspection cost in his price. Thus, in reinspecting the material, the customer pays for inspection twice. This is in sharp contrast to superior manufacturers who perform no inspection! It is paradoxical but understandable that, even after double inspection, defective purchased materials and components are still found during the production process. As Exhibit 6–10 indicates, innumerable defects are routinely identified in both supplier and user processes, because several types of defects can readily be seen or detected when they do not fit into the fixtures or assemblies into which they must be placed. The exhibit indicates the typical volume of rejects. (Note the size of the truck in which they are returned.) However, the point of greatest concern is not the return transportation cost but the fact that the possibility of rejection necessitates permanently carrying excessive, just-in-case inventories. The excess inventory presumably permits a company

SUPPLIER/USER INSPECTION

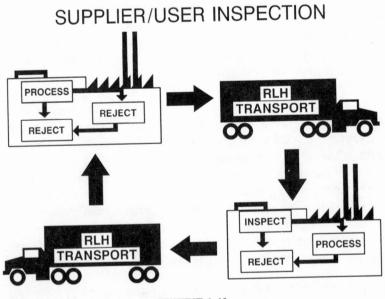

EXHIBIT 6–10

[13]A. Ansari and B. Modarress, *Just-in-Time Purchasing* (New York: Free Press, 1990), pp. 106–7.

to keep operating while defective material is being returned and replaced. In reality, as often as not, both the latest receipt and the surplus inventory are found to be defective when a quality problem is detected. Thus, the planned excess inventory provides only limited protection against rejection and line stoppage. The receiving inspection operation not only wastes money but also adds several additional days' supply of inventory and is a major bottleneck in the manufacturing operation. Many companies need expediters, who spend most of their time getting urgently required items out of the inspection backlog in time to avoid production stoppages.

Quality managers have used statistical techniques in their attempts to lower inspection costs. Statistical techniques sample a small quantity of an item, upon which to base the acceptance or rejection of a much larger lot of material. The decision is sometimes based on a small but acceptable amount of defects, but even if no defects are permissible, some might pass through undetected. While statistical techniques have reduced the costs of measurement, testing, and visual inspection, they are not able to assure perfect quality. It is always possible that at least one uninspected item will be defective. The real point, however, is not how to inspect, but rather how to work with suppliers. They must be brought to the point where they will honestly and accurately check or control quality with the result that they supply only perfect quality production. Globally, manufacturers have spent untold billions on defect detection over the years. It doesn't take much imagination to realize the gigantic improvement that could have been made if only a small fraction of these billions had been spent on improving process quality at the source, in the supplier's manufacturing operation.

In imperfect manufacturing environments, the necessity of receiving inspection is vital! To eliminate it completely could have disastrous results without some fundamental changes in the factory and in relationships between supplier and customer. As Hay wrote, "But incoming inspection cannot be eliminated by writing a memo that says: As of tomorrow there will be no inspection.[14] Even after a supplier has mastered the item's production quality, either through inspection and test or through process control, something still eventually goes awry. Sometimes, after months or even years of receiving defect-free production from a supplier, a customer suddenly receives poor quality parts. These few points are the basis for the assumption that inspection will always be

---

[14]Edward J. Hay, *The Just-in-Time Breakthrough: Implementing the New Manufacturing Basics* (New York: John Wiley, 1988), p. 119.

necessary. However, when it happens that parts that have long been of perfect quality are suddenly found to be defective, the reasons are actually quite limited. The reasons are as follows:

1. The process was not really under control, because once under control it should not be possible to produce a defective part.
2. The inspection/test procedure was not really under control since it should then be impossible to pass on a defective item without detecting the flaw and withdrawing it from production.
3. The supplier is burdened with an employee who knowingly passes defects (detected in the process or during inspection or test) to the customer.

In the past, to expect any supplier to invest much in quality improvement of the production process was impractical. Just about the time that the investment was about to yield benefits, the buyer might have switched suppliers because a competitor offered a better price. Suppliers know all too well that competitors (including themselves) will often "lowball" quoted prices when their order backlog drops or when they simply want to win over their competitor's customers. In the new world of superior manufacturing, one aim of the cooperative supplier program is to use the same suppliers in perpetuity. This alleviates two important business problems: (1) The supplier, equipped with the confidence that he will always be the supplier, more readily accepts the need to continuously improve the process and, inherently, the quality produced by the process. (2) Quality problems caused by changing suppliers are avoided.

A few years ago, while touring a diesel engine plant, I was struck by the very large number of rejected engines awaiting rework. In this dramatic example of the possible dangers of switching suppliers, the vendor of piston rings was changed to save a few pennies on the price of each ring. The new rings, although completely to specifications, caused a blow-by problem that was first detected at test. The rings were microscopically smaller than required to keep exploding, burning gases from blowing past the rings into the crankcase. Although meeting specifications, the ring diameter dimension was skewed toward the smaller end of the tolerance range. The combination of the stack of the piston cylinder dimension and the ring dimensions was enough to cause a problem. This problem had never before been experienced en masse, because the original vendor had always supplied rings with a normal distribution around the center of the tolerance range. This was due to the quality of the process, which always held the distribution of variances in dimensions close to the center of the range. The costs of this lesson were large. It will take thousands of years of saving pennies per ring set to repay the cost of tearing down completely assembled engines to replace the defective rings. Although not new, the message is nevertheless painfully clear. One of the most basic quality control principles is this: After a process has been brought under control, nothing should subsequently be changed, since changes will almost always cause the process that was in control to go out of control. The same applies to the vendor's processes.

In Sweden recently, the author saw a very new "flexible machining system" consisting of five "identical" machines and a pallet used in storing the raw castings in an automated storage and retrieval system prior to the first machining operation and between operations. An automated transport system delivered raw castings into and out of automated storage and back and forth to the "identical" machines. Of the twenty-five items machined in the system, any job was run on any of the machines that were available. Since, in reality, there are minute differences in the dimensions of every one of the "identical" machines, the parts produced by the different machines had variations in the skew of their dimensions. Therefore, the process had never been brought under control to the point of eliminating quality control checks of each unit produced. Incidentally, the tool magazines for the machines were immense since they were designed to hold the tools for all of the twenty-five parts for which they might be required. The author has always advocated assignment of parts to specific machines. This not only avoids unnecessary process quality control problems attributable to different machine attributes but also reduces the size and complexity of the machine's operating environment. Each machine could have been assigned an average of five parts, plus one or two parts that could have been used by exception, to balance loads between it and the other machines.

In the case of purchased parts, the randomness of the machine to which a job is assigned each time it is run is often even greater than in the company's own factory. Not only do vendors have more identical machines, but there is a great variety of vendors with whom the next order might be placed. Every supplier program must include working with vendors to persuade them to dedicate specific machines, cells, and lines to the customer's needs. This not only eliminates the competition for the vendor's machine time in peak demand periods but also supports quality improvements by eliminating the variation of facilities on which an item is produced.

In some receiving inspection departments, every receipt is sampled—despite the supplier's exemplary quality record—even in the case of some part numbers that have *never* been found to have had quality problems.

Even the best statistical sampling systems usually require sampling from suppliers with exceptionally good quality records (albeit either a minimum-sized sampling from each lot or else samples from every second or third lot received). Superior manufacturers, however, are speedily applying common sense and are eliminating inspection of highly reliable parts and suppliers. The risk of doing this is dramatically lower than in the past because of the new, superior manufacturing environment. Previously, the elapsed time between receipt of the item and its use in production was weeks or even months. Thus, if an uninspected or previously inspected item was first found to be defective during some stage of production or test, it might require reworking several weeks of work-in-process inventory and additional weeks of the item in material stores. Worse, it might stop production entirely. In the reinvented factory, the time between receipt of a purchased component and final test of the assembled product may be only hours. Therefore, the potential amount of rework is a fraction of that required in the old factory.

In the 1950s the author worked for a multiplant company that had extensive interplant shipments of components made by one factory and used by one or more other plants. Inspection and rejection of interplant receipts was a continuous source of production disruption as well as the reason for excessive receiving inspection costs. Both user and supplier inspected the items shipped—one in final inspection and the other in receiving inspection. In many cases both user and supplier used the same items. Interestingly, the supplier would often be using items that the supplied plant would be rejecting, even though the items were all made from one production lot. Finally, the author's boss, the corporate vice president of manufacturing, saw the folly of the practice and decreed the immediate and complete elimination of interplant receipt inspection. The results were astonishing! The volume of rejections and production stoppages dropped almost to the point of nonexistence, large numbers of inspectors were eliminated, and virtually no new quality problems occurred either in assembly and test or in use by the customer.

What are the messages and lessons learned during the preceding experience and others that followed? The most important was that many companies can radically reduce or eliminate receiving inspection with very little risk to offset the huge benefits. Further, it pays to eliminate receiving inspection because the "inspection" is often free when performed as part of the next operation. In addition, in those instances in which a defect is found after receiving a lot without inspection, the remedies of sorting good components from bad and/or reworking are almost always able to keep production going full blast.

As previously stated, many inspections, costly when performed by inspectors, are free when performed at the next machine or assembly operation. For example, checking a screw's maximum diameter is automatically done when the assembler tries to insert it and finds that it does not fit. This 100 percent inspection is completely free when no defects are found. However, when the assembler finds more than one defective part in rapid succession, he should push the line stop button, automatically summoning help. The line is then stopped only a few seconds, while the operator continues, using the screws that fit, while supervisors and others take one or more of the following actions:

1. Someone is assigned to sort bad screws from good. Thus, the operator is soon able to resume full speed.
2. If the screw has common use in other parts of the factory, supplies in those areas are checked and sorted, if necessary. Good screws are shared by all areas.
3. In the unlikely event that all screws are oversize, a rework procedure is developed almost at once. One likely rework procedure would use a thread cutting die to chase the threads, trimming them to size.
4. The supplier is contacted immediately to make arrangements for an emergency shipment of good screws.

It is now clear that every historical reason for receiving inspection rested on the assumption that accepting and living with poor quality was necessary. This is utter nonsense. If only the money spent on duplicate inspection and test had been spent on improving the process control, quality problems could have been eliminated years ago. And, more important, the productivity of the process would be vastly better. It is not too late to catch up. The trick is to eliminate wasteful inspection and redouble efforts to solve the real, evident problems by improving the process.

MATERIAL REVIEW BOARD

Many companies have a material review board (MRB) for the disposition of components and products that do not conform to specifications.[15] Several of the possible dispositions include (1) rework, (2) scrap, and (3)

[15]Armand V. Feigenbaum, *Total Quality Control* (New York: McGraw-Hill, 1983), pp. 705-7.

return to the vendor. However, the most interesting disposition is (4) use as is! When "use as is" is specified, the board has concluded that the material, while not conforming to specifications, fits and functions acceptably. Sometimes numerous items have repeatedly been identified as nonconforming and have always been dispositioned "use as is." This is a clear indication that the specified tolerances are probably tighter than necessary. In some of these cases, when the company eventually decides to get tough with its suppliers and insists on conformance to blueprint, the result is chaos, as the company discovers that conforming parts no longer fit or function in the product. This is usually due to the fact that managers in the customer and supplier factories have informally communicated the real dimensions needed to fit and function in the product. Not only vendors but also a company's own plants produce parts that are "not to print," making it possible to meet shipping schedules. This is commonly necessary because blueprints contain inaccuracies that, if adhered to, would make completed products inoperable. If and when the engineering specifications are finally corrected, the reason for the corrective engineering change order is usually "to conform to products as manufactured."

Often rejected items could be used while completely satisfying the customer's expectations. Engineering specifications are usually tighter than required to fit and function in the product more than adequately, because, as Ealey has written, "the conscientious engineer will typically set tolerances tighter than necessary to reduce the risk of premature failure in the field."[16] Improving the rationality of specifications can reduce the incidence of rejection.

The chief reasons for specifications that are more exacting than required for satisfactory fit and function are as follows:

1. Use of standard tolerances for all dimensioning, to avoid the extra work required to identify different ranges specific to each dimension. Standard tolerances are one powerful tool for reducing the cost of engineering and therefore should continue to be used. What is missing, however, is an exception routine, executed whenever it is difficult or impossible for the factory or vendor to increase performance to meet specifications without increasing the costs of manufacturing.

2. Design engineers are sometimes reluctant to spend the time required to revise specifications to conform to the way the product

[16]Lance A. Ealey, *Quality by Design: Taguchi Methods and U.S. Industry* (Dearborn, Mich.: ASI Press, 1988), p. 70.

is or should be produced. This stems from the self-pride that prevents one from admitting a mistake and the haughty and ill-advised conceit that considers no one but an engineer qualified to come to the conclusion that a change is necessary. This attitude leads the engineer to reject change requests out of hand. When requests are rejected frequently, the requestors stop asking for changes, but with the good of the company in mind, continue to produce the nonconforming items in order to continue to meet schedules.

Kaoru Ishikawa has a somewhat radical suggestion for teaching engineers to better appreciate what is in the best interest of the company. He says, "A common fault among engineers is to have a preconceived notion in their minds and play with data to match it, while ignoring the facts. To such engineers my suggestion is to join the work process (e.g. assembly line) and quietly observe it for one week or ten days. Without knowing what is going on in the work process, engineers cannot adequately perform their duties."[17]

Where the material review board is used, it continuously blocks the smooth flow of defects back to suppliers, to rework or to use as is. The typical board, incidentally, consists of representatives from Design Engineering, Manufacturing Engineering, Purchasing, Manufacturing, and Quality Control. Since all board members except the Quality Control person have other full-time duties, the quorum necessary to sign off on a disposition is quite difficult to gather. The board commonly assembles as infrequently as once a week. To make matters worse, some decisions require additional research and additional delays. Thus, some rejects spend weeks in material review board status until being dispositioned. Needless to say, the material review board roadblock is often the cause of production stoppages.

Since every item received might on occasion be found to deviate from specifications, receiving lead times and safety stocks are usually inflated for all purchased items, regardless of actual quality history. The material review board is one of the biggest reasons for large inventory investments. The elimination of receiving inspection will sharply reduce the number of items sent to the material review board. Also, lots containing both good and defective parts probably will have been sorted, based on practical fit and function criteria, prior to sending only defective parts to the material review board. (Inventories will be so lean that it will be necessary to sort and separate good parts immediately in order to keep

---

[17]Ishikawa, *What Is Total Quality Control?* pp. 109–10.

the line running.) Thus, the amount of work done by the board and the time elapsed until a disposition is made will also be reduced. Finally, when quality improves to the almost perfect level, the board will no longer be needed.

Unfortunately, the benefits of material review board elimination are unlikely to affect suppliers to military procurers. Although much ado has been made about the inflated cost of items sold to the government as compared to items sold to industry and to consumers, the blame really falls in the lap of government bureaucracy. It imposes mountains of unnecessary paperwork and inspection tasks on defense contractors through its myriad volumes of specifications and regulations. It seems to be unable to purchase the most mundane, off-the-shelf items without demanding all of the unreasonable documentation and unwarranted inspection and test suitable to purchases for exotic defense and space systems. The material review board is not optional to the defense contractor since the government insists on it. Years after the rest of industry has eliminated the waste, the government will still be requiring inspection and material review boards. Unfortunately, we, the taxpayers, pay.

FOCUSED RECEIVING: INSPECTION ELIMINATED

Giant strides in increasing quality levels and/or reducing the quality costs require parallel development of a superior supplier program, which means making a commitment to almost eternal sources of supply. Coordination with those responsible for receipts and storage in subplants within the factory is also required.[18] However, many factories can begin immediately to reduce the costs of receiving inspection. This can free up the time and the funds for attacking quality problems at their source. The source is the supplier's process, and the solution is to improve that process.

Two relatively simple analyses are useful for eliminating the waste of duplicate inspection. One of these, illustrated in Exhibit 6–11, is the Vendor Reject Analysis report. This report, organized by vendor, summarizes the number of lots received and the number containing defective material in recent years. In the exhibit, RLH Corporation has maintained a perfect quality history over the past three years. It has clearly solved the problems that led to the need for receiving inspection. The second vendor, Stanley, shows a drastic improvement in the quality of its prod-

[18]See Appendix 2.

SUPPLIER INSPECTION ELIMINATION

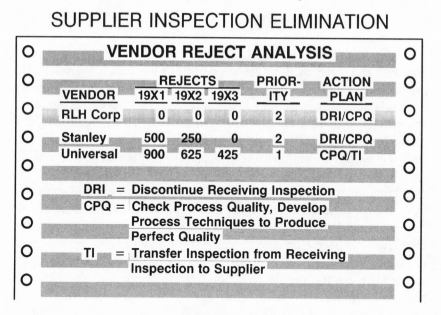

VENDOR	REJECTS			PRIOR-ITY	ACTION PLAN
	19X1	19X2	19X3		
RLH Corp	0	0	0	2	DRI/CPQ
Stanley	500	250	0	2	DRI/CPQ
Universal	900	625	425	1	CPQ/TI

DRI = Discontinue Receiving Inspection
CPQ = Check Process Quality, Develop Process Techniques to Produce Perfect Quality
TI = Transfer Inspection from Receiving Inspection to Supplier

EXHIBIT 6-11

ucts during the three-year time span. The third supplier, Universal, has a dismal quality history. All of the vendors have been assigned a priority number and an action plan based on their quality record. Universal, which has the worst record, is priority number one in terms of going to work on known quality problem suppliers. The action plans, coded CPQ and TI for Universal, indicate that its factory should be visited in order to identify problem processes and to help it get started on designing process quality improvements. This approach leapfrogs improved but outdated inspection procedures and goes directly to the problem's source. The code TI indicates that immediate action should be taken to transfer complete responsibility for inspection to Universal. Since its poor quality necessitates high inspection cost, successful transfer will yield large savings. However, the transfer can take place only after the transfer plan has been coordinated with the vendor's plan. This will include the formal selection of inspection and test procedures and equipment to be used. Further, it must be understood that the customer intends (1) to hold the vendor liable for any costs or monetary losses stemming from poor control of quality and (2) to accept receipts without inspecting them.

Since RLH Corporation and Stanley have superb quality records, they are given priority code two. The action code DRI means that immediate action should be taken to eliminate receiving inspection. Because their quality records are so good, these companies' items carry relatively little risk of causing problems.

The Vendor Part Reject analysis, Exhibit 6–12, is used only for vendors with imperfect quality records. Although a vendor's overall quality performance may be poor, various items supplied are likely to have different levels of quality since they might be produced on different processes or inspected with different procedures. The customer should discontinue inspecting individual items with perfect quality levels while working with the vendor to improve the process and inspection/test procedures for the severely problematic ones.

Although many receiving inspection improvements can and should be made independent of factory operation improvements, the ultimate objective should be to focus receipt and storage in new subplants, after inspection has been eliminated because it is no longer necessary. Exhibit 6–13 illustrates the transition period during which receipt, inspection, and storage are transferred from their old locations into the new subplant. This process is usually done one subplant at a time over an extended period. In the exhibit, all parts from the vendors with superb quality and individual parts with defect-free histories are being received at the subplant dock without inspection. Parts and materials from problem vendors and parts with problem histories are received at the old

PART INSPECTION ELIMINATION

VENDOR PART REJECT ANALYSIS
VENDOR: UNIVERSAL

PART NUMBER	REJECTIONS 19X1	19X2	19X3	PRIOR-ITY	ACTION PLAN
3	0	0	0	2	DRI/CPQ
7	500	250	0	2	DRI/CPQ
9	400	375	425	1	CPQ/TI

DRI = Discontinue Receiving Inspection

CPQ = Check Process Quality, Develop Process Techniques to Produce Perfect Quality

TI = Transfer Inspection from Receiving Inspection to Supplier

EXHIBIT 6-12

TRANSITION INSPECTION

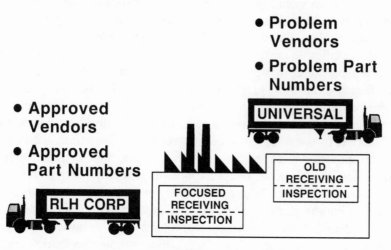

EXHIBIT 6-13

location, where they are inspected until a future time when the supplier will agree to accept the responsibility and potential liability for inspection. At that time it would be logical to start to receive and store them directly in the subplant.

RANKING A COMPANY'S QUALITY VALUES

Assuming that a company recognizes opportunities for quality improvement, it should then rank the various aspects of quality according to their importance to the enterprise's success. The objective, of course, is to develop a plan for bettering quality with emphasis on those aspects that will yield the greatest benefit. For a factory and its suppliers, the costs of achieving high quality production may appear high, but the opportunities for reducing inspection personnel and for lowering scrap and rework are enough to justify the expenditure. However, the long-term benefits of increasing the product's quality in the eyes of the customer may dwarf the other cost improvement potentials. The value of satisfied customers is, ultimately, that a business can maintain or gain market share. To fail to maintain share may sound the death knell for the company unfortunate enough to have convinced customers that it makes shoddy products.

The chief objective of this chapter is to discuss quality as it relates to defects created during the manufacturing process. However, improvements resulting from engineering design specification changes are far more likely to have greater impact on the customer's perceptions of the product's quality. Exhibits 6–14 and 6–16 contain widely (but not universally) applicable rankings of the quality criteria that have the greatest influence on the customer's evaluation of the manufacturer's products. The first and (for most products that are expected to function) most important criteria is performance. For example, a can opener is expected to open cans and to open them with comparatively little effort. A sports car is expected to reach high speeds in a relatively short time, while most cars are expected to use as little fuel as possible. Should these products fail to meet the customer's expectations, he is highly likely to switch to a competitor's product. Worse, he is likely to drop all products produced by the offending company, not just the product with inferior performance. Although some performance problems may be caused by defects created during the production process, most production defects are detected in final functional tests before the product is shipped. Improved engineering design is usually the most successful way to raise the product performance.

For product features other than those expected to function, aesthetics

RANKED QUALITY VALUES-1

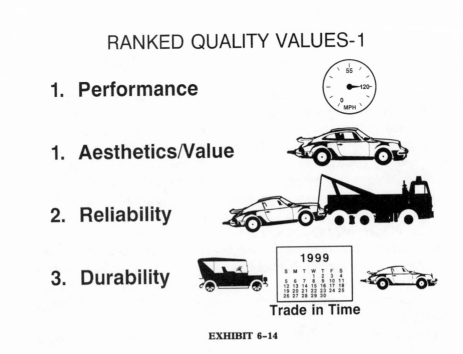

1. **Performance**

1. **Aesthetics/Value**

2. **Reliability**

3. **Durability**

Trade in Time

EXHIBIT 6-14

is the vital quality criterion.[19] Indeed, there are often no performance criteria to consider. Perfume is a good example. The purchaser of this type of product selects it for the ethereal quality of its aroma. Thus, although an error in production may result in a batch of perfume with an offensive odor, it is highly unlikely to occur since the process is quite simple. Therefore, a new, improved formula (engineering specification) that can gain wider customer acceptance will usually contribute much more to the business's growth than would factory quality control enhancements.

When a product's aesthetic appearance is the focus of manual inspection, varying quality perceptions of different inspectors will be a factor. Thus, a certain percentage of acceptable product as viewed by one inspector may be deemed unacceptable by another. For this reason, people who judge aesthetic quality must be trained to see the product in the same way that the typical customer might view it. For example, a U.S. Shoe Corporation project team at the Flemingsburg, Kentucky, plant found it relatively easy to develop standard quality criteria for inspecting shoe production, as illustrated in Exhibit 6–15. The well nigh impossible task was to standardize the perceptions of the different production operators to whom responsibility for inspection was ultimately shifted. The

QUALITY STANDARDS

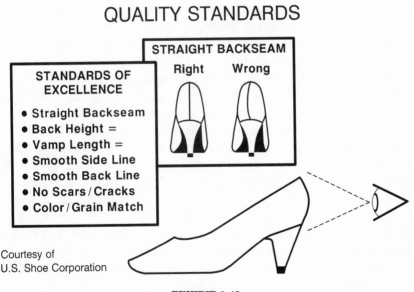

STANDARDS OF EXCELLENCE

- Straight Backseam
- Back Height =
- Vamp Length =
- Smooth Side Line
- Smooth Back Line
- No Scars / Cracks
- Color / Grain Match

STRAIGHT BACKSEAM

Right   Wrong

Courtesy of
U.S. Shoe Corporation

EXHIBIT 6–15

[19]David A. Garvin, *Managing Quality: The Strategic and Competitive Edge* (New York: Free Press, 1988).

team's goal: to eliminate the need for routine inspection by inspection specialists who do not improve the consistency of the quality evaluation. This sharply reduced the quantity of shoes that traveled through numerous operations before being discovered to be defective and in need of rework or scrapping. Although the inspectors at the end of the line were fewer in number (as contrasted to the operators scattered around the factory), and although they might use stricter judgment than the people who produce the shoes, the results will be better when all operators are trained to look at (inspect) their own work. Even better, the next person in a cell can also "inspect" the shoe (free inspection), thus interjecting group evaluation of quality. Since the group will contain a range of individuals, some inclined to be strict and others to be more lenient quality evaluators, the longer-term quality consensus will usually be more uniform and will tend to be more stringent than the most lenient individuals in the group. However, the most important reason for inspection by the production team itself is instant quality evaluation and correction. When problems are instantly recognized as they occur, where they occur, rather than detected and reported by inspection specialists much farther down the line, quality improvements will skyrocket!

For some functional products, like the sports car in Exhibit 6–14, aesthetics are every bit as important as performance. When a customer finds flaws in the paint finish or small dents on the body of a newly purchased car, he thinks twice before buying the same make again. These last types of *physical* defects *are* likely to originate in the manufacturing process.

In certain cases, customers perceive a company's products to be of poor quality when, in fact, the quality problems are not due to production defects. What they really see is *lower value material*. Executive management must be able to categorize improvement opportunities correctly as attributable to (1) inherent value, (2) aesthetic appearance, or (3) production defects. Distinguishing the difference between aesthetic and value criteria is often difficult. For example, consider two automobile seat cover options: leather and artificial leather. Many customers find leather to be inherently better and of intrinsically higher *value* than the synthetic product. However, with the best and latest technology, the artificial material can be improved to increase the product's useful life and sitting comfort and even to have an identical or even a superior aroma. The artificial material may even cost more than leather. Even if the cost, and therefore the price, of the artificial product is higher, many customers will still find leather to be more aesthetically pleasing and intrinsically greater in value than the synthetic alternative. Interestingly, on the converse side, even if the product's cost is lower than that of real leather, the purchaser is still likely to perceive the leather as being of higher value. An advertising campaign might be the key to converting buyers to enthusiasts for artificial leather. Armed with an accurate understanding of the differences between production defects, aesthetics, and the value of materials used, executives have three choices. They can focus on improving the value of material, solve production quality problems, or mold the market's perception of material value by advertising the superiority of "inferior" materials.

Incidents of failure to continue running, as in the case of an automobile that stops dead because of a defective voltage regulator, are likely to have disastrous results on the customer's next purchase choice, especially if such incidents occur frequently. Steve Jeoffrey, Ford Motor Company's Director of Process Quality Improvement, put it like this: "The customer doesn't mind going back to the dealership for a repair providing he or she gets timely and effective treatment. But by the third repeat repair you've lost their satisfaction and lost them as a repeat buyer."[20] Products with useful lives shorter than the customer expects are equally problematical. Although reliability and durability problems are of the utmost importance, the likelihood that they are caused by errors during the manufacturing process and that the errors would not be detected during final testing is quite low. Reliability and durability are such critical success factors that most companies continuously strive to improve the product design. Design and specification changes, including those to materials and components, usually have big payoffs, while process improvements gain little.

The next quality criterion listed in Exhibit 6–14 is reliability. The majority of customers accept as inevitable that products and their components will eventually show wear and even fail. However, they will continue to be tolerant only if skilled repairmen and spare replacement parts are readily available. All too often customers confuse acceptable levels of wear and failure with production-related defects. In these cases, companies must recognize that molding the market's perception of its ability to provide service can be of far greater importance than factory quality improvement. For example, innumerable brands of television sets are available to the consumer who takes the time to search them out. However, since there are relatively few differences in the appearance or performance specifications and only barely perceptible differences in the quality of the picture, it can be quite difficult to select one on these

---

[20]Jim Mateja, "Junk No More: U.S. Automakers Close the Quality Gap, but Public Remains Skeptical," *Chicago Tribune*, Transportation Section, February 10, 1991.

criteria. However, the wise buyer uses another important criterion, sales volume, to narrow the field. He shuns the brands that have markedly lower sales than the market leaders, knowing that spare parts and knowledgeable service personnel will be hard to find. Therefore, manufacturers with a history of poor repair and spare parts services and low volume manufacturers or new entrants into an established market could and should invest in service capabilities. Then they should focus their advertising on their premium service to overcome the logical reluctance toward their lesser-known brand. This tactic will help them begin to make inroads into the sales leader's market share.

Conformance to engineering specifications, the Holy Grail that quality control organizations slavishly pursue, is ranked very low on the list of quality criteria. The engineering drawing for the automobile in Exhibit 6–16 specifies the length of the car as 500 centimeters, plus or minus .01 centimeters. The customer, however, would be extremely unlikely to be aware of or disturbed by the fact if the actual length were found to be 499.98 centimeters and perhaps would be even less perturbed if it were found to be 500.02 centimeters, although both of these lengths would be outside the specified permissible tolerance range. As long as the car performs well and is aesthetically pleasing, reliable, and durable, conformance to specifications would seldom, if ever, be a serious competitive factor. This point, applied to the quality control process, can be a

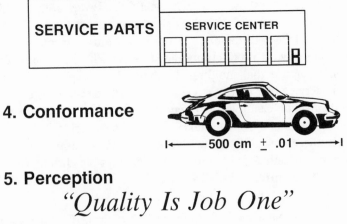

RANKED QUALITY VALUES - 2

4. Service/Serviceability

SERVICE PARTS   SERVICE CENTER

4. Conformance

|←——— 500 cm ± .01 ———→|

5. Perception

"Quality Is Job One"

EXHIBIT 6–16

powerful basis for reducing the many wasteful costs of blind, unquestioning conformance to design specifications.

Having explored the potential for quality improvement both in the production process and after distribution, the rest of this chapter will focus on quality improvement in manufacturing.

BACK TO BASICS

To understand the basic nature of quality, it is essential to accept the impossibility of repetitively producing exact duplicates. Every item produced will vary—even if only minutely—in dimensions and chemistry, as Oakland explains.[21] Because minor variation is unavoidable, products must be designed to function regardless of the variability of every one of their components. Therefore, one of the design engineer's chief responsibilities is to develop the tolerance ranges for each dimension, if the standard tolerance range normally used for any dimension is inappropriate.

Tolerance ranges are generally defined relative to the ideal dimension. For example, a perfect hole diameter might be the ideal target as illustrated in Exhibit 6–17. However, the engineer has specified that the ac-

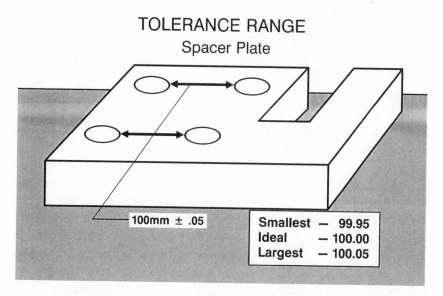

TOLERANCE RANGE
Spacer Plate

100mm ± .05

Smallest	— 99.95
Ideal	— 100.00
Largest	— 100.05

EXHIBIT 6–17

[21]John S. Oakland, *Total Quality Management* (Oxford, Eng.: Heinemann Professional Publishing, 1989), pp. 190–97.

ceptable range of deviation from the ideal is plus or minus .05 millimeters. To conform to specifications, spacer plates must have hole diameters in the range of 99.95 to 100.05 millimeters. When spacer plates are found to have hole sizes outside the acceptable range, either the plates are actually defective or the measurement tools or procedures are inaccurate. Upon closer scrutiny there might be a third possible scenario—the engineer's specifications may have called for tighter tolerances than were necessary. Thus, although the spacer plate may not conform to the blueprint, it performs the function for which it was designed and does it quite well. Finally, not all too infrequently, plates well within the tolerance range may not fit or function in the product because of a "stack" of the tolerance ranges of interrelated components. Even if the dimensions of all components are within their individual tolerances, a combination of the variances at either the high or low extreme may make the resulting product inoperable.

Millions, perhaps billions, of defect-free lots of manufactured and purchased components and materials are accepted every working day. In fact, companies that need to reject one or more pieces per lot in more than 5 percent of all lots are rare. The typical defect experiences the author has seen, as a result of experience in countless companies, include the following categories of items.

1. Items that have *never* been found to be defective
2. Items that have *rarely* been found to be defective
   - A *high percentage* of pieces in the defective lot were flawed. The probably causes are machine, tooling, and operator problems.
   - A *low percentage* of pieces in the defective lot were flawed. The most likely reason was that the process had drifted closer to the higher or lower tolerance limit. Thus, defective parts had been produced intermittently.
3. Items that have *usually* been found to have defective pieces in all or in most lots (These items are most likely to be produced by a process that has not yet been upgraded to yield the required tolerances. In these cases, process design improvement has great potential for improving quality.)

Given that the typical incidence of defective production is a relatively small percentage of the total but that some items are continually problems, how can a company simultaneously reduce the costs of quality control and increase the quality of its products? The use of statistics and the "seven tools of quality control" have been the most popular approaches in recent years.

SEVEN TOOLS OF QUALITY CONTROL

The seven tools of total quality control,[22] in the approximate order of their relative value, are:

1. Pareto analysis
2. Check sheet
3. Various charts
4. Histogram
5. Control charts
6. Scatter diagram
7. Cause/effect diagram

Pareto analysis is the process of eliminating the insignificant majority of any population from the most important few, in order to concentrate efforts on as few items as possible while achieving the greatest possible benefits.[23] Exhibit 6-18 is a classic example of the value of this tool (most important of the seven tools). Sixty percent of all items inspected, according to the company's historical records, have never been found to have defective pieces in any lot. At the opposite extreme, 1 percent of

PARETO ANALYSIS

PERCENTAGES		
Items	**Lots Rejected**	**Defects Per Lot**
60	0	0
30	1-10	1-10
5	1-10	10-100
4	10-100	1-10
1	10-100	10-100

EXHIBIT 6-18

[22]J. M. Juran, *Juran on Leadership for Quality: An Executive Handbook* (New York: Free Press, 1989), pp. 348–49.
[23]*Ibid.*, p. 136

the items inspected have had 10 percent or more of all lots rejected, with each rejected lot containing defective parts averaging 10 percent or more. This example is somewhat typical of the quality characteristics of the purchased component and material populations of many companies. Awareness of this fact can be helpful when trying to put quality problems in proper perspective and when assessing the degree of difficulty associated with achieving significant improvements with limited available resources. In fact, rather than being insurmountable, the quality arena is quite manageable in terms of the relatively few items with big improvement potential.

SOMETHING FISHY: THE FISHBONE CHART

The cause/effect diagram espoused by the Japanese Society of QC (Quality Control) Technique Development has sometimes been somewhat slavishly adopted as a standard tool by practitioners in the rest of the world. There is little question that diagrams bring a sense of methodology to investigating quality problems. However, such a ritualistic approach to problem solving runs the risk of adding unneeded complexity to problem analysis and solution. The various forms of relationship diagrams include those advocated by Shigeru Mizuno[24] and Kaoru Ishikawa.[25] Professors and consultants love to create documents that closely approximate the entire universe on a single page. In the process they contrive to depict tenuous lines of dependency relationships between the items portrayed. Of the two main forms of diagrams, the fishbone chart is superior in that it does not attempt to find all potential relationships between items.

The author's main reason for scoffing at diagramming approaches is that hundreds of factories have radically improved process designs and made giant gains in quality without ever having used a single diagram. Further, to have diagramed in these factories would only have added time and effort to the process of analysis and design. For example, consider a quality problem tackled by a project team at The Leather Center in Carrollton, Texas. Leather was once cut in a different location from where it was sewn into furniture coverings. Sometimes during the sewing process, some pieces that were cut with too little stock around the sewn seams were discovered. This often came to light days after the cutting opera-

[24]Shigeru Mizuno, ed., *Management for Quality Improvement: The 7 New QC Tools* (Cambridge, Mass.: Productivity Press, 1988), pp. 23–24.
[25]Ishikawa, *What Is Total Quality Control*, p. 63.

tion, when an assembler found the cover too tight to fit the frame properly. Reworking or scrapping of entire covers was expensive. Fortunately, the project team took only a few hours to both locate the problem source and develop a fail-safe solution. The problem source was the cardboard pattern used for cutting. The pattern was laid on the leather, and a utility knife was manually guided around the pattern. Over time, the knife gradually, continuously, and imperceptibly shaved the size of the cardboard pattern. The fail-safe solution was to develop all new patterns from a harder, permanent material that would not deteriorate over time. This permanently eliminated quality problems arising from pattern defects.

Finally, if one examines any two diagrams for different products, one must be struck by the following important points:

1. All elements of cause and effect apply to any product and its processes.

2. Each diagram omits some of the causes and effects of the other, although each cause and effect should apply universally.

3. With time, one could prepare a single gigantic cause and effect diagram, detailing every potential generic element. This would eliminate the need for unique diagrams for each of billions of different products and processes and would save trillions of wasted man-hours.

4. Even if such a giant diagram were available, its complexity would deter anyone from using it. It would include far too many causes and effects—most of which do not cause quality problems—for reasonable consideration. Because the few really important opportunities for improvement are usually relatively easy to find, most potential causes of quality problems never really warrant extensive investigation. A glance at Nagashima's sample chart[26] should help to understand how many of the possible causes and effects are not likely to be worth considering, how odd (versus standard) the categories are, and how mind-numbingly complex a chart can be. Unfortunately, charts like this are typical.

Why use the diagram and reinvent this wheel billions of times? One major reason is that the diagram's façade of implied methodology provides a security blanket for the problem solver. It removes the mystery from the analytical thought processes that, in reality, get the job done. This mental process is virtually impossible to explain in concrete, step-

---

[26]Soichiro, Nagashima, *100 Management Charts* (Tokyo: Asian Productivity Organization, 1987), pp. 128–29.

by-step terms. The methodical and not very glamorous part of creative invention is the plodding assembly of facts and the thorough review necessary to master understanding of the present product and process. One then picks the most important problems (or greatest opportunities) and, if required, studies them in even greater depth. Then, and only then, is one ready to invent potential solutions. The problem that most people have in designing improvements is that they select a single solution too early in the process, locking out consideration of the universe of all other alternatives. This narrow perspective can be attacked in two ways. The first, often costly and lengthy, is to use a big group (brainstorming) to analyze and design. The second is to train responsible individuals routinely to consider and evaluate multiple approaches while working on the selection of the best. Now the design alternatives considered and the one initially recommended (by the responsible individual) can be presented to one or more groups of involved and interested people. In this way group activity (and its expense) starts when much of the spadework has already been completed and the final solution is nearer. In some cases a group member may identify an entirely new alternative solution, but in the majority of instances the group enhances the proposed improvement and brings to light potential problems that necessitate additional study and design. In contrast, brainstorming the usual way (design by committee) usually starts with a blank piece of paper.

Another attraction of the chart is that it provides a substitute for education and training. In lieu of large investments in teaching and training in specialized job-related subjects, large masses of people can be taught the methodology of charting so they can be turned loose to do their best to master its use on their own products and processes. If a company does not have enough experienced people to supervise, educate, and train the workforce, this method will get several groups of people working on improvement. In the process they will start to stumble upon the problems and solutions as they invent their own versions of the chart that has already been reinvented millions of times, in numerous different versions. The real need, however, is adequate, experienced supervision, on-the-job training, and job-related education. Education and training should start with learning the universally applicable chart of source causes of problems, Exhibit 6–19. As the exhibit shows, every possible source cause can be classified into one of four categories: tools, people, material, and environment. Every material, in turn, is a product of the same four source causes, ad infinitum, down to the level of raw material in its natural state. The next lower lever chart, into which tool source causes can be further detailed, is shown in Exhibit 6–20. Note that the

THE UNIVERSAL CHART

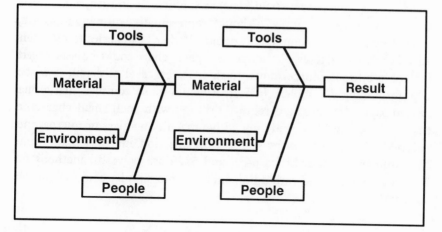

EXHIBIT 6-19

THE TOOLS CHART

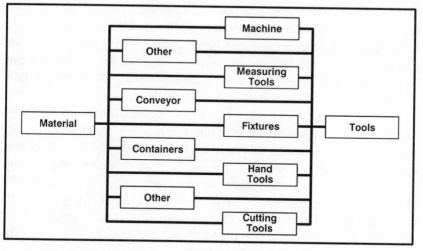

EXHIBIT 6-20

machine is deemed to be just one of numerous tools used to machine and assemble the product, albeit a complex tool. The machine itself, however, consists of its components (materials) each of which, in turn, comes from the four basic source causes. Although representative of many tools, this chart is by no means complete. It depicts "other" categories to represent all other types of tools. Although one giant chart could be assembled, including all four sources down to their lowest level of detail, it would look forbiddingly complex. In fact, it would be so complex that a one- or two-page version would require printing with such small characters that the chart could be read only with a magnifying glass or microscope. A level-by-level, segment-by-segment organization and presentation like those illustrated in Exhibits 6–19 and 6–20 are powerful methods for breaking complex and forbidding subjects into simple, comprehendible segments.

CONTROL CHARTS: LIMITED APPLICABILITY

Ranking control charts as number five relative to the rest of the seven quality control tools is not to imply that they cannot be of great value where they are applicable. The point is, however, that their applicability is quite limited. This fact is understated in most recent publications and in the minds of many people who have heard that they are the elixir for curing all quality ills. It is not the author's intention to describe charting here. Dorian and Peter Shainin have already described the basics more than adequately.[27] One particularly valuable lesson in their explanation relates to the number and size of samples required. These range from 4 to 100 per subgroup, and the charting technique is assumed to require measurement of 10 to 25 subgroups. The conclusion? Charting is least applicable to low volume, short-run production. In today's world, mastery of fast, low cost changeover of machines and processes makes it practical to set up routinely and run every required item every day. This being the case, all except the highest volume products, produced nearly continuously, are eliminated as practical charting candidates. Further, the new setup methods and tooling are designed to eliminate all the problems stemming from errors and inaccuracies during setup. This further reduces the applicability of charting these items. Where applicable, use of the seven tools can help lead to substantial defect reductions and, in some

[27]J. M. Juran, editor-in-chief, *Juran's Quality Control Handbook* (New York: McGraw-Hill, 1988), pp. 24.1–24.39.

cases, might signal that machine tools are drifting out of the center of the range of acceptable dimensions in time to correct the cause and avoid producing scrap or rework. However, charting just for the sake of charting may not serve a useful purpose and may add nonproductive work. For example, the Mitsubishi automobile plant (previously Chrysler) in Adelaide, Australia, has made remarkable strides in improving quality and productivity. For instance, as is typical of Japanese plants, all containers in the factory were on average 75 percent smaller than in the factories of Western counterparts. While touring the factory recently, the author saw hundreds of charts throughout the plant. But we stopped at the only four charts to show sharp changes. (All other charts we glanced at were virtually flat lines, basically without trend or periodic instances of out-of-limit production). The four exception charts were maintained by work teams at four factory locations at which major new or modified equipment had recently been installed, thus accounting for the dramatic productivity or quality improvements. The author's conclusions were, first, that charting does not automatically lead to improvement, as evidenced by the hundreds of charts that were essentially flat. The second was that most major improvements stem from major revisions to layout and equipment (equipment designed by responsible process engineers, not the teams). It was hard to resist commenting, as Shigeo Shingo once did, that the most important chart was missing: the chart to control the quantity of charts![28]

The charting and graphing methods of quality control are clearly impractical when the item includes innumerable dimensions and when variances from any one would be critical to the functioning of the product. For example, the spacer plate in Exhibit 6–17 has dimensions for four separate holes, thickness, length, width, and two cutouts. In addition, the plate's flatness and surface finish might be also be critical to the product's quality. This relatively simple part has at least eleven items to be charted if charting were indeed to be the preferred method for controlling quality. Imagine how many charts would be required to chart every component's specifications if the product were an automobile!

Finally, it may be helpful for the charting advocate to review the book edited by Hirano and Black.[29] This book, which contains numerous photographs of Japanese factory scenes, is devoid of quality charts, and the quality section of the book is similarly devoid of any such reference. Not

[28]Shingo, *Zero Quality Control*, p. 64.
[29]Hiroyuki Hirano and J. T. Black, *JIT Factory Revolution: A Pictorial Guide to Factory Design of the Future* (Cambridge, Mass.: Productivity Press, 1988; originally published by Nikkan Kogyo Shimbun, Tokyo, 1987).

that charting cannot be found in Japan. Since there are about 250,000 manufacturing entities, a wide variety of practices are found. Some factories are at the leading edge in terms of their performance while others still have a long way to go. In many respects, lifetime employment inhibits progress. Experience outside one's own company can be gained only by brief visits, and brief visits just do not satisfy the need.

AUTOMATION: HIGHER COST DEFECTS

Automation, one of the highly touted ways to increase product quality in recent years, has had mixed results in every aspect except one. In most cases, product costs have not declined in relation to the cost of automation. As Hajime Karatsu says, "There was a time when people would say, without much reflection, that once automation took hold in a company, QC [Quality Control] would be obsolete. This is an unrealistic view."[30]

Pitfalls of assembly and machining automation have been covered in *Reinventing the Factory*.[31] The primary pitfall of quality control automation has been that too much is being spent on automating inspection and too little on process control. Investments in computer controlled coordinate measuring machines, robot inspection, and vision inspection systems are examples of quality control improvements that detect defects only after they have occurred. Much higher returns result from expenditures for controlling the machining or assembly process, including quality checking and instant feedback when necessary. Integrating quality and production automation will inevitably cost less than permitting each to have separate sets of hardware and software. For example, a single computer could easily handle the requirements of both production operations and quality control. This would usually be preferable to a separate, stand-alone automated inspection system that would require its own computer in addition to the computer required to control production operations.

As long as inspection is a separate operation, not built into the process, the possibility of producing defective items that require reworking or scrapping will persist. If, however, the process is controlled, the need for inspection, scrap, and rework will disappear.

[30]Hajime Karatsu, *TQC Wisdom of Japan: Managing for Quality Control* (Cambridge, Mass.: Productivity Press, 1988), p. 109.
[31]See Appendix 2.

QUALITY COST: LOOKING FOR NEEDLES

Over the years, the author has had numerous opportunities to examine studies in which the sole objective of the projects was to develop statistics on the "Cost of Quality." The originators of these studies thought that identifying these statistics must be a prerequisite to going to work on quality improvement projects. Usually the studies have gone to great pains to identify not only the tangible costs but also the intangible ones (needles in the haystack). Philip Crosby has said: "Many managers wait, and fiddle, and never really do get a COQ [Cost of Quality] system installed. They collect endless lists and classifications of things that should be considered. They are too concerned with trying to obtain an exact cost figure and don't really understand the reason for doing the calculation in the first place. All this delays the rest of the program."[32]

The misguided rationale for studying the cost of quality is that it is necessary to convince management that the return is worth the investment. This is often an insult to good managers whose extensive knowledge of operations enables them to understand almost automatically the order of magnitude value of quality improvements. Although big companies follow project funding request/cost justification procedures, the required levels of return on investment are rarely actually achieved even though they were the basis for approval. Almost everyone knows that the request submitter must project the highest benefits and lowest costs possible if he wants his proposal to be in the running with other proposals. Competing proposals are also based on the rosiest estimates of benefits and cost. It is not that the proposals, if accurately and conservatively calculated, could not make money for the company, but rather that the cost justification process is not objective. The champions of various projects understand that their pet investments must appear more glamorous than the competing proposals in order to win a share of the limited pool of available funding. In addition, the process is much too detailed, requiring reams of information that can be produced only as a result of intense, in-depth study. (How the study can be done when there is no budget to do it is an interesting question.) It is unfortunate that any requests should be rejected or tabled since most of them would increase the company's competitiveness. Some, however, will have an unreasonably long payback period. Perhaps both short-term and long-term payback projects are necessary for the company ultimately to remain a viable, competitive force.

[32]Philip B. Crosby, *Quality Is Free: The Art of Making Quality Happen* (New York: New American Library, 1980), p. 104.

In any case, *good* executives and managers do not request avoidable expenditures if they know their operations well enough to operate them as an entrepreneur would. Having empowered them with authority for their small businesses should mean that they are capable of making capital expenditure decisions for their factory-within-a-factory.

The solution to the dilemma of spending too much time on cost justification (and, therefore, too little on quality improvement) starts with understanding that cost justification will always be necessary. However, using return on investment target criteria to screen out lower return projects and prioritize the remainder is not the best solution. It rewards the requester who uses the greatest imagination in finding a rationale for projecting big benefits and modest expenditures. A better way to approve expenditures is to use only the most tangible benefits and the most fiscally conservative cost estimates. If a project would have a payback anywhere under two years, it should be funded. The chief financial officer should arrange the financing necessary to improve the business continuously, not just limit expenditures to conveniently available funds.

In cases where a necessary investment cannot yield rapid payback, management should have the courage to proceed while insisting that methods be developed to continuously reduce the size of the required expenditures at every step of the process. Then, by the end of the project, the effort may indeed have a reasonable, tangible payback.

THE STEP-BY-STEP
QUALITY IMPROVEMENT APPROACH

Sometimes the poor quality of the output of manufacturing operations is obvious, as proved by scrap and rework costs traceable to defective machining and assembly operations. In these cases, the best quality improvement approach is to work on process design improvement, following the step-by-step approach outlined in *Reinventing the Factory*.[33] The biggest improvements in factory-produced quality will come automatically from better process design. Although increased productivity is the main goal, quality improvement is the automatic by-product. When defective machining and assembly operations are *not* the reasons for quality problems or when it appears that the only quality problems are the customer's false perceptions, a second, similar step-by-step approach applies. In both cases, the best overall way to develop solutions is to dedi-

[33]See Appendix 2.

cate full-time project teams and follow an established methodology. Quality improvement projects are usually performed in three phases: (1) quality planning and initial design, (2) design, and (3) implementation. Prior to phase I, the functional areas selected for analysis and design improvement should be chosen according to the biggest payback opportunities. The fast-moving, six-to-eight-week first phase, Exhibit 6–21, includes just enough design work to achieve the following:

1. Show that major improvements can be achieved. This entails designing some new components and revised processes, procedures, and systems for a small but representative portion of the functional areas within the scope of the project.

2. Quantify the approximate costs and financial benefits of the project. These order-of-magnitude estimates need only consider the most tangible benefits, if the improvements are of the impressive magnitude characteristic of most projects.

3. Develop a work plan for completing the next phase of the project.

At the end of phase I, management can revise project plans if business priorities have changed. It is now better equipped to juggle priorities of competing projects since the initial design work shows how to accomplish improvements, and the cost/benefit analysis assigns financial benefits to the changes.

Planning charts, a simplified form of critical path network, should be the roadmap for scheduling and managing the quality project (or any other type of project, for that matter). Exhibit 6–21, the highest level chart, illustrates the major segments of the quality planning and initial design phase. Each segment of the planning chart consists of several tasks, which in turn are made up of the fundamental steps of the step-by-step methodology. The first segment of phase I, organization and administration, consists of the tasks shown in Exhibit 6–22. Space does not permit discussion of all of the quality improvement charts, but a few points related to organization and administration require explanation.

1. Administrative and organizational tasks are performed in parallel with review and design tasks in the various functional areas. Typically, project team members make the mistake of spending too much time in the project team office and not enough in the functional areas that they need to learn and for which they need to design changes. Starting on day one of the project they should be where the action is!

2. One of the most important products of the organization segment

PHASE I PROJECT SEGMENTS

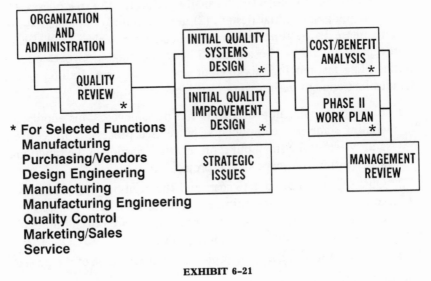

* For Selected Functions
Manufacturing
Purchasing/Vendors
Design Engineering
Manufacturing
Manufacturing Engineering
Quality Control
Marketing/Sales
Service

EXHIBIT 6–21

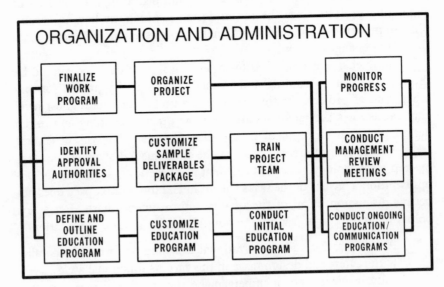

EXHIBIT 6–22

is the customized sample package of deliverables. The contents of the package are examples of what each team member must develop to present its findings and designs to all management levels.

3. Standard educational programs are customized and planned to match the needs of each functional area, based on the types of products and processes involved. In phase I, training programs are limited to those necessary to teach the project team how to do the job at hand. The best and most thorough training, however, comes on the job while doing the required tasks. During the implementation phase, training will be based on the specific procedures and systems developed for the company, but similar to corresponding procedures and systems used in hundreds of other companies.

Every quality project should include widespread education on statistical control topics since tough quality problems often require statistical analysis. Statistical methods can also be applied to designing quality into the product and the process. Education on small group improvement activities (quality circles) should be included in the program when top management has concluded that the company environment is ready or would simply like to start to introduce the concepts to the organization. The main thrust of education, however, should consist of programs tailored to the needs of each functional organization. They should focus primarily on case examples of specific operation improvements, procedures, and system features and the concrete benefits they can help to realize.

As a result of the phase I quality planning project, one or more of several quality programs might be launched. One such program could be the training and initiation of small group improvement teams (quality circles). For each type of quality program shown in Exhibit 6–23 (and for those not shown), detail planning charts are available. Thorough methodology for conducting quality improvement projects has been developed in conjunction with successful projects in hundreds of companies. Thus, reinventing the wheel is not necessary.

SUMMARY

That Western manufacturers are, on the average, lagging far behind the world's quality leaders is no longer debatable. One reason might be the focus of the professional and academic theorists who contribute most to the written body of knowledge. The bulk of the literature on the subject,

MULTIPLE QUALITY PROGRAMS

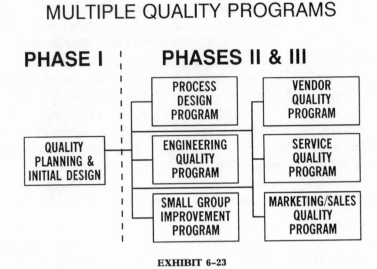

PHASE I | **PHASES II & III**

| QUALITY PLANNING & INITIAL DESIGN |

PROCESS DESIGN PROGRAM	VENDOR QUALITY PROGRAM
ENGINEERING QUALITY PROGRAM	SERVICE QUALITY PROGRAM
SMALL GROUP IMPROVEMENT PROGRAM	MARKETING/SALES QUALITY PROGRAM

EXHIBIT 6–23

not surprisingly, treats the matter theoretically and primarily as a statistical and mathematical problem. In discussing why the search for new methods for perfect quality took so long, Shigeo Shingo said: "The fact that quality control efforts in Japan were led by certain high-brow theorists with no real connection to the workplace has been, I suspect, one reason for the tardy pursuit of real quality control systems aimed at zero defects."[34] The author's opinions of academia would be less harsh. The study of theoretical and statistical approaches is vitally necessary to round out the knowledge needed to design the flaw-proof process modifications that our industries so urgently require. Nevertheless, far too few practitioners publish the practical, down-to-earth, low cost methods that we all need to emulate. Nevertheless, the body of knowledge is so convincing that there is no longer any excuse for delaying the quality revolution in our companies.

[34]Shingo, *Zero Quality Control,* p. 67.

7

□□□

Cost Management for Focused Subplants

CONSIDERING THE MAGNIFICENT SWEEP of innovative improvements in factory and office operations in the 1980s, the progress toward inventing imaginative *new* cost systems has been shockingly limited. The new systems must not only interface with the new superior factory and office but also simultaneously and drastically reform the productivity of the cost organization and systems through their simplification. Although cost systems have not been changing apace with factory and office improvements, most companies have been able to live with the old procedures, albeit with considerable unnecessary effort. In fact, some aspects of the conventional accounting systems actually hinder factory improvements. In a few limited cases, uninformed top executives have forced operating managements to discontinue implementing improvements because of erroneous indicators from these systems.

The search for new cost accounting concepts, management philosophy, and systems has been hampered by researchers who insist on continuing to pursue the same goals that have been so elusive in the past.[1] They would make a better contribution by focusing their efforts on developing pioneering visions of new ways to solve old problems and realizing that some perceived problems are not really problems but descriptions of the

[1]H. Thomas Johnson and Robert S. Kaplan, *Relevance Lost: The Rise and Fall of Management Accounting* (Boston: Harvard Business School Press, 1987), pp. 13–14.

realities of business. The following are examples of potentially disastrous "improvements" to cost systems:

1. Increasing the complexity of allocating overhead costs by developing different rates for different work centers.

2. Amortizing certain period expenses over future periods. This makes the current period look better but may mask the real need to cut costs of today's expenses. Unnecessary amortization of costs to future periods is always a gamble, since forecasting the volume of future sales, if any, is impossible. Preventive maintenance is an example of an expense that really benefits future production and thus would be a tempting amortization target.

3. Attempting to amortize engineering and other similar expenses by allocating them over the product life cycle. The misguided purpose would be to improve the accuracy of the product cost and to ensure that the burden charged to various products would reflect only their own product development costs, not those of other products. For example, Berliner and Brimson have said: "The practice of treating product- and process-development activities should be altered [and] major activities should be viewed as capital investments and ultimately charged to products that benefit from these investments." They go on to say, "Product costs that arise during the development, production and product logistics support phases must be linked to provide a long-term profitability picture and to support key management decisions about product line, mix and pricing."[2]

4. Persisting in the belief that there is or can be something called an accurate product cost, and increasing the detail and complexity of the cost system in its pursuit.

5. Increasing reliance on a computer system as a "vital communication link," rather than working toward increasing nose-to-nose communication, which is the most efficient of all communication methods.

6. Tinkering with machine depreciation methods to make high technology investments look better than when conventional depreciation methods are used.[3]

[2]Callie Berliner and James A. Brimson, eds., *Cost Management for Today's Advanced Manufacturing: The CAM-1 Conceptual Design* (Boston: Harvard Business School Press, 1988), pp. 140–42.
[3]Ibid., p. 30.

The stakes are high. Improvements to cost accounting and financial systems have the potential for major reductions in the accounting staff, perhaps by as much as 90 percent, if the sizes of these organizations in some of the world's best companies are indicative. (My colleague, Leroy Peterson, believes that 75 percent is a more reasonable number. Although my target is 20 percent higher than his, we both agree that there is room for *major* improvement.) Regardless of what accounting system is used, slavish belief in the financial numbers must be discarded. In most cases, simple common sense and arithmetic may be more valuable than the most "accurate" accounting. As Kanatsu says, "It is important to differentiate between precise calculations and the weight placed on these calculations for the purpose of business management decision making."[4]

CAVEAT: BEWARE OF THE AMATEUR'S ADVICE

The author is not an accounting specialist, nor has he been frequently involved in the development of accounting systems. His experience in the accounting area is limited to exposure in more than one hundred manufacturing companies during three decades. While it has been necessary for the author to use cost and financial systems information to develop cost-benefit analyses in conjunction with his processes and products projects, the author is still an amateur. In contrast, his colleagues have spent entire consulting and audit careers in the accounting and financial fields. Nevertheless, he has chosen to impart his often radical viewpoints in this chapter. Of one thing he is absolutely convinced: Much of the "new" accounting thinking is simply rehashed versions of the concepts that the author has heard in each year of the last three decades. Just as the factory has benefited from the unbiased thoughts of the inexperienced outsider, the author hopes that the accounting profession will eventually benefit from the viewpoints of those who are unafraid to challenge either the dogma of the past or the repackaged versions of accounting practices that are advocated by those who are too close to their mind-molding experiences of the past.

The author believes that the manufacturing world will not advance as rapidly as he would like and believes practical. Thus, some will choose

[4]Takashi Kanatsu, *TQC for Accounting: A New Role in Companywide Improvement* (Cambridge, Mass.: Productivity Press, 1990), pp. 25–26.

to view the world as it is likely to exist for many more years, and will opt for the course of least resistance, the "do nothing" route, or will rationalize delaying work on new accounting systems until the factory has reached its long-range potential. However, the fact is that every support function needs to start the process of reinventing its own "factory" in order to keep pace with the slow but continuous improvement in products and processes. This chapter is especially dedicated to the movers and shakers who are unafraid to open their minds to new ideas. They will understand that some of the ideas will fit neither the current nor the future environment in which their companies operate; they will be aware of the need to pick those ideas best suited to their own business.

My accounting specialist colleagues have reviewed the manuscript and identified those areas most likely to strike nerves, because of either the gulf between the state of business today and that of the factory of the future or the author's departure from conventional wisdom. As I consider my colleagues to be among the best in their field, their cautionary notes are liberally sprinkled throughout. For this valuable counterbalancing point of view, the author is especially indebted to two auditors, Robert Kutsenda and Charles (Chuck) Marx of Arthur Andersen & Co.

CHECKLIST: COST MANAGEMENT ZINGERS

Following is a checklist of the features of the superior cost management system of the future, summarizing the key messages of this chapter.

Inventory Accounting
1. Inventory transfers of finished products from work-in-process to finished goods accounts and to cost of goods sold can be based on estimated cost. Detail cost buildup will not be necessary for use in inventory accounting.
2. All material transactions and all payroll-related and other expense transactions can be charged to work-in-process at actual cost. Thus, standard costs and variance accounting will not be necessary.
3. A composite variance, calculated as the sum of actual period material, payroll, and expenses less the value of completed products at estimated cost, will replace all other variances.

4. All indirect payroll-related costs and other actual expenses will be charged to work-in-process inventory, eliminating the need to include them in overhead pools that would require allocation.

5. Detail reporting of purchases issued to manufacturing and of labor charged to inventory will be eliminated. A single report of the completion of a product will be used to charge material and labor automatically. This process, often called "backflushing," and the conditions that will make it a practical application are detailed in a prior work.[5]

6. Future material and work-in-process investments will be much smaller than today[6] and will therefore be a less significant portion of the company's balance sheet assets. Further, period-to-period inventory fluctuations will be minor. Therefore, as a practical matter, period beginning and ending inventories should be considered the same. Detail transactions will not need to be processed to maintain inventory balances. Instead, physical inventories will be taken once or twice a year, in a few minutes, to verify and adjust inventory balances.

Administrative Overhead

1. Administrative overhead (sales, engineering, and general and administrative costs) will never be used in evaluating a factory manager's performance. The managers of the administrative areas will be held accountable for controlling and improving their costs as a percentage of the cost of goods sold.

2. Budget-based responsibility reporting, modified only slightly to add target improvements, will be the key cost management tool for lowering not only administrative overhead but also factory burden expenses.

Material

1. Routine accounting for purchase price variance will be eliminated since the single supplier of an item will be paid at the annually negotiated price.

2. Material costs in the future will be maintained much as they have been maintained in the past.

---

[5]See Appendix 2.
[6]Richard T. Lubben, *Just-in-Time: An Aggressive Manufacturing Strategy* (New York: McGraw-Hill, 1988), p. 75.

Labor

1. Detail reporting of labor by item and operation for inventory accounting purposes will be unnecessary since period payroll will be charged to work-in-process inventory. Crow, Hronec, and Burns state, "Systems should accommodate a differential approach to transaction processing that will do away with the current practice of gathering data at all operations in sufficient detail to meet the lowest common denominator of detailed requirements."[7]

2. Operator and work center efficiency reporting will not be necessary. New cells and serpentine lines will produce precisely to schedule, regardless of the theoretical efficiency of doing this. The composite variance for the small, focused factory will be the only efficiency performance report required.

3. Labor estimates will be maintained by cell teams' operators and by the managers responsible for assembly line operations, not by industrial engineering specialists.

4. Conventional, single-operation routings can be used for recording estimated labor costs for cells, semicells, and assembly lines. Conventional, multiple-operations routings can continue to be used to cost functional department and subplant job shop operations.

Factory Burden

1. Burden (factory overhead) will be allocated to the sum of material and direct labor, instead of allocating to labor.

2. Plantwide burden rates will be preferred to different rates for different work centers.

Regarding the point concerning almost immaterial inventory levels of the future, my colleagues make the point that most companies are still far from attaining minimal inventory levels; thus, their managements might be inclined unduly to delay going to work on improved cost systems. While I agree that this is the case (and also that this is the danger), I cannot agree that companies can afford to set their inventory reduction goals any lower than drastically less than current levels. Indeed, in individual, small factories-within-the-factory, the reductions are almost always as radical as they should be. The *real* need is not for one system or the other, but for a system that can achieve most of the opportunities for

[7]David A. Crow, Steven M. Hronec and James K. Burns, "Cost Management in a JIT/CIM Environment," in John Mortimer, ed., *Just-in-Time: An Executive Briefing* (Bedford, Eng.: IFS, Ltd., 1986), p. 172.

improvement while the transition from just-in-case to just-in-time inventory levels is occurring.

CLUES FOR CREATIVE THINKING

Few factories have come close to achieving the attainable objectives of virtual elimination of inventories, setup (changeover) costs, quality defects, late production, and all other forms of waste. At the current rate of progress, another decade will pass before many factories can compare with leading Japanese companies. The people now contemplating new cost systems are understandably unable to disregard completely their present factory's status, since upgrading it will take years. Therefore, they must begin realistically to envision the new operating environment in which the new system will operate while developing systems suitable for both old-fashioned and superior manufacturing operations. The author does not intentionally minimize the complexity of managing the costs of an enterprise during the lengthy period of transition from old-fashioned techniques to the near-perfect superior factory. To force all of the radical, pioneering cost management practices enumerated in this chapter into production operations that have not yet been upgraded could have disastrous results. However, it certainly would be feasible and advisable to start to practice these new management philosophies, procedures, and systems in each of the new focused subplants shortly after they go on stream. Only by understanding and accepting the new factory environment will companies begin to see opportunities for radical departure from past preconceptions. Even after intellectually accepting the shining new world of near-perfect factories, we shall continue to be hampered by the ill-founded assumptions basic to the structures of past and current accounting systems. For example, the standard cost accounting system is almost universally used for the following:

1. Maintaining inventory accounts for the purpose of having accurate, timely information for the balance sheet. The chief concern of inventory accounting is to avoid surprise shortages of inventory resulting from year-end physical inventory taking.

2. Developing product costs with the objective of providing a basis for pricing products or dropping unprofitable products from the product line. Few companies have found either of these to be practical objectives because of the extreme difficulty or impossibility of calculating meaningful, "accurate" product costs.

3. Generating operating variances as a form of management by exception. Unfavorable variances should presumably trigger investigation to determine ways to avoid future variances.

In the future factory, inventories of materials and work-in-process will be a small fraction of what they are today.[8] The inventories that remain will be located in and controlled by small new focused factories within the large plant. This means that detecting and correcting inventory errors throughout the year will be fast and simple. Complete physical inventories will take only minutes to complete, as against hours or days in today's factories. Radical new ways of accounting for inventory start to surface once the inventory investment is so low that it has little materiality and once both factory and vendors start to adhere strictly to schedule. For one example, starting and ending inventories of materials and work-in-process could be considered to be constant, at historical average levels, for eleven months of the year. A complete physical inventory could be taken and valued at the end of the fiscal year. This type of procedure will eventually eliminate almost all detail inventory accounting activity for materials and work-in-process. A basic change in operating characteristics is most important to achieving the conditions to justify the assumption that work-in-process inventory is relatively constant. In the new focused subplants, production (capacity) will be controlled at the level required to meet the final assembly schedules. Fluctuations above and below the required level will no longer occur. It is the wild, uncontrolled fluctuation of work-in-process that has made routine detail accounting for it necessary. Nevertheless, *accurate* work-in-process accounting is extremely difficult and one of the major reasons that accountants and executives are fired (surprise inventory losses often come to light when physical inventory is taken). Perpetually consistent inventories will, therefore, be a major factor in making executive positions more secure.

In the new world of long-term vendor relationships, all purchase prices will be fixed annually, semiannually, or quarterly. The vendor's target costs, like those of the company, will be achieved. The target costs (in constant dollars) will always be lower than in previous periods as long as all suppliers in the pipeline are observing the practice of continuous improvement. Since all receipts from the long-term vendors will be priced at the agreed-upon fixed rate, purchase price variance accounting will be obsolete. In rare instances in which material is received at prices

[8]William L. Duncan, *Just-in-Time in American Manufacturing* (Dearborn, Mich.: Society of Manufacturing Engineers, 1988), p. 100.

other than the contract price, an exception procedure will be followed. (My audit colleagues note that if management permits more than minimal changes in price, the resulting exception procedure will deteriorate into a price variance system.)

This vision of customer–supplier relationships of the future will undoubtedly be one of the points that some will find to be most unrealistic. The author feels justified in optimistically anticipating that the vision will become reality in the majority of these relationships in the not-too-distant future. The primary reason for such optimism is the very large number of such relationships that already exist. In his experience, almost every company has some suppliers with which it already works in the cooperative mode, and some even in the mode of single source of supply. However, because of the difficulty and time required in converting almost all vendor–customer relationships to the new cooperative and permanent relationship, improved systems will need to accommodate both old- and new-style relationships in a transition period longer than the author would prefer.

Since manufacturing lead time will be slashed to merely hours or days and since the work-in-process levels will be correspondingly lower, all payroll and payroll-related costs, both direct and indirect, can flow directly out of inventory accounts and into the period cost of goods sold. This simplifying feature will completely eliminate the need to maintain any type of labor standard information at the operation, part, or subassembly levels. Further, once this assumption is accepted, it leads to understanding the notions of using estimated product costs to value transfers of completed products to (1) finished goods and (2) the cost of goods sold.

Exhibits 7-1, 7-2, and 7-3 are based on Takao Makido's description of the basic estimated cost accounting method, one of three blockbuster recent trends in Japanese accounting systems.[9] Exhibit 7-1 shows how the actual material usage, payroll, and payroll-related expenses and all other expenses could flow into work-in-process at actual cost. Material usage can be determined in one of two simple, low cost ways. The first would be to relieve the material from the inventory account by computer process when completions to finished goods are reported. The other would be based on the assumption that beginning and ending inventories are always considered to be the same, except when a physical inventory

[9]Yasuhiro Monden and Michiharu Sakurai, eds., *Japanese Management Accounting: A World Class Approach to Profit Management* (Cambridge, Mass.: Productivity Press, 1989), p. 8.

ACTUAL COSTS & EXPENSES

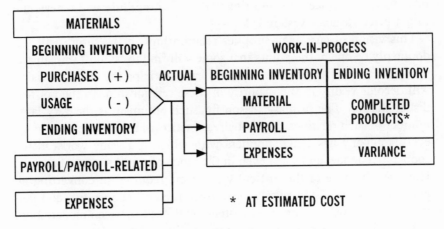

EXHIBIT 7-1

FINISHED GOODS ACCOUNT

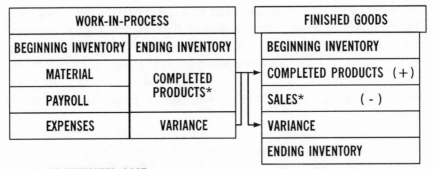

EXHIBIT 7-2

is taken. In this case, material usage would be equal to material purchases. In Exhibit 7–1, the ending inventory is calculated as beginning inventory plus actual material, payroll, and expenses less completed products valued at the estimated cost.

The composite variance, depicted in Exhibit 7–1, embodies a critically important new management philosophy, consistent with the new, near-perfect factory. This includes the presumption that the simplest measure

COST OF SALES

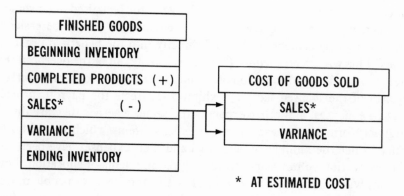

EXHIBIT 7-3

of period performance is the total amount that the actual costs of production exceed or fall short of the estimated product costs for the units sent to finished goods. Since continuous improvement must be a routine part of every focused factory's daily routine, the variance will be favorable in most periods and will be quite small in proportion to the finished products' value. The focused factory manager will be responsible for controlling the total costs of production and will continuously be presented with budget reports that inform him of the cost trends. Thus, neither he nor his superior should be concerned with a breakdown of the variance into its components. The proper response to an unfavorable variance will not be to isolate the reason for variance. Rather, it should be to identify the best way to lower expenditures in *all* categories of payroll and operating expense and then to implement changes to yield the biggest cost reduction. The action-oriented continuous attack on all cost elements will preclude the possibility of a recurring unfavorable variance.

Personnel who have previously been part of factory service (maintenance, for example) and office staff organizations and whose payroll and expenses have always been allocated to manufacturing operations will be far fewer in number in the twenty-first-century factory. Of those remaining in the new focused factory, as many as feasible will be moved out of central offices and into the new focused organization. Incidentally, Ishikawa contends that staff (administrative overhead *and* factory overhead) should work 70 percent of the time performing services and 30 percent as general staff.[10] His point is this: When management insists on such a ratio of service, it helps to minimize the risk that staff will begin to believe and to act as though they are in charge of the benefited organization. Further, when the 70 percent target is achieved, it should be easier to transfer that percentage of the staff directly into the benefited organizations. This will greatly reduce (but not eliminate) all of the overhead that needs to be allocated to various focused factories. The cost management system of the focused factory, Exhibit 7–1, treats the payroll, payroll-related expenses, and other expenses the same, whether they are direct, indirect, former overhead, or those expense items which are still allocated. Since the number of personnel and their expenses have been cut, the transaction volumes and processing requirements of allocation transactions will plummet. With overhead and factory services people moved into the focused factory organization, their costs will be more accurately reported than under any allocation scheme.

Since actual direct labor will be charged to the work-in-process inventory account, reporting production by part number, operation number, or production order number will not be necessary. Actual payroll and related benefits are the lowest level of detail necessary. Many factories have always had detail production reporting for the combined purposes of reporting detailed operator and workcenter efficiencies, maintaining inventory accounts, and tracking production progress. Since twenty-first-century subplants will start and complete almost any job in less than one day, tracking progress will not be necessary. New management techniques for operating cells, lines, and focused subplants will make efficiency reporting obsolete.

Exhibit 7–2 tracks the completion of products from work-in-process into the finished goods inventory account. The reported completion of products, at estimated cost, is used to reduce the work-in-process account while simultaneously increasing that of finished goods by the same amount. At period end, the composite variance, described previously, is calculated and transferred to the finished goods account. As the exhibit shows, the ending inventory is derived by adding completed products at estimated value to beginning inventory and subtracting sales (at estimated cost). The next exhibit, 7–3, shows that the cost of sales consists of sales valued at estimated cost, less the composite variance.

This section has covered the basics of the superior inventory accounting system. Following sections of the chapter will further explain some

---

[10]Kaoru Ishikawa, trans. David J. Lu, *What Is Total Quality Control? The Japanese Way* (Englewood Cliffs, N.J.: Prentice-Hall, 1985), p. 108.

past false perceptions of accounting systems needs and several new, superior concepts.

PRODUCT COST: FACT OR FICTION

The Japanese are gravitating toward the elimination of standard cost in favor of estimated cost at the end product level. We should find this of compelling interest. Many Japanese recognize that it would be extremely difficult and costly, if not impossible, to develop an "accurate" product cost. After all, standard costs are a result of a best attempt to forecast several unforecastable factors, including the future mix and volume of product sales. If a normally low volume, high cost product has a sales volume much higher than normal, it may determine whether every other product was profitable. Total sales volume is what finally determines the amount of profit or loss.

Virtually every theoretician says determining sales price is one of two primary uses of product cost. Yet, in decades of experience in hundreds of factories, the author has never yet found a factory able to set prices based on a formula for adding a standard profit margin to product cost. (The author, as an amateur, might be mistaken. Formula pricing might have been applicable in some of these companies. However, the author is supported in his opinion by the works of experts like Berliner and Brimson. Of the twelve factors they list that affect prices, the last is product cost.[11] The author believes their sequence reflects the relative importance of cost in pricing). The primary reason that product cost is of such little importance to pricing is not that product costs are inaccurate (although this is true) but that the market (supply and demand)[12] and chief competitor (not the seller) determines prices. When an industry is working at capacity, and when customer order backlogs are high, fast-acting executives will increase prices. Conversely, when order backlogs are low, prices must be reduced in an attempt to increase sales to as close to the break-even point as possible. A new product that has no competitors should be priced as high as possible (but not so high as to dampen sales). Further, even when an item is found to have high cost, typically because it is a low demand item, it is likely that applying a formula calculation will set the price higher than competitors' prices. Since few

[11]Berliner and Brimson, *Cost Management for Today's Advanced Manufacturing*, pp. 86–87.
[12]Isao Shinohara, *NPS New Production System: JIT Crossing Industry Boundaries* (Cambridge, Mass.: Productivity Press, 1988), pp. 113–16.

customers would choose to buy from the company offering higher prices, the price must be lowered. Most product lines must include numerous loss leaders since dropping them from the product line might drive customers to lower price competitors. As Schonberger wrote, "There is no good reason for costs to be ultra-accurate. For pricing and product-line decisions, roughly accurate costs are good enough."[13]

EFFICIENCY REPORTING: DEAD AS A DOORNAIL

In the heyday of incentive standards, under which a factory worker was paid for the number of pieces he produced, every worker was an island. The same has been true for people working under a measured day work plan. These workers have not been paid for the number of pieces produced. However, their production has been measured against a standard for the purpose of evaluating their performance. In the author's experience, incentive pay and measured day rate (both standards systems) have worked, in that they cause more pieces to be produced, per hour, than when employees are not paid incentives or when their performance is not measured.

Employees working under these systems have, however, been isolated from other workers by the distances between operations and insulated from them by large piles of inventory between operations. They have been little islands of production, with no direct contact with other workers from whom they receive work and to whom they send work. Incentive pay and performance measurement are necessary to provide incentive to take parts out of one big container, perform the operation, and put what they have finished into another big container as fast as possible all day long. No wonder the worker who receives neither extra pay nor recognition for this type of operation works well below his maximum potential. All of this will change in the superior factory of the future.

Someday the factory will be a completely synchronized network of assembly, subassembly, and manufactured component operations. In the network each serpentine line and U-form cell will be directly linked to prior and next operations, with no more than a single unit of inventory between operations. Given these characteristics, every worker can work only as fast as the employees stationed before and after his operation. Thus, individual incentive and measurement standards no longer make

---

[13]Richard J. Schonberger, *Building a Chain of Customers: Linking Business Functions to Create The World Class Company* (New York: Free Press, 1990), p. 181.

sense. Group incentives will usually be equally nonsensical, since there may be up to several hundred workers in the network, none of whom will be able to change the entire network's output rate. Also, the entire network will be expected to produce only as much each day as the schedule calls for—no more and no less. So using incentive pay to try to squeeze more than is required from the network does not make good business sense.

Fortunately, the people in the network will no longer be islands unto themselves. They will be in close proximity to the people performing operations before and after them and among large numbers of other network teams. In the new gamelike environment, they will automatically be motivated to perform well. In the work "game" they can constantly struggle to complete their operation before the next person is ready to accept the item and before the preceding operator completes the unit on which he is working. In the well-designed new cells and lines, the physical organization of the equipment and the new team spirit have spurred teams to perform at levels at least as high as under incentive pay. Since use of standards requires small armies of industrial engineers, timekeepers, and payroll clerks, their elimination will cut deeply into overhead costs without sacrificing productivity.

ALLOCATION: PRECISION VERSUS MANAGEMENT PERSPECTIVE

For decades some consultants and most theoreticians have been advocating better, more detailed allocation of services to the products or factory processes receiving the benefit of the services. From a purist theoretical viewpoint, it seems logical to assume that if a given service benefits one product more than another, the "real" costs of the two products will be distorted if the amounts allocated to both are not proportionate to the cost of the service provided. However, the executive whom the author credits with management perspective has always doubted if the fuss and bother of precise allocation recommended by the theorist is warranted when viewed from a pragmatic, hard-headed business standpoint.

Adopting a system for detailed charging of services to the benefited areas would cause major increases in cost and transaction activity, which has usually precluded doing so. However, some would like to make a case for taking advantage of the continuing decrease in computer hardware costs to increase the amount of activity and processing performed in the allocating process.[14] Sadly, they do not realize that the computer age has not contributed to better operating results on either a national or an international scale. As computer costs have decreased, companies are spending ever greater proportions of their budgets on new systems development, software, hardware, and personnel. At the same time, the number of the white collar employees whose jobs are involved in computer support is constantly increasing. Nor have any other tangible benefits (such as reductions in inventory) surfaced. The folly of the "let the computer do more" philosophy should be clear by how. The computer cannot acquire information out of thin air. It takes people to create and to input transactions. Then, given the transactions on which to work, the computer can execute up to hundreds of millions of operations every second, in the process generating a vast sea of analytical information. Unfortunately, the computer not only can but does generate an overwhelming amount of data. The mountain of data is either stored (waste?) or fed to people who are then expected to take some type of action. As . if any company could afford to have that many data recipients! But the cycle continues—every day people are feeding computers more and more data, the computers are generating more and more data for people! As a result, businesses need either to add more people or simply to ignore most of the generated data. Most enterprises are doing both.

The author believes that much more intelligent use can and must be made of the computer. To do so means finding ways to *reduce* the amount of transactions, *simplify* computer logic, and *limit* information processed and stored. This will greatly improve the productivity of the white collar force by reducing the amount of unnecessary work that computer systems are causing and will also reduce the computer's operating costs.

The author recognizes two types of overhead, the first of which is often thought of as corporate overhead. The author calls it administrative overhead since it consists of the sales, engineering, and general and administrative costs. The second is factory overhead, which the author calls burden (since the burden of paying for it falls on the direct labor worker). It consists of factory, factory service, and staff function costs. This distinction is important in terms of the future methods of accounting for these costs in the new, superior factory. It is also important in determining the methods that will be suitable during the lengthy transition period when both old-style and new-style departments and focused subplants will be operating.

---

[14]See H. Thomas Johnson and Robert S. Kaplan, *Relevance Lost: The Rise and Fall of Management Accounting* (Boston: Harvard Business School Press, 1987), p. 5.

As a point of reference, the product line operating statement, Exhibit 7–4, shows a company's operating results for two products. Sales, engineering, and general and administrative costs are corporate expenses subject to allocation to the products, on some predetermined base. In the example, some factory-related costs, such as equipment depreciation, have been distributed on the basis of direct labor and are part of the cost of sales. Other costs, such as the sales, engineering, and general and administrative categories, are typically distributed to products on some other base—for example, sales volume.

The following example assumes that the cost of the purchasing organization is a general and administrative cost and that the question needing an answer is, "On what base should purchasing be allocated?" This raises a second question: "Should the allocation be based on a predetermined distribution or on actual period data?" Let us review a few of the possible bases for allocation and the difficulties of using these to calculate accurate cost.

On the surface, material usage value would appear to be a logical allocation base for purchasing cost as long as purchasing costs are proportionate to the amount spent on material. However, this is highly unlikely since ordering a low cost and a high cost material are likely to require the same amount of time and administrative expense. That being the case, a better base would appear to be the number of orders placed for the materials required for each product. However, if products require the same materials, another dilemma arises. The cost of purchasing could logically be split equally between the two products since each order

PRODUCT LINE PROFITABILITY

Operating Statement ($000)		
	Product A	Product B
Sales	$2,000	$1,000
Cost of Sales	1,000	500
Gross Margin	1,000	500
Sales	300	150
Engineering	300	150
General & Administrative	200	100
Pretax Profit	200	100

EXHIBIT 7–4

would be likely to contain some material for each product. If, however, the lower volume product B were to be discontinued by reason of the high cost of the overhead charged to it, 50 percent more would suddenly have to be allocated to product A. But the volume of purchase orders that would be required would not change if the common materials continue to be delivered just-in-time, daily. Finally, if marketing must offer both products in price ranges set by numerous competitors and must offer both products in order to sell either successfully, the value of finely apportioning costs to products seems questionable.

The point of this example is that allocating purchasing cost on *some* base is possible even though the base may be neither entirely accurate nor rational from the standpoint of business necessity. However, the "real" cost changes dynamically as usage volumes change. Is a dynamic system that changes the allocation as volume fluctuates warranted, or is the practical alternative of moving purchasing personnel and costs into the focused factory whenever possible a much simpler, better alternative? The author believes the latter to be the best. If different orders could and should be placed for each product, the logical conclusion should be to move the purchasing function into the focused product factories, not to allocate purchasing costs. This would mean that the purchasing cost could be charged to inventory as previously discussed. If some remaining purchasing cost needs to be allocated, the simplest base and the simplest system should be used to allocate it. Sales volume of a product is one of the least likely of the bases to have a close correlation between the amount of purchasing effort and the benefits by product, and hence it requires little additional discussion.

From this single simple example of the difficulties associated with allocating purchasing costs, one can see that as long as costs must be allocated and the allocation must have some base, finding a base that "accurately" allocates them will be difficult (if not impossible). More important, the real question is whether any valuable business purpose is served by fussing about what base to use or whether the allocating needs to be dynamically revised. Reasons for using the simplest possible allocation base with a minimum amount of analysis are as follows:

1. The resulting product costs will not be used to set sales prices in most businesses.
2. If all allocated services were to be carefully analyzed and calculated, the summary results for all product lines are likely to have relatively little spread between the highest and the lowest costs.

When the costs do differ, competent executives will probably already have a rough idea of the correct weight to assign to each. However, the important question is whether or not more accurate allocation will make any difference in operations or in profitability.

3. The real payoff, if any, will not come from knowing which products get what percentage of the services. Rather, it will come from cutting the costs of the services and controlling them in the target ratio of service cost to total gross margin.

4. The Japanese are allocating the highest percentage of their administrative costs based on sales, using mainly predetermined percentages (versus attempting to allocate "actual" costs).[15]

The total amount of allocated costs should be minimized by continuously reducing and subsequently controlling them. The simplest, lowest cost base on which to allocate would be sales. It would be even simpler to stop allocating altogether, and instead to manage the costs within a narrow band of acceptable variance from a target ratio of cost to gross margin. This would ensure that profit targets would be met.

The majority viewpoint regarding administrative overhead is that the factory organizations (divisions) of a company cannot control these costs.[16] Therefore, according to this viewpoint, they should not be allocated to the factory manager or his organization. However, in most organizations these allocations are made and go into the financial evaluation of the manager's performance. The author's conclusion is that the consensus has been right all along, and these costs should not be allocated to the factory. They also should not be accounted for as a part of the product cost. The superior cost system will not allocate them. Instead, it will operate on a new set of cost management philosophies, as follows:

1. The managers of overhead services, not the recipients of the benefits of the services, will be deemed by executive management to be responsible for controlling their costs and equitably performing services to the organizations benefiting from them directly or abstractly.

2. If the services and the transactions of the overhead area are easily segregated by the organization benefited, the people involved

---

[15]Monden and Sakurai, *Japanese Management Accounting.*
[16]Takeyuki Tani, "How Japanese Companies allocate Corporate Cost," in *ibid.,* p. 295.

should be moved into that organization and managed directly by its manager.

3. Cost comparisons, one product to another, for the purpose of comparing profitability, will be based on marginal profit contribution. The managers of the overhead organizations will be responsible for controlling the costs of their operations. Even more important, the managers must regulate these costs dynamically to keep them at a consistent percentage of the cost of sales, while continuously working to reduce that percentage in the long run.

4. To the extent that calculated product costs are used as one factor in setting prices, the ratio of total administrative overhead costs to the total cost of sales of all products will be used to "burden" products with this overhead. Thus, all products will have the same burden rate, a procedure of the utmost simplicity, and the only logical way to treat costs that defy practical tracing of services performed to the organizations and products benefiting.

For some time, while factories are being transformed into superior manufacturers, allocating administrative overhead to products will continue to be necessary. Knowing this to be true, companies should allocate in the simplest, most productive way. Sakurai's conclusions concerning Japanese accounting practices should be of particular interest. He says: "Japanese managers prefer simple systems, especially in overhead allocation. They do not wish to use sophisticated methods such as activity costing."[17] Companies continuing to pursue ways to apportion more "accurately" costs that have no direct relationship between services performed and products benefited are engaging in an exercise in futility. The idea was a beautiful dream, but the reality is a nightmare.

TRANSITION ALLOCATION OF BURDEN

Manufacturing burden has been applied almost universally based on direct labor hours. However, consensus is developing that this practice is questionable given that direct labor, for most companies, is only 5 to 10 percent of the total product cost. The cost breakdown, Exhibit 7–5, represents a somewhat typical distribution of product costs. With only

---

[17]Michiharu Sakurai, "The Influence of Factory Automation on Management Accounting Practices: A Study of Japanese Companies," in Robert S. Kaplan, ed., *Measures for Manufacturing Excellence* (Boston: Harvard Business School Press, 1990), p. 58.

BURDEN ALLOCATION
BASED ON LABOR

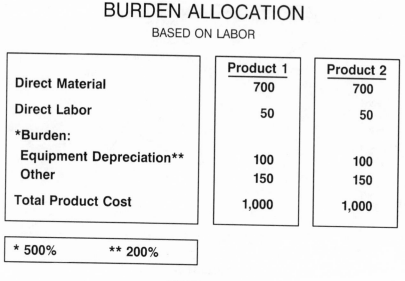

	Product 1	Product 2
Direct Material	700	700
Direct Labor	50	50
*Burden:		
Equipment Depreciation**	100	100
Other	150	150
Total Product Cost	1,000	1,000

* 500%   ** 200%

EXHIBIT 7-5

minor variation, the author has found this structure of costs in every country in which he has worked. Most companies develop a burden rate, 500 percent in this case, and in calculating product costs or in accounting for inventory apply this rate to every standard hour of labor. Some make a case for applying burden based on machine hours rather than labor hours. This would presumably result in more "accurate" costs for assigning new technology to the products using it. In the example in Exhibit 7-5, the rate of equipment depreciation is 200 percent of labor cost. This figure would disturb those who would all too readily assume that because new technology is expensive (and especially expensive in relation to the labor required), it requires less labor. New technology is always perceived to require less labor, although all too often this is not the case. There are two reasons for refuting the universality of this assumption or even its applicability to more than a minority of enterprises. First, in Japan where the state of automation is assumed to be most advanced, the ratio of direct labor costs to total product cost has *not* changed appreciably in more than two decades.[18] Second, an analysis of the annual reports of the largest manufacturing companies on the Fortune 500 list, Exhibit 7-6, shows that total plant and equipment depreciation charges average close to 4 percent of sales. Since roughly half of that number is factory equipment, the 10 percent of cost of sales used for depreciation in Exhibit 7-5 seems

[18]Monden and Sakurai, *Japanese Management Accounting*, Chapter 16.

DEPRECIATION TRENDS

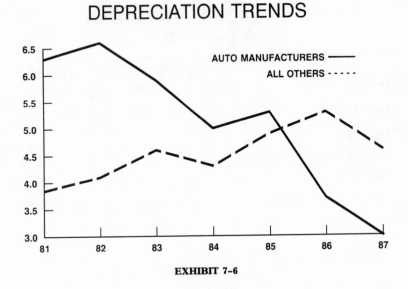

EXHIBIT 7-6

quite liberal. Despite these arguments, some people would still insist that new, technologically advanced processes would represent a much larger proportion of product cost. Thus, they would still prefer to see examples that amplify the differences between allocation of burden by machine-hour and by direct labor. This skewing of examples simply cannot be allowed to win the case since allocation of depreciation by machine-hour adds complexity and cost to the accounting system. As a generalization, the logic that holds that new technology costs (in the form of depreciation) must be a greater part of product cost is flawed. Why? It fails to recognize that the higher the process cost, the higher the output is expected to be. Thus, very expensive processes should have high volumes of output over which to spread their costs. If this is not the case, something must be wrong. Perhaps uneconomical equipment has been purchased. One must be able to expect output to increase as much as, or more than, the cost increases when the latest technology is adopted.

The Computer Aided Manufacturing-International (CAM-I) project advocates consideration of allocating burden to products based on the machine-hours used (among other, perhaps less practical, alternatives).[19] Exhibit 7-7 shows the machine-hours that would be used for allocating burden for each of two products, if indeed machine-hours were to be

[19]Berliner and Brimson *Cost Management for Today's Advanced Manufacturing*, pp. 29–31.

BURDEN ALLOCATION
BASED ON MACHINE-HOURS

	Product 1	Product 2
Direct Material	700	700
Direct Labor	50	50
Burden:		
Equipment Depreciation	25	175
Other	150	150
Total Product Cost	925	1,075

Hours of Machine Use	25	175

EXHIBIT 7-7

used as the allocation base. In the example, Product 2 uses seven times as many machine hours as Product 1. As a consequence, the "accurate" costs of the total product are now 7.5 percent different from the result when allocating the burden based on labor, as Exhibit 7-5 shows. However, one must remember that these standard costs are based on an inaccurate forecast or prediction of the total sales volume as well as the product mix. Further, inaccurate standard material costs are always used, as evidenced by routine occurrence of purchase variances. Worse yet, labor standards are typically highly inaccurate as evidenced by large manufacturing efficiency variances. Even the forecast of future burden costs are inaccurate.

One must seriously consider the ramifications of discovering that the "accurate" product costs of some products are greater than reported under the labor allocation basis. If prices of the two products in the example had previously been set based on the "erroneous" cost of a thousand dollars each, it is logical to suppose that these prices would usually be close to the average of competitors' prices. If so, raising the price of Product 2 is likely to lower it sales volume while the converse would happen with Product 1. In this example, the overall results would be to reduce sharply the utilization of the new machine, perhaps risking the feasibility of recouping its cost. Finally, Monden and Sakurai report that Japanese companies have found that switching to allocation by machine-hours is quite complex, effectively limiting the number of companies using or planning to use the machine rate technique.[20]

When an executive consensus agrees that the most "accurate" practical product cost is still only relatively accurate, the next step will be to agree that adding a standard percentage to product costs to cover administrative overhead and profit is a reasonable practice. The result can then be viewed as a minimum price target (although actual prices may still need to be higher or lower than the target in response to competitors' prices and market conditions). Next, examination of another way to allocate burden should be undertaken, in light of the fact that material cost, 70 percent of the total product cost, may be high for some products requiring an hour of machine time, and low for others (also requiring one machine hour), as illustrated in Exhibit 7–8. One should really wonder, when the difference in the amount or value of the material in Product 2 is so much higher than in Product 1, if the absolute price markup for recovering administrative overhead costs and profit should be so proportionately higher for Product 1.

If burden were to be allocated based on the total of direct costs (material and labor), Exhibit 7–9, it would raise the target price of Product 2. Now Product 2, with total material and labor costs higher than those of Product 1, will have a higher target sales price, based on having been assigned a larger amount of overhead than would have been the case

VARIABLE MATERIAL CONTENT

	Product 1	Product 2
Direct Material	250	1,150
Direct Labor	50	50
Burden (500%)	250	250
Total Product Cost	550	1,450

EXHIBIT 7–8

[20]Monden and Sakurai, *Japanese Management Accounting*, p. 267.

BURDEN ALLOCATION
BASED ON DIRECT COST

	Product 1	Product 2
Direct Material & Labor	300	1,200
Burden (33 1/3%)	100	400
Total Product Cost	400	1,600

EXHIBIT 7-9

when labor alone was the allocation base. Having greater material value, Product 2 would logically be expected to have higher inherent value and thus should be able to command higher prices. Further, when the higher material costs are caused by the use of larger amounts of material in the product, the larger amounts of material will substantially increase several indirect categories of cost, including receiving, transport, and storage of the material. Since burden allocation is not based on the cost of material used in each product, the material-related costs are not equitably shared by the products. Allocating burden on the basis of the combined total of material and labor costs has two important advantages. First, it is logical to burden a product's material with overhead cost. The method is not only simple but also effective for minimizing product cost "inaccuracies." The resulting product costs will be heavily influenced by the cost of material, and since material cost standards are the least inaccurate of all standards, the product costs will come a little closer to being "accurate." Allocation of burden to total direct material and labor cost will be an important feature of the transition cost system.

PRODUCT COST: STANDARD OR ESTIMATE

Material, labor, and overhead (burden) are the fundamental elements of virtually every existing cost management system. To calculate the costs of a complete product, systems today maintain labor and overhead costs for every routing operation and all three costs for every completed manufactured part, subassembly, assembly, and final product. For all of modern history, accountants have bemoaned the "accuracy" of their cost systems and the data used by the systems, because they have known the following reasons for inaccuracy:

1. Numerous overhead costs simply defy logical allocation. Because there are no such logical bases, it is impractical or impossible to define bases for allocation.
2. Inflation and other market factors always make the actual costs of purchases today different from the standard costs. Usually standard cost is lower than actual.
3. Actual labor costs are almost never the same as standard. When employees are paid for the amount produced, actual labor is usually much less than standard. When employees are paid on an hourly basis, the amount of production is rarely as high as the standard.

Considering the inaccuracies in the detail elements of a product's cost, one can quickly conclude that rolling these elements up to final product costs yields a result that might be considered an estimated cost at best!

Whether or not to be concerned with the accuracy of the product cost estimate is an interesting question. If the proportionate amounts of total sales are like those in Exhibit 7–10, one can see that the accuracy of labor by itself would have limited impact on the total product cost. However,

OPERATING RESULTS

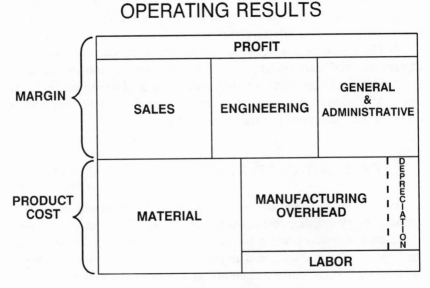

EXHIBIT 7–10

since manufacturing overhead, a very large portion of the total cost, is allocated to labor, any inaccuracy is magnified. This will change in new systems in which manufacturing overhead (burden) will be allocated based on the total of direct materials and labor.

Since the best possible "accurate" standard costs are, in reality, merely an approximation (estimate) of the cost, one must begin to wonder if the voluminous detail and precision that go into the development of a standard cost are necessary. Estimated product cost is one alternative to conventional standard cost as previously explained. The superior inventory accounting system, previously discussed, credits work-in-process inventory and debits finished goods by extending the quantities of end products transferred by an estimated cost. On the surface, that would seem to eliminate the need for costing any of the components or subassemblies. In most companies that assemble products from both purchased and manufactured components, many of the components are also products for service or for other factories of the company. Thus, the cost management system must have cost data for both products and components.

The author's definition of standard, estimated and actual costs is somewhat different from the types that are generally accepted. When discussing a product cost system or a new target cost system, the author's definition are as follows:

Materials

1. *Standard cost.* The conventional standard cost, which for most companies would mean the most recent prices at the time of the once-a-year setting of standards.

2. *Estimated cost.* For new purchases for which no purchase history is available, potential suppliers are asked to submit either estimates or quotations, which are then used to develop a standard cost.

3. *Actual cost.* When the goals of superior manufacturing have been achieved, standard and actual cost will not differ, since an annually negotiated purchase price will be used as both the material standard and as the basis for paying the vendor.

Labor

1. *Standard cost.* Although the standard cost might be developed by time study or by motion-time measurement techniques, it could also be based on the actual history. However, when the author mentions standard labor cost, he means the formal, engineered standard.

2. *Estimated cost.* The author advocates actual cost history and favors

elimination of costly engineered standards. The estimated cost will be maintained by the factory people and will be updated as frequently as improvements cause costs to change. This will typically be monthly. Once (perhaps twice) a year, the latest estimated cost will be used as a basis for the standard cost for the new fiscal period.

3. *Actual cost.* Last month's actual cost will become the current estimated cost.

The words "estimated cost" should not be construed to mean that estimates should be drawn out of thin air. Every estimate should be based on the best, lowest cost (for their development), most readily available cost data. For example, material cost has always been and will continue to be one of the most accurate elements of product cost. In both transition and superior cost systems, therefore, material costs should be maintained in about the same way as they are now and should continue to be summed up for each assembly level, including that of the end product.

Accounting for labor requires more changes in systems and procedures than do other cost areas, although labor is no longer one of the biggest costs. As illustrated in the upper left of Exhibit 7–11, superior factories of the future will be able to revise drastically the concept of the routing.

MANUFACTURING ROUTING

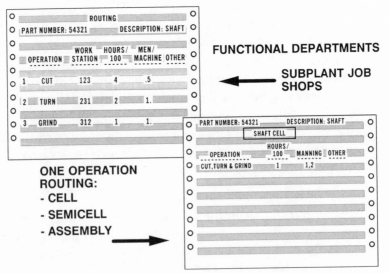

EXHIBIT 7-11

In the past the routing has been a document useful only for listing the sequence of manufacturing operations performed on each manufactured part. Each operation on a part tended to be performed in different workcenters or departments by operators who attended a single machine. The routing was always a "home" for labor standards for each operation. The labor standard might have been based on time study, predetermined time/motion elements, or even estimates, in the case of newly released engineering designs. When all operations on a part are performed in cells or semicells (a group of machines in close proximity),[21] a single-step routing provides all routing information needs as illustrated in the lower right portion of Exhibit 7–11. A team of cell operators now performs all operations on the shaft, and the estimated or approximate man-hours per 100 pieces produced are applicable to the entire team. In this example, the cell can be manned with either one or two people, which usually has only a minor effect on the productivity of the cell. When two people man the cell, there are brief periods when all machines are cycling, which means that both must sometimes wait for a machine to complete its cycle before they have something productive to do. When one person is manning the cell, this idle time is reduced, but the average machine idle time is usually higher.

In the conventional cost management system, a specialist, the industrial engineer, sets standards for labor operations based on stopwatch timing of the operation or a compilation of predetermined standards for the various elements of the motion and distances involved. The new philosophy of management would place responsibility for maintaining estimated labor (posted to the routing) on the cell team. It need only enter the number of hours required on the routing when it first produces it or when changes have been made to increase output. When new designs are released, the team would enter its best estimate of the required time, based on its experience with similar items or, if it has not had a similar item, simply its best expert estimate.

Only time will tell if any company will be able to eliminate multiple operation routings completely. The author thinks it may be a long time, if ever, before all operations will be performed on assembly lines, in cells, or in semicells, thus eliminating the multiple operation routing. In the meantime, it will continue to be necessary to use multiple operation routings, like those on Exhibit 7–11, for the operations still organized as functional departments or reorganized into subplant job shops.

[21]See Appendix 2.

The beauty of the one-operation routing concept for new cells, semi-cells, and assembly lines is that most companies use computer systems,which already handle costs of single-operation routings. The only difference in labor costs in future systems will be where their responsibility will rest—in the hands of the industrial engineers or in those of the factory team. In the case of assembly lines, some of which are manned with hundreds of operators, the single-operation routing can also be used to capture and maintain the most basic cost data (for example, the man-hours per 100 units produced and the various manning levels required by various levels of market demand). Whenever the large number of people on an assembly line precludes the assembly team from being responsible for units per man-hour and manning level information, the manager responsible is a better choice than the industrial engineer. After all, observing the number of units produced per hour and the number of people manning the line to determine the estimated hours required is not very difficult. In the future, assembly line estimates need not distinguish between direct and indirect labor categories. Employees such as material handlers and supervisors who are dedicated to servicing a line can be lumped with direct labor, thus reducing the amount of burden requiring allocation. The same would be true of cells, if machining cells were large enough to need dedicated indirect personnel. However, this is rarely the case, as the majority of cells in the world have a small number of machines and operators.

Even in the remaining functional departments and subplant job shops of the future, superior manufacturers will make changes that will affect the way one must think of cost management. Historically, most machining operations have been designed as one-man, one-machine operations. Because man and machine work cycles rarely, if ever, match precisely, great waste of labor has resulted. The main thrust of improvements in this area will be to increase man-to-machines ratios. In most factories in which the author has worked, man–machine ratios can be doubled or even tripled by simply moving machines close enough to make it practical for one person to attend more machines. Where the variety (size and shape) of items machined is very low and their required volumes are high, the man–machine ratio can always be improved by low cost loading and unloading devices. Eventually, as more and more machines can be attended by one person, the output per hour will be determined by the machine cycle time. The labor cost of that machine will then be a function of how many machines are kept in operation by one person. It does not make sense to try to determine how much labor is applied to a specific item versus that applied to other parts. To involve people responsible for manufacturing in the development and maintenance of initial estimates of machine-hour output for a newly released design, the subsequent recording of the actual production rate and the updating of the changes that always ensue will not be difficult in the focused factory environment.

For executive management, at the outset of planning and developing new, superior cost systems, the top business priority is to review the impracticality of developing "accurate" costs for the companies' products. The inevitable conclusion must be that accurate costs are not achievable for most companies. The second business priority must be to determine which types of cost are easily maintained and the procedures necessary to maintain them with the highest practical accuracy. The inevitable executive conclusion of those dedicated to achieving focused factories-within-the-factory and committed to the delegation of complete authority and responsibility for performance must be as follows: Those responsible for purchases will continue to maintain purchase cost information, and those responsible for manufacturing operations should maintain labor cost estimates.

However powerful and simple these new concepts of product costing are, success will be limited unless they are managed the way they must be, as changes in actual practice and not simply as changes in terminology. The best possible force for assuring industrywide success will come from developing standard definitions for new techniques. The standard definitions will serve to guide the accounting profession in the regulation of the design of new systems.

TARGET COST: A COST REVOLUTION

Thinking executives must embrace the concept of continuous product cost improvement, given hundreds of examples of success stories in both Japan and the West. More important, they must begin to implement the improvements fundamental to its achievement. The target cost methods of the Japanese are one systematic approach for planning and achieving cost targets. Today's cost accounting systems are not suitable for planning improvements. They have been developed for the primary purpose of providing financial report information and have no single feature designed to support continuous improvement. For example, standard costs are the foundation on which operating statements and financial projections are based. But freezing standard costs for one year (one-half year in a few cases, one-quarter year in very rare cases) is necessary to establish a baseline for use in a practical system designed to prepare financial projections and subsequently report actual versus planned results.

In an environment in which every cell and line in the factory and in the vendor's factories are expected to lower operating costs at least slightly, every month, based on companywide targets, new procedures and systems must be developed. The systems should support broadcasting of the *target* and measuring the progress various departments have made toward achieving them. Target costing may be the key to diverting attention from engineered standards and accumulation of actual cost information on a monthly basis. Integration of target costs into the financial system may well bridge the gap between theoretical standards and reality. Cross and Lynch point out: "Variances, rather than serving to update goals [i.e. standards] are merely bled off to the general ledger. The underlying assumption, of course, is that the standards are right and reality is wrong."[22]

Target cost concepts are different during the new product design phase and after the new product is released for production. Following are ideas for target costs for the product design phase. A simplified explanation of how a target cost should be developed for a new or significantly revised product starts with marketing, which determines the target volume and sales price. Aggressive pricing is necessary to ensure that the product will win a large share of the worldwide market by virtue of having the lowest price among competing products. Once the target price has been established, management's target margin is subtracted, and the remainder is the target product cost.

The purpose for setting a target cost is to initiate a self-fulfilling prophesy. The target cost inevitably becomes the actual cost when used to control the cost of the product designed and the cost of plant and equipment designed to produce it. The new product target cost process may sound more like black magic than science. However, most companies' marketing departments usually keep their fingers on the market's pulse. They know what types of product features have excited the market historically and thus have a reasonable experience base for anticipating the market's reaction to new planned features. If they doubt their own knowledge, or even if they are confident in their knowledge and want to verify it, they conduct market surveys to be absolutely positive of the projected market reaction. Marketing executives must also have a good feel for the prices that a product could be expected to demand and the target prices that their competitors are likely to ask.

[22]Kelvin F. Cross and Richard L. Lynch, *Measure Up! Yardsticks for Continuous Improvements* (Cambridge, Mass.: Blackwell, 1991), p. 160.

The establishment of target *costs* can proceed independently from the determination of target *price*. But a target cost that is too high when finally compared to the target price less target margin will need to be improved. This is done by revising and improving both product design concepts and manufacturing process concepts until the target cost is reduced to or below the level determined by the target price. The development of target costs for new and updated models of existing product lines is really not that difficult for design and manufacturing engineers experienced in their fields. The target cost, for example, could quickly be set at slightly below that of a quite similar existing model or even one that is generally similar. Take automobiles, for example. The new 1993 model, Exhibit 7-12, differs very little from the 1992 model. Although the styling *is* different, the body is still a body. Thus, the cost difference between the basic 1992 and 1993 automobiles will not be significant.

Actually, the 1993 model changes in Exhibit 7-12 are not limited to styling; they also include a new carburetor, using the latest technology, and passenger television. The latter was not available on the 1992 model. The product cost target buildup, Exhibit 7-13, illustrates how the 1992 model cost has been reduced by components (systems) not used in 1993 (carburetor) and the 10 percent cost reduction that management expects engineering to save in the process of finalizing the 1993 model design. The engineer's estimates for the new carburetor and passenger television are then added, giving the final target product cost. Given a list of other

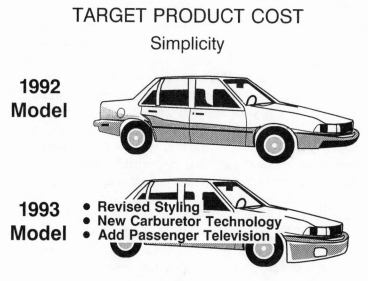

TARGET PRODUCT COST
Simplicity

1992 Model

1993 Model
- Revised Styling
- New Carburetor Technology
- Add Passenger Television

EXHIBIT 7-12

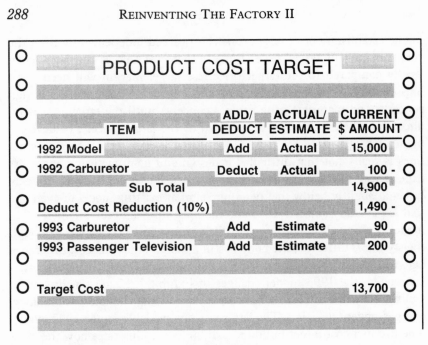

ITEM	ADD/ DEDUCT	ACTUAL/ ESTIMATE	CURRENT $ AMOUNT
1992 Model	Add	Actual	15,000
1992 Carburetor	Deduct	Actual	100 -
Sub Total			14,900
Deduct Cost Reduction (10%)			1,490 -
1993 Carburetor	Add	Estimate	90
1993 Passenger Television	Add	Estimate	200
Target Cost			13,700

EXHIBIT 7-13

minor differences, but none that is truly revolutionary compared to the current state of the art, it is likely that after the engineers have taken a new pass at the design, they will certainly be able to lower its cost compared to earlier models. Where planned product features are completely new or radically different from older models, their costs can be estimated, and the product cost can be developed based on a similar product minus the features that will be discontinued and plus the new and radically different features.

When target costs are quickly and easily developed at the level of the completed product and when the product is as complex as an automobile, the target cost must next be apportioned to the lower level components or the systems of the car. Examples of items that are both systems and components would be engines, bodies, wheels, and carburetors. Some functional system examples are lighting, exhaust, braking, and steering. When the new or revised model's components and systems are not radically different from current models, a low cost, practical way to apportion target costs for the automobile to the lower levels is as follows: The overall target should be prorated to each component and system based on their percentage of the total cost in a current model. When some planned features consist of entirely new components or systems not yet designed, engineering's best estimates are used as target cost. (The estimate may contain a combination of historical costs, material quotations from vendors, and pure estimates.) Therefore, proration of the complete automobile cost back to these new or revised features is not necessary. For experienced automotive engineers, sketches of a proposed new car and simple lists of differences compared to prior models is often enough to set the initial cost targets. If these targets, in total, are higher than the target selling price would support, the company has several options: (1) discontinue planning for the new product (almost never); (2) revise the design concept as depicted in sketches and lists of new and revised features (sometimes); or (3) reduce the target costs to the necessary level and get into design at the still lower level of detail, continuously improving the design until the target cost has been achieved or bettered (usually).

Some of my colleagues correctly argue that the system for developing target costs will need to be more complex than outlined above. As a realist, the author agrees that we always find complicating factors that defy short-term simplification. Thus, we will add complexity where it is unavoidable. However, the world's superior manufacturers have gained their positions by unswerving devotion to "impossible" simplification, so every effort should be made to avoid compromising the ideal before exhausting all possible avenues of simplification. In the case of target cost, it is of the utmost importance to realize that the target is something that might be missed. When it is, it is revised. Even when it is attained, the next target is higher still. And no one has yet gone before the firing squad as a result of missing a target.

The process of design cost reduction may also be simpler than it might seem. For example, the lion's share of cost reduction effort can focus on materials and purchased components since they usually make up 70 percent of the product cost. Material costs can be reduced in two fundamental ways: (1) by reducing the amount of the material used (by size reduction, for example) and (2) by finding a different material of equal or better performance but of lower cost. The vendors' costs of materials and components are also usually 70 percent of their product costs. Therefore, vendors should also be expected to participate in the target cost process for items they supply.

VALUE ENGINEERING AND VALUE ANALYSIS

Never in the history of the world has a product been designed that has not been subsequently and substantially improved. Often the intervals between major advances in product improvement are short, as they have been in the computer industry in recent decades. Some advances have been results of major technological breakthroughs, such as the invention of the transistor, the integrated circuit, and superconductivity. Most incremental improvements, however, have been evolutionary, not revolutionary. They involve continuous refinement of product design and manufacturing processes.

Why are the initial product and process designs not the ultimate? Value engineering is a method for applying value analysis techniques to the initial product and process before releasing the designs for production. When successful, value engineering will help engineers to leapfrog one or two generations of product improvements. Value analysis techniques have been around for three decades, but few companies are applying them. The question remains. Why, at the time of initial design, are products not as good as they ultimately will be? Why is value engineering valuable in the design phase? The answer is simple, but understanding it and applying the techniques that lead to leapfrogging generations of improvements are powerful means for not only improving the product but also reducing its cost.

The product designer faces two virtually immovable roadblocks. First, he does not and cannot recognize every possible design alternative. Since the alternatives are innumerable, the likelihood of identifying the best or even close to the ultimate is extremely remote. The second roadblock is that once the designer picks a design alternative, he starts to view his selection as the only possible design path. He bases all subsequent design decisions on the less-than-ideal path he has chosen to pursue. Consequently, his design often shifts farther and farther from the ideal with each subsequent revision.

What is the magic solution? It is bringing the power of a larger group's thinking to bear. Unfortunately, those who write and lecture on value analysis and value engineering have always complicated rather than simplified the methodology for capitalizing on this simple but powerful message. What is needed is to involve more people in design improvement and to persist in improving every best effort of the responsible designers. For example, Tanaka's "practical" example of cost planning for a pencil is a notably hypothetical example versus a real-world case.[23] In the real world, in the same time it would take to develop the target cost allocation that Tanaka suggests, most engineers could have gone through one or

[23]Masayasu Tanaka, Chapter 4 in Monden and Sakurai, *Japanese Management Accounting*.

two generations of design and design improvement, achieving the best cost possible. The practical approach recommended is as follows:

1. Do not waste too much time developing target cost. It should be either simply estimated or prorated as previously described.

2. Every component and assembly design should be reviewed by a group from diverse functional areas. The purpose of review is not to design by committee but to generate ideas that the responsible designer should pursue.

3. A designer other than the original one should be assigned responsibility for the improved design. The one with the original responsibility will find it hard to discard the design ideas so firmly entrenched in his head, his brainchildren. An impartial new designer will usually make faster progress—up to the point when he too becomes blinded to opportunities other than those embodied in his own design.

4. Assign responsibility for pursuing opportunities to the group members in their areas of expertise. For example, the buyer of raw materials should investigate the alternative materials and should put the suppliers to work on improving the material and components they supply.

PRODUCTION TARGET COST

The production output of cells, lines, and processes can and should be continuously improved by the team of operators or assemblers, the focused factory-in-a-factory manager, and the responsible design and process engineers. Every month, month after month, continuous work on improving tooling, machines, and work methods should reduce costs. In some months improvements in one cell might be lower than in other months. Overall, at the end of a year, plantwide improvement should average at or above executive management's 10 percent target.

Although companies generally and perhaps erroneously believe that labor cost is and will continue to decrease as a percentage of total cost, the cost in most factories is still millions of dollars per year. It still makes sense, therefore, to have a philosophy as well as a systematic method and systems for planning and tracking continuous improvements. Although it is conceivable that in some circumstances it would be advisable to target different improvement levels for different areas of the factory, to do so would complicate the procedures and systems. The simplest system would be based on a single improvement target for the entire factory.

The procedures for targeting profit improvements and for maintaining estimated standards might take the form of a computer display or report, like the one illustrated in Exhibit 7-14 (simplified for ease in understanding). The (estimated) standard cost in the example is merely the latest best estimate and would typically be roughly the same as the previous target cost (assuming that most targets, on the average, will be met). The procedure might also be based on manual forms. Whether the target product improvement and standard cost systems are integrated is not a critical issue, but integration would appear to be desirable. The important points of the example are as follows:

1. The report is prepared for every cell, semicell, or line. It lists all of the products produced in the manufacturing unit (a gear cell in the exhibit).

2. The standard hours per unit, as previously discussed, will be updated annually by replacing the old standard with the latest (current) estimated hours. Actually, the estimate is based on the most recent actual hours and thus should be more accurate than standards of the past.

TARGET PRODUCT IMPROVEMENT

Cell/Line Number: 221   Cell/Line Description: Medium Gears

PRODUCT NUMBER	PRODUCT DESCRIPTION	STANDARD HOURS/100	ESTIMATED HOURS/100		
			CURRENT	TARGET	NEXT
1234	HP Gear	1.75	1.66	1.64	TURNAROUND INPUT
3456	RLH Gear	1.90	1.80	1.78	
4567	LDP Gear	2.45	2.32	2.29	

EXHIBIT 7-14

3. Although different target hours could be input for every cell or line, most will be plantwide targets and will be specified by management as a percentage of improvement. The percentage in this example has been converted by the computer into the target hours.

4. The blank column headed "next" is for the estimated hours that cell teams and line managers will update when changes in tooling or methods cause an improvement in the hours per 100 pieces.

Advocates (not the author) of the use of machine versus employee hours as the basis of standard cost will note that the type of system outlined above will easily support a combination of one or the other for different cells or lines, with only a little additional logic. The basic information presented in Exhibit 7–14 will be enhanced in logical ways in actual practice. For example, the percentage of the target achieved for each product would be calculated and displayed. Management, however, will realistically expect that month-by-month achievements by product will be variable and that only by year-end will the overall improvement be achieved. As always, improvement efforts will focus on the products with the greatest potential for improvement. In the example, the third gear requires more hours per 100 than the other two and thus would be the highest priority item for improvement, assuming the same requirements for all three gears.

BUDGETING: THE BEST OVERHEAD
REDUCTION TOOL

Factory subplants, support services and offices, sales, engineering, and administrative departments should all continuously improve the ratio of their payroll-related costs and other expenses to sales or the cost of sales. The author subscribes wholeheartedly to an observation by Nagashima, who wrote: "Cost control is an excellent system. . . . But however excellent it may be, it is of little value from a business point of view unless it is related to profit."[24] One easy way to relate cost to profit is to track it as a percentage of margin. Some of my colleagues are quick to point out the shortcomings of ratios as compared with other alternatives. They argue, for example, that increased sales should not automatically trigger

---

[24]Soichiro Nagashima, *100 Management Charts* (Tokyo: Asian Productivity Organization, 1987), p. 17.

increased expenditures in all expense categories. If the system that the author describes were not a combination of target *plus* the ratio, this might be a danger. Or if executives and their managers were slavishly to follow a single number such as the ratio as the basis for their decisions, there would be a danger. The author credits management with the intelligence to use the ratio the way intended, as an upper limit and as a tool for tracking progress toward achieving the main goal of continuous improvement, lowering all costs in relation to revenues, or at least containing them.

Since comparatively little creative thinking has been focused on implementing exciting new ways to reduce costs in these areas dramatically, they are goldmines of opportunity. As the author writes this section, memories of cutting electricity costs while in Japan come flooding back. The experience may serve to highlight the simple but major changes that are possible. Shortly after the second energy crisis in the 1970s, a small group of Americans came to visit. Their purpose was to sell the author's client a package of control hardware and computer software for monitoring and consequently shifting energy loads. This would yield savings in the use and cost of electricity. After politely listening to the long sales presentation and praising the complex system and its outputs, my Japanese colleague, with typical modesty, explained that the company had already installed a system that had reduced electric consumption by as much as 50 percent in the office and as much as 25 percent in the factory. He ended the meeting by describing the system: on/off switches and pull chains! Prior to the two energy crises, triggered by the Arab producers' cutting of shipments of petroleum, electricity consumption discipline in Japan had been almost as lax as in the United States. Rows of lights in the factory and the office were controlled by master switches, each of which controlled lights in areas of hundreds and thousands of square feet. When anyone worked in any area, the entire area was usually lighted, rather than just the small area in which perhaps only one person was working. Further, machines in the factory tended to be turned on all day regardless of whether or not they were in continuous use. By putting pull chains or switches on every light, air conditioner, and heater and by instructing every employee in the importance of using electricity only when needed, electricity use was slashed. Somewhat similar but less draconian measures were adopted in the West during that period but were dropped as soon as the oil started to flow again. The practices in Japan, however, are still in use, with enhancements.

This example is being written in a brightly lit office (ten 4-foot fluorescent tubes) used solely by the author. Outside the sun is blindingly bright, so the blinds are almost completely closed. It would be just as light with the blinds slightly open and the lights off. Even on cloudy days a desk lamp would be adequate light by which to work and would consume only 5 percent as much electricity as the overhead lights. This simple example points first to the easy but excitingly large improvements that can be made to overhead costs. Secondly (a point not quite so obvious), while motivation is important, it will not by itself be enough to sustain savings. In Japan it was necessary to modify the lighting physically in order to shift the responsibility to small groups. The physical change made it easy for the manager, the members of the production team, and everyone else in the range of sight to monitor the energy awareness of the small group. Lights that are on in an unoccupied area or in areas adequately lit by the sun are easily recognized by all as indicators of bad performance.

Companies using budget-based responsibility reporting of expenses will find that these systems will have continued usefulness in the future. With minor modifications for including targets for improvement, responsibility reporting will be even more useful. The simplified responsibility report for an order entry cell, Exhibit 7-15, includes not only the budget and actual expenses but also a separate target. This example presumes that the monthly budget base is the amount based on past experience as

MONTHLY RESPONSIBILITY REPORT

Responsibility Number: 2140   Description: Order Entry Cell

ACCOUNT NUMBER	ACCOUNT DESCRIPTION	BUDGET	ACTUAL	TARGET
2345	Payroll	$ 100,000	$ 95,000	$ 90,000
4567	Space Rental	2,000	2,000	1,800
5678	Office Supplies	4,000	3,800	3,600
6789	Telephone	10,000	9,000	7,000
6790	Fax	1,000	1,500	2,000

EXHIBIT 7-15

modified, required to maintain a target ratio of expenses to sales (or cost of sales). The target in the example is the management-determined goal for the enterprise for the budget year. In the example, the target improvement for telephone expense is even greater than the management target since the cell has a plan to reduce telephone use in favor of facsimile. Incidentally, it is necessary to be assured that the *total company cost* would be reduced. This would be easy to verify if all telephone and facsimile costs for an area were included on its responsibility report. This would enable comparison of actual costs of each before and after the change. If some costs are on two different responsibility reports, the solution is simple. Since the fundamental principle of responsibility reporting should be to assign *all* costs to the person (organization) that can control them, all of the costs should be switched to the telephoning area.

Also of interest is that each area is charged for the space occupied, based on either building depreciation or actual rental if the building is leased. As in the factory, the most efficient use of office space will simplify operations and communications, lower costs of office operations, and shorten throughput time. Therefore, it makes lots of sense to charge each cell (department) for the space it occupies. It motivates them to find ways to cut the space required. Perhaps the president should be charged with the responsibility for unoccupied space since he will be the person most likely to find new products to fill it. Alternatively, he may rent or sell the space in order to realize a tangible benefit from the space reduction.

THE OVERHEAD ABSORPTION ROADBLOCK

In businesses managed by the numbers, accounting numbers sometimes cause bad decisions, including canceling projects that are actually reducing operating costs. This happens when the numbers used to evaluate manufacturing performance show worsening rather than improving results, regardless of the fact that there are offsetting gains in other accounts. Executives must not permit their companies to be run solely by the numbers. When they are forced to, they must *manage the numbers* to manage the business. In the simplified example, Exhibit 7–16, between the end of month 1 and the start of month 2, a company has converted operations to the use of highly productive assembly lines and machine cells. While labor costs have been cut in half, all other cost factors remained the same in month 2, including overhead costs. However, only $1 million of the overhead was absorbed, causing an equal amount of

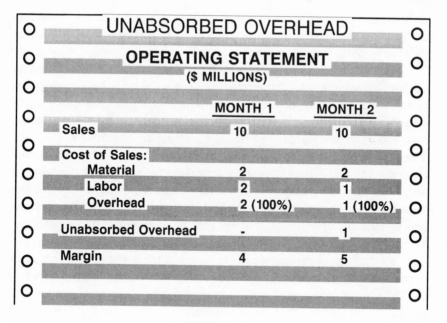

UNABSORBED OVERHEAD OPERATING STATEMENT ($ MILLIONS)	MONTH 1	MONTH 2
Sales	10	10
Cost of Sales:		
Material	2	2
Labor	2	1
Overhead	2 (100%)	1 (100%)
Unabsorbed Overhead	-	1
Margin	4	5

EXHIBIT 7-16

unabsorbed overhead. Therefore, a manufacturing variance, unabsorbed overhead, suddenly appeared in the operating statement in month 2. Since variances are the cornerstone of the financial performance measurement system, the executive who manages by the numbers would find manufacturing's performance unsatisfactory. The superior executive, however, would *manage* the numbers, because he can see the favorable improvement in margin. In order to manage the numbers, he merely needs to change the overhead rate from 100 to 200 percent. When labor was cut in half, it should have been obvious that overhead would need to be absorbed at twice the previous rate. The reasons that the overhead rate is typically not synchronized with changes in the amount of labor required are as follows. (1) The majority of cost systems are designed and operated to permit overhead rates to be adjusted only once a year. (2) Many companies use different overhead rates for different cost centers. In these cases, changing one rate is difficult when that change would usually require that all other rates also be revised. Incidentally, the author believes that a single overhead rate for a company is simpler and results in cost data that is as precise as most businesses require. (3) In the real factory the conversion of operations cannot occur overnight as it did in this example. Changes are made over a longer period of time, sometimes a few each month. As changes occur month by month, the unfavorable, unabsorbed overhead account grows continuously but irregularly. Therefore, to time overhead changes to correspond with changes in labor is not a simple matter.

In reality, if changes in the factory reduce actual costs, there should be no possible way in which the improvement would not be a component of the *total* operating profit or loss. When wrong decisions are made based on misleading accounting information, it indicates a larger problem. That problem can only be that the responsible executive's statement does not include *all* favorable and unfavorable costs and benefits. For example, the benefits of inventory reduction are usually attributable to operations improvements. But the interest charges on inventory are not included in costs of manufacturing and, perhaps, should not be. In companies with low debt-to-equity there may be no interest charges attributable to manufacturing, either because there is no debt or because the debt is a very small percentage of the assets of the company. In this case, it may be nonsensical to try to decide whether to charge interest expense to the need for money to finance operations, the equipment and tooling assets, the factory building or the inventory.

Incompetent and/or shyster consultants (fortunately outnumbered by savvy, honest advisers) inside and outside the company recommend using inflated cost of inventory numbers to justify projects. The rationale is based on the assumption that opportunities to reduce storage and handling costs or, alternatively, rates of return expected from other investments will produce improved results. The problem is that if the storage space occupied and the number of storeroom personnel employed is not separately targeted and monitored, these benefits usually evaporate. The reason some prefer to use high costs is that this makes inventory reductions look more attractive than when using more conservative and, perhaps, more realistic numbers. Further, it is easier than the better route—identifying the target storage space and manpower, and ensuring that they are achieved. The fact is that management becomes disenchanted with advisers who follow this tack because the actual savings just do not materialize on the profit and loss statement, even if the inventory on the balance sheet has improved as projected.

As Buehler and Shetty point out, it has long been recognized that conventional return on investment calculations, based solely on labor savings, are inadequate.[25] In order to have tangible operating benefits from

[25]Vernon M. Buehler and Y. K. Shetty, eds., *Competing Through Quality* Cambridge, Mass.: Productivity Press, 1988), p. 10.

inventory reduction, the company must have a carefully formulated plan for reducing people in areas such as stores and material handling and must execute the plan. Reducing inventory does not automatically yield increased profitability. On the balance sheet, for example, inventory reduction should be offset by a corresponding increase in cash, or a reduction of indebtedness. These changes should logically cause a reduction in operating expense (interest paid) or an increase in income (interest earned). However, it will cost something to implement the changes that bring about the inventory reduction. If the cost (often capital investment) is equal to the inventory reduction, what occurs is simply a switch of assets from inventory into plant and equipment. In other words, the improvement is self-financing. Since no real net investment is required, it would seem illogical to subject the "investment" to the alternative return on investment test. (Some would correctly argue that there is often a delay between expenditure and benefit, thus there will actually be *some* expense. However, on the best-managed projects, this delay should not be material.) Many, perhaps most, capital expenditure authorization procedures would fail to recognize the principle of exchanging inventory for capital equipment. Whenever this is the case, executives must manage the numbers in order to make the right decision for the company.

Even accountants who understand the sometimes misleading numbers embedded in financial reports must counsel their executives to take actions that are not really in the best interests of the company, for fear that the board and investors will view unfavorable numbers as indicative of poor management. This is simply not logical or acceptable behavior, however, when the alternative would be to make changes in the system or its factors to report more accurately on the favorable (or unfavorable) actual versus theoretical results.

SUMMARY

Cost accounting professionals, more than anyone, are aware of the inaccuracies of cost information. They must be the leaders of the new age of cost management. They must find inventive new ways to live with the inevitable inaccuracies by applying business logic to the data available, no matter how "inaccurate." Too many popular accounting techniques produce numerical indices that bear no relevance to the realities a company does its best to include in its operating statements and on its balance sheet. Such techniques or their results must be changed to simple, hence understandable, financially compatible amounts if accounting simplification is to be as successful as simplification in the factory has been.

Emphasis must shift dramatically from accounting only for historical cost and from using standard costs for financial reporting to accounting that fosters continuous, major reductions of cost. This makes target costs and target expenses the most important features of the superior cost management system of the future.

8

□□□

Capacity:
Constraint or Opportunity?–Plus Other Factory Issues

BETTER CAPACITY MANAGEMENT HAS THE POTENTIAL for unlocking vast reservoirs of additional capacity in existing factories and on present machines. In the worst cases, where it is not practical to increase the output of a critical bottleneck process, decisions to build and equip entire new factories are often found to be unnecessary since the need may be only to add capacity for a few processes. However, there are few points in the history and future of a manufacturer at which new capacity strategies for existing product lines are needed. Most capacity management tasks involve *decisions*, not strategy.[1] In many respects the capacity strategy, when significant enough and long-range enough to be described as a strategy, is really deciding issues related to a combination of manufacturing location and method. How *much* capacity to provide is a condition on which the manufacturing method is based, not a separate strategy. Although the capacity issue is rarely equivalent to a companywide strategy, it can be an issue that differentiates the industry leader from the also-rans. Adequate capacity of the right type is vitally important. However, few people understand what capacity is, let alone how to plan it.

---

[1]Robert W. Hayes and Steven C. Wheelwright, *Restoring Our Competitive Edge: Competing Through Manufacturing* (New York: John Wiley & Sons, 1984), p. 46.

Superior manufacturers will add capacity earlier than their competitors since they understand that the first company to win a customer's business is likely to be the company that keeps it.

Failure to deliver products when customers need them is perceived by executives as a cardinal sin.[2] Accordingly, every company strives to achieve the highest practical level of delivery performance. In most cases, when customer-requested shipping dates are missed, the underlying reason is inadequate capacity (people or equipment) somewhere in the network of a factory's processes and those of suppliers. Yet the potential capacity of most factories is woefully underutilized, and many have only a few processes that are operated at levels approaching the maximum practical capacity limit. On the surface this appears to contradict government statistics, which usually summarize the national level of factory utilization near 80 percent.[3] However, the factory managers who report their utilization levels know full well that their report is at best a Kentucky windage estimate based on the factory's past record of shipments. Most of their factory's processes have enough capacity to meet projected demand while only a few constrain the production flow. Unlocking the flow of the entire factory by adding capacity to a few critical processes has the potential for major increases in profitability. It supports increased production but should not require corresponding increases in overhead.

A case example, taken from the Lennox Industries productivity improvement in the Columbus, Ohio, plant, highlights the disparity between perceptions of capacity and reality. In this case, before the project started, the company had thought the air conditioner factory to be operating near maximum capacity. This perception was in large part due to the fact that the coil-slitting process, one of the largest in the factory, was operating around the clock. A fast hitting setup reduction project cut the very lengthy slitter changeover time in half, freeing a considerable amount of time and helping to avoid a capital outlay. As Dennis Blanchard, Corporate Vice President of Manufacturing, said, "Freeing up capacity [on the slitter] helped us avoid a million dollar outlay." After subsequent work throughout the factory, production was doubled using half as many people. These measures helped Lennox avoid an expenditure of several million dollars by eliminating the need for a new plant and new equipment.

As Bane and Garwood indicate, defining capacity of a manufacturing

---

[2]Thomas M. Hout and George Stalk, Jr., *Competing Against Time: How Time-Based Competition Is Reshaping Global Markets* (New York: Free Press, 1990), p. 1.
[3]82 percent in January 1990. Council of Economic Advisers, *Economic Indicators* (Washington: CEA, March 1990), p. 17.

process is difficult, to say the least.[4] Part of the difficulty results from the wide gulf between what many managers define as the capacity week–three shifts, five days a week–versus the real maximum available: twenty-four hours, seven days a week. Most managers immediately equate hours on the weekend to overtime work, and rightly believe that peoples' attitudes and productivity will suffer if seven-day work weeks are planned for extended periods of time. However, if one or two machines or processes need to be operated nonstop to meet demand and to match the output of other departments that have enough capacity to meet demand within the five-day week, special crews and working schedules can be developed. For example, six teams, each working thirty-two hours a week, could keep an operation running twenty-four hours every day, seven days a week, (A thirty-two-hour week would provide compensation for holidays and weekend work schedules.)

Second, an operation where it is not feasible to increase production capacity is indeed rare. Thus, to assume that the current rate of production is the same as the capacity of the process would overlook the potential for increased output or yield. In the author's experience, a reasonable output or yield improvement target would be no less than 5 percent and often up to 35 percent. Such improvement involves low cost machine and tooling changes, machine loading/unloading methods improvements, quality yield improvements, and reduction of setup/changeover time, to name a few of the more common opportunities. Incidentally, working with equipment manufacturers who are capable of fast delivery would minimize many of the problems of trying to project capacity needs. Further, equipment specifications could be developed well in advance of actual need—ready to release to the machine manufacturer when actual demand trend makes it clear that the additional capacity can no longer be delayed. Another way is to maintain relationships with outside vendors who have capacity that they will make available for both temporary peaks and until the company is able to increase its own capacity.

Finally, people-paced capacity is extremely variable since the natural pace of individuals is different based on such factors as age, agility, size, and physical condition. Further, each individual's pace varies day to day and hour to hour. It is little comfort to know that the average pace of all workers is used to plan capactiy and schedule operations, especially if you are the customer whose part takes the longest rather than the average time to produce and thus have to live with late delivery.

[4]Michael Bane and Dave Garwood, *Shifting Paradigms: Reshaping the Future of Industry* (Atlanta: Dogwood Publishing, 1990), p. 94.

CHECKLIST: CAPACITY PLANNING ZINGERS

Precise matching of manufacturing capacity and a company's market share is rarely a practical business strategy. Superior manufacturers will need to increase their capacity faster than their competition in order ultimately to gain market share. This simple but powerful truism is a simplifying fact that should be the primary driver of every company's capacity expansion strategy. Following is a summary list of the most powerful methods of increasing capacity while maximizing flexibility and minimizing capital investment requirements:

1. Base *process industry* capacity addition decisions on the industry backlog of customer orders, and expect to fill the added capacity immediately after it becomes available in all but the most unusual cases.

2. Base *job shop and assembly industry* capacity addition decisions on recent past capacity and short-term load projections. Plan the capacity addition before actually needed to avoid operating for a long period at maximum practical capacity.

3. Routinely perform Pareto analysis to identify the few machines and processes with loads close to maximum capacity, and focus attention on these exceptions.

4. Recognize that every long-range forecast and prediction used to project capacity needs is likely to be far from accurate. Therefore, place more emphasis on recent trends in process loads than on future projections.

5. Routinely set goals for increasing the capacity of existing equipment through low cost modifications. Focus on processes operating closest to maximum capacity.

6. Plan and use the third shift and weekends to meet short-term demand peaks.

7. Negotiate with unions to establish work rules and pay scales for special twenty-one-shift-per-week manning of overloaded machines and processes during extended periods of operating at near maximum capacity.

8. Avoid one-of-a-kind machines and processes.

9. Reduce the size or output of the equipment purchased to provide greater flexibility for various mixes of product demand peaks and valleys.

10. Develop skilled staffs of machine designers and builders. Use their

skills to develop custom-designed machines superior to those of competitors.

11. Reduce the lead time between capacity addition decisions and the delivery of completed machines or processes.

EVALUATING CAPACITY UTILIZATION

The broad assumption of this chapter—that the capacity of most processes in the majority of factories is underutilized—applies least to process industries, many of which almost always operate perpetually. Examples are paper mills, chemical plants, and several types of food processing plants. Other factories, however, usually have numerous departments and work centers that work far fewer hours than they are capable of working. Exhibit 8–1 illustrates the approximate capacity of several areas of one typical factory based on the hours currently worked. In this example, small presses work sixty hours (approximately one and one-half shifts) per week. They rarely, if ever, work on a Saturday or Sunday. Thus, if they were ever required to work at maximum potential, they could increase their output by 180 percent (if only temporarily). Not coincidentally, small presses, in the example, are operated half as many hours as large presses. The cost of the small machines is low and the useful life virtually eternal if well maintained. The company is thus led to believe that it can acquire and keep more than enough equipment since the cost is so low.

APPROXIMATE CAPACITY

DEPARTMENT/WORK CENTER/ LINE/CELL/MACHINE	APPROXIMATE HOURS WORKED				% POTENTIAL INCREASE
	MONDAY - FRIDAY	SATURDAY	SUNDAY	TOTAL	
MAXIMUM HOURS	120	24	24	168	-
PRESS DEPARTMENT	80	-	-	80	110
SMALL PRESS WORK CENTER	60	-	-	60	180
LARGE PRESS WORK CENTER	120	-	-	120	40
PLASTIC MOLDING DEPARTMENT	120	24	8	152	10
MACHINE CENTER	120	24	-	144	17

EXHIBIT 8-1

Plastic molding, in Exhibit 8–1, is the department closest to reaching the real limits of its capacity. Since it works all but two shifts per week, it can increase its output by only 10 percent by working those additional shifts. The large investment required for each machine, compared to the relatively low value of the machine's output, dictates maximum utilization in order to absorb the high cost of depreciation and to maximize the return on capital invested.

Managers of factories like the one in this example often characterize their entire factories as operating at or close to maximum practical capacity and want their internal or external consultants to help formulate a strategy for building a new plant or a new addition to an existing plant, or even to assist in identifying the new equipment required to increase capacity in the existing factory. The first easy step is to gather a minimal amount of information on which decisions can be made on which few operations to focus–those near or at capacity limits. Exhibit 8-2 is a worksheet designed for this fast, simple analysis. The worksheet includes a block of identification information and can be used to record capacity at the highest level [plant or subplant cluster],[5] the lowest level (machine, cell, or line), or anywhere in between. The approach for analyzing capac-

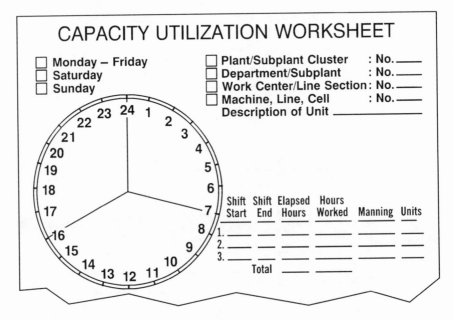

EXHIBIT 8-2

[5]See Appendix 2.

ity is top down. If an entire plant works only one shift, there is no question that production should be capable of increasing by 200 percent or more. Thus, there would be no need to look deeper. However, in many departments of the factory, there may be one or a few machines or machine groups (machines with identical capacities and capabilities) that routinely operate close to maximum capacity and therefore appear to have little additional capacity. The worksheet is also useful for the first cut at analyzing these machines. To illustrate the use of the worksheet, a case example of a punch press department, Exhibit 8–3, will be used. Although it may later be shown that many of the presses would best be grouped with machines from other departments into cells, capacity analysis can still start with a rough cut toward understanding current and potential capacities. Exhibit 8–4 illustrates how the process identification block of the worksheet is used to identify the unit or units being analyzed. In this example, the 10-ton presses are the subject of analysis. Their complete identifier includes department *20,* work center (*1*), machine group *A* and *10-ton presses*. The date part of the worksheet, by shift, is demonstrated in Exhibit 8–5. The date for each shift includes the shift start and stop times and the elapsed hours per shift. The elapsed hours usually differ from the hours worked because of lunch and break interruptions and sometimes time provided to clean up at the end of the shift. If the machines in the area are routinely and materially operated

CASE EXAMPLE OVERVIEW

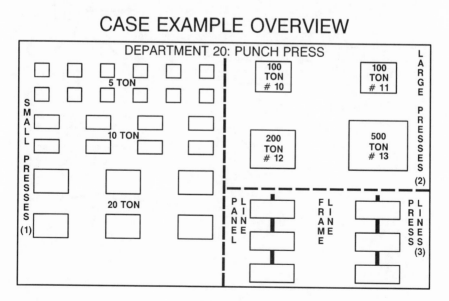

EXHIBIT 8-3

INTERCHANGEABLE CAPACITY EXAMPLE - 1

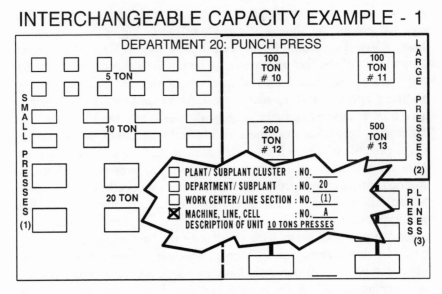

EXHIBIT 8-4

INTERCHANGEABLE CAPACITY EXAMPLE - 2

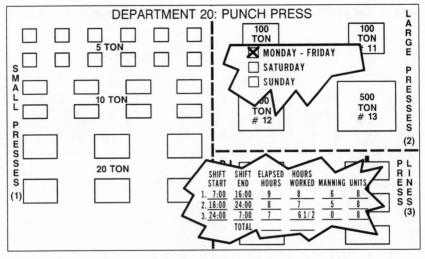

EXHIBIT 8-5

on Saturdays and Sundays, three worksheets would be used–one for the normal five-day week, and two more for Saturday and Sunday. Although there are eight units (presses) in the 10-ton group, only six are manned on the first shift, five on the second and none on the third. The number of shifts worked, by department, is perhaps the most important question the author asks when visiting a factory for the first time. For example, at a railroad maintenance equipment factory, the answer to the shift question was that the final assembly department worked two shifts. The equipment assembled was very large and very complex, and only a few units were assembled each week. During a factory tour, the author could see that the average number of assemblers working on each unit in work-in-process was less than one, although each large and complex unit contained enough work and had enough space around it to permit several workers to work simultaneously. Clearly, it would have been better to have all workers from both shifts work on a single shift, reduce the number of units in work-in-process, and increase the number of assemblers on each unit. The benefits would be reduced inventory investment, shorter time required to assemble each customer's order, and shorter and simpler operations for each assembler, reducing the potential for errors and providing an opportunity to increase productivity.

In Exhibit 8–5 hands are drawn on the twenty-four-hour clock face for each capacity unit. This divides a day into the shifts worked. The actual hours worked usually differ somewhat depending on the number of shifts the department works. Exhibit 8–6 shows how the data are graphically displayed for the purpose of subsequent presentations. The theoretical maximum daily capacity of the eight presses, working twenty-four uninterrupted hours would be 192 press hours. Based on the number of presses currently manned on each shift, the number of work hours per shift, the average actual approximate utilization of the presses is eighty-three press hours, less than half of the maximum possible.

By analyzing capacities as shown, one can narrow the need for a more in-depth analysis to the few units that are likely to represent real capacity constraints. Having done so, the next question is whether or not the way in which the highly utilized units are operated can be improved. The objective will be to squeeze every bit of additional production from the available equipment and facilities to delay the need for additional capital investment.

Exhibits 8–7 and 8–8 are sections of a worksheet used to analyze utilization in greater depth but still in a relatively simple form. In the example on Exhibit 8–7, a group of ten turret lathes with identical capabilities are analyzed, stating with the development of net shift hours as the differ-

INTERCHANGEABLE CAPACITY EXAMPLE - 3
10-TON PRESSES: 8 UNITS

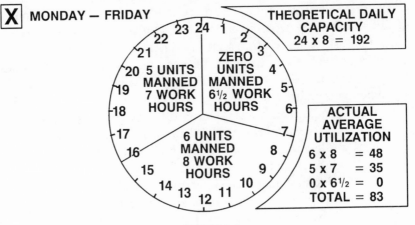

EXHIBIT 8-6

CAPACITY DETAIL EXAMPLE - 1

UNIT NAME: VERTICAL TURRET LATHES	ACTUAL: PER SHIFT/TOTAL				
	1	2	3	TOTAL	MAXIMUM
TOTAL UNITS	10	10	10	30	30
UNITS/SHIFT MANNED	10	5	2	17	30
PERSONNEL	10	5	2	17	30
TOTAL SHIFT HOURS	9	8	7	24	24
BREAKS/LUNCHES*	1	1	1	3	N/A
NET SHIFT HOURS	8	7	6	21	24
HOURS OPERATING	6	5	5	16	24
CUTTING	5	4	4	13	24

* POTENTIAL CAPACITY GAIN

EXHIBIT 8-7

ence between total shift hours and lunches and breaks. As indicated by the asterisk, if the lathes could be kept in operation during lunch and break times, three hours of capacity per day would be gained. This is often accomplished by staggering lunch hours for various groups of machines and by using relief teams to keep the machines in operation when their assigned teams are eating or breaking.

The hours operating (running) in Exhibit 8–7 are sixteen hours per day versus twenty-one working hours. Thus, further study will be performed to identify ways in which the five hours of lost time can be reduced. Although many view hours operating as synonymous with cutting hours, there is usually a noteworthy difference. In Exhibit 8–8 this difference is the sum of the time required to load and unload the machines and plain idle time. The lost cutting time is therefore three hours per day. This might be reduced through improved tooling and methods. Other major opportunities for increasing utilization and production volume that are illustrated are setup/changeover and downtime for machine repair and maintenance. Targets for improvement in these catagories should be in the range of 75 to 90 percent.

Where production increases are urgently required, high priority should be given to settling goals for improvement and initiating projects to achieve them. Exhibit 8–9 is a worksheet that lists all major areas in which improvements might be expected for a machining operation or

CAPACITY DETAIL EXAMPLE - 2

UNIT NAME: VERTICAL TURRET LATHES	ACTUAL: PER SHIFT/TOTAL				
	1	2	3	TOTAL	MAXIMUM
TOTAL UNITS	10	10	10	30	30
NET SHIFT HOURS	8	7	6	21	24
HOURS OPERATING/UNIT	6	5	5	16	24
CUTTING	5	4	4	13	24
LOAD/UNLOAD/IDLE*	1	1	1	3	-
OTHER HOURS/UNIT	2	2	1	5	-
SETUP*	2	1	-	3	-
REPAIR/MAINTENANCE*	1	1	1	2	-
OTHER*	-	-	-	-	-

* POTENTIAL CAPACITY GAIN

EXHIBIT 8-8

MACHINING/PROCESS GOALS

UNIT:_____   **NUMBER OF UNITS:_____**

PERFORMANCE CATEGORY	CURRENT	GOAL	%	$
MAN/MACHINE RATIO				
CHANGEOVER HOURS/MONTH				
CHANGEOVER FREQUENCY/MONTH				
CHANGEOVER MINUTES AVERAGE				
SCRAP RATE (%)				
REWORK HOURS (%)				
QUEUE HOURS				
MACHINE REPAIR HOURS/MONTH				
ROUTINE MAINTENANCE HOURS/MONTH				
MACHINE REBUILD FREQUENCY (YEARS)				
OUTPUT/HOUR/UNIT				
OTHER:				
AUTOMATION/UPGRADE IDEAS:				

EXHIBIT 8-9

process. By improving the operation, scrap and rework might be virtually eliminated, increasing the yield of the operation and, thus, increasing its capacity. Chapter 6, "Quality Engineering: Replacement for Quality Control," describes quality improvement concepts. Exhibit 8–10 is a similar worksheet for recording goals for assembly, test, and packaging operations.

Incidentally, one additional goal of assembly design is the integration not only of all assembly, test, and packaging operations into a focused factory but also of major related machining cells.

ASSEMBLY LINE ZINGERS

In a recent review of Briggs & Stratton's new large engine plant layout design, the author had an opportunity to reexamine the features of superior assembly. This led to the discovery that he had not addressed a few important assembly design issues in his previous book. One such issue relates to the overall scheme for locating assembly operations vis-a-vis machining. Exhibit 8–11 shows two alternatives: end-to-end and surrounding. In the example, each of the two similar assembly lines (used to assemble two different product families) has corresponding, dedicated machining cells that make its components. Whenever practical, a layout in which machining surrounds assembly is superior because it can bring

ASSEMBLY/PACKAGING GOALS

UNIT:_____ NUMBER OF UNITS:_____

PERFORMANCE CATEGORY	CURRENT	GOAL	%	$
CYCLE TIME				
HOURS/WEEK MANNED				
NUMBER OF ASSEMBLY STATIONS				
COMPONENTS PER STATION AVERAGE				
NUMBER OF END PRODUCTS/YEAR				
CHANGEOVER HOURS/MONTH				
CHANGEOVER FREQUENCY/MONTH				
CHANGEOVER MINUTES AVERAGE				
SCRAP RATE (%)				
REWORK HOURS (%)				
EQUIPMENT REPAIR (DOWNTIME) HOURS/MONTH				
ROUTINE MAINTENANCE HOURS/MONTH				
OTHER:				
AUTOMATION/UPGRADE IDEAS:				

EXHIBIT 8–10

ASSEMBLY/MACHINING LOCATION

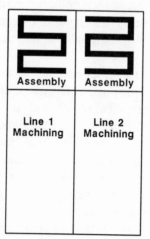

Assembly | Assembly

Line 1 Machining | Line 2 Machining

End-to-End

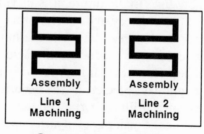

Assembly | Assembly

Line 1 Machining | Line 2 Machining

Surround Assembly

EXHIBIT 8–11

both machining and assembly operations into the most compact area, simplifying supervision and communications. In this example, the maximum number of machining cells can be located as closely as possible to the points on the serpentine assembly lines at which their machined parts are used. Since inventory between supplying cells and the assembly line points-of-use increases as distance increases, the surround alternative will require less investment in inventory and conveyors or conveyance devices to transport machined components to the line.

The most powerful argument favoring the end-to-end alternative is that in some factories the machining operations generate airborne particles that would invade the assembly area and cause quality problems. Or the machining operations, although not the creators of particles, might be contaminated as raw materials are delivered, and this contamination could drift into assembly operations. This would be the case when the materials are dirty or when dust enters through material receiving docks. In the author's experience, certain machining operations should not pollute, and others are clearly a problem. However, all too frequently black-and-white decisions are made without understanding whether there really might be a potential problem. Few factories hve taken the trouble to formally collect and analyze the air around each machine and on the assembly line. In the future, it is inevitable that if such pollution exists, it will be mandatory to do such testing to ensure the safety of the people working in the area. After all, the human body is usually much more sensitive than the products manufactured.

The few factories that have formally studied samples have found what they might have predicted. The majority of *cutting* operations (lathe, machine center, drilling, boring) do not contribute measurably to air pollution, while the majority of *abrasive* operations (grinding, sanding) pollute the air in their immediate vicinity and in the areas into which air currents are permitted to carry the particles. This knowledge makes it easier to reduce or eliminate the danger of particle contamination. In extreme cases, curtain walls can be constructed between machining and assembly. However, in most cases the best long-term solution will be to limit pollution to the immediate vicinity in which it is created and to control the air flow to preclude pollutant travel. The solution is really quite simple: design a cocoon for each problem machine and isolate the generated particles not only from the assembly area but also from machine operators and other machines. After all, most machines are as subject to damage from foreign particles as are the products that speed down the assembly line.

Many products (television sets, for example) require numerous assembly operations before the partially or completely assembled product can be tested. If the test reveals a need to repair and reassemble the unit, it is common practice to loop back in the assembly line to a point where the units can rejoin the original process. Such loops are often wide bulges somewhere along the otherwise uniform-width assembly line. Therefore, the areas that do not bulge are wasted space (the assembly line is most often designed to be as wide as its widest bulge). For this reason it makes sense to lift the unit and to return it overhead (above the line) to the point required. In some instances this will require overhead structure for repair operations or for the conveyor, but the cost of such a limited structure is usually much less than that of the space wasted by return loop bulges.

Incidentally, bulges along the assembly line are often caused by large equipment that occupies more space than do the operators and materials. Provisions of extra space along the line as a contingency for possible future large equipment (automation) should not be permitted. The specifications for any such new equipment should be controlled to limit its dimensions to the size occupied by the line and the operator. However, the designer cannot possibly envision every future possibility and should proceed to finalize a practical design and to implement it as quickly as possible. As Apple has said, "It is the task of the facilities designer to design as much of the total system flow as is currently practicable, implement the portions that are feasible, and continue to work on other portions of the theoretical system."[6]

SMALL FACTORY CAPACITY MANAGEMENT

In focused factories, responsible managers, cell and line supervisors, and operators become intimately familiar with their current and maximum capacity. Thus, organization of small factories-within-the-factory eliminates the need for forms and procedures with which to analyze capacity as previously described. However, large out-of-focus factories often have no single individual with the equivalent knowledge of all departments, because the factory is simply too large for any one person to manage personally. Nevertheless, even in the largest factories, operating personnel are usually familiar with the production units with which they are involved. Most of the data needed are readily available (often in manual

[6]James M. Apple, *Plant Layout and Material Handling* (New York: John Wiley & Sons, 1977), p. 94.

rather than computer form). Thus, information gathering for capacity analysis does not require that systems be developed to supply necessary data. Operating personnel are usually able to make ballpark estimates to cull out operations with sufficient capacity, thus narrowing the scope of closer examination to operations that have critical capacity limitations.

Having to refuse a customer's order for lack of capacity is one of the greatest business disappointments. Therefore, once a company has identified the processes that constrain production it should immediately try to increase production through improvements in existing operations and by acquiring additional capacity in the few operations that limit the output of the entire factory. In process factories, setup/changeover reduction is often one of the biggest opportunities for increasing capacity.

SETUP/CHANGEOVER IN PROCESS INDUSTRIES

The author's previous book contained numerous examples of many of the blockbuster concepts of superior manufacturing applicable to machining, assembly, and material storage operations.[7] It also touched on seemingly minor details of factory design that have explosive impact when applied plantwide. (Consider, for example, the dramatic effect of cutting the size of all contianers in half.) Following are a few food processing case examples that the author feels would add important examples to the body of knowledge.

The target of every setup/changeover reduction project team must be to eliminate completely the time and cost required to change from producing one item to another. Although complete elimination will rarely be economically or technically practical in the short term, there are almost always at least some elements of changeover that lend themselves to complete elimination. For example, one element of the changeover of Nabisco's Barquisimeto, Venezuela, plant was the removal of the roller drive chain, Exhibit 8–12. The roller contained different cutting patterns for different crackers and thus required changing for each change in cracker type. (The roller detachment and reattachment time reduction is not shown here.) By replacing direct drive by chain with a wheeled pulley, Exhibit 8–13, Nabisco no longer had to remove the chain in order to replace the roller. This single change saves the company 100 percent of the time previously required for this element.

Process industries, like all other manufacturers, tend to treat the pro-

<hr>

[7]See Appendix 2.

ROLLER CHAIN ADJUSTMENT
BEFORE

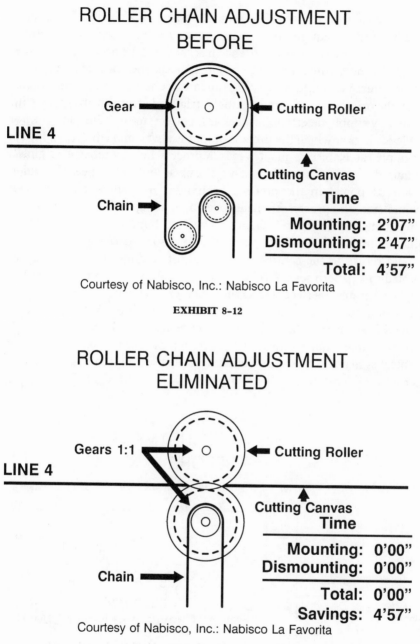

LINE 4

Gear ➡ ← Cutting Roller

Cutting Canvas

Chain ➡

Time	
Mounting:	2'07"
Dismounting:	2'47"
Total:	4'57"

Courtesy of Nabisco, Inc.: Nabisco La Favorita

EXHIBIT 8–12

ROLLER CHAIN ADJUSTMENT
ELIMINATED

LINE 4

Gears 1:1 ➡ ← Cutting Roller

Cutting Canvas

Chain ➡

Time	
Mounting:	0'00"
Dismounting:	0'00"
Total:	0'00"
Savings:	4'57"

Courtesy of Nabisco, Inc.: Nabisco La Favorita

EXHIBIT 8–13

cess of changeover almost like something akin to alchemy. The process is perceived to require "old timers" to set various speed, temperatures, etc. at settings that their experience has shown to be necessary, and then to tweak the settings until the product meets specifications. Trial and error adjustments end up costing much more in both time and expense than the original setting. Interestingly, trial and error can always be eliminated by simply determining standard, perfect, measurable, and controllable settings at which the process output is alway immediately right. For example, at Nabisco's plant, cracker process line Number 4 originally required nine separate adjustments of canvas and roller speeds at widely scattered points in the process, as Exhibit 8–14 illustrates. Workers would start the process of changeover by making each approximate setting at the control board. Then they walked hundreds of feet along the line to observe slow speed operations. Based on their observations, they would return to the control board to adjust settings. They typically repeated this pattern several times until the process was running smoothly. By determining perfect settings for each cracker type and permanently inscribing these on the control panel dials (Exhibit 8–15) for each of the nine line segments, the Nabisco project team was able to slash radically the total time required. Eventually, through the use of modern electronic control systems, Nabisco converted nine separate dials to a single control for all nine locations.

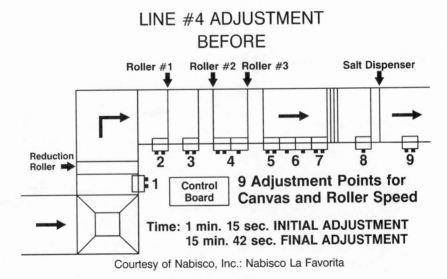

Courtesy of Nabisco, Inc.: Nabisco La Favorita

EXHIBIT 8–14

ONE TOUCH

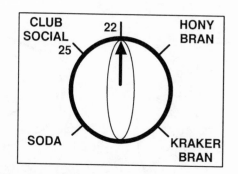

Time After: 4 min.
Reduction: 12 min. 57 sec.

Courtesy of Nabisco, Inc.: Nabisco La Favorita

EXHIBIT 8–15

A large percentage of process factories fill various containers (boxes, bottles, cans, barrels, and buckets, for example) with the proudcts they produce. Most use more than one size of container and have long, costly changeover related to changes in container size. For example, conveyors on filling and packaging lines have "fences" to channel containers through the process. These "fences," often hundreds of linear feet, must be repositioned for different container sizes. An example from Kraft General Foods Cannada's Mont Royal Plant in Montreal illustrates the opportunity for improvement. The small section of conveyor shown in Exhibit 8–16 is part of the jar cleaning process. Prior to improvement, several adjustment devices along the jar guides on both sides of the line required loosening, adjusting, tightening, and additional trial and error iterations before high speed production could resume. Changing to one fixed "fence" and using replaceable, fixed guides for each jar size, Exhibit 8–17, were some of the improvements that reduced changeover elapsed time on this line by 91 percent and changeover labor by 80 percent. Exhibit 8–18 addresses an additional aspect of changeover improvement, elimination of threaded fasteners. This example illustrates the nature of the change when switching from production of 1-kilogram to 500-gram jars in Kraft's Cheez Whiz filling and packaging line. Since the smaller jar could run in three parallel channels, whereas the larger could run in only two, part of the changeover involved removing or putting

CONVEYOR "FENCE" MOVEMENT
BEFORE

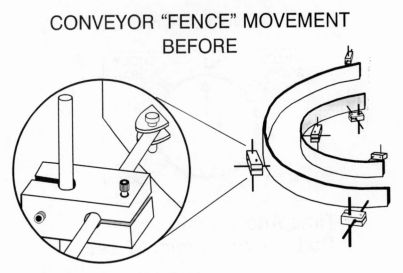

Courtesy of Kraft General Foods Canada

EXHIBIT 8-16

CONVEYOR "FENCE"
AFTER

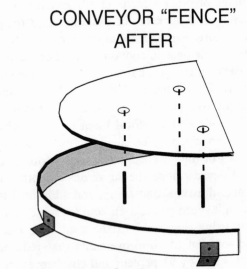

Courtesy of Kraft General Foods Canada

EXHIBIT 8-17

LINE SEPARATOR FASTENERS -- BEFORE

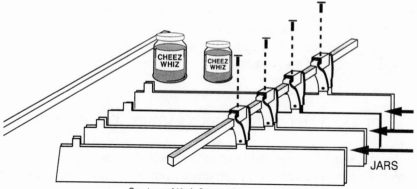

Courtesy of Kraft General Foods Canada

EXHIBIT 8-18

back the fences between the lines of jars. Originally this required the removal (and, later, the replacement) of fasteners and the trial and error adjustment of the fence positions. This small part of the line changeover was reduced from seven minutes to just under two minutes by the changes illustrated in Exhibit 8–19. The quick-attach clamp eliminated the need to turn threaded fasteners laboriously while a permanent set of

QUICK CONNECT CLAMPS -- AFTER

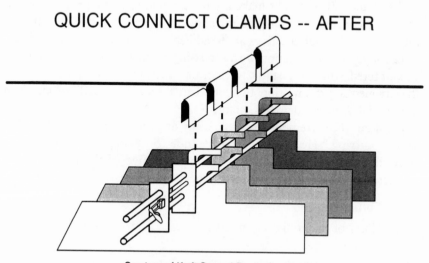

Courtesy of Kraft General Foods Canada

EXHIBIT 8-19

spacers for each jar size completely eliminated trial and error adjustment. Further, the lane guide no longer needed to be added or removed, because flat, thin guides made it possible merely to slide one over to touch another. These and other changes cut more than forty minutes of change-over time from the case packer section of the line.

The next key question to address is what *types* of production processes should be acquired and constructed.

PLANNED TIMING OF CAPACITY ADDITIONS

Although some factories add capacity well in advance of the time at which demand exceeds the maximum output of the existing factory or factories, the author is convinced that companies in this category are the exception. He has worked exclusively with factories that add capacity only after a period of operating full blast, but at levels lower than the market demand. The timing of capacity additions may make or break a company. Major investments in added capacity that are made immediately before deep and lengthy periods of economic downturn might mean ruin. If, however, capacity is added immediately before a major and continuing surge in demand, the enterprise may steal a march on the competition and capture an increased share of the market. As all competitors know, once lost, market share is extremely difficult to regain.

Hayes and Wheelwright make a scholarly and valuable presentation of the three conceptual strategies for adding capacity,[8] as depicted in Exhibit 8-20. These alternatives are to add capacity earlier than, later than, or in rough synchronization with the rising market. The problem always encountered when one starts to plan or strategize capacity additions is the erroneous presumption that one can forecast or predict long-term trends and accurate demand quantities. Even Michael Porter neglected to point out the extremely low probability of various forecasts and predictions occurring.[9] He does, however, allude to the degree of uncertainty as if this might be forecastable. He explains five of the forecasts and predictions that go into the capacity decision process:

1. Future demand
2. Costs of materials/commodities

---

[8]Hayes and Wheelwright, *Restoring Our Competitive Edge*, pp. 48–50.
[9]Michael E. Porter, *Competitive Strategy: Techniques for Analyzing Industries and Competitors* (New York: Free Press, 1980), pp. 326–28.

THE ACADEMIC VIEWPOINT

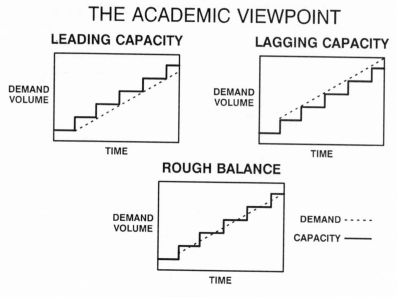

EXHIBIT 8-20

3. Technological changes and obsolescence potential
4. Competitor's capacity plans
5. Industry prices and costs

After executives and their staff expend considerable time and effort to forecast, predict, and analyze the future, real decisions are most frequently made according to the executives' gut feel for their business. The gut feel decision is often contrary to those indicated by the results of systematic analysis based on forecasts and probably at least as unsuccessful at anticipating the future. Although every company must make forecasts and predictions and must consider them when planning capacity additions, actual demand is at least as likely to decrease as increase. This being the case, the financial viability of the enterprise should not be jeopardized if the potential loss could be of such proportion.

Long-term demand trends in over 90 percent of all manufactured products are relatively gradual, while extreme peaks and valleys of long duration occur in cycles of four to seven years. In combination, these facts sharply reduce the number of companies needing major changes in capacity attributable to increased demand.

In process manufacturing the graph of typical capacity and demand, Exhibit 8-21, bears little resemblance to the academic viewpoint of planning alternatives. Because of the very high cost of process facilities and

PROCESS CAPACITY ADDITION

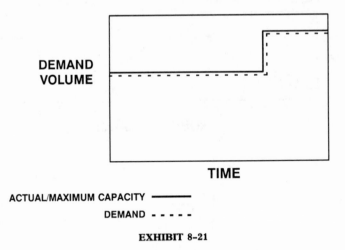

ACTUAL/MAXIMUM CAPACITY ————

DEMAND - - - - -

EXHIBIT 8–21

equipment, they must usually run at maximum capacity. Customers' orders are therefore scheduled into the first available capacity. In process industries the order backlog is often equal to several weeks of capacity, which means the shipment date of the next customer order received will be several weeks in the future. As Exhibit 8–21 shows, when the new process comes on-line, demand often fills the new capacity instantly. This is possible for the following reasons:

1. Most process industries have many times more total capacity than any single company in the industry. The entire industry has even more capacity, proportionately, than the amount of any single company's contemplated capacity addition. Thus, just one company's new capacity would usually drop the backlog of the entire industry by only hours or days.

2. Some companies are always in need of immediate delivery of some items; therefore, when industrywide backlogs are several weeks, customers with immediate needs flock to the one company with capacity available and thus able to make delivery almost at once.

Even process manufacturers experience long periods of demand higher and lower than normal. When demand rises, order backlogs increase, and customers must wait longer for delivery. When it falls, the backlog will fall until demand is too low to keep all of the process lines in operation. When this happens, a process line must be shut down until the demand once again climbs. Because demand can be seriously depressed over a long period of time, every process industry learns to master the science of reducing overhead costs to avoid catastrophic operating results. The survivors learn how to accomplish this and do it once every several years.

In assembly and job shop factories, the profile of customer demand, as compared with the maximum capacity of most machines, lines, and cells, is most frequently like that illustrated by the graph in Exhibit 8–22. In this example, the long-term trend of demand is up. However, in most periods, demand is substantially less than capacity. In the unusual peak periods in which potential sales are higher than capacity, the actual hours worked, including overtime, are at or close to maximum capacity. It is glaringly obvious when sustained demand finally comes close to maximum capacity, because the facility must operate continuously for twenty-one shifts per week. Even so, output per hour starts to decline. As Cox and Goldratt explain, when demand approaches maximum practical capacity, throughput drops.[10]

What do these typical patterns of demand versus capacity mean in terms of executive decision criteria? For one thing, in the process industry the company that adds capacity earlier than its competitors will probably capture the long-term market increase and will also increase existing market share. However, should the long-term market trend be flat or

ASSEMBLY/JOB SHOP

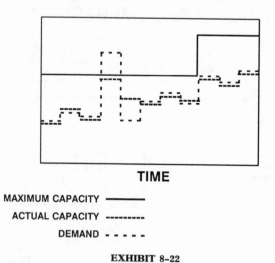

TIME

MAXIMUM CAPACITY ——————
ACTUAL CAPACITY ----------
DEMAND - - - - -

EXHIBIT 8–22

[10]Jeff Cox and Eliyahu M. Goldratt, *The Goal: A Process of Ongoing Improvement* (Croton-on-Hudson, N.Y.: North River Press, 1986), p. 86.

declining, the last company to have added capacity is likely to have the costliest plant and equipment and is thus the most likely to suffer. The executive decision criterion for job shop and assembly manufacturers is based on the fact that capacity is usually more than demand. Therefore, management attention should focus on the few processes for which demand is approaching capacity. Whenever this occurs, capacity of those processes should be increased as soon as possible. Increasing the capacity of just a few processes is likely to raise the total output of the facility substantially. Having thus solved a capacity constraint problem, other processes are likely to emerge as limiting the facility's output. Then management should again focus on the relatively few true capacity constraints. If the capacity-limited processes are low cost, the penalty for having "excess" capacity is correspondingly low. The company policy should therefore permit a greater margin of capacity for these low cost processes.

The lead time required to purchase new factory equipment is often assumed to be much longer than it really is. In the case of the first bar on Exhibit 8–23, decisions for authorizing capital are based on the eighteen-month acquisition lead time. Although it should be theoretically possible to avoid commitment until after quotations have been processed, once the process has been started, it tends to progress inexorably through each step in the process, up to the receipt of the completed equipment. Be-

LEAD TIME COMPRESSION

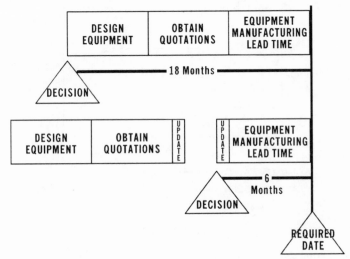

EXHIBIT 8-23

cause of the long lead time, the forecast required date is usually quite inaccurate. By contrast, if the new equiment designs and quotations are always processed far in advance for the few processes at or near maximum capacity, and if they are updated when technological changes occur, the decision-to-receipt lead time can be reduced to only the equipment manufacturer's lead time. Now the projected required date can be expected to be much more accurate than it would have been one year earlier.

The primary reason that this logical procedure is virtually never followed is that most companies do not have enough equipment designers. As discussed later in this chapter, this must change. However, even when only high level specifications are given to equiment suppliers for bidding, the specifications could be developed and delivered earlier, quotes could be obtained, and the supplier could be selected pending updates and ordering at the start of the manufacturer's lead time, based on the very latest forecast.

DUPLICATE PROCESSES: FLEXIBILITY, ECONOMY, AND BACKUP

During the first substantive seminar on "Japanese" techniques,[11] an attendee asked one of the Toyota executives if one of Toyota's secrets for reducing setup costs was to dedicate a machine to the production of a single item, thus completely eliminating setup cost. The answer was a vitally important message in terms of a policy that makes sense to *any* factory. The answer was, in essence, that Toyota would never consider having dedicated processes because of the problems that would arise when the demand rate of the item would vary drastically from the level on which the equipment decision was made. Superior manufacturers will purposely plan duplicate or near duplicate processes for every type of process. (Like every policy, exceptions will be allowed when they make good business sense.) Some of the advantages of redundancy of processes are as follows.

1. Backup is provided against the possibility of repair downtime.
2. More than one product can be produced at the same time; thus, customer service is better.

[11]Robert W. Hall, *Driving the Productivity Machine: Planning and Control in Japan* (Falls Church, Va.: American Production and Inventory Control Society, 1981).

3. Future incremental increases in capacity will be less costly than if bigger, faster equiment were used.

4. Overloads on one of the duplicate processes can often be moved to another duplicate process.

5. Because there are more than one identical process, the output of each is lower; thus, lower demands are more easily met by adjusting the capacity to match it. This will mean lower levels of inventory investment.

The policies of redundancy and down-scaling even apply to the largest of processes, such as paint lines and plating facilities. In appliance and automotive factories, paint lines are almost always mammoth installations which set the inflexible rate of production for the rest of the factory for all eternity. Eventually, every process becomes outmoded or destroys itself through corrosion, as is the usual case with plating installations. When this point is reached, the factory must often be shut down to disassemble the old process and install the new one. The alternative is to construct the replacement process in a new location that is remote from the rest of the inbound and outbound processes. This inevitably leads to the tortuously long, costly, illogical production paths that plague so many of the world's factories.

SIZING PRODUCTION EQUIPMENT: BIG IS NOT BEST

Factory management tends to put far too much emphasis on the speed and batch size of production equipment and facilities. They seem to confuse the valid economies of scale (discussed by Abegglen and Stalk)[12] related to the volume of sales with the decisions they make in sizing new equipment. The end result is a continuous progression to every bigger and faster equipment. As the speed and size of equipment increases, inventory investment usually increases proportionally, while the company's flexibility to respond rapidly to changing demand decreases in inverse proportion. The costs of larger production processes and facilities and their operating costs (*when running*) tend to increase at the rate of six-tenths per increment of speed/capacity increase,[13] as illustrated by Exhibit 8–24. However, as Hayes and Wheelwright indicate, as econ-

---

[12]James C. Abegglen and George Stalk, Jr., *Kaisha: The Japanese Corporation,* (New York, Basic Books, 1985), pp. 72--79.
[13]Hayes and Wheelright, *Restoring Our Competitive Edge,* pp. 58–67.

6/10 RULE OF THUMB

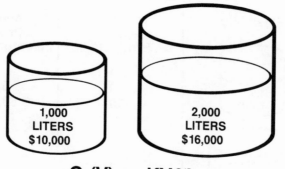

$$C\ (V)\ =\ KV^{2/3}$$

C (V) - Cost of Capacity Increment of Size V
K = Constant

EXHIBIT 8–24

omies of scale lower some costs, diseconomies of scale counterbalance them. These diseconomies include distribution costs (the larger facility may produce enough to cover a larger geographic area), added bureaucracy, chaotic complexity, and vulnerability to natural disaster. These diseconomies of scale are mostly of the intangible variety, and it is well nigh impossible to meaningfully calculate their costs by formula. However, the *very* tangible results of bigger, faster processes, in terms of the increased inventory investment required, are calculable and can be quite enormous. As Exhibit 8–25 shows, inventories attributable to lot size increase in the same ratio as the production output of a process. This increase may be insignificant when there is only a single product but becomes very material when the production unit is used to produce hundreds of products.

To date, in almost every instance the author has analyzed, companies that have completely abandoned small, slow equipment in favor of bigger, faster equipment have increased rather than decreased the total operations costs. For example, a factory producing small, sintered-metal products progressed to larger and larger sintering furnaces over the years. Since each different product requires slightly different programs of ideal furnace temperature and duration, it became necessary to accummulate furnace "charges" of numerous products of approximately the same formula and to process them using a formula for the average product processed. The furnace was large enough, and the product formulas were

VESSEL SIZE =
INVENTORY INVESTMENT

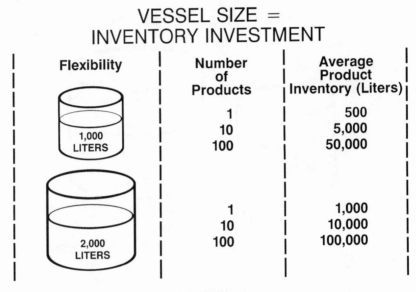

Flexibility	Number of Products	Average Product Inventory (Liters)
1,000 LITERS	1	500
	10	5,000
	100	50,000
2,000 LITERS	1	1,000
	10	10,000
	100	100,000

EXHIBIT 8-25

variable enough, for it to take two or more weeks to accummulate a full charge. The output of a complete charge then formed large queues of work ahead of the following machining operations, which could not process an accumulation of two weeks of production in just a few hours. Worse yet, the compromise in the actual furnace program used versus the ideal program caused yields to drop by approximately 10 percent. The extremely long lead times caused by the big furnaces and the variability of the time required to accumulate a furnace charge meant that it was impossible to fill large orders for custom products in a competitive time frame. Even standard products, stocked in finished goods, required exorbitant replenishment lead time. Thus, the long lead time and the unpredictable yield coupled with inaccurate forecasts necessitated monstrous amounts of safety stocks. Management concluded, when all of this was presented, that all future furnaces would be sharply downsized.

The problem of getting bigger and faster processes to run and to continue running is all too often overlooked. In one electronic assembly factory, a $5 million circuit board assembly tester–the first of its kind ever produced–was continuously worked on by a team of engineers for three years before finally being abandoned. It never performed a satisfactory test in all that time. Its problem? The machine was designed to test virtually any size and type of board and every imaginable type of condition. Had it worked properly, it would have been the most efficient tester in the world. Unfortunately, however, its specifications were just too complex for a mere mortal to be able to coax it to work. Sadly, engineers could walk on water as readily as they could master its complexities and get it to work.

The superior competitor of the future will be the one with the flexibility to produce every day what the market requires that day. As a result, it will have the lowest imaginable investment in inventory and the highest return on investment. Therefore, the best answer to the size and speed of equipment is neither the smallest and slowest nor the largest and fastest but rather a range of sizes to correspond to the demands of different products. This is illustrated in Exhibit 8–26, which includes several different vessel sizes. Incidentally, superior manufacturers, when starting production of new products, will base the size of their equipment on the share of the worldwide market they intend to capture. That planned share will be very ambitious. When they target more than any competitor, and tool up accordingly, the economies of scale can help to guarantee them that they will achieve the goal. Timid competitors, unable to lower their costs adequately, will not be serious contenders. As long as the bold company matches equipment size and speed to the most probably demands, the economies of scale will apply. Most new product lines include both high and low volume demand items. Accordingly, equipment applicable to each demand level should be considered.

Note in Exhibit 8–26 that the number of vessels of any one size is two

THE BEST TARGET

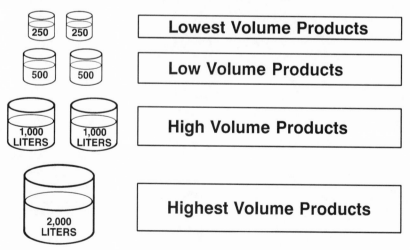

EXHIBIT 8-26

or more in all but one case. This is not an accident. By purposely planning to have at least two of each vessel, a company provides automatic backup for each. In addition, it can respond more rapidly to changing requirements since it will be able to produce more than one product at a time.

SUMMARY

Ultimately, the factory that best utilizes its capacity will have a competitive advantage. However, natural demand includes peaks and valleys as well as trends. The peaks and valleys are of both short and long duration. Therefore, to plan to maintain capacity exactly equal to actual demand is unreasonable. A superior strategy would call for focusing on selling available capacity. Numerous companies have found ways to manipulate peak sales into periods of low demand and vice versa (for example, by delayed billing agreements and sales promotions).

Placing the responsibility for capacity planning on the managers of small focused factories-within-a-factory is one effective way to simplify capacity planning. The small factory manager knows his loads and capacities through direct daily involvement where it counts–on the shop floor. For the superior manufacturer, greatly expanded staffs of machine designers and skilled machine builders will be the ultimate key to managing capacity.

9

□□□

Instant, Free Machine Maintenance and Repair

AT THIS VERY INSTANT, in each of hundreds of thousands of the world's factories, at least one machine is idle for repair. In most of these factories, such breakdowns will delay shipments of customer orders. A large percentage of these machines are not being repaired because maintenance specialists are already busily working on other machines. Paradoxically, potentially repairmen—the operators of the shut-down machine or cell— are standing idly by, waiting for the machine to be repaired.

As in most aspects of manufacturing, specialization and centralization have crippled our factories' ability to perform as well as they once did— before they became too big to permit people to have broader responsibilities for all aspects of their jobs. Machinists in the small factory took pride in their work and in their knowledge and mastery of machines. They performed both preventive and repair maintenance, for example. When factories grew to a much larger size, they fell victim to generally accepted beliefs concerning productivity. One such belief was that production workers should specialize in only *direct* production tasks: loading and unloading machines and pushing the machine start button. This forced factories to hire or train a new elite classification, the maintenance repairman.

Expectations of worker and machine productivity were certainly met. The simplified task of the new production worker enabled him and his machine to work at fever pitch *as long as the machine was running.* The problem was that the machines were more frequently not running. Whenever a setup or changeover was necessary, the operator and machine were idled until the setup specialist had time. As often as not, the setup man would already be working on another machine. The problems of lost time for machine and operator, due to repair, became even more severe. Among these were the following.

1. Machine repair specialists (maintenance men) were far fewer in number than the types and numbers of machines they were expected to service and repair. In the centralized maintenance organization, highly paid specialists were expected to repair any machine since their scarcity made specializing on one machine type impractical. Thus, these specialists never became as intimately familiar with machines as the small factory's machinist.

2. As indirect employees, maintenance workers have always been subject to cutback in every cost reduction program. As a result, manpower resources rarely suffice to cover repair and preventive maintenance adequately. Thus, preventive maintenance falls by the wayside, exacerbating the problem of machine breakdowns.

3. Even when a progressive management recognizes the need for increasing maintenance and repair capacity and decides to increase the maintenance organization, it is almost impossible to hire experienced people. And it takes years to train specialists to the point of being reasonably proficient since proficiency depends so much on experience with specific machine types.

It is now much better understood that the most effective machine maintenance and repair is performed as it always has been in small factories—by the machinist. Thus, superior manufacturers are hard at work decentralizing maintenance. In the process, the goals of such reorganization are as ambitious as in every other factory area and typically include such improvements as the following:

Percent

90	Machine downtime
40	Maintenance cost
50	Machine spare parts inventory
75	Direct labor loss due to downtime
50	Computer system support

Not surprisingly, one of the tricks behind improved machine maintenance is simplification. The most powerful tool for simplification is making problems visible to everyone. The author learned one example of fast, low cost visibility while working in Japanese factories. Each cell team member was given a bright pink pad of ink and a circular stamp. Each time a machine broke down, it was prominently stamped with a large, bright pink dot. Since almost all machines were green, the most problematic ones soon came to resemble blossoming cherry trees (Exhibit 9–1). Anyone in the company, from the chief executive officer down, had no trouble identifying machines with maintenance problems. A walk in the factory was sufficient to spot quickly machines that would benefit most from rebuilding or from other problem solving methods. Interestingly, the author's clients have taken the messages of simplification and making problems visible even farther than some Japanese companies, as will be seen in this chapter.

CHECKLIST: MACHINE MAINTENANCE AND REPAIR ZINGERS

The author's previous book contains a much shorter section on equipment maintenance.[1] For harried executives with too much to do and too little time to do it, reading that brief introduction and the following sum-

CHERRY BLOSSOM METHOD

EXHIBIT 9–1

[1] See Appendix 2.

marized list of this chapter's most important messages might be a valuable shortcut to a basic understanding of the opportunities.

1. Machine operators and assemblers should be expected to perform their own preventive maintenance and should perform it when they would otherwise be idle. This helps to make preventive maintenance almost free.

2. Directed by maintenance specialists, machinists and assemblers can rapidly learn to do the routine, simple repair tasks (such as machine disassembly and reassembly) on the portion of the machine in which there is a problem. The operators will rapidly become more expert at these tasks than the repair specialists. Instead of being idle while the repairmen work, the operators can perform some of the necessary repair.

3. One new role of maintenance specialists should be to train and supervise machinists in performing maintenance and repair. In the past, one specialist could work on only one machine at a time. In the future, the specialist can keep repairs of several machines under way simultaneously by periodically supervising each operator's repair work instead of doing the work himself.

4. Another new role of the maintenance specialist will be to develop and install fast maintenance features (for example, fast detach/attach mechanisms for removing machine covers and for replacing components like motors).

5. Maintenance specialists can use some of their newly available spare time (resulting from maintenance and repair work performed by operators) to develop fail-safe maintenance methods. These would preclude operator oversight and errors when they perform preventive maintenance.

6. Every factory should foster the development of its own skilled machine makers and designers. The world's most important innovations flow out of the invention of new machines and processes that can most economically produce new products. The superior manufacturers of the twenty-first century will attain this status only if they have these important personnel resources.

7. Every factory must have the systematic plans and personnel skills necessary to rebuild machines periodically. Even the best preventive maintenance procedures cannot stop the continuous wear of moving components. Electronic components also deteriorate, because they are continuously subjected to variation in temperature.

Machines that have deteriorated from wear can best be restored to original condition by rebuilding.

8. Advance procurement of spare parts and organization of disassembly/assembly teams can sharply reduce the time and cost involved in rebuilding machines. Too many companies first start to procure parts when a disastrous breakdown occurs and use only one or two people to do the rebuild work.

9. As many machine spare parts as possible should be moved from centralized storage to the machine's subplant or cell. This slashes the time wasted in retrieving them and helps to cut machine downtime.

10. Operator teams should be responsible for maintaining a reasonable supply of spare parts unique to the machines in the subplant or cell. They will be better able to understand the frequency with which items fail than is the central storeroom clerk. Thus, they will be able to maintain inventory at adequate, not excessive, levels.

11. Machine specialists should become more actively involved in developing specifications for new machine features related to low cost and free maintenance. A machine's uptime performance and effective, low cost maintenance features should be major factors in selecting single-source machine suppliers.

12. In the long term, choosing single-source machine suppliers will help to standardize maintenance and repair procedures and reduce the variety of spare machine parts stocked, greatly simplifying maintenance operations.

13. Tracking status and accounting for the costs of machine repair work orders will no longer be necessary. The small, focused subplant manager and cell teams will participate in and be responsible for repairs, so they will always automatically know the status of repairs. Since they will perform the majority of the maintenance work, transferring repair costs from the central maintenance department to the department for which work has been performed will not be required as much.

14. Bright paint will be used to highlight lubrication points and other components requiring preventive maintenance inspection. This will make them easy to see and hard to forget.

15. The instant camera will be used to make pictures of important parts of machines and related maintenance and repair procedures. These pictures cost a fraction of the cost of producing drawings

or even sketches of the same items. And photos are infinitely easier to decipher than formal drawings.

JOB ENRICHMENT: A POWERFUL INDUCEMENT

Whenever we have reasoned together on productivity-related issues, managements, unions, and consultants have always been able to come to agreement on acceptable ways to make the changes necessary to stay or become superior competitors. This is not to say that there have not been issues that take a long time to resolve. Chief among these is the one topic of this very chapter—shifting the responsibility for equipment maintenance and repair from specialists to operators. There are two reasons for difficulties. One is that maintenance personnel are often members of a separate, elite union. Where this is the case, union officials and rank-and-file members are often likely to fear that changes will lead to reductions in their membership and thus an erosion of union power. when a single union represents both production and maintenance workers, maintenance specialists often fear losing the prestige of the elite maintenance classification. Managements with long histories of dealing with the union in good faith (demonstrating an almost equal commitment to the well-being of stockholders and employees) have the least difficulty working in harmony with their unions and rank-and-file to improve competitiveness. Regardless of management or union attitude, in almost every case the rank-and-file consensus favors improvement. They see that the methods of greater productivity can and should not only ensure continuing jobs but also enrich them.

Operators already have much greater and more valuable knowledge of their machines than management thinks. Therefore, the production workforce majority does not view the proposed new responsibilities with trepidation. Nor do they fear that added responsibilities will cause a reduction of jobs in their classifications. Although everyone knows that increased productivity will reduce the labor required per piece, they also understand that it holds the potential for increasing sales. Therefore, the long-term prospects for retaining or even for increasing the number of jobs will be bright. This is not automatically the same outlook of maintenance specialists who have little basis for believing that they are prepared for the new roles that they must adapt to in the new environment (although it *will* be feasible for them to master prestigious new jobs). New roles for them include: (1) trainers and supervisors of production workers in maintenance and repair activities, (2) maintenance engineers, responsible for designing and installing maintenance improvements in present equipment, (3) equipment maintenance procurement specification engineers, responsible for specifying maintenance features for new machines, and (4) designers and developers of equipment rebuilding methods. The solution to the maintenance specialists' trepidation is to initiate an intensive education and training program designed to upgrade their skills and give them confidence in their ability to perform their new responsibilities. At the same time, nothing works as successfully as success itself. So a pilot project in a limited area of the factory can prove to production workers and maintenance specialists that both will find that the new job parameters can enrich their working lives, and both can easily learn how to perform their new duties. However, overcoming the powerful resistance of specialists who are fearful of the erosion of their elite status will not be an easy task. For example, Dick Faucett, the United Auto Worker Local 933's synchronous manufacturing coordinator, points out that craft workers, a small percentage of the rank-and-file, control the union with their almost 100 percent attendance at union meetings. Although Dick feels this will make it impossible to shift responsibilities from specialists to production personnel in the near term, the author remains confident that as soon as management does its part (developing important new jobs for the specialists), the highly intelligent craft people will recognize the advantage to themselves and their companies of new, more responsible positions. Incidentally, several top union officials share the author's optimism and enthusiasm for continuously improving labor–management relations. For example, Donald Ephlin, retired International Vice President, United Auto Workers, attributes General Motors' rise to the position of best in the domestic industry to union–company teamwork.[2]

MACHINE DOWNTIME: CUSTOMER SERVICE BANE

The job stress of almost every manufacturing executive and manager would be eased immeasurably if only machines and assembly equipment were never down for repair. Next to late supplier deliveries, machine downtime is one of the most serious deterrents to achieving on-time shipment of customer orders. To assume that breakdowns will be completely eliminated any time in the foreseeable future would be naïve. Therefore, superior manufacturers must take steps to minimize the risk of downtime

[2]Ross E. Robson, *The Quality and Productivity Equation: American Corporate Strategies for the 1990s* (Cambridge, Mass.: Productivity Press, 1990).

and to cut its duration when it does occur. The most powerful risk avoidance tactic is extremely simple: planned backup. Backup entails having more than one machine, cell, or process and having more potential capacity than usually required. And, because customer demand of job shops and assembly factories fluctuates in a wide range on both sides of average demand, this surplus capacity is, to some extent, automatically available in many factories. However, even if backup capacity is available, being forced to use it interrupts the normal smooth flow of production. For example, the backup capacity might be made available by working a third shift and weekends, whereas the rest of the factory operates only two shifts. Thus, even if backup is available, the duration of machine downtime must be minimized.

Often, during most of the time machines are down for repair, no one is actively working on the machine. Among the innumerable periods of delay are the following:

1. Waiting for a machine maintenance man to become available and to be assigned to work on the machine.

2. After being assigned to repair a machine, the maintenance specialist must make a long trip from the maintenance workshop to the machine location.

3. After analyzing the machine's problem, the maintenance specialist must usually take trips back to the maintenance shop for tools and to the central maintenance storeroom for repair parts.

4. The required spare parts are often either not stocked or out of stock. If so, they have to be ordered. In some cases, days or weeks might pass before the parts become available.

5. In some cases defective machine parts must be repaired or replaced by the maintenance machine shop or the tool room. This is most often the case when machines are old and no longer serviced or are purchased from overseas suppliers.

6. Work on one machine is often interrupted when another machine is deemed to be of even more urgent priority. However, to determine the relative priority of dozens of out-of-order machines in shops with hundreds of machines is not easy and may even be impossible.

7. Repair specialists often work only the first shift or with skeleton staff on other shifts. Therefore, repair work typically comes to a screeching halt at the end of the first shift. Long repair jobs take

three times as long to complete if the work is done on one shift instead of three.

8. As a consequence of insufficient expertise, repair is often done on a trial and error basis—replacing some component in the hopes that this will solve the problem, only to discover that the machine still does not work properly. All too often the repair specialist turns machine operation over to production people who quickly discover that the machine is still not working. In these instances, all of the above delays are experienced again.

Decentralization of selected maintenance functions will help to reduce these delays.

THE SUPERIOR MAINTENANCE ORGANIZATION

The typical maintenance organization includes specialists of various craft and industrial disciplines. Among these are millwrights, carpenters, pipe fitters, welders, and electricians. The craft divisions are often the root cause of disruption of the smooth execution of machine repair. Union work rules often restrict work performed during machine repair to the craft worker specializing in the particular discipline. For example, any work on any electric aspect of the job are deemed to require a qualified electrician. When the repair might be as straightforward as replacing a simple wire between two points, this seems somewhat ludicrous. This roadblock is one on which executive management and its unions need to start negotiations. In general, however, maintenance workers tend to specialize in one of two general types of work: plant (building) and equipment (air conditioning, power plant) maintenance, and production equipment maintenance. In the superior factory of the twenty-first century, plant and plant equipment maintenance will most often continue to be a centralized function, as shown in Exhibit 9–2.

Incidentally, Higgins's handbook should be a standard reference for maintenance managers and specialists but is not yet updated to reflect all of the latest thinking.[3] For example, Erikson, the author of Chapter 5, recognizes the possibility of decentralized maintenance but describes it more as an option than a vital necessity.

[3]Lindley R. Higgins, editor-in-chief, *Maintenance Engineering Handbook* (New York: Mc-Graw-Hill, 1988), section 1, chapter 5.

The amount of plant and plant equipment maintenance work in most subplants does not justify specialists of the various required disciplines for each organization. Therefore, plant engineering will usually continue to be a responsibility of the central maintenance department. By contrast, almost all millwrights (the factory machine maintenance specialists) will be moved into the factory organization. In Exhibit 9–2, the millwrights become part of the subplant organization. However, in many subplants the maintenance workload would be too low to justify a full-time millwright. Thus, in these cases the millwright would be part of the subplant cluster organization and would serve more than one subplant.[4]

In addition to people, machines (used to repair and to manufacture machine parts) and repair part inventories will be assigned to either central maintenance or the factory organization. For example, spare parts for building and building equipment would be the responsibility of the central maintenance organization, as would maintenance supplies and components commonly used by several subplants and/or in building and building equipment maintenance. In addition, in the best maintenance shops, each specialist has his own workbench, to which he can go to repair small machine components and subassemblies. His home is also where he stores his tool set and processes paperwork. In the new organization, the factory layout should include places in the subplant (or clus-

NEW MAINTENANCE ORGANIZATION

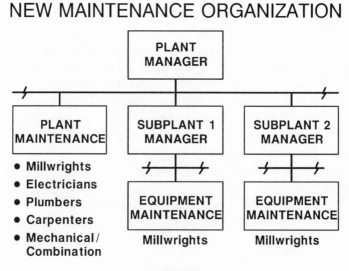

EXHIBIT 9–2

[4]See Appendix 2.

ter) for the specialist's "home base" and for storage of repair parts and supplies.

REBUILD: THE ONLY SURE CURE

Some of the best factories (from the standpoint of the reliability of their machines) in which the author has worked have been high volume producers whose machines are destroying themselves as rapidly as any in the world because of their high operating speeds and high production volume. One cannot help but notice that many such factories achieve near-perfect utilization—thanks to an almost complete lack of machine downtime. How do these factories keep machines running almost continuously, even though they are just as much subject to wear as any other machine? The answer is that these companies have scheduled points at which every machine is removed from production, completely rebuilt, and then put back into production. Processing high volume, over time, makes it possible to develop histories of machine repairs. The histories are used to determine which types of machines need to be rebuilt after a year in operation, after two years, three years, and so forth.

Improving the quality of preventive maintenance does not guarantee reducing the frequency of breakdown, although in the author's experience it does yield improvements. Nevertheless, too many factories that have ignored preventive maintenance for too many years are inclined to place far more value on preventive maintenance than is warranted. In these factories, the machines that continuously break down are often the same ones on which it is virtually impossible to consistently produce parts within the required tolerance limits. This inability to hold tolerances is caused by "play" in the machine. For example, a worn bearing in a drill press might cause the drill bit to wobble very slightly, causing holes to be larger than the diameter of the drill bit. The problem with these machines is so severe that, after years of neglect, the only effective solution is to rebuild them completely, replacing all worn components and upgrading them by incorporating the most recent features developed for the machines most recently produced by the machine's manufacturer. (Too few companies systematically review new machines for the purpose of learning of new ideas and designing modifications to older machines to install the same type of improvements). Rebuilding the machine not only reduces downtime, it also increases the consistency of the quality of items produced.

Failure to perform preventive maintenance is not the reason that the best companies systematically rebuild machines. As Nakajima has said, "Equipment slowly deteriorates over time and breakdowns occur as fatigues develop."[5] Thus, no matter how diligently preventive maintenance is performed, eventually the condition of the equipment deteriorates to the point where breakdowns become rampant. At this point many companies treat the most obvious breakdown cause, only to see the machines continue to break down time and time again. The reason is that every other part of the machine has also been fatigued, and it is only a matter of time before other machine components also start to fail. The total machine time loss and cost of repair to fix the obvious problem of the moment is several times greater than the alternative, a one-time, well-planned machine rebuilding. This means completely rebuilding the machine and replacing all parts subject to deterioration, regardless of their degree of deterioration.

Even in factories that regularly schedule and execute rebuilding of machines, the process of rebuilding takes the machine out of production for longer than necessary and costs more than it should. Why? Too often machine rebuilding is done on a learn as you go basis, without preplanning every disassembly and reassembly step. The productivity of rebuilding machines can be improved as methodically as any other factory operation. Advance preparation (such as procuring parts to be replaced) and planning and documenting disassembly and reassembly methods are the most important ingredients of the most productive, speedy machine rebuild programs. Assembly and disassembly are usually performed by a single individual. The author has found that any low volume assembly involving physically large and complex items such as machines can be broken into numerous small tasks to be performed by a team of two or more. This simplifies the task of each team member, which drastically cuts the time required. Complex tasks require time for thinking and for referencing documentation, whereas people performing simple tasks spend more time working and less time thinking. In addition, the larger team slashes the elapsed time. When two individuals' tasks are well planned, both the total man-hours worked and the elapsed hours should be less than one-half those of a single individual working alone. This occurs because the tasks of each team member require less time, and the work of the team members overlaps.

[5]Seiichi Nakajima, ed., *TPM Development Program: Implementing Total Productive Maintenance* (Cambridge, Mass.: Productivity Press, 1989), p. 97.

VIBRATION: THE INSIDIOUS LOOSENING TOOL

The typical machine uses thousands of fasteners, most of which could become sources of a machine breakdown should they become too loose. As J. B. Catlin points out in his excellent chapter on the analysis and correction of vibration,[6] one of the reasons that fasteners become loose is that machines vibrate, in varying degrees. Vibration, over time, causes some fasteners to loosen. One way to prevent or minimize machine damage due to loose fasteners is to inspect and tighten them periodically before they become a serious problem. Fastener inspection can even be an automatic, free by-product when performed as part of the routine cleaning of machines that should be a cornerstone of the preventive maintenance program. It is hard to clean an area without noticing loose fasteners in the vicinity. Regardless of the fact that loose fasteners can be detected earlier, this does not get to a permanent solution to the problem.

Human error can also cause loose fasteners. The last person who should have tightened the fastener sometimes forgets to tighten it enough or just did not understand how tight it should have been. Although inspection might detect some of these people errors, detection does not address the source of the problem. Immediate steps to eliminate the potential for error can and should be taken. One such permanent solution might be to use fasteners that lock with such force that even continuous vibration will not dislodge them. Another would be to mark the fastener and the immobile machine part to which it is attached with paint or with a scribed line. The fastener would be seen to be adequately tightened only when the lines are perfectly aligned.

Fasteners are not the only machine elements that are subject to loosening or movement as a result of machine vibrations. Many machines have one or more built-in, calibrated measuring devices. Over time, or even when the machine is new, these devices are found to be inaccurate and thus are not used. The most frequent reason for inaccuracy is simply that there are no routine procedures for checking measuring devices' accuracy and adjusting them to make them correct. Again, vibration is the chief reason for wandering away from accuracy.

Since vibration, noise, and heat are signals that wear or damage have caused machine components to deteriorate, electromechanical devices can be installed to provide early warning signals. Machines subject to frequent problems should be the earliest candidates for the use of such

---

[6]Higgins, *Maintenance Engineering Handbook*, section 10, chapter 3.

devices, as soon as operating personnel have been trained to understand their signals. After all, as Suzaki has said, "the use of diagnostic equipment is like the use of robots or any other sophisticated equipment. Without understanding the functions and utilizing people's capabilities to evaluate alternative methods, the cost effectiveness of such equipment will be greatly reduced."[7] Bloch and Geitner have provided one source of information that is of value in understanding the basics of vibration and equipment condition monitoring signals. Further, they point out that such equipment has helped many companies to change from periodic rebuild programs to replacing specific components when indicated by the signals of sensing devices.[8] Savings can be quite significant in terms of delaying the replacement of slightly worn components that have not yet deteriorated to the point of reducing the controllability of the machine or causing additional damage.

MAINTENANCE–CHANGEOVER INTERRELATIONSHIP

There is usually a strong correlation between a machine's condition and the time and cost associated with its setup (changeover). Although the author views setup reduction and maintenance productivity projects as separate, the goals of each are impacted by improvements undertaken to achieve the goals of the other. For example, devices originally intended for setting the machine for different parts are often not used because they have become inaccurate over time. If the devices are restored to their original accuracy, the time it takes to adjust machine settings by trial and error can often be eliminated.[9] Subsequent periodic checking and calibration of the devices is much less time-consuming than trial and error adjustment during setup.

Excessive "play" (looseness of machine component fit) most frequently stems from normal deterioration of machine parts as the machine ages and from additional deterioration that comes from inadequate maintenance (i.e., lack of lubrication). "Play" in machines, until corrected, is one of the most difficult setup problems to overcome. Improving the accuracy of built-in measuring devices will be of little use if "play" is

[7]Kiyoshi Suzaki, *The New Manufacturing Challenge: Techniques for Continuous Improvement* (New York: Free Press, 1987), p. 121.
[8]Heinz P. Bloch and Fred K. Geitner, *Major Process Equipment Maintenance and Repair* (Houston: Gulf Publishing, 1985), Chapter 13.
[9]See Appendix 2.

going to cause the devices to give different results from one minute to the next.

Finally, the combined effect of setup reduction and maintenance productivity enhancement is often to improve quality sharply. Accurate, failsafe setup precludes producing defective parts that result from setup errors. Reducing the degree of "play" in the machine also reduces the tendency of the machine to produce parts with dimensions that vary widely from the center of the acceptable range of tolerances (some even falling outside the range). All of these arguments in favor of improved maintenance deal with intangible and difficult-to-predict benefits of improved maintenance. Although the tangible benefits of productive maintenance are great enough by themselves to make improvements self-financing, the less tangible benefits must not be overlooked. If improvements in setup and quality do not ensue, something might have been overlooked.

MAINTENANCE SYSTEMS: AID OR BURDEN?

The classical maintenance systems that predominate in the field today are burdens, not aids. They exemplify the wrong way to solve a problem—by reporting it—as opposed to getting to the root of the problem and resolving it with the simplest possible approach. The main functions these systems are intended to address include (1) scheduling and prioritization of maintenance jobs, (2) accounting for the costs of maintenance by the factory area in which the work is performed, and (3) maintaining inventory status and usage history of maintenance parts and supplies. The need for these functions virtually disappears as soon as most of the central maintenance organization is moved into the factory's small, focused subplants. As Grief has written, "data processing should be decentralized . . . the volume of data argues for decentralization."[10] However, data and data processing for supporting maintenance can be taken farther than just decentralization. The amount of computer processing can be sharply reduced.

The author has said and fervently believes that the manager of the centralized maintenance organization has the toughest of all factory jobs. Every executive and manager in both factory and office believes that his maintenance needs are the most critical and therefore expects instant

[10]Michel Greif, *The Visual Factory: Rebuilding Participation Through Shared Information* (Cambridge, Mass.: Productivity Press, 1991), pp. 177–79.

service. However, the number of maintenance personnel is *always* far less than the number of pending repair and maintenance jobs. Even if there were some magic way to determine the real priority of each job in relation to all others, the priority would be valid only until the next breakdown occurred, or until the production schedule changed. (In the case of machines, their repair urgency is a function of the schedule of the products in which the components produced by the machines are used. Thus, whenever the production schedule changes, the relative repair priority of machines would also change.) Further, the repair time for each job is so unpredictable that accurate completion estimates are impossible. Given the impossibly difficult circumstances, it is easy to see why maintenance managers find system logic for prioritizing jobs to be worthless. If one must still have a priority-determining system, as Wireman suggests, "the simpler the priority system is, the more widely accepted it will be."[11] Simplicity is as powerful a tool in maintenance as in every other area of business. It is incredibly simple for each subplant manager to know his pending maintenance jobs for the relatively few machines and cells for which he is responsible, Thus, he can easily assign them a relative priority and communicate the priority to the maintenance specialist in his own organization. The job becomes even simpler when the most basic problem, lack of adequate repairmen, is alleviated by turning the entire workforce into competent repairmen.

The foundation on which the traditional maintenance system rests is the maintenance work order. Until the paperwork establishing a work order is prepared, work can not even be started. The new, focused subplant has no need for the work order—either for scheduling and prioritizing maintenance or for collecting the maintenance costs for charging the subplant with the labor costs of maintenance (since the maintenance is performed by the subplant's own employees). To create and use the work order would only add cost to the maintenance task. However, the work order will probably continue to be used for work performed by the remaining central maintenance organization. The volume of work orders will be much more manageable than when the order backlog included machine repair and preventive maintenance work orders.

Whether or not a subplant's maintenance inventories and spare parts usage history is complex enough to warrant maintaining data at all should be determined on a case-by-case basis. In most cases, the inventory of spare parts in a given focused factory will contain few enough items that it will be practical to maintain superb control by eye.

[11]Terry Wireman, *World Class Maintenance Management* (New York: Industrial Press, 1990), p. 94.

PREVENTIVE MAINTENANCE SCHEDULING

Preventive maintenance is not even performed in many factories the author visits. The reason is crystal clear. Every machine maintenance specialist in the factory has a backlog of repair jobs waiting for him. Since repair has higher priority than preventive maintenance, it is impossible ever to get the backlog of repair so low that there is time to work on prevention rather than repair. To make matters worse, in older factories there is seldom even any substantive documentation of maintenance procedures for each machine. Therefore, most preventive maintenance projects must start with the development of maintenance procedures. The logical source of preventive maintenance information would be the machine manufacturer's manual. However, we find that machine manufacturers have done very little to support superior maintenance by developing and documenting comprehensive procedures. At least a little information can usually be gleaned from the supplier's manuals, and even more becomes available when the manufacturer is consulted. Nevertheless, whenever preventive maintenance has been superficially performed or completely ignored, starting from scratch to gather procedural data is almost always necessary. If an improvement team plans to do all of the groundwork itself, it may take forever to complete procedures for every machine. The author's approach gets a lot more work done in a shorter time span. Developing preventive maintenance procedures is a task for which the assistance of the entire workforce can be recruited. The machine operator could do the initial groundwork for the machine with which he works all the time in mere minutes (or at most a few hours). The most valuable function that the full-time project team can perform is to develop preventive maintenance checklists to guide operators in the investigation necessary to identify preventive maintenance needs. For instance, operators should clean machines thoroughly and, in the process, should be looking for the oil holes, grease zerks, and lubrication caps that will be the focus of the lubrication program.

LUBRICATION: DO NOT GREASE
THE SQUEAKING WHEEL

When one greases the squeaking wheel, it is already too late. The noise indicates not only that the wheel bearings are devoid of lubricant but also that the resulting friction has started to accelerate the deterioration of the wheel components. Thus, although it is true that damage can be detected early by sensing devices that "listen" to machine vibrations, the main line of attack on deterioration should be frequent lubrication. And, of course, machine, cell, and line operators should be the front-line troops, grabbing each opportunity to use time that might otherwise be idle to check and replenish lubrication.

In many factories that have tried operator preventive maintenance programs, there have been instances where operators have missed a lubrication point or have used the wrong lubricant. Where these instances have led to machine breakdown, the solution has been to shift the preventive maintenance responsibility to a crew in the central maintenance organization. This approach, which fosters specialization and thus disperses the responsibility for performance, has its own drawbacks. They include the following:

1. The tendency is to cut the preventive maintenance crew every time cost-cutting drives occur.

2. Production schedules interfere with preventive maintenance. Interrupting urgently needed production to perform maintenance on schedule proves impractical.

3. Maintenance people's time is more urgently required to assist in machine repairs. Accordingly, preventive maintenance can rarely be done on schedule.

4. Managers and executives do not see significant decreases in output or even machine utilization in direct proportion to cutbacks in preventive maintenance lubrication. Nor do they see instant results from increasing its frequency. This leads them to doubt the wisdom of spending money on an activity that cuts into short-term profitability.

Many factories, especially large, bureaucratic ones, have specialists who work full-time on preventive maintenance. One advantage of this is that they are not called upon to do repair work when machines are down, thus stinting on their own preventive maintenance job. Using preventive maintenance specialists to avoid conflicts with priorities for downtime repair is not only the easy way out but also the wrong way. The rationale for using specialists—because operators might make mistakes (such as using the wrong lubricants)—is terribly flawed. It only adds a layer of specialization and contributes to the blight of bureaucratic bloat. After all, even the specialist could make a mistake. The best solution would be to develop fail-safe methods that make oversight and error virtually impossible, no matter who performs the required task. For example, every superior manufacturer should make lubrication points highly visible. It is not enough just to clean all machines, removing the grease and grime that has hidden the lubrication points. The next step is to paint a bright ring of color around each point. Doing this lessens the possibility of overlooking that point when performing maintenance. Incidentally, color highlighting should be used wherever it will help to call attention to routine maintenance and maintenance inspection points. For example, motor brushes should be periodically inspected and replaced when worn. Color highlighting of the ring around the brush location would be desirable. Color highlighting of maintenance points can and should be started tomorrow, if not today. If all operators take part in the process of developing fail-safe methods, all machines and equipment in the factory can be done in just a few days. As soon as possible, additional color bands should be added to both lubrication points and the lubrication containers. When the lubrication container color and that of the lubrication point are the same, the wrong lubricant will not wind up in the wrong place. This color coding will usually need to wait until the team has done enough study to know which lubricants will be used and to establish a factory-wide color code. (Incidentally, Anne Bernhardt's chapter on lubricants[12] is a fine source of guidelines for lubricants that is of value when the machine manufacturer's lubrication recommendations cannot be found).

After implementing fail-safe methods, there is certainly nothing so difficult about maintenance tasks, such as lubrication, that operators cannot be trained to do the work. Even Taylor, who said, "The man suited to handling pig iron is too stupid to train himself,"[13] had no reservations about that same man's being trainable. Taylor appears to have mistakenly attributed slowness to learn to low native intelligence. In fact, the qualities of intelligence that he prized so highly were mostly gained through education (a form of training) and experience.

The color highlighting method and the instant camera are important tools for simplifying maintenance procedure documentation and, thus, for reducing its development cost. Interestingly, the author's clients are apparently outperforming some Japanese companies in this regard. For example, Exhibit 9–3 is a small part of a large procedure matrix used by Tokai Rubber Industries.[14] The full matrix also includes the maintenance and inspection criteria, maintenance tools, time estimates for each main-

---

[12]Anne Bernhardt, Chapter 2–1, in Robert C. Rosaler and James O. Rice, eds., *Industrial Maintenance Reference Guide* (New York: McGraw-Hill, 1987).
[13]Frederick Winslow Taylor, *The Principles of Scientific Management* (Easton, Pa.: Hive Publishing, 1985), p. 63.
[14]Nakajima, *TPM Development Program*, p. 197.

TYPICAL MAINTENANCE DOCUMENTATION

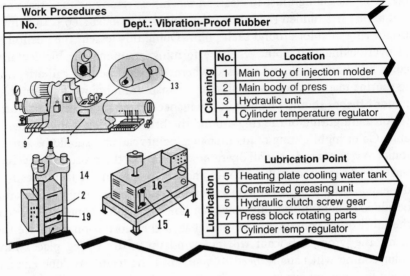

Work Procedures		
No.	Dept.: Vibration-Proof Rubber	

	No.	Location
Cleaning	1	Main body of injection molder
	2	Main body of press
	3	Hydraulic unit
	4	Cylinder temperature regulator

Lubrication Point

	No.	
Lubrication	5	Heating plate cooling water tank
	6	Centralized greasing unit
	5	Hydraulic clutch screw gear
	7	Press block rotating parts
	8	Cylinder temp regulator

EXHIBIT 9-3

tenance item, person responsible, and the maintenance interval. How much simpler to color code the maintenance points and/or make instant camera pictures of their locations and applicable tools than to draw sketches of the various locations and try to describe in words where the locations are!

DEVELOPING BETTER MACHINES: SKILLED CRAFTSMEN SHORTAGE

Several personal experiences with engine failure and fires while on international flights aboard big jets have strengthened the author's contention that it is unlikely that machine breakdown will ever be completely eliminated. After all, aircraft and their engines are probably more zealously maintained that any other equipment category. However, this should not deter anyone from striving for perfection. It should be encouraging to note that the frequency of jet engine breakdowns is measurable only in instances per million flights, as are breakdowns of some factory machines. Every aircraft breakdown in flight triggers intensive investigation. And, if the design of the failed component were found to be of less durability than necessary, a new design would be developed and aircraft in service updated. Similar attention must be paid to upgrading present and planned factory equipment based on its breakdown history.

A factory that does not design and manufacture its own machines will find it much more problematic to design improvements to increase the durability of existing and future machines than factories that do. After all, where can the improved machine designs come from if a company does not have people with this background? This is somewhat harder to do than to say. In the factory of the past, a somewhat elite group of young people learned the trade of machine makers through a long program of apprenticeship. Today, union rules and economics have made it difficult to follow the same course. However, since these skilled resources will be a vital competitive sword, industry, institutions of education and training, and government would all be well advised to get to work on rebuilding and improving their numbers.

Skilled maintenance workers, freed from the drudgery of routine repair and maintenance of machines (because of operators' expanded maintenance and repair roles), will have time available for exciting new responsibilities. Maintenance engineering will be one of the chief new challenges. The maintenance engineer will be responsible for designing and specifying improved maintenance features for present machines as well as machines to be built or purchased. Improved machine design is such a natural adjunct to maintenance responsibilities that it is a wonder it has been overlooked. Even such maintenance experts as Heinzelman make no mention of this aspect of maintenance.[15]

At the practical, what-to-do-tomorrow level, enterprises and their unions should start immediately to discuss how best and most equitably to do the necessary job. The most fundamental need is to start a program of education and training for present employees.

CLEANLINESS: THE MAINTENANCE IMPACT

It is fascinating that Nakajima chose to introduce the topic of total productive maintenance with comments on factory cleanliness.[16] However, the author's experience supports this notion. Improved maintenance must start with cleaning machines (if they have been allowed to become begrimed—a terrible mistake). Nor is machine cleanliness a one-time

[15]John E. Heinzelman, *The Complete Handbook of Maintenance Management* (Englewood Cliffs, N.J.: Prentice-Hall, 1988).
[16]Seiichi Nakajima, *Introduction to TPM: Total Productive Maintenance* (Cambridge, Mass.: Productivity Press, 1988), p. 4.

thing. Cleanliness is one prerequisite to achieving continuous uptime. When foreign matter gets into the machine's moving parts, it is likely to accelerate the natural deterioration of the machine. For example, microscopic dust particles or metal chips can invade the machine's openings and start to scratch and deform moving components. They can hinder free flow of part conveyors into and out of the machine, causing jams that might in turn cause machine damage. However, dirt not only causes damage but also helps to hide it. For example, lubricant leaks are one of the major causes of machine breakdown. Thus, when dirt masks a leak that would otherwise be instantly detectable on a clean machine, it permits the leak to go undetected until the inadequate lubrication causes major damage. Lack of cleanliness can cause machine breakdown in several other places. One such example is the ventilation passages of electric motors. When these passages become even partially blocked, the motor can overheat and eventually burn out. Every maintenance improvement project team should develop, maintain, and expand a master list of machine component types that are especially subject to breakdown when dirty. This list should double as a checklist for every machine, to ensure development of maintenance procedures that stress their importance.

Finally, thorough cleaning automatically provides an opportunity to inspect the machine visually, which is an important way to detect developing problems before they cause breakdowns. For example, periodic maintenance inspection checklists might call for visually checking belts to detect fraying. Alternatively, cleaning in the area where the belt is located provides for much more frequent inspection and is free.

THE STEP-BY-STEP MACHINE MAINTENANCE
IMPROVEMENT APPROACH

The basic framework of the methodology for any factory improvement project is essentially the same. The author's previous work introduced the framework and its most important first step, project organization.[17] Exhibit 9–4, the planning chart for maintenance improvement design, differs from the standard methodology mainly in the steps illustrated as (1) maintenance methods design, (2) maintenance work station design, (3) preventive maintenance design, and (4) maintenance storage design. Each of these steps is supported by its own planning chart and methodology. For example, Exhibit 9–5 is the chart for designing new and im-

[17]See Appendix 2.

MAINTENANCE PLANNING CHART

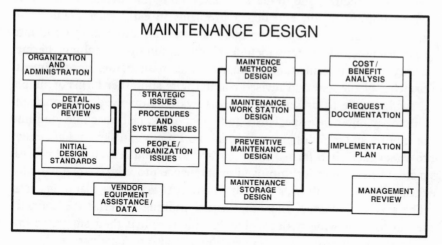

EXHIBIT 9–4

MAINTENANCE METHODS DESIGN

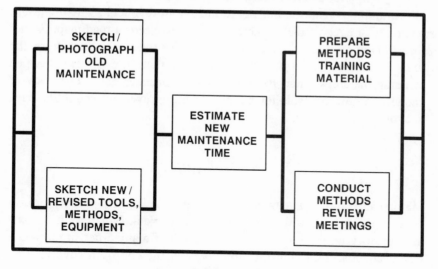

EXHIBIT 9–5

proved maintenance methods. These steps are applicable to repair maintenance procedures and to machine and tooling improvements to reduce wear, simplify repair, and detect problems in early stages. They also apply to features that machine manufacturers are directed to build into new machines. The steps include photographing or sketching the machine, its components, and its maintenance tools before improvement. Sketches of the new and revised counterparts and other forms of simple drawings serve to present new ideas to various involved personnel, including maintenance specialists and supervisors; cell, machine, and line operators; and tool designers and makers. Photos and sketches are easier to understand than formal drawings and are much less costly. The estimates of new times for improved maintenance procedures are a basis for the cost-benefit analysis, a step for which there is another planning chart. The sketches, photos, and other visual training material are not only useful for reviewing with involved people to solicit their suggested improvements, approval, and cooperation, but also become part of the permanent procedural documentation and training material. They are also attached to normal change request documents used to trigger necessary tooling and machine changes.

The complete, detailed methodology of maintenance improvement is too voluminous (and too boring) to include in this book. The important point is that every project, like every journey, needs a road map. Rather than wander around in unknown territory like the original explorers, the thinking traveler would get a copy of the map that the explorer developed to guide his steps when he returned at some later date. The body of knowledge now available for maintenance improvement should be used to avoid reinventing it.

SUMMARY

Maintenance improvement has never been the highest priority project for companies with which the author has worked. Nor does it become high priority until after the implementation of many other fundamental improvements. This contrasts sharply with the approach advocated by McNair and Stasey. Their first steps of actual factory improvement are housekeeping and preventive maintenance.[18] The author has rarely found it necessary to start with gains of inches (preventive maintenance and

---

[18]Carol J. McNair and Robert Stasey, *Crossroads: A JIT Success Story* (Homewood, Ill.: Dow Jones–Irwin, 1990), pp. 31–33.

quality measurement) when higher priority fundamentals advance progress by miles. Examples of higher priority fundamentals are forming new cells and lines and reducing setup/changeover costs. In almost every instance where operations have been reorganized into smaller factories and cells within a large factory, companies have been able simultaneously to make improvements in reducing downtime attributable to repair. A good deal of improvement stems from the intangible impact of giving small teams complete responsibility and authority for their operations. The average improvement in downtime in General Motors' factories, for example, has been 75 percent. It may not be practical to achieve 100 percent uptime in the foreseeable future, but there is no reason not to try and to get started as soon as possible.

10

Conclusion

THE MOST IMPORTANT MESSAGE of my two books lies not in the factory techniques that thrust an enterprise into the forefront of progress. Nor is it the methodology used to design and implement these techniques. The indomitable will to improve is the ingredient that separates the leaders from the pack. Champions of Western manufacturing who have blazed the trail for the army of their counterparts soon to follow include Tom Gelb of Harley-Davidson, Mr. Hans-Joachim Beyer of Siemens AG, and Glen Bloomer of 3M. Each had the spark that ignites and unites an entire organization's determination to propel its company into the forward ranks of the world's best. The past success of our Western industries is no accident, having resulted from the ingrained "can do" attitude. Current successes have sprung from an even stronger "can do better" spirit.

Our industries need to nurture tens of thousands of champions to infuse every employee with the thirst for betterment that is slaked only by outstanding performance in their field. Medieval kings had a single champion to represent them on the battlefield. Industry leaders are smarter today. They understand that they alone are the champions who must breed additional champions throughout their organization. Further, they cannot be lofty generals, directing the battle from remote command centers, but must be in the thick of the fray, continuously urging the troops to ever greater heights of accomplishment.

The battlefield champion earns his spurs by virtue of his superior knowledge of the strategies, tactics, and weapons of war. On the battle-

358

field of competitive manufacturing, the central strategies must be to organize focused factories-within-a-factory in clusters of permanent, single-
source supplier and user plants. The winning tactics including forming
serpentine lines and U-form cells, slashing setup/changeover costs, reducing container sizes, wiping out most factory inventory, and pursuing fail-
safe product quality, to name just a few. Nor can logistics be forgotten.
Resupply lines are not overextended, because the strategy of clustering,
like the circling of the wagons, minimizes the distances between the
fighting units and the central supply of ammunition. Nor are huge stock-
piles of ammunition and supplies at risk, since deliveries in small lots
are made by a just-in-time transportation shuttle.

The battle is not joined precipitously, with untrained troops. Pilot
projects of limited scope serve the same purpose as training maneuvers;
they permit the troops and their chain of command to shoot their
weapons and operate the machines of war without risking the entire
army. The maneuver strengthens the confidence and cooperation of all
and helps to identify weaknesses that must be corrected before entering
a full-scale war. But basic training precedes maneuvers. Training and
education are the foundation of the modern fighting machine. General
Schwartzkopf repeatedly attributed the success of the allies over the Iraqi
forces to two things. The first was superior training, and the second, the
invincible will to win. The author hopes this book will contribute to the
education and training of both generals and troops. The time for hunker-
ing down in defensive positions is long past. Let the battle begin!

Appendix 1

□□□

The New Achievers

THIS LIST INCLUDES some of Andersen Consulting's over more than six hundred clients and more than eight hundred factories that have implemented some of the superior manufacturing techniques described in this book. The achievers appendix in a previous book[1] listed more than a hundred additional companies. An Andersen Consulting person to contact and his office are shown in parentheses for the convenience of the reader desiring more information.

Cabot Safety Corporation, Indianapolis, IN, ear plugs and hearing protection devices. (Robert Christianson, Indianapolis, Indiana). Manufacturing lead-time reduction, 73%. Space reduction, total, 30%. Inventory investment, total, 58%.

Concurrent Computer Corporation. Oceanport Plant: Printed Circuit Board Assembly Subplant, Oceanport, NJ (A. William Kapler, III, Florham Park, NJ, and Daniel J. Emmi, New York). Manufacturing lead time reduction, 58%. Space reduction, assembly, 15%. Labor savings: direct, 10%; indirect, 10%. Inventory investment: work-in-progress, 23%; materials, 18%. Quality defects, 25%.

Concurrent Computer Corporation. Oceanport Plant: Final Assembly Subplant, Oceanport, NJ (A. William Kapler, III, Florham Park, NJ, and Daniel J. Emmi, New York). Manufacturing lead time reduction,

[1]Roy L. Harmon and Leroy D. Peterson, *Reinventing the Factory: Productivity Breakthroughs in Manufacturing Today* (New York: Free Press, 1990).

50%. Space reduction: assembly, 25%; storage, 25%. Labor savings: direct, 10%; indirect, 10%. Inventory investment: work-in-process, 25%; materials, 10%. Quality defects, 30%.

Delta Air Lines. Technical Operations Center, Atlanta, GA, jet engine maintenance and rebuild (Ron Stewart, Atlanta, GA). Manufacturing lead time reduction, 81%. Labor savings, direct, 30%. Spares inventory investment, 40%. Payback period, 13 months.

Duriron Company, Inc., The. Valve Division: Plug Valve Subplant, Cookeville, TN, industrial valves (Gary H. McClimans, Cincinnati, OH). Manufacturing lead time reduction, 84%. Setup/changeover cost, 95%. Inventory investment: work-in-process, 96%; finished goods, 79%. Quality defects, 79%.

EG&G Sealol. Engineered Products Division, Subplant 1, Warwick, RI, seals (Steven Kruger, Boston, MA). Manufacturing lead time reduction, 43%. Space reduction, 23%. Labor savings, direct, 22%. Inventory investment: work-in-process, 39%; finished goods, 18%. Quality defects, 40%. Payback period, 24 months.

EG&G Sealol. Engineered Products Division, Subplant 2, Warwick, RI, seals (Steven Kruger, Boston, MA). Manufacturing lead time reduction, 50%. Space reduction, total, 52%. Labor savings, direct, 25%. Setup/changeover cost, 52%. Inventory investment, total, 33%. Quality cost, 43%.

EG&G Torque Systems, Watertown, MA, servo motors (Steven Kruger, Boston, MA). Manufacturing lead time reduction, 94%. Space reduction: machining, 31%; storage, 31%. Labor savings, direct, 45%. Inventory investment: work-in-process, 94%; materials, 25%. Quality defects. 38%. Payback period, 10 months.

Esperanza y Cia, Marquina, Vizcaya, Spain, mortars and ammunition (Angel Diaz-Miguel, Bilbao, Spain). Manufacturing lead time reduction, 25%. Space reduction: machining, 30%; assembly, 30%. Labor savings: direct, 40%; indirect, 58%. Setup/changeover cost, 70%. Inventory investment: work-in-process, 25%; materials, 80%. Payback period, 12 months.

Fergat, Turin, Italy, automobile wheels (Federico Feyles, Turin). Manufacturing lead time reduction, 50%. Space reduction, storage, 30%. Inventory investment, work-in-process, 30%. Payback period, 6 months.

Forjas Taurus S.A., Porto Allegre, Rio Grande Del Sul, Brazil, revolvers (Ernesto Kuperman, Saõ Paulo). Manufacturing lead time reduction, 72%. Space reduction, machining, 30%. Direct labor savings, 24%.

Setup/changeover cost, 82%. Inventory investment, work-in-process, 65%. Payback period, 16 months.

General Motors. Allison Transmission Division, Plant 3, Off-highway Converter Elements, Indianapolis, IN, medium and heavy duty transmissions (Robert L. Christianson, Indianapolis, IN). Manufacturing lead time reduction, 95%. Space reduction, machining, 45%. Setup/changeover cost, 73%. Inventory investment, total, 93%.

General Motors. Allison Transmission Division, Plant 7, Gear Unit Subassembly, Indianapolis, IN, medium and heavy duty automatic transmissions (Robert L. Christianson, Indianapolis, IN). Manufacturing lead time reduction, 94%. Space reduction, assembly, 43%. Setup/changeover cost, 80%.

General Motors. Allison Transmission Division, Plant 12, On-highway Torque Converter Focused Factory, Indianapolis, IN, medium and heavy duty automatic transmissions (Robert L. Christianson, Indianapolis, IN). Manufacturing lead time reduction, 80%. Space reduction, machining, 32%. Productivity, 13%. Inventory investment, total, 65%.

General Motors. Inland Fisher Guide, Grand Rapids, MI, automotive seat covers (Robert L. Wilson, Jr., Cincinnati, Ohio). Manufacturing lead time reduction, 93%. Space reduction: assembly, 15%; storage, 58%; office, 10%. Labor savings: direct, 22%; indirect, 31%; office, 38%. Inventory investment: work-in-process, 90%; materials, 63%; finished goods, 40%. Lift trucks, 30%. Machine downtime, 50%. Quality defects, 64%.

Hamilton Industries. Columbus Street Plant, Two Rivers, WI, Wood and metal laboratory furniture (Thomas E. Arenberg, Milwaukee, WI). Manufacturing lead time reduction, 50%. Space reduction, total, 61%. Inventory investment: work-in-process, 57%; finished goods, 62%. payback period, 6 months.

Harley-Davidson, Inc. Holiday Rambler Division, Wakarusa, IN, recreation vehicles (Thomas E. Arenberg, Milwaukee, WI). Manufacturing lead time reduction, 99%. Space reduction, inside plus outside, 50%. Setup/changeover cost, 77%. Inventory investment, work-in-process, 96%.

Holiday Rambler. Motorized Vehicle Assembly, Wakarusa, IN, recreational vehicles (Thomas E. Arenberg, Milwaukee, WI). Manufacturing lead time reduction, 33%. Space reduction, assembly, 52%. Labor savings, direct and indirect, 16%. Inventory investment, total, 60%. Quality defects, 83%.

Holiday Rambler. Steel Weld, Wakarusa, IN, recreational vehicles

(Thomas E. Arenberg, Milwaukee, WI). Manufacturing lead time reduction, 99%. Space reduction, total, 50%. Inventory investment, work in process, 96%.

Holophane Company, Inc. Newark, OH, industrial lighting fixtures (John Rife, Columbus, OH). Manufacturing lead time reduction, 75%. Space reduction, storage, 40%. Inventory investment: work-in-process, 60%; materials, 40%. Payback period, 12 months.

Indux, S.A. de C.V. Mexico City, Mexico, rivets and eyelets (Gabriel Bravo, Mexico City, Mexico). Manufacturing lead time reduction, 15%. Space reduction, office, 10%. Labor savings, indirect, 10%. Setup/changeover cost, 30%. Inventory investment, finished goods, 40%. Payback period, 7 months.

INTA. Buenos Aires, Argentina, textiles (David Stilerman, Buenos Aires, Argentina). Manufacturing lead time reduction, 42%. Setup/changeover cost, 46%. Inventory investment: work-in-process, 42%; materials, 50%.

I.P.R.A. Turin, Italy, radiators (Federico Feyles, Turin). Manufacturing lead time reduction, 50%. Space reduction, machining, 30%. Labor savings: direct, 20%; indirect, 20%. Inventory investment, work-in-process, 40%. Payback period, 12 months.

Kennametal Inc. Mining and Metalurical Division, Bedford, PA, coal mining and construction tools and tool systems (Mike Sullivan, Pittsburgh, PA). Manufacturing lead time reduction, 25% to date. Setup/changeover cost, 75%. Inventory investment: work-in-process, 44% to date.

Kraft General Foods Canada. Cobourg Plant, Cobourg, Ontario, cereal, beverages, powdered mixes, desserts (S. L. Brant, Montreal). Manufacturing lead time reduction, 50%. Setup/changeover cost, 70%. Inventory investment, finished goods, 10%. Payback period, 18 months.

Kraft General Foods Canada. Ingleside Plant, Ingleside, Ontario, natural cheese (S. L. Brant, Montreal). Manufacturing lead time reduction, 66%. Inventory investment, finished goods, 49%. Quality (yield) 15%. Payback period, 6 months.

Kraft General Foods Canada. Mount Royal Plant, Montreal, Quebec, cheese, dinners, salad dressing. (S. L. Brant, Montreal). Manufacturing lead-time reduction, 66%. Setup/changeover cost, 90%.

Leather Center Holding, Inc. Carrolton, TX, leather furniture (Louis J. Grabowsky, Dallas). Manufacturing lead time reduction, 66%. Space reduction, 50%. Labor savings, direct, 30%. Inventory investment:

work-in-process, 67%; materials, 50%; finished goods, 67%. Quality defects, 30%. Payback period, 6 months.

Lennox Industries Inc. Fort Worth, TX, air conditioning and heating equipment (Gerald R. Gallagher, Dallas). Manufacturing lead time reduction, 50%. Direct labor savings, 60%. Setup/changeover cost, 60%. Payback period, 14 months.

Lennox Industries Inc. Columbus, OH, air conditioning and heating equipment (Gerald R. Gallagher, Dallas). Space reduction, assembly, 50%. Labor savings, direct, 75%. Setup/changeover cost, 50%.

Lord Corporation. Industrial Products, Cambridge Springs Plant, Cambridge Springs, PA, elastomer products (Scott A. Smith, Rochester, NY). Manufacturing lead time reduction, 20%. Inventory investment, work-in-process, 67%. Quality defects, 50%.

Marketing Displays International. Farmington Hills, MI, marketing displays (Kirk Jabara, Detroit). Manufacturing lead time reduction, 93%. Space reduction, machining and assembly, 21%. Labor savings: direct 50%; indirect, 70%. Setup/changeover cost, 75%. Inventory investment, work-in-process, 60%. Lift trucks, 92%.

Microsoft Ireland. Dublin, Ireland, computer software (Andrew Hunter, Dublin). Manufacturing lead time reduction, 85%. Space reduction, storage, 40%. Setup/changeover cost, 50%. Inventory investment, materials, 70%.

Nabisco, Inc. Nabisco La Favorita, C.A., Caracas, Venezuela, crackers and cookies (José Luis Gonzalez, Caracas). Manufacturing lead time reduction, 58%. Space reduction, assembly, 40%. Labor savings: direct, 30%; office, 19%. Setup/changeover cost, 81%. Inventory investment, finished goods, 32%. Machine downtime, 65%. Payback period, $2\frac{1}{2}$ months.

Nestle Beverage Company. Suffolk, VA, New Orleans, LA, and Union City, CA, coffee (E. T. Kennedy, San Francisco, CA). Space reduction, assembly, 25% minimum to 50% maximum. Inventory investment: materials, 25% minimum to 50% maximum; finished goods, all locations, 25%. Payback period, 12 months.

Nestle Beverage Company. Suffolk, VA, Plant, coffee (E. T. Kennedy, San Francisco, CA). Space reduction, assembly, 10% minimum to 15% maximum. Labor savings: direct, 10%; indirect, 10%. Setup/changeover cost, 20%. Payback period, 12 months.

Pharmacia Diagnostics AB. Uppsala, Sweden, pharmaceutical-diagnostic kits and instruments (Carl Lilljeqvist, Stockholm, Sweden). Inventory investment, total, 32%.

Productos Plasticos Para Hogar. Plasticos Division, Mexico City, Mexico, plastic home appliances (Eugenio Kuri, Mexico City). Manufacturing lead time reduction, 30%. Setup/changeover cost, 92%. Inventory investment, finished goods, 30%. Payback period, 11 months.

PT Mayer Indah Indonesia. Embroidery, Knitting, and Finishing Plants, Cibinong, West Java, Indonesia, textiles (S. Adhiwidjaja, Jakarta). Manufacturing lead time reduction, 64%. Setup/changeover cost, 76%. Inventory investment, work-in-process, 64%. Payback period, 4 months.

Raychem Corporation. Circuit Protection Division, Menlo Park, CA, circuit protection devices for computer, telecommunication, and automotive applications (Edward T. Kennedy, San Francisco). Manufacturing lead time reduction, 90%. Space reduction, assembly, 50%. Labor savings: direct, 40%; indirect, 50%. Inventory investment, work-in-process, 90%. Payback period, 18 months.

Rolscreen Company. Casement Subplant, Pella, IA. casement windows (Leroy D. Peterson, Chicago, IL). Labor savings, direct and indirect, 15%. Inventory reduction, work-in-process, 41%.

Rowe International, Inc. Whippany Manufacturing, Whippany, NJ, vending equipment (A. William Kapler, III, Florham Park, NJ). Manufacturing lead time reduction, 60%. Space reduction, assembly, 20%. Labor savings: direct, 10%; indirect, 30%. Setup/changeover cost, 45%. Inventory investment, work-in-process, 70%. Lift trucks, 30%. Quality defects, 40%.

Sargent-Essex. Mortise Lock Subplant, New Haven, CT, architectural hardware (Stephen Schaus, Hartford, CT). Labor savings, direct and indirect, 24%. Inventory investment, work-in-process, 60%.

Sirma. Venice, Italy, refractory materials (Federico Feyles, Turin). Manufacturing lead time reduction, 50%. Space reduction: machining, 20%; storage, 50%. Labor savings, indirect, 20%. Setup/changeover cost, 30%. Inventory investment, work-in-process, 30%. Quality defects, 50%. Payback period, 12 months.

Syntex, S.A. de S.V. Cuernavaca, Morelos, Mexico, chemicals (Gabriel Bravo, Mexico City). Manufacturing lead time reduction, 30%. Space reduction, storage, 60%. Labor savings: direct, 25%; indirect, 30%. Setup/changeover cost, 45%. Inventory investment, work-in-process, 45%. Lift trucks, 50%. Machine downtime, 10%. Payback period, 8 months.

Technographics. Fitchburg CPI, Scranton, PA, coated paper products (Steven Kruger, Boston, MA). Manufacturing lead time reduction,

41%. Setup/changeover cost, 25%. Machine downtime, 60%. Payback period, 3 months.

Teksid. Avigliana, Italy, aluminum castings. (Federico Feyles, Turin). Labor savings, indirect, 30%. Setup/changeover cost, 70%. Quality defects, 50%.

TTI, Inc. Connector Division, Fort Worth, TX, connectors (David J. Scullin, Fort Worth). Manufacturing lead time reduction, 77%. Labor savings, direct, 90%. Inventory investment, work-in-process, 90%. Quality defects, 85%.

U.S. Shoe Corporation. Crothersville, IN, women's shoes (Dean Truitt and Robert L. Wilson, Jr., Cincinnati). Manufacturing lead time reduction, 70%. Inventory investment: work-in-process, 50%; materials, 70%. Quality defects, 75%. Payback period, 4 months.

Venmar Ventilation Inc. Drummondville, Quebec, Canada, residential ventilating equipment (Steve L. Brant, Montreal). Manufacturing lead time reduction, 75%. Space reduction: machining, 33%; assembly, 19%; storage, 50%. Labor savings: direct, 32%; indirect, 12%. Setup/changeover cost, 75%. Inventory investment: work-in-process, 75%; finished goods, 94%. Payback period, 20 months.

Vicente Puig Oliver, S.A. Exterior Door Division, Alicante, Spain, wooden doors (Eduardo de Quinto, Valencia, Spain). Manufacturing lead time reduction, 50%. Space reduction: machining, 10%; assembly, 15%. Labor savings, direct, 15%. Setup/changeover cost, 60%. Inventory investment, work-in-process, 50%. Payback period, 12 months.

PROJECTS IN PROCESS

As the book neared completion, a large number of Andersen Consulting's clients had productivity improvement projects in process but had not yet implemented the results of the changes designed. A separate list of some of these companies follows.

Agritec. Saves Viejo, Sante Fe, Argentina (David E. Stilerman, Buenos Aires, Argentina). Manufacturing lead time reduction: machining, 60%; assembly, 45%. Space reduction: machining, 41%; assembly, 60%. Direct labor savings, 22%. Setup/changeover cost, 73%. Inventory investment: machining work-in-process, 60%; assembly work-in-process, 43%.

Cartonajes Suner, S.A. Alzira, Spain, printed packages (Eduardo de

Quinto, Valencia, Spain). Labor savings: direct, 30%; indirect, 20%. Setup/changeover cost, 45%. Inventory investment, materials, 67%. Payback period, 7 months.

Duriron Company Inc. Pump Division, Dayton, OH, industrial pumps and components (Gary H. McClimans, Cincinnati). Manufacturing lead time reduction, 90%. Space reduction: machining, 15%; storage, 20%; office, 15%. Labor savings: direct, 5%; indirect, 25%; office, 10%. Setup/changeover cost, 25%. Inventory investment: work-in-process, 85%; finished goods, 25%. Lift trucks, 15%. Machine downtime, 25%. Quality defects, 25%. Payback period, 6 months.

EG&G Wakefield Engineering. Components Division, Wakefield, MA, heat sinks and active cooling devices (Steven Kruger, Boston). Manufacturing lead time reduction, 87%. Space reduction: machining, 30%; storage, 30%. Labor savings: direct, 25%; indirect, 25%. Setup/changeover cost, 73%. Inventory investment: work-in-process, 87%; materials, 15% finished goods, 31%. Payback period, 11 months.

Fagor Electrodomesticos S. Coop. Planta De Lavavajillas, Bergara, Guipuzcoa, Spain, dishwashers (Angel Diaz-Miguel, Bilboa, Spain). Manufacturing lead time reduction, 30%. Space reduction: machining, 35%; assembly, 40%; storage, 25%. Labor savings: direct, 10%; indirect, 10%. Setup/changeover cost, 50%. Inventory investment: work-in-process, 55%; materials, 30%; finished goods, 25%. Payback period, 12–36 months.

Frudesa. Frio, Frutos y Derivados/Benimodo, L'Alcudia-Valencia, Spain, frozen food (E. De Quinto, Valencia, Spain). Manufacturing lead time reduction, 60%. Space reduction, storage, 25%. Labor savings: direct, 30%; indirect, 5%. Setup/changeover cost, 65%. Inventory investment, finished goods, 40%. Lift trucks, 15%. Quality defects, 30%. Payback period, 8 months.

GICSA. Groupo Industrial Columer, S. A. Columer Plant, Saint Francesco Vic, Spain, leather (Federico Montllonch, Barcelona, Spain). Manufacturing lead time reduction, 60%. Labor savings, direct, 7%. Inventory investment, work-in-process, 30%. Payback period, 12 months.

Gomez Sepulcre Sal. Crevillente, Alicante, Spain, carpets (Eduardo de Quinto, Valencia, Spain). Manufacturing lead time reduction, 80%. Space reduction, storage, 50%. Labor savings, direct, 25%. Setup/changeover cost, 40%. Inventory investment: work-in-process, 85%; finished goods, 80%. Payback period, 6 months.

Graforegia, S.A. de C.V. Monterrey, Mexico, labels and packaging products (Eugenio Kuri, Mexico City). Manufacturing lead time reduction,

10%. Setup/changeover cost, 70%. Machine downtime, 30%. Payback period, 12 months.

Greenwood Mills, Inc. Greige Division (7 plants), Greenwood, SC, woven cloth (Rick Embree, Charlotte, NC). Labor savings, direct and indirect, 3%. Inventory investment: work-in-process, 12%; materials, 18–47%; finished goods, 47%. Quality defects, 27%. Payback period, 20 months.

Guilford Mills, Inc. Automotive Division, Kenansville, NC, fabrics (automotive and other industrial applications) (H. R. Embree, Charlotte). Manufacturing lead time reduction, 70%. Inventory investment: work-in-process, 65%; materials, 60%.

Guria, S. Coop. Irun, Guipuzcoa, Spain, Construction machinery (Angel Diaz-Miguel, Bilbao, Spain). Manufacturing lead time reduction, 60%. Space reduction: machining, 30%; assembly, 40%. Labor savings, direct, 25%. Inventory investment: work-in-process, 60%; materials, 15%. Payback period, 24 months.

Industrias Nardini S.A. Americana, Brazil, lathes (José Schettino, Rio de Janeiro, Brazil). Manufacturing lead time reduction, 65%. Space reduction: machining, 20%; assembly, 50%. Labor savings: direct, 20%; indirect, 10%. Setup/changeover cost, 70%. Inventory investment: work-in-process, 75%; finished goods, 50%. Payback period, 12 months.

INMOT, Koper, Yugoslavia, chain saws, motorcycles, and outboard motors (Alessandro Falchero, Milan, Italy). Space reduction: machining, 40%; assembly, 40%; storage, 40%. Labor savings: direct, 40%; indirect, 37%. Inventory investment, work-in-process, 70%. Payback period, 13 months.

Johnson & Johnson. Codman & Shurtleff, Inc., New Bedford, MA, medical/surgical instruments (Steven A. Kruger, Boston). Manufacturing lead time reduction, 80%. Space reduction, 25%. Labor savings, total, 31%. Inventory investment: work-in-process, 86%; finished goods, 59%. Quality defects, 75%. Payback period, 3 months.

Kraft General Foods Canada. Lasalle Plant, Lasalle, Quebec, coffee and chocolate (S. L. Brant, Montreal). Manufacturing lead time reduction, 75%. Setup/changeover cost, 95%. Inventory investment, finished goods, 25%. Payback period, 6 months.

Magneti Marelli SPA. Milan, Italy, spark plugs, alternators, start motors, windshield wipers, fan motors (Alessandro Falchero, Milan, Italy). Setup/changeover cost, 65%. Quality defects, 25%.

Nabisco, Inc. Nabisco La Favorita, C.A., Caracas, Venezuela, crackers and cookies (José Luis Gonzalez, Caracas). Space reduction, storage, 72%. Lift trucks, 95%.

PTC Aerospace, Inc. Bantani Division, Bantani, CT, airline passenger seats (Stephen J. Schaus, Hartford, CT). Manufacturing lead time reduction, 80%. Space reduction: machining, 20%; assembly, 30%; storage, 30%. Labor savings, 11%. Machine downtime, 60%.

PT Pacific Utama Rattanesia. In-House Division, Tanggerang, West Java, Indonesia, rattan furniture (S. Adhiwidjaja, Jakarta, Indonesia). Manufacturing lead time reduction, 90%. Space reduction: machining, 42%; assembly, 68%, finishing, 42%. Labor savings, direct, 24%. Setup/changeover cost, 74%. Inventory investment, work-in-process, 90%. Payback period, 7 months.

Reece Corporation, The. Gorham, ME, industrial sewing machines (Steven Kruger, Boston). Space reduction, storage, 54%. Labor savings, indirect, 40%. Payback period, 2 months.

Tecna SPA. Ferrara, Italy, plastic tubes (Alessandro Falchero, Milan, Italy). Setup/changeover cost, 50%.

Technographics. Fitchburg CPI, Scranton, PA, coated paper products (Steven Kruger, Boston). Quality defects, 60%. Payback period, 6 months.

Valores Industriales SA. Cerveceria Cuauahtemoc Plant, Monterrey, Mexico, beer (Chris Coleman, Milwaukee, WI). Space reduction, assembly, 13%. Labor savings, indirect, 22%. Inventory investment: work-in-process, 93%; materials, 80%.

Vicente Puig Oliver, S.A. Interior Door Division, Alicante, Spain, wooden doors (Eduardo de Quinto, Valencia, Spain). Manufacturing lead time reduction, 50%. Space reduction, machining, 25%. Labor savings, direct, 20%. Setup/changeover cost, 40%. Inventory investment, work-in-process, 40%. Payback period, 12 months.

Villares. Acos Villares, Sao Caetano Do Sul, Saõ Paulo, Brazil, rolled and forged steel products (Ernesto Kuperman, Saõ Paula). Manufacturing lead time reduction, 88%. Space reduction, machining, 20%. Labor savings, direct, 17%. Setup/changeover cost, 80%. Inventory investment, work-in-process, 45%. Payback period, 6 months.

Villares. Pindamonhangaba Plant, Saõ Paulo, Brazil, iron and steel rolls, forged and cast parts, roller cylinders (Ernesto Kuperman, Saõ Paulo). Manufacturing lead time reduction, 80%. Space reduction, machining, 10%. Labor savings, direct, 16%. Setup/changeover cost, 80%. Inventory investment, work-in-process, 80%. Quality defects, 80%. Payback period, 2 months.

West Bend Company, The. West Bend, WI, aluminum cookware (Thomas E. Arenberg, Milwaukee, WI). Manufacturing lead time reduction, 80%. Space reduction, 30%. Setup/changeover cost, 60%. Inventory investment: work-in-process, 90%; finished goods, 60%. Quality defects, 60%.

Wrightech (Pty) Ltd. Barlows Equipment Manufacturing Company, Boksburg, South Africa, earth moving and construction equipment (Uri Galimidi, Johannesburg, South Africa). Manufacturing lead-time reduction, 76%. Labor savings, indirect, 22%. Inventory investment, work in process, 65%. Payback period, 17 months.

Zettelmeyer Baumaschinen GMBH. Werk Konz, Konz-Koenen, Germany, wheel loader (Thomas D. Follett and Wolfgang Gattermeyer, Frankfurt-Main Germany). Manufacturing lead time reduction, 83%. Space reduction, outside storage, 86%. Setup/changeover cost, 75%. Inventory investment: work-in-process, 35%; materials, 75%; finished goods, 90%. Production output per month, 50%. Lead time, customer order to delivery, 62%.

Appendix 2

◻◻◻

Footnote References to the Author's Previous Book

Reinventing the Factory: Productivity Breakthroughs in Manufacturing Today By Roy L. Harmon and Leroy D. Peterson

THE AUTHOR'S PREVIOUS BOOK is a frequently footnoted source of definitions and background information for the subject matter covered in *this* book. To help minimize the clutter that numerous footnote references to the one source would cause, this appendix was developed. Footnotes in the book, referencing *Reinventing the Factory,* will direct the reader to this appendix. Readers interested in selected chapters of this book may wish to read first the portions of the prior book in which important background material can be found. This appendix is organized to facilitate such use.

Bibliography

BOOKS

Books not listed in the author's previous work, *Reinventing the Factory: Productivity Breakthroughs in Manufacturing Today,* are identified with an asterisk for the convenience of readers of that book.

*Abegglen, James C., and George Stalk, Jr. *Kaisha: The Japanese Corporation.* New York: Basic Books, 1985.

*Akao, Yoji, ed. *Quality Function Deployment: Integrating Customer Requirements into Product Design.* Cambridge, Mass.: Productivity Press, 1990.

*Anderson, Alan D., and Ernest C. Huge. *The Spirit of Manufacturing Excellence: An Executive's Guide to the New Mind Set.* Homewood, Ill.: Dow Jones–Irwin, 1988.

*Ansari, A. and B. Modarress. *Just-in-Time Purchasing.* New York: Free Press, 1990.

Apple, James M. *Plant Layout and Material Handling.* New York: John Wiley, 1977.

*Asaka, Tetsuichi and Kazuo Ozeki, eds. *Handbook of Quality Tools: The Japanese Approach.* Cambridge, Mass.: Productivity Press, 1990.

*Athos, Anthony G., and Richard Tanner Pascale. *The Art of Japanese Management: Applications for American Executives.* New York: Simon & Schuster, 1981.

*Aubrey, Charles, and Patricia K. Felkins. *Teamwork: Involving People in Quality and Productivity Improvement.* Milwaukee: Quality Press, American Society for Quality Control, 1988.

*Bane, Michael and Dave Garwood. *Shifting Paradigms: Reshaping the Future of Industry*. Atlanta: Dogwood Publishing, 1990.

*———. *A Jumpstart to World Class Performance*. Marietta, Ga.: Dogwood Publishing, 1988.

*Belcher, John G., Jr. *Productivity Plus: How Today's Best Run Companies Are Gaining the Competitive Edge*. Houston: Gulf Publishing, 1987.

*Belohlav, James A. *Championship Management: An Action Model for High Performance*. Cambridge, Mass.: Productivity Press, 1990.

*Beranger, P. *Les Nouvelles Règles de la Production: Vers l'Excellence Industrielle*. Paris: Bordas, 1987.

Berliner, Callie and James A. Brimson, eds. *Cost Management for Today's Advanced Manufacturing: The CAM-1 Conceptual Design*. Boston: Harvard Business School Press, 1988.

*Berry, William Lee; Thomas E. Vollmann; and D. Clay Whybark. *Manufacturing Planning and Control Systems*. Homewood, Ill.: Business One–Irwin, 1988.

*Birkholz, Charles R., and Jim Villella. *The Battle to Stay Competitive: Changing the Traditional Workplace*. Cambridge, Mass.: Productivity Press, 1990.

Blache, Klaus M., ed. *Success Factors for Implementing Change: A Manufacturing Viewpoint*. Dearborn, Mich.: Society of Manufacturing Engineers, 1988.

*Blackstone, John H., *Capacity Management*. South-western, 1989.

*Blauth, Robert E., and Carl Machover, eds. *The CAD/CAM Handbook*. Bedford, Mass.: Computervision, 1980.

*Bloch, Heinz P., and Fred K. Geitner. *An Introduction to Machine Assessment*. New York: Van Nostrand Reinhold, 1990.

*———. *Practical Machinery Management For process Plants*. Four Vols: *Improving Machine Reliability; Machinery Failure Analysis and Troubleshooting; Machinery Component Maintenance and Repair;* and *Major Process Equipment Maintenance and Repair*. Houston: Gulf Publishiung, 1985.

*Boothroyd, G., and P. Dewhurst. *Design for Assembly: A Designer's Handbook*. Amherst: University of Massachusetts, 1982.

*Bossert, James L. *Quality Function Deployment: A Practitioner's Approach*. Milwaukee: ASQC Quality Press, 1991.

*Boyes, William E., ed. *Jigs and Fixtures*. Dearborn, Mich.: Society of Manufacturing Engineers, 1982.

*Bralla, James G. *Handbook of Product Design for Manufacturing: A Practical Guide to Low-Cost Production*. New York: McGraw-Hill, 1986.

*Buehler, Vernon M., and Y. K. Shetty, eds. *Competing Through Productivity and Quality*. Cambridge, Mass.: Productivity Press, 1988.

*Burnham, John M. *Just-in-Time in a Major Process Industry: Case Studies of JIT Implementation at Alcoa*. Falls Church, Va.: American Production & Inventory Control Society, 1986.

*Camp, Robert C. *Benchmarking: The Search for Industry Best Practices That Lead to Superior Performance.* Milwaukee: ASQC Quality Press, 1989.

*Carlisle, John A., and Robert C. Parker. *Beyond Negotiation: Redeeming Customer–Supplier Relationships.* New York: John Wiley, 1989.

Chassang, Guy. *Gerer la Production avec l'Ordinateur [Production Control in the Computer Age].* Paris: Dunod, 1983.

*Claunch, Jerry W.; Michael W. Gozzo; and Peter L. Grieco, Jr. *Supplier Certification: Achieving Excellence.* Plantsville, Conn.: PT Publications, 1988.

*——, *Just-In-Time Purchasing: In Pursuit of Excellence.* Plantsville, Conn.: PT Publications, 1988.

*Claunch, Jerry W., and Philip D. Stang. *Set-up Reduction: Saving Dollars with Common Sense.* Palm Beach Gardens, FL: PT Publications, 1989.

*Coombs, Clyde, and W. Grant Ireson, eds. *Handbook of Reliability Engineering and Management.* New York: McGraw-Hill, 1988.

*Cox, Jeff, and Eliyahu M. Goldratt. *The Goal: A Process of Ongoing Improvement.* Croton-on-Hudson, N.Y.: North River Press, 1986.

*Crosby, Philip B. *Quality Is Free.* New York: New American Library, 1979.

*Cross, Kelvin F., and Richard L. Lynch. *Measure Up! Yardsticks for Continuous Improvement.* Cambridge, Mass.: Blackwell, 1991.

Dallas, Daniel B., ed. *Tool and Manufacturing Engineers Handbook.* New York: McGraw-Hill, 1976.

*Davidow, William H., and Bro Uttal. *Total Customer Service: The Ultimate Weapon.* New York: Harper & Row, 1989.

*Deming, W. Edwards. *Out of the Crisis.* Cambridge: Massachusetts Institute of Technology, Center for Advanced Engineering Study, 1986.

*Dertouzos, Michael L.; Richard K. Lester; and Robert M. Solow. *Made in America: Regaining the Productive Edge.* Cambridge: MIT Press, 1989.

*Dholakia, N.; J. R. Hauser; and G. L. Urban. *Essentials of New Product Management.* Englewood Cliffs, N.J.: Prentice-Hall, 1987.

*Dore, Ronald. *British Factory–Japanese Factory: The Origins of National Diversity in Industrial Relations.* Berkeley: University of California, 1973.

*Drucker, Peter F. *Managing in Turbulent Times.* New York: Harper & Row, 1980.

Duncan, William L. *Just-In-Time in American Manufacturing.* Dearborn, Mich.: Society of Manufacturing Engineers, 1988.

*Ealey, Lance A. *Quality by Design: Taguchi Methods and U.S. Industry.* Dearborn, Mich.: ASI Press, 1988.

*Eloranta, Eero. *Advances in Production Management Systems.* Amsterdam: North-Holland, 1991.

*Eureka, William E., and Nancy E. Ryan. *The Customer-Driven Company: Managerial Perspectives On QFD.* Dearborn, Mich.: ASI, 1988.

*Feigenbaum, A. V. *Total Quality Control.* New York: McGraw-Hill, 1983.

*Ford, Henry, *Today and Tomorrow.* Cambridge, Mass.: Productivity Press, 1988 (reprint).

*Fox, Robert E., and Eliyahu M. Goldratt. *The Race.* Croton-on-Hudson, N.Y.: North River Press, 1986.

*Fuchs, Jerome H. *The Prentice-Hall Illustrated Handbook of Advanced Manufacturing Methods.* Englewood Cliffs, N.J.: Prentice-Hall, 1988.

*Fucini, Joseph J. and Suzy Fucini. *Working for the Japanese: Inside Mazda's American Auto Plant.* New York: Free Press, 1990.

Fukuda, Ryuji. *Managerial Engineering: Techniques for Improving Quality and Productivity in the Workplace.* Cambridge, Mass.: Productivity Press, 1983.

*Garvin, David A. *Managing Quality: The Strategic and Competitive Edge.* New York: Free Press, 1988.

Gilbreth, Frank B. *Motion Study: A Method for Increasing the Efficiency of the Workman.* Easton, Pa.: Hive, (1911) 1985.

*———. *Primer of Scientific Management.* Easton, Pa.: Hive, 1985 (reprint).

Goddard, Walter E. *Just-in-Time: Surviving by Breaking Tradition.* Essex Junction, Vt.: Oliver Wight, 1986.

*Gotoh, Fumio. *Equipment Planning for TPM: Maintenance Prevention Design.* Cambridge, Mass.: Productivity Press, 1991.

*Gozzo, Michael W., and Peter L. Grieco, Jr. *Made In America: The Total Business Concept.* Plantsville, Conn.: PT Publications, 1987.

*Grazier, Peter B. *Before It's Too Late: Employee Involvement—An Idea Whose Time Has Come.* Chadds Ford, Pa.: Teambuilding, 1989.

*Greif, Michel. *The Visual Factory: Building Participation Through Shared Information.* Cambridge, Mass.: Productivity Press, 1991.

Gunn, Thomas G. *Manufacturing for Competitive Advantage.* Cambridge, Mass.: Ballinger, 1978.

*Hackman, J. Richard, ed. *Groups That Work (and Those That Don't): Creating Conditions for Effective Teamwork.* San Francisco: Jossey-Bass Publishers, 1990.

Hall, Robert W. *Attaining Manufacturing Excellence.* Homewood, Ill.: Dow Jones–Irwin, 1987.

———. *Driving the Productivity Machine: Production Planning and Control in Japan.* Falls Church, Va.: American Production & Inventory Control Society, 1981.

———. *Zero Inventories.* Homewood, Ill.: Dow Jones–Irwin, 1983.

*Harmon, Roy L., and Leroy D. Peterson. *Reinventing the Factory: Productivity Breakthroughs in Manufacturing Today.* New York: Free Press, 1990.

———. *Effective Cycle Counting: A Foundation for Profitable Inventory Management.* Chicago: Andersen Consulting, Arthur Andersen & Co., 1980.

——. *Inventory Record Accuracy.* Chicago: Andersen Consulting, Arthur Andersen & Co., 1980.

——. *Reinventer la Production.* Paris: InterEditions, 1991.

——. *Reinventar la Fabrica: Como Introducir Mejoras Sensibles en la Produccion Industrial.* Madrid: CDN (Ciencias de la Direccion), 1990.

*——. *Reinventando a Fabrica: Tecnicas Modernas de Produtividade Aplicadas na Pratica.* Rio de Janeiro: Editora Campus, 1991.

*——. *Die Neue Fabrik: Einfacher, Flexibler, Produktiver-Hundert Faelle Erfolgreicher Veraenderung.* Frankfurt, Germany: Campus Verlag, 1990.

*Harper, Ann, and Bob Harper. *Succeeding as a Self-Directed Work Team.* Croton-on-Hudson, N.Y.: MW Corporation, 1990.

*Hatakeyama, Yoshio. *Manager Revolution: A Guide to Survival in Today's Changing Workplace.* Cambridge, Mass.: Productivity Press, 1985.

Hay, Edward J. *The Just-in-Time Breakthrough: Implementing the New Manufacturing Basics.* New York: John Wiley, 1988.

Hayes, Robert H., and Steven C. Wheelwright. *Restoring Our Competitive Edge: Competing Through Manufacturing.* New York: John Wiley, 1984.

Hayes, Robert H.; Steven C. Wheelwright; and Kim B. Clark. *Dynamic Manufacturing: Creating the Learning Organization.* New York: Free Press, 1988.

*Heinzelman, John E. *The Complete Handbook of Maintenance Management.* Englewood Cliffs, N.J.: Prentice-Hall, 1988.

*Hernandez, Arnaldo. *Just-in-Time: A Practical Approach.* Englewood Cliffs, N.J.: Prentice-Hall, 1989.

Higgins, Lindley R., ed. *Maintenance Engineering Handbook.* New York: McGraw-Hill, 1988.

*Hirano, Hiroyuki, ed. *JIT Factory Revolution: A Pictorial Guide to Factory Design of the Future.* Cambridge, Mass.: Productivity Press, 1988.

*Hoffman, Edward G., ed. *Fundamentals of Tool Design.* Dearborne, Mich.: Society of Manufacturing Engineers, 1984.

*Hout, Thomas M., and George Stalk, Jr. *Competing Against Time: How Time-based Competition Is Reshaping Global Markets.* New York: Free Press, 1990.

*Huge, Ernest C., ed. *Total Quality: An Executive's Guide for the 1990s.* Homewood, Ill.: Dow Jones–Irwin, 1990.

*Hunt, V. Daniel. *Smart Robots: A Handbook of Intelligent Robotic Systems.* New York: Chapman & Hall, 1985.

*——. *Industrial Robotics Handbook.* New York: Industrial Press, 1983.

*Hutchins, David. *Just-in-Time.* Aldershot, Eng.: Gower Technical Press, 1988.

*Imai, Masaaki. *Kaizen: The Key to Japan's Competitive Success.* New York: Random House, 1986.

Isikawa, Kaoru. Trans. David J. Lu, *What Is Total Quality Control? The Japanese Way.* Englewood Cliffs, N.J.: Prentice-Hall, 1985.

*Johnson, H. Thomas, and Robert S. Kaplan. *Relevance Lost: The Rise and Fall of Management Accounting.* Boston: Harvard Business School Press, 1987.

*Jones, Daniel T.; Daniel Roos; and James P. Womack. *The Machine That Changed the World.* New York: Macmillan, 1990.

*Juran, J. M. *Juran on Leadership for Quality: An Executive Handbook.* New York: Free Press, 1989.

*———. *Juran on Planning for Quality.* New York: Free Press, 1988.

*———, editor-in-chief. *Juran's Quality Control Handbook.* New York: McGraw-Hill, 1988.

Juravich, Tom. *Chaos on the Shop Floor: A Workers View of Quality, Productivity, and Management.* Philadelphia: Temple University Press, 1985.

*Kanatsu, Takashi. *TQC for Accounting: A New Role in Companywide Improvement.* Cambridge, Mass.: Productivity Press, 1990.

*Kane, Victor E. *Defect Prevention: Use of Simple Statistical Tools.* New York: Marcel Dekker, Inc., 1989.

*Kaplan, Robert S., ed. *Measures for Manufacturing Excellence.* Boston: Harvard Business School Press, 1990.

Karatsu, Hajime. *TQC Wisdom of Japan: Managing for Total Quality Control.* Cambridge, Mass.: Productivity Press, 1988.

*———. *Tough Words for American Industry.* Cambridge, Mass.: Productivity Press, 1987.

*Kaydos, Will. *Measuring, Maximizing, and Managing Performance.* Cambridge, Mass.: Productivity Press, 1991.

*Keller, Maryann. *Rude Awakening: The Rise, Fall, and Struggle for Recovery of General Motors.* New York: William Morrow, 1989.

*King, Bob. *Better Designs in Half the Time: Quality Function Deployment in America.* Methuen, Mass.: GOAL/QPC, 1989.

*Kobayashi, Iwao. *20 Keys to Workplace Improvement.* Cambridge, Mass.: Productivity Press, 1990.

Lu, David J., trans. *Kanban: Just-in-Time at Toyota: Management Begins at the Workplace.* Cambridge, Mass.: Productivity Press, 1985.

*———. *Inside Corporate Japan: The Art of Fumble-Free Management.* Cambridge, Mass.: Productivity Press, 1987.

Lubben, Richard J. *Just-in-Time: An Aggressive Manufacturing Strategy.* New York: McGraw-Hill, 1988.

*Maskell, Brian H. *Just-in-Time: Implementing the New Strategy.* Carol Stream, Ill.: Hitchcock Publishing, 1989.

*———. *Performance Measurement for World Class Manufacturing: A Model for American Companies.* Cambridge, Mass.: Productivity Press, 1991.

*Mather, Hal. *Competitive Manufacturing.* Englewood Cliffs, N.J.: Prentice-Hall, 1988.

*McNair, Carol J.; William Mosconi; and Thomas F. Norris. *Beyond the Bottom Line: Measuring World Class Performance.* Homewood, Ill.: Dow Jones–Irwin, 1989.

*McNair, Carol J., and Robert Stasey. *Crossroads: A JIT Success Story.* Homewood, Ill.: Dow Jones–Irwin, 1990.

*Melman, Seymour. *Profits Without Production.* 2d ed. New York: Alfred A. Knopf, 1988.

*Merli, Giorgio. *Total Manufacturing Management: Production Organization for the 1990s.* Cambridge, Mass.: Productivity Press, 1990.

*Millman, Gregory J. *The Floating Battlefield: Corporate Strategies in the Currency Wars.* New York: AMACOM, 1990.

Mizuno, Shigero. *Company-Wide Total Quality Control.* Tokyo: Asian Productivity Organization, 1988.

——, ed. *Management for Quality Improvement: The 7 New QC Tools.* Cambridge, Mass.: Productivity Press, 1988.

Monden, Yasuhiro. *The Toyota Production System: Practical Approach to Production Management.* Atlanta: Institute of Industrial Engineers, 1983.

*——, ed. *Applying Just in Time in America: The American/Japanese Experience.* Atlanta: Industrial Engineering & Management Press, 1986.

*Monden, Yasuhiro, and Michiharu Sakurai, eds. *Japanese Management Accounting: A World Class Approach to Profit Management.* Cambridge, Mass.: Productivity Press, 1990.

*Montgomery, Douglas C. *Introduction to Statistical Quality Control.* New York: Wiley, 1985.

*Moody, Patricia E. *Strategic Manufacturing: Dynamic New Directions for the 1990s.* Homewood, Ill.: Dow Jones–Irwin, 1990.

*Moran, Linda: Ed Musselwhite; Jack Orsburn; and John H. Zenger. *Self-Directed Teams: The New American Challenge.* Homewood, Ill.: Business One–Irwin, 1990.

*Mortimer, John, ed. *Just-in-Time: An Executive Briefing.* Bedford, Eng.: IFS, Ltd., 1986.

*Murphy, S. *In-Process Measurement and Control.* New York: Marcel Dekker, 1990.

*Muther, Richard. *Practical Plant Layout.* New York: McGraw-Hill, 1955.

*Nagashima, Soichiro. *100 Management Charts.* Tokyo: Asian Productivity Organization, 1987.

Nakajima, Seiichi. *Introduction to TPM: Total Productive Maintenance.* Cambridge, Mass.: Productivity Press, 1988.

*——. *TPM Development Program: Implementing Total Productive Maintenance.* Cambridge, Mass.: Productivity Press, 1989.

*O'Grady, P. J. *Putting Just-in-Time Philosophy into Practice.* New York: Nichols Publishing, 1988.

*Oakland, John S. *Total Quality Management.* Halley Court, Oxford, Eng.: Heinemann Professional Publishing, 1989.

Ohno, Taiichi. *Toyota Production System: Beyond Large-Scale Production.* (Trans. not credited.) Cambridge, Mass.: Productivity Press, 1988.

———. *Workplace Management.* Trans. Andrew P. Dillar. Cambridge, Mass.: Productivity Press, 1988.

———, with Setsuo Mito. *Just-in-Time: For Today and Tomorrow.* Trans. Joseph P. Schmelzeis, Jr. Cambridge, Mass.: Productivity Press, 1988.

*Ouichi, William. *Theory Z: How American Business Can Meet the Japanese Challenge.* Reading, Mass.: Addison-Wesley, 1981.

*Perigord, Michel. *Achieving Total Quality Management: A Program for Action.* Cambridge, Mass.: Productivity Press, 1991.

*Peters, Tom. *Thriving on Chaos; Handbook for a Management Revolution.* New York: Knopf, 1988.

*Peters, Thomas J., and Robert H. Waterman. *In Search of Excellence: Lessons from America's Best-run Companies.* New York: Warner Books, 1984.

*Phadke, Madhav. *Quality Engineering Using Robust Design.* Englewood Cliffs, N.J.: Prentice-Hall, 1989.

*Porter, Michael E. *The Competitive Advantage of Nations.* New York: Free Press, 1990.

———. *Competitive Strategy: Techniques for Analyzing Industries and Competitors.* New York: Free Press, 1980.

———. *Competitive Advantage: Creating and Sustaining Superior Performance.* New York: Free Press, 1985.

*Reid, Peter C. *Well Made in America: Lessons from Harley-Davidson on Being the Best.* New York: McGraw-Hill, 1990.

Robson, Ross E., ed. *The Quality and Productivity Equation: American Corporate Strategies for the 1990s.* Cambridge, Mass.: Productivity Press, 1990.

Rosaler, Robert C., and James O. Rice. *Industrial Maintenance Reference Guide.* New York: McGraw-Hill, 1987.

———. *Plant Equipment Reference Guide.* New York: McGraw-Hill, 1987.

*Rosaler, Robert C., editor-in-chief, and James O. Rice, associate editor. *Standard Handbook of Plant Engineering.* New York: McGraw-Hill, 1983.

*Ross, Philip J. *Taguchi Techniques for Quality Engineering.* New York: McGraw-Hill, 1988.

*Sandras, William A. *Just-in-Time: Making It Happen.* Essex Junction, Vt.: Oliver Wight Limited Publications, 1989.

*Sandy, William. *Forging the Productivity Partnership: The Path-breaking Blueprint for a High-Performance, Lightning-Reflex, Smooth-running Business Force.* New York: McGraw-Hill, 1990.

Schonberger, Richard J. *Japanese Manufacturing Techniques: Nine Hidden Lessons in Simplicity.* New York: Free Press 1982.

——. *World Class Manufacturing.* New York: Free Press, 1986.

*——. *Building a Chain of Customers: Linking Business Functions to Create the World Class Company.* New York: Free Press, 1990.

*——. *World Class Manufacturing Casebook: Implementing JIT and TQC.* New York: Free Press, 1987.

*Sedlik, Harold. *Jigs and Fixtures for Limited Production.* Dearborne, Mich.: Society of Manufacturing Engineers, 1970.

*Sephri, Mehron. *Just-in-Time, Not Just in Japan: Case Studies of American Pioneers in JIT Implementation.* Falls Church, Va.: American Production & Inventory Control Society, 1986.

Shingo, Shigeo. *Non-Stock Production: The Shingo System for Continuous Production.* Cambridge, Mass.: Productivity Press, 1988.

——. *A Revolution in Manufacturing: The SMED System.* Cambridge, Mass.: Productivity Press, 1985.

——. *The Savings of Shigeo Shingo: Key Strategies for Plant Improvement.* Cambridge, Mass.: Productivity Press, 1987.

——. *Study of the Toyota Production System.* Tokyo: Japan Management Association, 1981.

——. *Zero Quality Control: Source Inspection and the Poka-Yoke System.* Cambridge, Mass.: Productivity Press, 1986.

*——, introduction. *Poka-Yoke: Improving Product Quality by Preventing Defects.* Cambridge, Mass.: Productivity Press, 1988.

Shinohara, Isao. *NPS New Production System: JIT Crossing Industry Boundaries.* Cambridge, Mass.: Productivity Press, 1988.

*Sink, D. Scott, and Thomas C. Tuttle. *Planning and Measurements in Your Organization of the Future.* Norcross, Ga.: Industrial Engineering & Management Press, 1989.

*Smith, David A. *Quick Die Change.* Dearborn, Mich.: Society of Manufacturing Engineers, 1991.

*Sugiyama, Tomo. *The Improvement Book: Creating the Problem Free Workplace.* Cambridge, Mass.: Productivity Press, 1989.

Suzaki, Kiyoshi. *The New Manufacturing Challenge.* New York: Free Press, 1987.

*Suzue, Toshio, and Akira Kohdate. *Variety Reduction Program: A Production Strategy for Product Diversification.* Cambridge, Mass.: Productivity Press, 1990.

*Tanner, William R., ed. *Industrial Robots.* Dearborn, Mich.: Robotics International, Society of Manufacturing Engineers, 1981.

Taylor, Frederick W. *The Principles of Scientific Management.* Easton, Pa.: Hive, (1911) 1985.

Tompkins, James A., and John A. White. *Facilities Planning.* New York: John Wiley, 1984.

*Tompkins, J. *Winning Manufacturing: The How-to Book of Successful Manufacturing.* Norcross, Ga.: Institute of Industrial Engineers, 1989.

*Trucks, Dr. H. E. *Designing for Economical Production.* Dearborn, Mich.: Society of Manufacturing Engineers, 1987.

*Varney, Glenn H. *Building Productive Teams: An Action Guide and Resource Book.* San Francisco: Jossey-Bass, 1988.

Voss, C. A. *Just-in-Time Manufacture.* London: IFS Publications, 1987.

*Wantuck, Kenneth A. *Just-in-Time for America: A Common Sense Production Strategy.* Milwaukee: The Forum, Ltd., 1989.

Waterman, Robert H., Jr. *The Renewal Factor: How to Best Get and Keep the Competitive Edge.* New York: Bantam Books, 1987.

Wicks, Charles, ed. *Tool and Manufacturing Engineer's Handbook-Volume 4.* Dearborn, Mich.: Society of Manufacturing Engineers, 1988.

Wild, Ray. *Mass Production Management: The Design and Operation of Production Flow-Line Systems.* London: John Wiley, 1972.

*Wilson, Frank W., ed. *Handbook of Fixture Design.* New York: McGraw-Hill, 1962.

*Wireman, Terry. *World Class Maintenance Management.* New York: Industrial Press, 1990.

*Wolferen, Karel van. *The Enigma of Japanese Power.* New York: Knopf, 1989.

*Yamada, Kenjiro. *The Idea Book: Improvement Through Total Employee Involvement.* Cambridge, Mass.: Productivity Press, 1988.

*Yasuda, Yuzo. *40 Years, 20 Million Ideas: The Toyota Suggestion System.* Cambridge, Mass.: Productivity Press, 1991.

*Zeyher, Lewis R. *Cost Reduction in the Plant.* Englewood Cliffs, N.J.: Prentice-Hall, 1965.

ARTICLES

Appel, Efrem. "Il CIM Nell 'Industria Farmaceutica: L'Automazione Del Batch Record." *Societa Editoriale Farmaceutica,* (Notiziario Chimico Farmaceutico), November 1989, pp. 115–16.

Arenberg, Thomas E. "Engineering Productivity: JIT in the Product Development Function." *Just-in-Time Seminar Proceedings* (American Production & Inventory Control Society), July 9–11, 1990, pp. 58–61.

Bandyopadhyay, Jayanta K. "Product Design to Facilitate JIT Production." *Production and Inventory Management Journal* (American Production & Inventory Control Society), fourth quarter 1990.

Bhide, Amar. "Hustle as Strategy." *Harvard Business Review*, September–October 1986, pp. 59–65.

Brandy, Scott; Robert C. Farwell; and Bradley A. Rosencrans. "MRP in a JIT environment." *The Journal of Manufacturing* (Frost & Sullivan, Inc.), Winter 1990, pp. 5–12.

Brant, Stephen L. "Invisible Barriers to Productivity Improvement." CAPICS Conference *Proceedings*, March 1990, pp. 157–92.

Centrone, Angelo, and Paolo Valario Pennino. "Il Sistema Nell' Industria Farmaceutica." *Notiziano Chimico Farmaceutica*, July–August 1990, pp. 44–46.

Chassang, Guy. "Manufacturing World Class Management." *Manufacturing Technology International* (Sterling Publications Limited), 1989.

Chua, Richard C. H., and Steven J. Poniatowski. "The Soft Side of JIT: A Framework for Success." *1990 International Industrial Engineering Conference Proceedings* (Institute of Industrial Engineers, Norcross, Ga.), May 1990, pp. 399–404.

Conrad, Guenter. "Warum CIM sich doch rechnet." *VDI-Z* (VDI Verlag), October 1990, pp. 22–24.

Cooper, Jeffrey H. "The Soft-side Issues of CIM." *CIM Review* (Auerbach Publishers, Inc.), Spring 1989, pp. 23–24.

Cuartero, Alejandro. "Sinergias: Como Integrar la Gestion en la Revolucion Industrial de los 90." *Capital Humano* (Madrid), January 1989, pp. 33–35.

———. "Alunas Herramientas del Software Para el Just-in-Time." *CIMWORLD* (CW communications, SA, Madrid), October 1987, pp. 53–56.

Dias, Miguel O. "Techologia E Innovacion: El Reto de la Industria Espanola." *El Pais* (Madrid), June 1990.

———. "Las Tecnologias en la Fabrica del Futuro." *Novamaquina*, Noviembre 1990, pp. 103–8.

Galimimi, Uriel C. "Computer Integrated Manufacturing: Is Your Company Ready?" *Electronic 2000 Conference Proceedings* (Systems Publishers, Johannesburg, South Africa), March 1990, pp. 214–24.

Gattermeyer, Wolfgang, and Horst Polzer. "Japanische Methoden Greifen Durch." *Computerwoche*, September 28, 1990, pp. 25–25.

Harmon, Roy L. "Breakthroughs in Manufacturing Today." *APMS '90: International Conference on Advances in Production Management Systems Proceedings* (International Federation for Information Processing, Helsinki), August 20–22, 1990, pp. 1–12.

———. "Tecnicas Modernas de Fabricacion." *Gestion de Calidad y Productividad como Estrategia de Desarroll: Memorias* (República de Colombia, Departamento Nacional de Planeación Seminario Internacional, Cartagena, Colombia), June 13–15, 1990, pp. 111–116.

———. "La Productividad: Tendencias Mundiales." *Gestion de Calidad y Productividad como Estradegia de Desarroll: Memorias*. (República de Colombia, Departamento Nacional de Planeación Seminario Internacional, Cartagena, Colombia), June 13–15, 1990, pp. 171–183.

Harmon, Roy L., and Leroy D. Peterson. "Reinventing the Factory." *Across the Board*, March 1990, pp. 30–36.

——. "Focusing the Factory." *Robotics World*, January–February 1990, p. 2.

——. "La Fabrica Reinventada." *Oficina Eficeinte* (Cali, Colombia), October–November 1990, pp. 36–45.

Johnson, H. Thomas; R. Steven Player; and Thomas P. Vance. "Pitfalls in Using ABC Cost-Driver Information to Manage Operating Costs." *Corporate Controller* (Faulkner & Gray, New York), January–February 1991, pp. 26–32.

Krahn, Richard R. "Beyond Process Control." *International Conference and Exhibit Proceedings* (Instrument Society of America), October 14–18, 1990, pp. 1321–25.

Lamb, Peter. "How To Improve U.S. Productivity." *Washington CEO Magazine*, May 1990, p. 34.

Liss, Arthur S. "Planning, Justification and Implementation of a CIM Solution." *Proceedings of the Technology Assessment and Management Conference of the Gottlieb Duttweiler Institute* (Elsevier Science Publishing Company, Inc.), November 24–25, 1986, pp. 57–81.

Mateja, Jim. "Junk No More: U.S. Automakers Close the Quality Gap, but Public Remains Skeptical." *Chicago Tribune*, February 10, 1991.

Peterson, Leroy D. "How to Tell if Your Manufacturing Operations Are Non-Competitive." *Industrial Engineering* (Institute of Industrial Engineers), January 1990, pp. 41–44.

Raghavan, Sadeesh. "Migrating to a JIT Environment." *The New Straits Times* (Kuala Lumpur), March 30, 1989, p. 24.

Rosencrans, Bradley A. "Traditional Cost Accounting Can Get in the Way." *Gateway Engineer* (Ad More Publishing), April 1989, pp. 32–35.

——. "MRP III—MRP in a JIT Environment." *Gateway Engineer* (Ad More Publishing), May 1989, p. 42.

——. "CAD Is Just a Starting Point." *Gateway Engineer* (Ad More Publishing), June 1989, p. 25.

——. "Network Is Integral to CIM." *Gateway Engineer* (Ad More Publishing), August 1989, pp. 24–25.

Sarfatti, Jacques. "Productividade na Manutenacaõ [Maintenance Productivity]." *Manutencaõ* (Abraman), May–July 1990, p. 26.

Skinner, Wickham. "The Focused Factory." *Harvard Business Review*, May–June 1974, pp. 113–21.

Stauffer, Robert N. "In-Process Gaging for Real Time Quality Control." *Manufacturing Engineering* (The Society of Manufacturing Engineers, Dearborn, MI), April 1990, pp. 40–43.

Stevens, Mark. "JIT Implementation at GM-Allison Transmission: A Change in Attitude." *1990 Manufacturing Principles and Practices Seminar Proceedings* The American Production & Inventory Control Society, (Falls Church, VA), May 14–16, 1990, pp. 181–85.

Storm, David J., and Steven J. Sullivan. "CIM Justification: The 'Fresh Start' Approach." *Journal of Cost Management,* Spring 1989, pp. 4–13.

Susffalich, Miguel Angel. "Productividad y Apertura Economica." *Oficina Eficeinte* (Bogota, Colombia), August–September 1990, pp. 46–47.

Sutton, John R. "America in Search of a Competitive Advantage in World Class Manufacturing." *Industrial Engineering* (Institute of Industrial Engineers, Norcross, GA), May 1990, pp. 14–15.

——. "Rearranging the Furniture." *Industrial Engineering* (Institute of Industrial Engineers, Norcross, GA), June 1990, pp. 12–13.

——. "Start with the People." *Industrial Engineering* (Institute of Industrial Engineers, Norcross, GA), August 1990, pp. 16–17.

——. "From Total Chaos to Total Quality." *Industrial Engineering* (Institute of Industrial Engineers, Norcross, GA), September 1990, pp. 18–19.

——. "Total Preventive Maintenance." *Industrial Engineering* (Institute of Industrial Engineers, Norcross, GA), October 1990, pp. 18–19.

——. "The Factory: A Home Away From Home." *Industrial Engineering* (Institute of Industrial Engineers, Norcross, GA), December 1990, pp. 14–15.

——. "The New Benchmark of Competition." *Industrial Engineering* (Institute of Industrial Engineers, Norcross, GA), January 1991, pp. 16–17.

Treece, James B. "The Corporation: War, Recession, Gas Hikes . . . GM's Turnaround Will Have to Wait." *Business Week,* February 4, 1991, pp. 94–96.

Underwood, Michael L. "Productivity in the 1990 Factory." *Financial Executive,* March–April 1988, pp. 40–42.

Watkins, Warren H. "Reinventing the Factory." *Manufacturing Engineering* (The Society of Manufacturing Engineers, Dearborn, MI), January 1991, p. 96.

Willis, Roger G. "The Laws of CIM: Case Studies of Optimizing Manufacturing." *Manufacturing Systems* (Hitchcock Publishing Company), February 1990, pp. 54–58.

Zipkin, Paul H. "Does Manufacturing Need a JIT Revolution?" *Harvard Business Review,* January–February 1991, pp. 40–50.

Index